VOLUME THREE OF

THE PLANNING OF INVESTMENT PROGRAMS

ALEXANDER MEERAUS AND ARDY J. STOUTJESDIJK, EDITORS

A World Bank Research Publication

The Planning of Investment Programs
Alexander Meeraus and Ardy J. Stoutjesdijk, Editors

Vol. 1. *The Planning of Industrial Investment Programs: A Methodology* David A. Kendrick and Ardy J. Stoutjesdijk

Vol. 2. *The Planning of Investment Programs in the Fertilizer Industry* Armeane M. Choksi, Alexander Meeraus, and Ardy J. Stoutjesdijk

David A. Kendrick
Alexander Meeraus
Jaime Alatorre

The Planning of Investment Programs in the Steel Industry

Published for the World Bank
The Johns Hopkins University Press
Baltimore and London

Manufactured in the United States of America
First printing March 1984

The Johns Hopkins University Press
Baltimore, Maryland 21218, U.S.A.

The views and interpretations in this book are the authors' and should not be attributed to the World Bank, to its affiliated organizations, or to any individual acting in their behalf. The maps have been prepared for the convenience of readers of this book; the denominations used and the boundaries shown do not imply, on the part of the World Bank and its affiliates, any judgment on the legal status of any territory or any endorsement or acceptance of such boundaries.

Editor: Jane H. Carroll
Figures: Pensri Kimpitak
Maps: Larry Bowring and Julio Ruiz

Library of Congress Cataloging in Publication Data

Kendrick, David A.
The planning of investment programs in the steel industry.
(The Planning of investment programs; v. 3)
"A World Bank research publication"
Includes bibliographical references and index.
1. Steel industry and trade—Planning—Mathematical models. 2. Steel industry and trade—Mexico—Planning—Mathematical models. I. Meeraus, Alexander, 1943– II. Alatorre, Jaime. III. World Bank. IV. Title. V. Series.
HD9510.5.K46 1984 338.4′3669142 83-18722
ISBN 0-8018-3197-0
ISBN 0-8018-3198-9 (pbk.)

Contents

Tables

Figures

Maps

Editors' Note to the Series

THIS IS THE THIRD VOLUME in a series dealing with the use of mathematical programming methods in investment analysis. The volume focuses on the use of such methods to analyze production and investment problems in the steel industry. The exposition of the methodology follows closely that adopted in the first volume of the series, *The Planning of Industrial Investment Programs: A Methodology*, by David A. Kendrick and Ardy J. Stoutjesdijk. The other applications volumes in the series are *The Planning of Investment Programs in the Fertilizer Industry* by Armeane M. Choksi, Alexander Meeraus, and Ardy J. Stoutjesdijk; *The Planning of Investment Programs in the Forest Industry Sector* by Hans Bergendorff, Peter Glenshaw, and Alexander Meeraus (forthcoming); and *Multi-Country Investment Analysis* by Loet B. M. Mennes and Ardy J. Stoutjesdijk (forthcoming).

ALEXANDER MEERAUS
ARDY J. STOUTJESDIJK

Preface

THE STEEL INDUSTRY is one of the cornerstones of the industrial sector of most countries. It has strong linkages to other activities, either as a provider of materials for further processing or as a supplier of capital equipment. Its cost structure therefore has a substantial impact on the cost structure and competitiveness of other activities. At the same time, the cost structure of the steel industry itself depends to a large extent on the efficiency of past investments. These factors suggest that the sector is a fitting subject for a volume in this series.

The thesis of this series is that industrial investment projects should be evaluated not individually but rather in groups of interdependent projects. Moreover, it is the investment analyst's responsibility not only to evaluate projects but also to play a significant role in the design of projects. "Design" here means the choice of timing, size, location, technology, and product mix.

Consider the problem of the design of projects in the steel industry. As an example, take a country in which existing steel plants are using coal and ore from various mines and supplying products to markets; the demand for steel products is growing and the quality of ores and coal in the mines is declining. What additions to capacity should be made in existing plants and mines and where should new plants and mines be developed? The answer to this question requires the study of a set of interdependent investment projects for different parts of the productive facilities in the existing mines and plants and at the new sites.

Furthermore, the size and technology of each project in the system will have substantial effects on the best design of other projects in the system.

The analysis of interdependent projects was difficult in the past because of the long and tedious calculations. These difficulties are being removed by steady improvements in computer hardware and software. For example, the research for this volume has benefited greatly from a new economic modeling language called GAMS, which was developed by Alexander Meeraus. This language considerably decreases the time and effort required to construct and use industrial sector models.

The book is in two parts. The first part provides an overview of the technology of the steel industry and the problems of doing investment analysis in this industry. The second part contains an application of investment analysis to the Mexican steel industry.

We are indebted to Ardy Stoutjesdijk for his support and help from the inception of this project, through the model formulation and the data collection, to the writing and editing of this volume. The officials and executives of the Mexican steel industry have been most cordial in helping us develop the models and obtain the data needed to complete this study. Lic. Jorge Leipen Garay, the director general of SIDERMEX, gave us permission to visit the plants of that government corporation. Alejandro Reyes of SIDERMEX assisted both in the development of the models and the collection of data. Ing. Juan Autrique, the former director of the Coordinating Commission for the Steel Industry, shared with us his understanding of the industry. Aristeo Plehn of that commission worked with us for several weeks on the project in Washington, D.C., and made a Spanish translation of one of the models. Oscar Garaza and David Yanez of Hojalata y Lámina (HYL) in Monterrey provided particularly helpful comments during a seminar on the models.

At the World Bank, we were assisted in the computational work by Albert Cheung, Wilfred Chow, and Sethu Palaniappan. Vivianne Lake provided valuable editorial help. The typing of numerous drafts with many tables and equations was done by In-Ae Lee, Geri Mitchell, and Charlotte Robinson. Also Maurice Meunier and Claus Westmeier provided comments on the steel technology chapter. Finally, J. Scott Rogers of the University of Toronto provided many valuable suggestions for improvement of an earlier draft.

At the University of Texas in Austin, David Kendrick's graduate students provided useful comments on various versions of the small models. Particularly helpful were the comments of Ilene Kelfer-Lodde, Mina Mohammadioun, and Jung Sun Suh.

For the help of these individuals and many others we are most grateful. The responsibility for the final product remains our own.

David Kendrick
University of Texas

Alexander Meeraus
Development Research Department
The World Bank

Jaime Alatorre
Mexican Ministry of Programming
and Budget

October 1983

PART ONE

General Methodology

1
Introduction

TRADITIONAL INVESTMENT ANALYSIS has employed cost-benefit and rate-of-return calculations to make investment decisions about single projects. In the first volume in this series, Kendrick and Stoutjesdijk (1978) argued that it is more useful to evaluate groups of interdependent projects. Furthermore, they argued that the emphasis should be largely shifted from the *evaluation* of projects to the *design* of projects. That is, most of the important economic decisions about projects are made at the design stage and not at the evaluation stage. Consider the following list of decisions:

Size of productive units
Location of productive units
Choice of technology
Time phasing of the stages of the project
Mix of final products.

Most of these design decisions are interdependent. For example, the optimal size of a project may depend on its location, as well as its product mix. The advent of computers has made it possible for the investment analyst to participate in the design of projects by developing models to consider alternatives.

The particular kinds of models outlined in Kendrick and Stoutjesdijk (1978) are for an industry or sector. They consider a set of plants and a set of markets. Each plant may contain various productive units. These units transform raw material into final products which are then shipped to markets. The demand for these products is growing, and the investment analyst is faced with the question of which productive units in the existing plants should be expanded and where new plants should be constructed.

The model is constructed to find the capacity expansions which will satisfy the growing market requirement at least cost. This is done by developing a linear programming model of the industry. The model is solved to find the set of investment, production, and shipping activities that will minimize cost while satisfying market requirements without violating capacity constraints for the productive units. If there are economies of scale in investment cost—as there usually are in heavy industry—then the linear programming model needs to be converted into a mixed integer programming model.

Typically, to make best use of the effort of constructing a sector-wide investment planning model, the model is not solved once to obtain a single optimal set of investment projects, but is solved many times to study the basic economics of the industry. A variety of models with different types of aggregation may be used just as is done in this volume. For example, in the steel industry the following types of questions might be studied:

- As the quality of ores in inland mines decreases, should existing plants near mines be expanded or should new plants be constructed at ports to receive imported iron ore?
- As natural gas and coal prices change relative to one another, should investments be made in direct-reduction units which use natural gas and pellets to produce sponge iron or in blast furnaces which use coke and iron ore to produce pig iron?
- Should large productive units be constructed with plans to export substantial quantities of steel products or should smaller units be built to satisfy only the domestic demand?

The models presented in this book do not provide foolproof answers to all these questions, but they do provide a very useful methodology for obtaining quantified insights into these problems. It is important to stress from the outset, however, that the models cannot substitute for sound judgments by sector specialists, whose views should also be sought before decisions are made. That is, the models are used to consider a broad range of issues and so must ignore the details of any given alternative, which only the experts can evaluate.

What are the limitations of the models used here? A lengthy discussion is provided in chapter 7 of Kendrick and Stoutjesdijk (1978). Here it suffices to mention a few of these limitations.

- The methodology assumes fixed demand for final products.
- No substitution between final products is permitted, unless explicitly specified in the model.
- The prices of many inputs and outputs are treated as fixed.
- No uncertainty is considered in the analysis.
- The degree of disaggregation is limited by the size of model that computers can solve and humans can understand.

Several of these limitations can be mitigated by methods discussed in the chapter cited above.

Previous Work

Since the previous volumes in this series provide references to the general methodological development in this field, this section will be confined to references to investment analysis work in the steel industry.

A mixed integer programming model of the steel industry was constructed and applied to the Brazilian steel industry by Kendrick (1967). A dynamic programming model of the Venezuelan steel industry was developed by Wein and Sreedharan (1968). Westphal (1971) constructed an economy-wide model of the Republic of Korea with special attention to the steel and oil refining industries. Alatorre (1976) built a mixed integer programming model of the Mexican steel industry, which laid the foundations for the present study. A linear programming model of the U.S. steel industry with a focus on pollution control was developed by Russell and Vaughan (1976).

Reader's Guide

Like the other books in the series this volume is divided into two parts. The first part provides an overview of the technology used in the steel industry and a discussion of the investment problems faced by that industry. The second part provides an application of the methodology to the steel industry in Mexico. Three models are developed: two are static and one is dynamic; two are small and one is large. They are not arranged in a hierarchy, since different models are useful for different kinds of analyses. The two static models are useful for studying operational problems, and the dynamic model is helpful in analyzing investment decisions. The two small models can be solved repeatedly in doing sensitivity analysis. The large model provides much more useful levels of disaggregation for studying the operation of particular productive units in each plant.

We believe that the development of multiple models is an extremely useful way to study an industry. The small models are easier to construct, to solve, and to understand, but they are not disaggregated enough to answer many questions of interest.

Separate chapters provide a mathematical description of each of the models and a discussion of the sets, parameters, variables, constraints, and objective function. Appendix A of each model chapter gives a notational equivalence to a bridge between the mathematical description of the model and the computer-readable (GAMS) statement of the model that follows in appendix B.

After the models are described, chapter 10 gives extensions of the model, a summary, and conclusions about the application of this kind of model to the steel industry. The book concludes with some observations on industrial modeling.

2
The Production of Steel

THIS CHAPTER PROVIDES a brief introduction to the technology of steel production. Those who wish more details about the technology are referred to classic works on the subject, such as United States Steel (1971).

The making and shaping of steel can be divided into the following steps: mining and preparation of raw material, iron production, steel production, rolling of products, and coating of products. Figure 2-1 gives an overview of these processes. First, iron ore is mined, concentrated, and turned into pellets or sinter, and coal is mined and converted to coke. Then the iron ore and coke are charged to a blast furnace and heated to remove oxygen from the iron ore and thereby produce molten pig iron (hot metal). The molten pig iron is transported to basic oxygen furnaces where it is oxidized—that is, oxygen is blown into the liquid to remove carbon and thereby make steel. At the same time, other impurities are removed by additives such as lime. The steel is then poured into continuous casting units to make billets or slabs. The billets are rolled into shapes such as reinforcing rods, and the slabs are rolled into flat products such as plate and hot or cold sheet. Cold sheet can be coated with zinc or tin to produce galvanized sheets and tin plate.

In the mathematical modeling of the steel industry, it is useful to divide the entities in figure 2-1 into three groups: the *commodities* which are transformed from inputs to outputs in the system, the *productive units* which are used to transform these commodities, and the *processes* by which the commodities are transformed. Table 2-1 lists these three groups. The distinction between productive units and processes may seem subtle, but it is basic to the mathematical modeling of the industry.

Figure 2-1. *The Making and Shaping of Steel: Conventional Technology*

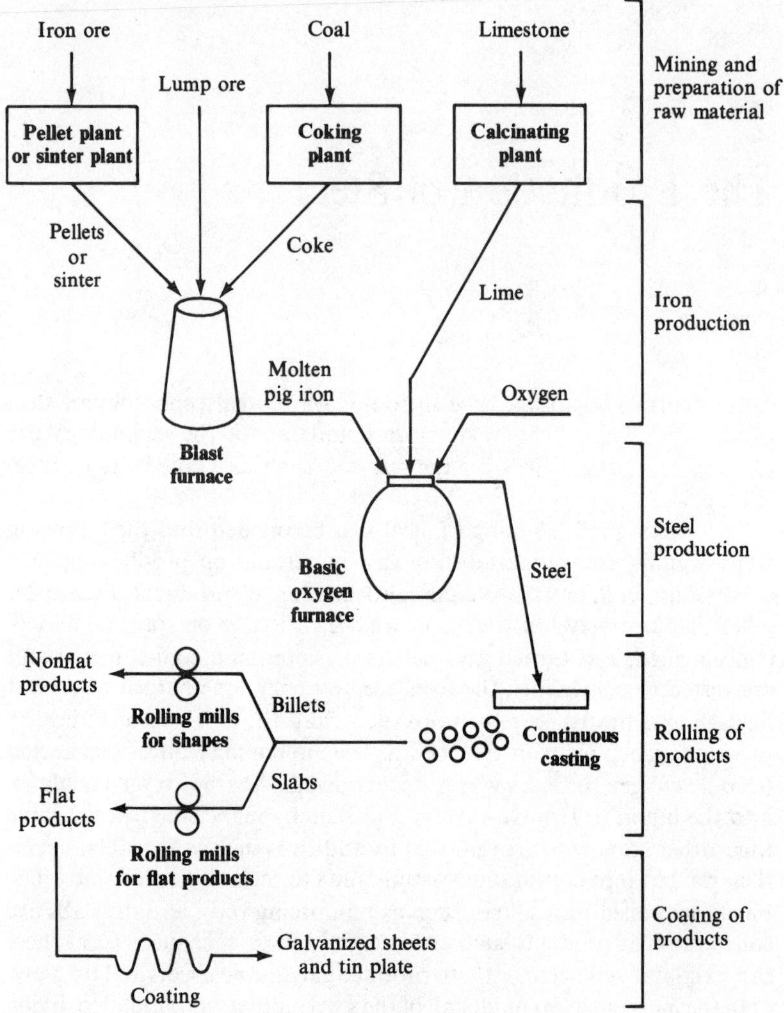

Table 2-1. *Entities in Steel Production*

Commodities	*Productive units*	*Processes*
Iron ore	Sinter plant	Sinter production
Coal	Pellet plant	Pellet production
Pellets	Coking plant	Coke production
Coke	Blast furnace	Molten pig iron production
Molten pig iron	Basic oxygen furnace	Steel production
Water	Direct reduction unit	Continuous casting
Oxygen	Continuous casting unit	Rolling of shapes
Electricity	Rolling mills for shapes	Rolling of flat products
Fuel oil	Rolling mills for flat products	
Natural gas		
Steel		
Billets		
Slabs		
Shapes		
Flat products		

A productive unit is a machine or a piece of capital equipment such as a blast furnace. A process is equivalent to a recipe. For example, two different processes for making pig iron might be used in the same blast furnace. One process would use pellets as an input and a second would use lump ore.

Figure 2-1 provides an overview of the most widely adopted technology in the steel industry. There are other methods of producing steel, however, one of which is shown in the schematic diagram in figure 2-2. Natural gas is used instead of coke to reduce the ore to iron, and sponge iron (reduced pellets) is produced instead of molten pig iron. The sponge iron is then charged to an electric arc furnace where it is transformed into steel. The steel is passed through continuous casting units and rolling mills in a manner identical to that used in the conventional technology. Direct reduction uses natural gas instead of coal, which is an advantage in some places where natural gas is abundant and cheap. As the price of natural gas rises relative to coal, however, the direct reduction process becomes less attractive. Direct reduction may be done with other gases, which may be substituted if natural gas prices continue to rise.

In the remainder of this chapter each step in the production of steel will be discussed in greater detail.

Figure 2-2. *Direct Reduction Technology*

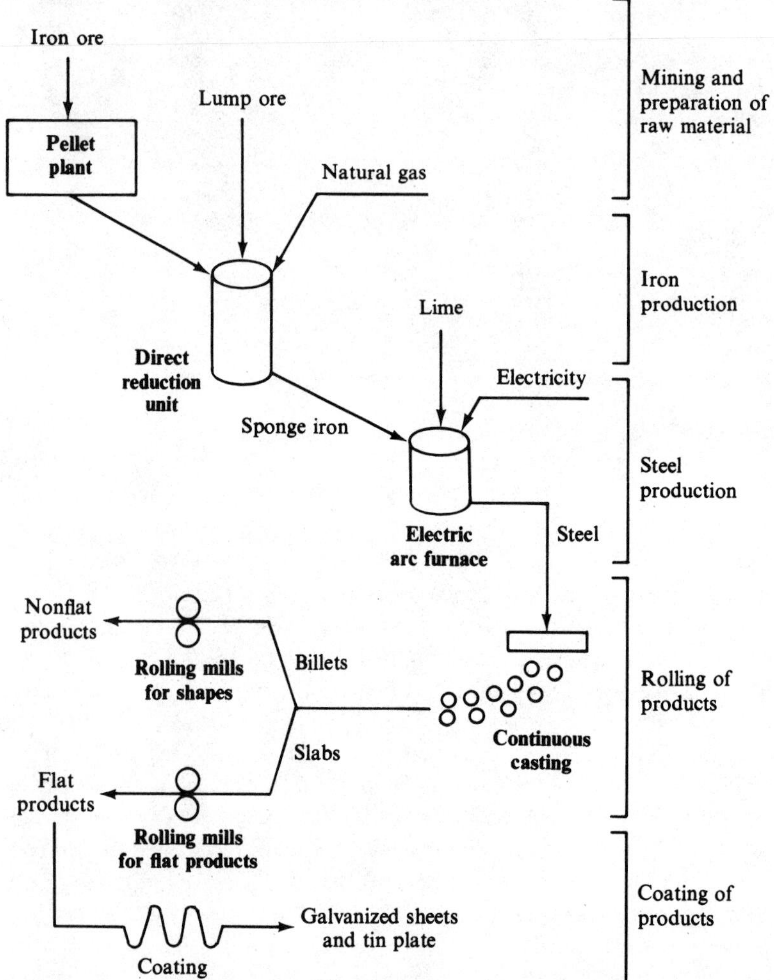

Mining and Preparation of Raw Material

Figure 2-3 provides an overview of the mining and preparation of ores. Iron ore is mined from open pit mines which have roughly 45 to 65 percent iron content. The ore is crushed and sized before it is sent to a concentrator. The type of concentrate produced depends on whether the

Figure 2-3. *Mining and Pellet Production*

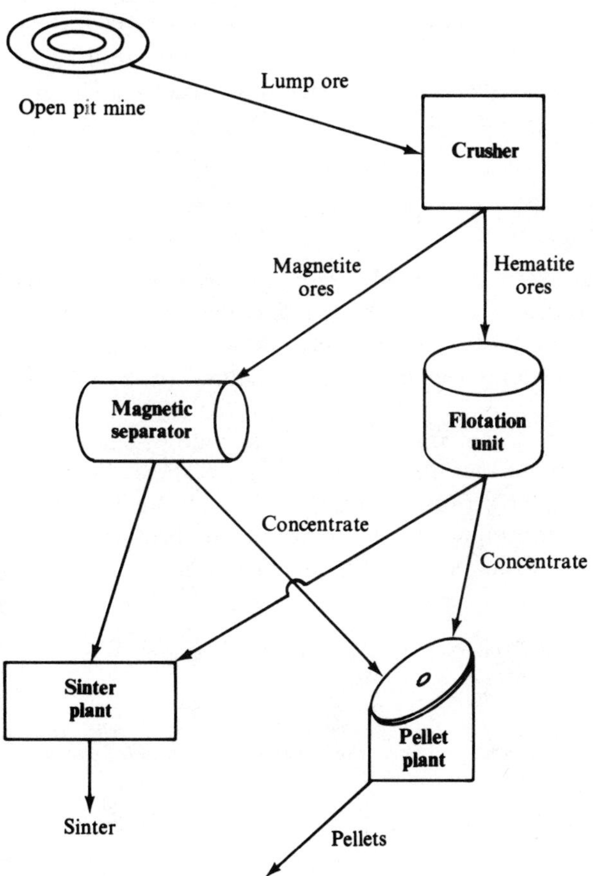

ore is magnetite or hematite. Magnetite can be concentrated by magnetic means: after it is crushed and ground, it is passed near large magnetic drums so that the iron can be separated from sand and other impurities. If the ore is hematite, magnetic separation cannot be used and a more expensive flotation process is required. With either one, the result of the concentration process is a slurry of rich ores suspended in water. This slurry can be piped to a pellet plant where the water is removed and the ore is agglomerated into small balls a quarter to a half inch in diameter. These balls (pellets) are baked so that they become hard before they are charged to the blast furnace or to the direct reduction units.

Coal is mined from either open pit or underground mines. It is then washed and shipped to coking plants, which are usually located at the steel mills. The coal is heated to very high temperatures to drive off volatile matter and thus reduce it to coke (almost pure carbon). The coke is then charged with pellets to the blast furnace.

Iron Production

Two technologies for iron production are described here: the conventional blast furnace and the direct reduction process. The first uses sinter, pellets, lump ore, and coke to produce pig iron, and the second uses pellets or lump ore, or both, and natural gas to produce sponge iron.

In the blast furnace technology sinter, pellets, lump ore, coke, and limestone are charged to the top of a blast furnace. Three alternative processes for running a blast furnace are given in table 2-2. Inputs are shown as negative numbers and outputs as positive numbers. Thus in the pellets-only process, 1.6 tons of pellets are combined with 0.6 ton of coke

Table 2-2. *Alternative Processes for Pig Iron Production*
(metric tons)

Inputs and outputs	*Pellets-only process*	*Pellets and lump ore process*	*Sinter pellets and lump ore process*
Sinter	0	0	−0.6
Pellets	−1.6	−1.4	−0.6
Lump ore	0	−0.2	−0.3
Coke	−0.6	−0.6	−0.5
Limestone	−0.1	−0.1	0
Molten pig iron	1.0	1.0	1.0

and 0.1 ton of limestone to produce a ton of pig iron (all tons in this book are metric). In the second process some lump ore is substituted for pellets to produce a ton of molten pig iron. In the third process the burden includes 40 percent lime-fluxed pellets, 40 percent sinter, and 20 percent lump ore to yield a ton of molten pig iron. Sinter is a mixture of ore fines and coal which is baked into small lumps about an inch in diameter and then charged to the blast furnace.

A typical steel mill will have one to five blast furnaces, each of which produces 1 million to 3 million tons of pig iron. So each steel mill produces 1 million to 15 million tons.

In contrast to blast furnaces, direct reduction units use natural gas or lower quality coke to reduce the iron ore. Pellets are heated under pressure in the presence of natural gas and are reduced to sponge iron. Sponge iron looks just like pellets—balls roughly a quarter inch in diameter—but it is slightly less dense. The iron content of pellets ranges from 92 to 96 percent. One process for direct reduction of iron ores is the HYL process developed in Mexico. Another, the Midrex process, was developed in Germany. An input-output vector for the HYL process is:

Pellets (metric tons)	– 1.38
Natural gas (thousand cubic meters)	– 0.38
Sponge iron (metric tons)	1.00

The natural gas input of 0.38 thousand cubic meters per metric ton of sponge iron is controversial. This is the reported usage at the HYLSA (Hojalata y Lámina S.A.) plant in Puebla, Mexico. The other HYLSA plant, in Monterrey, Mexico, reportedly uses 0.58 thousand cubic meters per metric ton of sponge iron. New processes under development are said to require only 0.28 thousand cubic meters of natural gas but require 77 kilowatt-hours of electricity per metric ton of sponge iron. Although the blast furnace technology is so widespread that it is relatively easy to check input-output coefficients, the relatively new direct reduction processes are not so widely used, and information on technical characteristics is closely held by a few companies.

The next section describes the processes by which molten pig iron and sponge iron are transformed into steel.

Steel Production

Figure 2-4 provides an overview of steel production and ingot and continuous casting. Three productive units for steelmaking are shown:

Figure 2-4. *Steel Production and Ingot and Continuous Casting*

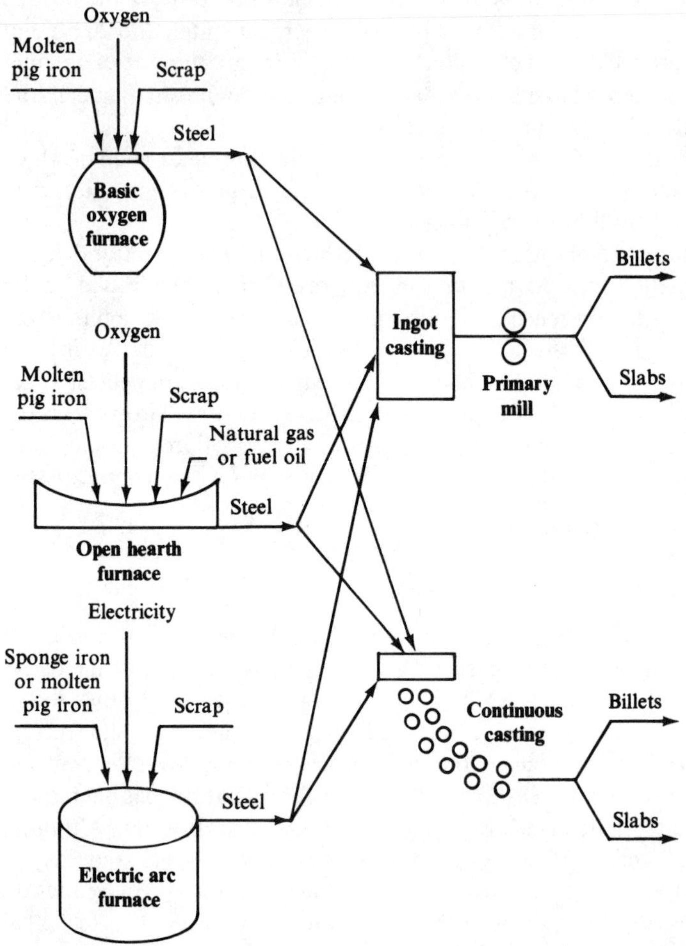

the basic oxygen furnace (BOF), open hearth furnace, and electric arc furnace. BOF is also called BOP (basic oxygen process) and LD (Linz-Donawitz). The BOF has replaced the open hearth technology as the most widely adopted of the three. The electric arc furnace can take a 100 percent cold metal charge such as sponge iron and scrap, while the BOF must have at least a 60 percent hot metal (molten pig iron) charge.

Table 2-3. *Input-Output Vectors for Steel Production*

Inputs and outputs	*Basic oxygen*[a]	*Open hearth*[a]	*Electric arc sponge*[b]	*Electric arc scrap*[b]
Hot metal	−1.02	−0.77	0	0
Sponge iron	0	0	−1.09	0
Scrap	−0.11	−0.33	0	−1.06
Electricity	0	0	−0.68	−0.50
Oxygen	−0.05	−0.05	0	0
Steel	1.00	1.00	1.00	1.00

a. From AHMSA (Altos Hornos de Mexico S.A.).
b. From HYLSA (Hojalata y Lámina S.A.).

Therefore, the electric arc furnace is frequently used to melt scrap or to reduce sponge iron. Two casting technologies are also shown in figure 2-4; ingot casting is the older and is being replaced by continuous casting.

Input-output vectors for the three steelmaking processes are shown in table 2-3. Two processes for the electric arc furnace are displayed, one using a sponge iron charge and one using a scrap charge. Mixtures of these two charges may also be used. The basic oxygen steelmaking process uses a mixture of hot metal (molten pig iron) and steel scrap in a large vessel about 20 feet high. Once the furnace is charged with the metal, an oxygen lance is inserted at the top. The furnace is blown for about 30 minutes and then tilted to pour the liquid steel into a ladle which carries the steel to the ingot casting or continuous casting operations. Two or three BOFs are usually installed side by side, and one of the furnaces is relined while the others are in operation. The capacity of such a grouping of furnaces is 1 million to 4 million metric tons of steel a year. Thus a large steel mill may have several "steel shops" with two or three BOFs in each shop.

Open hearth furnaces are being replaced by BOFs because the energy input and the time required for each heat in the open hearths are much greater, and therefore both the operating cost and cost per unit of capacity are higher. There are comparative advantages, however, which can be exploited in steel mills that have not already retired their open hearth furnaces. The BOFs can take no more than about 40 percent of the metal charge as cold metal such as scrap or sponge iron; in contrast, the open hearths can be operated even with a 60 to 70 percent cold metal charge, though heat times are much longer. This has advantages as well, since it is possible to do more exact quality control on open hearth steel than on BOF steel. Open hearth furnaces did not originally have oxygen lances, but most now have them installed, with a commensurate decrease in heat times and an increase in capacity.

In both the basic oxygen furnace and the open hearth furnace, the heat in the hot metal charge and the burning of the contained carbon are the principal sources of energy for the processes. In contrast, the electric arc furnace uses electricity which arcs between two electrodes in the furnace and heats the metal. For this reason, the electric arc furnace can take a 100 percent cold metal charge, but heat times are longer and capital costs per ton of capacity are higher.

Pollution problems may be severe for all three technologies. Open hearth furnaces were infamous for the clouds of red smoke that emanated from their chimneys before modern pollution control equipment was installed. Similarly, a BOF furnace or an electric arc furnace without proper controls would significantly pollute the air. Thus an important part of the capital cost for all three technologies is the pollution control equipment.

After production by one of the three technologies, the steel is taken either to an ingot casting or a continuous casting shop. In the ingot casting shop, the liquid steel is poured into ingot molds that are about 6 feet high, 2 feet thick, and 3 feet wide. The ingots are allowed to cool and, when scheduled for use in the rolling mills, they are moved to the soaking pit where they are uniformly heated. In the primary mill, the ingot is passed back and forth as the rollers are moved closer and closer together to form the ingot into a slab about 30 feet long, 8 inches thick, and 4 feet wide or into a bloom about 10 feet long and 10 inches by 10 inches in cross section. The slabs are later rolled into flat products, and the blooms are rolled into shapes.

In continuous casting operations, liquid steel is poured into a container with several holes in the bottom. If the continuous caster is a billet casting machine, the liquid steel slides down tubes below these holes as it is cooled, and then it is guided between rollers that gradually reduce its size to form a strand 4 inches by 4 inches in cross section. The strands are then cut into 20 to 50 foot lengths to become billets. A normal billet casting machine will have four strands. In contrast, a slab casting machine emits a single slab that is roughly 8 inches by 48 inches in cross section. The strand is cut into 20 to 30 foot lengths to form slabs.

Since the liquid steel is not allowed to cool until the billets or slabs are formed, the continuous casting process is more energy efficient than ingot casting. Also, the capital cost for a continuous casting machine is much less than for the equivalent capacity in ingot casting, soaking pits, and primary mills. The capacity of a single continuous casting machine can be anywhere from half a million to several million tons per year.

The slabs and billets are next rolled into final products, flat or shapes.

Rolling of Products

Figure 2-5 provides a schematic drawing of rolling operations for flat products. Slabs are sent either to the plate mill or to the hot strip mill. The plate mill rolls the slabs into steel plates an eighth to three-quarters of an inch thick and 10 or 20 feet in length and width. These plates will be used to build storage tanks or ships or other steel vessels.

The preponderance of the slabs are sent to the hot strip mill where they are reheated and then rolled through the mill. The mill usually has four or five stands, each of which rolls the product into a thinner form. The entire mill may be a third of a mile long, with slabs entering one end and coils of hot sheet leaving the other end. The coils contain several hundred feet of hot sheet less than an eighth of an inch thick and 3 to 5 feet wide. Some of these coils are sold as hot sheet and some are sent on to the pickling line for further processing. The pickling line is an acid bath that the unrolled coils are passed through to remove rust and scale before they are rolled up again and sent to the cold strip mill.

The cold strip mill has three to five stands located within a few feet of one another, where the pickled sheets are further reduced in thickness. Some of the resulting coils of cold sheet are sold to make automobile bodies, appliances, furniture, and other products. Others are passed through the annealing furnace where they are heated, held at an elevated temperature for several hours, and cooled in a neutral atmosphere to give the metal desirable ductile properties. Then the annealed strip is run through a temper mill and recoiled to be sold as tempered sheet. The rest of the coils are delivered to the tinning lines or galvanizing lines where they are coated with tin or zinc and then recoiled and sold as coils of tin sheet or galvanized sheet. This completes the flat product rolling operations.

Shapes are rolled from either blooms or billets. Blooms may be either round or square in cross section with a diameter of about 1 to 2 feet. Billets are square in cross section and about 1 to 5 inches on a side. Blooms are used for the heavy shapes such as beams for bridges and buildings, and billets are used for light shapes, reinforcing bars, and wire rods. Special blooms are used to produce seamless pipe by extrusion.

Figure 2-5. *Rolling of Flat Products*

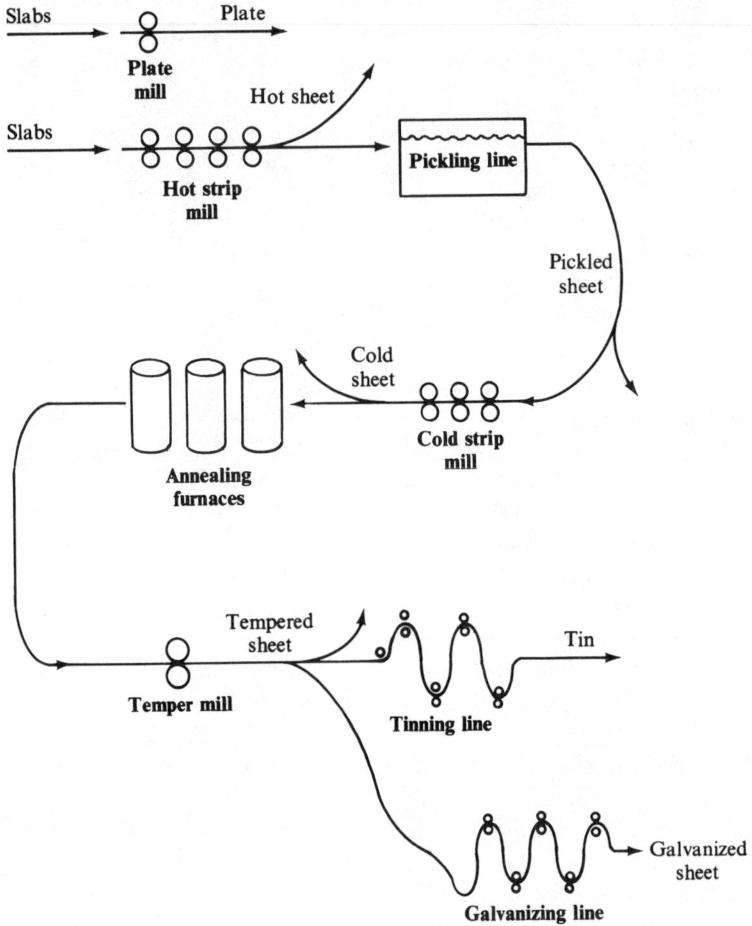

Mills that roll flat products are fairly standardized, but a profusion of different collections of rolling mills and stands is used to roll light shapes, bars, and wire rods. Furthermore, the same mills may be used to roll several different products. Therefore, figure 2-6 should be viewed as only a rough approximation of the reality of rolling shapes. Basically, billets are reheated and rolled through a collection of different mills to produce

Figure 2-6. *Rolling of Shapes*

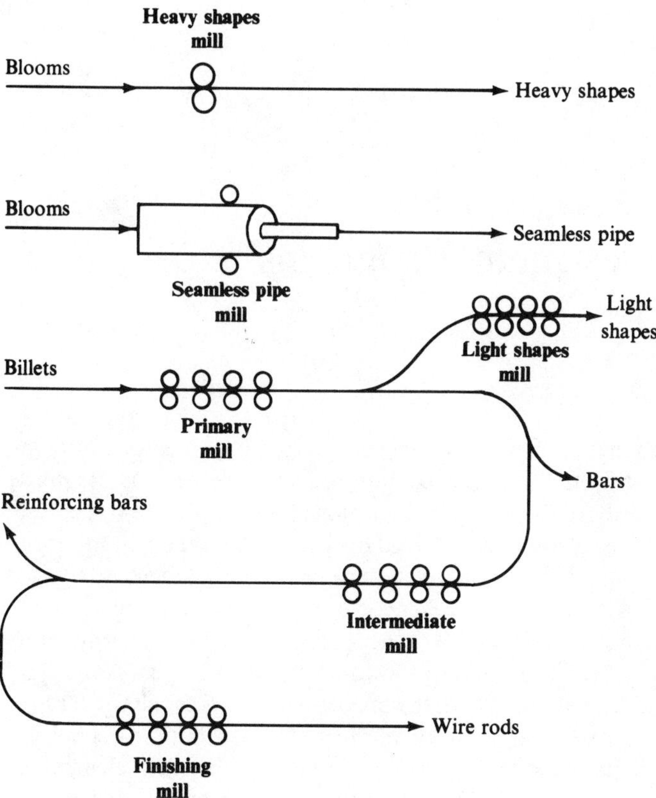

light shapes, bars, reinforcing rods, and wire rods. The capacity of such a collection of mills will range from several thousand to half a million tons of shapes and bars per year.

This discussion has outlined the technology of steel production in integrated steel mills. In most countries, there is also a collection of nonintegrated steel mills, most of which use electric arc furnaces to melt scrap and cast billets or which buy billets directly. The billets are then reheated and rolled into light shapes, reinforcing rods, and wire. The models in this book do not attempt to include the nonintegrated steel mills.

3

Model Specification and Investment Programs

WHEN INVESTMENT ANALYSIS is done by calculating rates of return on individual projects, the specification of the problem is relatively straightforward. All the inputs and outputs of the project are valued, and these values are discounted, summed over time, and set equal to zero to permit calculation of the rate of return. When investment analysis is done by considering *interdependent* sets of projects, as is advocated in this book, the specification of the problem is considerably more complicated. The reason is that if all inputs, outputs, processes, plant sites, and markets are included, the problem becomes much too large to analyze and to understand. It is therefore useful to formulate a simplified version of reality, a model, in which one must decide which elements to include and which to exclude. Therefore, in the first part of this chapter the specification of the planning problem is discussed in terms of the size and complexity of the model.

The second part of the chapter is devoted to the formulation of investment programs: how one uses a model to focus on the crucial investment issues for the industry. Examples are investments to break bottlenecks in capacity, selection of new sites, choice of technology, size of new units to be installed, and the timing of capacity expansion.

Set Specification

The three principal parts of the process of model specification are set specification, development of the constraints and the objective function, and data input and transformation. This section is devoted primarily to the first of these, set specification. Although the constraints and objective function have a similar structure for models of different industries (see Kendrick and Stoutjesdijk 1978), the set specification differs considerably across industries. Therefore, this section provides a discussion of set specification for models of the steel industry. The sets considered are mines, plants, productive units, processes, commodities, markets, time periods, new sites, and expansion units. Following this is a brief discussion of the modeling of transport.

Mines

Mines may be of crucial importance in determining the overall pattern of investment in the industry, or they may be of little or no importance and therefore omitted from the model specification. If the ores or coking coal for the industry are supplied from domestic mines and if the quality of ores is declining rapidly, the mines should be included in the model. If, however, the ores and coking coals for the industry are mostly imported or if the output of existing domestic mines is unlikely to decline in quality during the planning period, then the mines may be excluded from the set specification, thus simplifying the model.

When mines are used, one must decide how many of them to include in the model. In some countries, there are so many small coal mines and ore mines that it is impossible to include all of them. In this case, one may include only the largest mines or collections of smaller mines aggregated into a single mine in the model.

Plants

Two kinds of steel mills exist in the industry: integrated and nonintegrated. The integrated mills contain the entire set of processes from iron and steel production through rolling of final products. The nonintegrated steel mills do not have the processes for iron production and in many cases do not have the processes for steel production. These plants may have an electric arc furnace in which scrap is melted to make steel or they may simply buy billets from the integrated mills. The billets or slabs are reheated and rolled into light shapes, bars, reinforcing rods, plates, cold rolled products, and coated products. These plants are also called rerolling mills.

Since there are usually only a few large integrated steel mills but many small nonintegrated mills, it is common to include only the integrated mills in models of the steel industry. The part of domestic steel demand that is satisfied by the rerollers is subtracted from the total, and the models are solved without including these small plants.

The model may be further reduced in size and complexity by excluding nonflat products. This is a useful abstraction since economies of scale are more pronounced in flat product rolling mills than in those for nonflat products. Thus, the model may be restricted to include only flat products. In most countries, however, a variety of integrated steel mills produces both flat products and shapes so that separation is not useful.

Productive Units

Table 3-1 provides a list of the major productive units in an integrated steel mill. A small, highly aggregated model would include only a few of these productive units: blast furnaces, basic oxygen furnaces, continuous casting units, and hot and cold strip mills. A large, disaggregated model would include all of them.

Obviously, every steel mill does not include all these productive units. But the set of productive units for the model includes all the large productive units used in one or more of the steel mills.

Table 3-1. *Productive Units*

Mines
- Trucks and crushers
- Coal washing units
- Magnetic concentrators
- Flotation concentrators

Preparation of raw material
- Pellet plants
- Sinter plants
- Coke ovens
- Oxygen plants

Iron production
- Blast furnaces
- Direct reduction units

Steel production
- Basic oxygen furnaces
- Open hearth furnaces
- Electric arc furnaces

Ingot and continuous casting
- Ingot casting units
- Continuous casting units for billets
- Continuous casting units for slabs

Rolling mills
- Flat products
  - Slabbing mills
  - Plate mills
  - Hot strip mills
  - Pickling lines
  - Cold strip mills
  - Annealing furnaces
  - Temper mills
  - Tinning lines
- Nonflats
  - Blooming mills
  - Heavy section mills
  - Billet mills
  - Merchant bar mills
  - Wire rod mills
  - Seamless pipe mills

The art of model building is to include in the model only the elements that significantly affect the outcome. For example, if two adjacent productive units in a process line are always installed at the same size, it would be necessary to include only the one joint unit in the model. An example is the pickling line and the cold strip mill. If all the materials which pass through the pickling line also pass through the cold strip mill, the two units would have the same capacity and could be treated in the model as a single productive unit.

Processes

Table 3-2 lists the production processes that might be included in a large model. A smaller model would include only a few of these processes. For the most part, there is one process listed for each

Table 3-2. *Production Processes*

Mines
- Mining coal
- Washing coal
- Mining ore
- Crushing ore
- Magnetic concentration
- Flotation concentration

Preparation of raw material
- Pellet production
- Sinter production
- Coke production
- Oxygen production

Iron production
- Pig iron production with lump ore
- Pig iron production with pellets
- Sponge iron production

Steel production
- Steel production in open hearths
- Steel production in basic oxygen furnaces
- Steel production in electric arc furnaces with a high percentage of scrap iron in the charge
- Steel production in electric arc furnaces with a high percentage of sponge iron in the charge

Ingot and continuous casting
- Ingot casting
- Continuous casting of billets
- Continuous casting of slabs

Rolling
- Flat products
  - Rolling of slabs
  - Rolling of plate
  - Rolling of hot strip
  - Pickling
  - Rolling of cold strip
  - Annealing
  - Tempering
  - Production of tin plate
  - Production of galvanized sheets.
- Nonflats
  - Rolling of blooms
  - Rolling of heavy sections
  - Rolling of billets
  - Bar production
  - Wire rod production
  - Seamless pipe production

productive unit in table 3-1. In some cases, however, two or more processes can be run in the same productive unit. For example, a blast furnace may be run with either a high percentage of lump ore or a high percentage of pellets in the metal charge. An electric arc furnace may be charged with a high percentage of scrap steel or with a high percentage of sponge iron. Thus, as the mix of inputs is changed for a given productive unit a new process is specified. In principle, an infinite number of processes can be used in a given productive unit, and table 3-2 shows only a small number of these. Again, the art of modeling is to include only the processes that are necessary to capture the essential economics of the industry. Some of the inputs and processes for which substitution is important are:

- Coke, natural gas, and fuel oil in the blast furnace
- Lump ore, sponge iron, pellets, and sinter in the blast furnace burden
- Scrap, sponge iron, and molten pig iron in the basic oxygen and open hearth furnaces
- Scrap and sponge iron in electric arc furnaces.

The simplest way to model these substitution possibilities is to include two processes—one at each extreme of the substitution possibilities—and let the model solution give the best mix of the two activities. For example, one activity for the basic oxygen furnace might include 35 percent scrap and 65 percent pig iron, and another activity would include no scrap and 100 percent pig iron.

It is by now apparent that the choice of elements in each set is not independent of other choices. For example, the choice of plants to include in the model necessitates the choice of certain productive units, which in turn require that certain processes be included in the model. Likewise the choice of processes dictates that certain commodities be included in the model.

Commodities

The model should include in the set of commodities all the major inputs to and outputs from the processes. For example, a process for steel production in a basic oxygen furnace would have inputs of pig iron, scrap, refractories, and oxygen, and the output would be liquid steel. The model may or may not include minor inputs such as ferroalloys and lime. Putting them in the model permits all the significant items of cost to be included but does so at the expense of increasing the size of the model.

Table 3-3. *Commodities*

Mines
- Iron ore of various types and qualities (magnetite and hematite with different concentrations of iron, sulfur, and phosphorous)
- Coal of various qualities
- Washed coal
- Concentrated ore

Preparation of raw material
- Pellets
- Sinter
- Coke
- Coke oven gas
- Limestone
- Oxygen

Iron production
- Pig iron
- Sponge iron
- Fuel oil
- Blast furnace gas

Steel production
- Scrap steel
- Ferroalloys
- Refractories
- Dolomite
- Lime
- Electrodes
- Liquid steel
- Electricity
- BOF gas

Ingot and continuous casting
- Ingot steel
- Billets
- Slabs
- Electricity

Rolling operations
- Flat products
  - Electricity
  - Plates
  - Hot sheets
  - Pickled sheets
  - Cold sheets
  - Annealed sheets
  - Tempered sheets
  - Tin
- Nonflats
  - Blooms
  - Heavy shapes
  - Light shapes
  - Bars
  - Reinforcing rods
  - Wire
  - Seamless pipes
  - Rails

All processes
- Labor

Table 3-3 provides a list of commodities that might be used in a disaggregated model. A smaller model would include only a fraction of these commodities.

One commodity, labor, deserves special attention. Under certain circumstances, it can be argued that labor should be treated in the model not as a commodity but as a productive unit. The argument is that labor inputs cannot change as production fluctuates, but that once people are hired to run the mill at full capacity, they are employed no matter how output levels change. Thus, the cost of labor would not be related to the production of the plant but rather to the capacity of the plant.

Markets

Steel products are used at many different locations, but the model would become much too large if all possible locations were included. Thus, representative market centers are used, and it is assumed that all the steel used in the area around the center is consumed at the center. For example, a small model might include three market centers and a large model would have twenty or so. This might seem like a small number of market centers to have in a large model, but the model includes shipment activities from every plant to every market. If it is important to include many more markets, creating subsets of plants that are permitted to ship to each market would keep the model from becoming too large.

Time Periods

The dynamic models must cover a long enough time horizon to permit an interesting study of the investment possibilities in the industry. Because of distortions caused by the finite horizon of the models, it is common practice to solve them for a number of years past the period of interest. For example, if the gestation time to design and construct projects is five years, the planning period of interest is fifteen years, and the allowance for finite horizon effects is five, then the planning horizon would need to be twenty-five years.

If each time period were to cover a single year, then the model would have twenty-five time periods. Since this would make the model too large to solve, it is customary to include two to five years in each time period. Thus a model with a time horizon of twenty-four years might include eight time periods of three years each or six time periods of four years each.

New Sites

The set of new sites is like the set of plants. A static model would include in the set of plants only those already in existence. A dynamic model would include both the existing plants and potential sites for new plants. For example, a model might include eight existing plants and potential sites for three new plants. The investment problem is then to determine what productive units should be installed at these new sites as well as what increases in capacity should be made at the existing plant.

Of course, considerable engineering and design work may go into the selection of the new sites. They may be located at ports, near mines, or near markets. They must already have infrastructure or the potential for it to be constructed at reasonable cost. They may be near pools of relatively low-cost labor. Thus, the original screening of many potential sites may be done outside the model. Then a small group of the choice candidates is included as new sites in the model. Depending on the solutions obtained, it may be desirable to add to the model some of the sites which did not at first look promising. Thus, model building is not done in a single pass but rather by moving backward and forward as one's understanding of the economics of the industry or subsector increases.

At both the existing and new sites, one must consider which productive units might be increased in capacity. These units are called the expansion units for the industry.

Expansion Units

Expansion units are the productive units that are considered in expansion plans. Thus, the set of expansion units may exclude some of the types of productive units in existing plants and some productive units not yet installed in any of the existing plants.

Some of the productive units in the existing plants may embody technologies that have become outmoded. These units will be excluded from the set of expansion units. For example, open hearth furnaces, ingot casting facilities, and primary mills would be included in the set of productive units but excluded from the set of expansion units. The set of expansion units may also include some types of capital equipment not yet installed in the existing plants. For example, direct reduction units may not exist in some countries, but new discoveries of natural gas may make them a viable alternative for capacity expansion. They would not be included in the set of productive units in a static model but would be included in both the set of expansion units and the set of productive units in a dynamic model.

Transport

Although transport is not included as a set in the model, it is useful to discuss it here. Most of the major inputs to and outputs from the steel industry are moved by rail. However, there are important exceptions. Trucks often carry a significant share of the final products. Ships may also be used both to move ore and coal and to ship final products out of—and sometimes even within—a country.

It would be possible to introduce alternative modes of transport into the model and let the solution indicate the most efficient mode for each commodity in each shipment link. This is usually a needless complication, however, because the most efficient mode of transport for each commodity in each link in the transport system is well known, and that mode and the associated cost should be built directly into the model.

Within-plant transport may be a major item of cost. It has not been modeled in this book but is large enough in some cases to merit special attention.

Formulating an Investment Program

Once the planning model is fully specified, it can be used to formulate an investment program for the industry. Such a program would consider:

- Additions to capacity in existing plants
- Construction of plants at new sites
- Choice of technology
- Size of capacity expansions
- Timing of additions to capacity
- Product mix
- Transport
- Foreign trade policy
- Budget constraints

In the following subsections, these aspects of the program are considered in turn.

Additions to Capacity in Existing Plants

In the steel industry, a substantial part of the total additions to capacity come from investments in existing plants. In part, this is because the infrastructure and skilled labor are already available at those plants, and it is therefore less expensive to expand existing facilities than to build entirely new ones. In addition, certain aspects of steel technology often make this attractive. For example, in a steel shop with two basic oxygen furnaces, one of the furnaces operates while the other is being relined. Much less than half the operating time is required to reline the furnace, but a steady throughput of steel can be maintained by operating one furnace at a time. If a third basic oxygen furnace is installed to add to the capacity of the plant, then two furnaces will be operated at a time while the third is being relined. Thus, a 50 percent increase in the capital cost of the original facility results in a doubling of output.

In anticipation of this situation, the blast furnace of the original facility may have been designed with a capacity to produce enough pig iron for twice the original steel production. For a time, the steel shop would therefore have half the capacity of the blast furnace and would be a bottleneck on the production capacity of the plant. The investment in the third basic oxygen furnace would remove the bottleneck.

Since this kind of addition to capacity within existing plants is important in the steel industry, the model includes a constraint for the capacity of each productive unit rather than for each plant. Furthermore, the investment alternatives considered in the model include both additions to capacity within existing plants and expansion at new sites.

Construction of Plants at New Sites

When plans are made to expand steel production, a variety of new sites is usually considered. The sites may be at ports with good access to imported pellets and coal. Alternatively, they may be near demand centers or at points near iron ore and coal deposits where the raw materials can be brought together at low cost. New sites may be chosen for their potential for market incursion on a rival steel company or as a result of direct or indirect government intervention to achieve political balance or to decentralize the industry. Defense and security considerations may also be important in selecting sites.

No matter what the reasons were for choosing the alternative sites, the model offers a means of calculating the implications of the choice to build steel mills at any combination of the potential sites. For example, the model may be used to study how the construction of a new plant near existing facilities will cause the existing plants to lose parts of their established markets and be forced to serve more distant and less lucrative markets. Or the model may be used to cost-out quickly the implication of building a new plant at a port, near a mine, or near a market. Moreover, the calculations do not assume that the existing plants continue to operate in the same way but rather that they adapt to the presence of the new plant. Finally, the model may be used to study which technology to use—for example, direct reduction units or blast furnaces—at the new site or sites.

Choice of Technology

One of the most difficult problems in the development of expansion programs in the steel industry is the choice of technology. At times, this problem is caused by the development of new technologies, such as the basic oxygen furnace or continuous casting methods. At other times, it is due to a shift in the relative prices of inputs, such as a change in the cost of natural gas, so that the choice between direct reduction units and blast furnaces becomes a difficult one.

In such cases, it is not sufficient to calculate the total cost of inputs for each of the competing technologies and to choose the technology with the lowest cost of inputs. One productive unit may have a much higher cost of inputs but a lower capital cost than the other. Moreover, one unit may have strong economies of scale and the other little or no economies of scale in investment cost. Thus, a small unit would favor one technology and a large unit the other technology. Moreover, the choice of technology may be influenced by the location of plants.

As is the case for energy inputs in many countries, government policies may strongly affect the relative prices of inputs. It may be desirable to use the models to ask "what if" questions about government policy, such as: What will be the best technology to use for capacity expansion if the government should suddenly decontrol natural gas prices, or slowly but surely let natural gas prices rise over a ten-year period, or offer lower natural gas prices and electricity prices in some locations than in others.

The models are designed to address these questions by including production activities for alternative technologies and the associated capacity expansion options in alternative types of productive units.

Size of Capacity Expansion

One of the most important aspects of investment decisions is what size of unit to install. Should one large plant be built at a central location or a number of small plants at decentralized locations? Should a large plant be built now even though there is not yet enough demand or should a number of small plants be built, spread out over time? These two questions give examples of the tradeoff between economies of scale on the one hand and transport cost and time discounting on the other. If transport costs are low and economies of scale are pronounced, one large central plant should be constructed. But if transport costs are high and economies of scale small, a number of small plants at decentralized locations will be more economical (see Vietorisz and Manne 1963 or Kendrick 1967). If economies of scale are small and discount rates high, small plants should be constructed every few years. But if economies of scale are pronounced and discount rates are low, large plants should be constructed only infrequently (see Manne 1967). The timing may also be affected by the price of imports and exports. If exports are priced relatively high, it may be advantageous to build capacity ahead of domestic demand and export the surplus. If import prices are relatively low, it may be useful to let domestic capacity fall below domestic demand and provide the needed materials with imports for a time (see Chenery 1952).

Economies of scale also have a tradeoff with reliability which may be important. If the probability of breakdown is independent across plants, a system of many small plants will be more reliable but also more expensive than a system with a few large plants.

These four tradeoffs with economies of scale—space, time, international trade, and certainty—make the problem of the size of additions to capacity an interesting one. (In this book, however, only the first three tradeoffs are included in the models.) Furthermore, when additions to capacity are considered in the context of existing plants, the best size may be determined by the presence of complementary slack capacity in existing units.

Timing of Additions to Capacity

The best timing for the construction of new units was discussed above as it is affected by economies of scale and discount rates. Timing may also be affected by the cost of imports and the value of exports. For example, it might be economical in some cases to build a fairly large blast furnace and steel shop together with a smaller facility for rolling shapes. The excess steel might then be sold as billets to rerollers or exported in the form of billets or slabs for a time until demand had grown enough to justify the installation of rolling facilities for flat products. The timing decision in this example is whether or not to delay the construction of the flat product rolling facility while exporting billets and slabs and importing flat products.

Usually, new steel mills are constructed and existing steel mills are expanded in stages. For example, the plan for stage one might include two basic oxygen furnaces and the plan for stage two would include a third. The timing of these stages depends on the growth of demand and even on capacity expansions that may be occurring at other steel mills in the area. The model allows the careful study of the costs associated with changes in timing of all the interdependent projects in a system of plants. The plants may belong to different corporations or some may be owned by the government and others by private companies. Nonetheless, the investment decisions in them are interdependent and the model provides a means of analyzing these interdependencies.

Product Mix

If there are substantial economies of scale in the investment cost of productive units, one would expect different plants to specialize in different products. For example, one would not expect every plant to have a rolling mill for large shapes since there are substantial economies of scale in the investment cost for such a mill. Nor would one expect that every integrated steel mill would have flat product rolling mills. Instead, some mills would be expected to specialize in flat products and others in shapes. Thus, the problem of product mix is an important one in the design of investment projects.

Table 3-4 lists the final products that might be included in a disaggregated model. It is unlikely that any steel mill would produce all these products. Thus, the problem is to find a niche for the new productive units. The new units may be installed in the existing plants to permit more efficient use of the existing capacity or they may be installed at new plants. For example, a new cold strip mill might be added to take advantage of excess capacity in the hot strip mill.

The possibility of interplant shipments further compounds the choice of product mix. For example, a company may want to install a plate mill in order to produce welded pipe but may lack the steelmaking capacity to service this unit. If another plant should have some excess steel capacity, a shipment of slabs might be arranged. This would allow the

Table 3-4. *Final Products*

Nonflat products	*Flat products*
Billets	Plates
Heavy shapes	Hot sheets
Light shapes	Cold sheets
Bars	Tin plates
Reinforcing bars	Galvanized sheets
Wire rods	
Seamless pipes	
Rails	

one plant to enter the welded pipe market and permit the other to make more efficient use of its steelmaking facilities.

Once the products are fabricated, the question is how they will be transported to market.

Transport

The shipment not only of products to markets but also of raw material to plants makes transport problems important in the design of investment projects.

There are occasional bottlenecks in the transport structure of any country, and the steel industry's demand for transport services is substantial. For example, a country may experience shortages of railroad cars or bottlenecks on certain links in the rail system. Anticipation of these kinds of difficulties may substantially affect the choice of where to construct new facilities. This can be studied in the models by adding constraints to certain shipments or by increasing the cost of transport in parts of the system. One can then study the implications for investment in the steel industry of bottlenecks in the transport system.

Foreign Trade Policy

If there are large economies of scale in investment cost, one would expect plants to expand beyond the level of the domestic market and to export the excess output for a time. As demand grows, a new plant will not be built as soon as domestic supply equals domestic demand; instead, imports will be used until there is sufficient demand to justify the installation of another large facility. Thus, international trade policy may play a key role in the design of investment projects in the steel industry.

The economics of the steel industry at some locations may look favorable enough to support a facility that is largely or entirely devoted to the export market. A study of this possibility can be carried out by including export possibilities in the model. If the facility is thought to be large enough to have some impact on prices within a certain part of the world, declining export prices can be built into the model.

The model may also be used to study the question of whether to use domestic or imported raw material. If the domestic raw material is declining in quality, then the new facilities should probably be built at ports, and the remaining ores or coal should be used by the plants already located nearby.

Finally, trade in intermediate products may play a role in the design of steel investment projects. A small country might find it advantageous to invest first in rolling mills for nonflat products and to import the billets. At a later stage, it might install electric arc furnaces and import sponge iron or scrap. Later still it might invest in the facilities to produce sponge iron and import pellets.

Thus, trade policy may affect the design of investment projects with respect to raw material, intermediate products, and final products.

This chapter has provided a discussion of the specification of the planning problem and of the formulation and design of investment projects in the steel industry. The application chapters of this volume will translate this first into mathematical statements and then into a language that can be read by computers.

PART TWO

The Mexican Steel Sector: A Case Study

THE CASE STUDY INCLUDES a chapter describing the situation in the Mexican steel industry in 1979 when this study was begun, a chapter on a small static model, two chapters on a large static model, and two chapters on a small dynamic model of the industry. These models provide a slow increase in complexity from small to large and from static to dynamic; each has its own comparative advantage in analyzing the industry. The static models can be used for studies of operational efficiency, and the dynamic model is useful for analyzing investment possibilities. The small models are easier than the large to explain and less expensive to solve when sensitivity tests are performed.

The two small models are calculated in dollars and in millions of metric tons of inputs and outputs. The large model is calculated in pesos and in thousands of metric tons of inputs and outputs.

4
The Steel Sector in Mexico

THE MEXICAN STEEL SECTOR provides a useful example for this volume on investment analysis in the steel industry. It is large enough to include a diversity of production technologies and products. Yet it is small enough that a relatively small model can capture the essential economics of the industry. Furthermore, a variety of interesting economic issues confronted the industry at the time of this study. First, natural gas prices in Mexico were lower than international prices by roughly a factor of ten. This fact influenced the choice of technology for the future: direct reduction with natural gas or blast furnace reduction with coke. Second, the domestic iron ores in Mexico were severely limited, and it appeared likely that the industry would have to rely on imported iron ore in future years. This had important implications for *where* new capacity should be built. Third, the government of Mexico was attempting to encourage the decentralization of industry by offering lower natural gas prices in uncongested areas. These differences in price were great enough to affect decisions about where to add to capacity. Finally, the oil boom in Mexico was causing demand for steel products to grow rapidly so that the industry was likely to expand markedly in the coming decades.

Against this background, this chapter provides a brief overview of the steel sector in Mexico. It begins with overall demand for and supply of steel products and then discusses in turn raw material, transport, and imports and exports.

Demand for Steel Products

Since the mid-1940s, Mexico has been engaged in an industrialization process that has produced a steady growth in the demand for steel

Table 4-1. *Apparent National Consumption, 1970–79*
(thousand metric tons)

Year	*Steel*	*Increment (percent)*	*Flat products*	*Increment (percent)*	*Nonflat products*	*Increment (percent)*	*Seamless pipe*	*Increment (percent)*
1970	3,965	9.3	1,367	11.3	1,367	5.5	174	9.4
1971	3,735	– 5.8	1,361	– 0.4	1,268	– 7.2	160	– 8.0
1972	4,276	14.5	1,585	16.5	1,410	11.2	183	14.4
1973	5,351	25.1	2,062	30.1	1,670	18.4	207	13.1
1974	6,205	16.0	2,420	17.4	1,954	17.0	203	– 1.9
1975	6,444	2.6	2,365	– 2.3	2,127	8.9	238	17.2
1976	5,951	– 7.7	2,100	– 11.2	2,036	– 4.3	241	1.3
1977	7,018	17.9	2,322	10.6	1,919	– 5.9	246	2.1
1978	8,056	14.8	3,049	31.3	2,203	14.8	286	16.2
1979	9,096	12.9	3,278	7.5	2,694	22.3	392	47.0

Source: Department of Economic Studies, CANACERO.

Note: Doubt can be raised about the validity of a few numbers in the table (in thousands of metric tons). The total consumption of steel in 1977 should be 6,098 instead of 7,018 if it is to be consistent with the projected growth from 1976. The growth from 1976 to 1977 is given as

Flats	222
Nonflats	– 119
Seamless	5
	108

Then using a ratio of 1.359 tons of steel per ton of products one obtains a growth of (108) (1.359) = 147 thousand tons of steel. This added to the apparent consumption in 1976 of 5,951 yields an apparent consumption in 1977 of 5,951 + 147 = 6,098 in contrast to the figure in the table of 7,018. Our manpower resources have not been sufficient to enable us to track down the source of the inconsistency.

products. In the mid-1940s, there was only one major steel plant, and it had an installed capacity of 120,000 tons. Because the demand for iron and steel products was estimated to be over 350,000 tons, imports played an important role in satisfying internal demand. Traditionally, demand for finished steel products has always exceeded supply, and increments to capacity have been a result of large excess demand. It is only in recent years that Mexico has had installed capacity that exceeded current demand.

Since the 1970s, the steel industry's main concern has been to maintain an adequate exploration rate for iron ore reserves and to improve productivity in some of the older steel mills. Aggregate demand for steel from 1970 to 1979 is given in table 4-1. The figures correspond to "apparent national consumption," a term frequently used as an estimate for demand and obtained by the relation: production + imports − exports.

The fluctuations in demand for steel shown in table 4-1 follow the world pattern. The leading steel-producing countries, such as the United States, Japan, and the European Economic Community, had a record steel consumption in 1974 followed by a decrease in 1976 as a result of the world economic recession and a reduction of international steel trade because of the protectionist actions of some major countries. The fluctuations in the Mexican steel industry also present a cyclical pattern that reflects the economic slowdown following a change of administration every six years—in this case, 1970–76.

Classification of Steel Products

Traditionally, Mexican steel products have always been classified under the categories of flat, nonflat, and seamless pipe products. The relative share of the market that each of these holds has been: flat products, 51 percent; nonflat products, 44 percent; and seamless pipes, 5 percent. In view of the future expansion of the Mexican petroleum industry and the requirement it will have for seamless pipe and flat products, however, their relative share of demand is expected to increase in the near future. As shown in table 4-1, from 1972 to 1974, when the Mexican economy was expanding, the relative shares and the percentage increments of seamless pipe and flat products increased considerably. This result would be expected in a country trying to establish capital goods industries, and with an oil industry becoming increasingly important.

Regional Distribution of Demand

Even though Mexico has a surface of 2 million square kilometers, industrial activity is heavily concentrated within three relatively small areas surrounding Mexico City, Monterrey, and Guadalajara. Approximately 85 percent of total demand for steel products takes place within these cities, but it is expected that a decentralization program of the government, along with the natural development that the oil-producing areas will generate, will more evenly spread the demand for steel.

If the regional distribution of demand were to continue its historical pattern, 60 percent would be in Mexico City, 25 percent in Monterrey, and 15 percent in Guadalajara. As shown in map 1, these three locations form a triangle that leaves out the northwestern and southeastern regions of the country. In the next few years, the oil-associated activity offshore in the Gulf of Mexico will do little to change the isolated situation of Campeche, but inshore activity in Chiapas will improve conditions there.

For the near future, it is expected that four major demand regions—Mexico City, Monterrey, Guadalajara, and Coatzacoalcos—will have about 75 percent of total demand. The regions are identified by the major city in each, which can be considered a center of distribution for steel products. Depending on the success of the decentralization program, the northwestern region could be included as an important potential consumer, having its distribution center in Culiacán.

Projections of Future Demand

Recent dramatic increases in Mexico's oil reserves have prompted a large expansion plan in the petrochemical industry and corresponding expectations of a boom in Mexican industrial development. Steel plays a vital role in such development, mainly because steel pipe and steel sheet are essential inputs for the petrochemical sector. In addition, the growing capital goods sector will continue to demand steel ingots and various special steel products.

To obtain a more disaggregated demand for steel products, it is necessary to determine the relative shares of demand for each type of flat and nonflat product. In the near future, the structure of demand is expected to be:

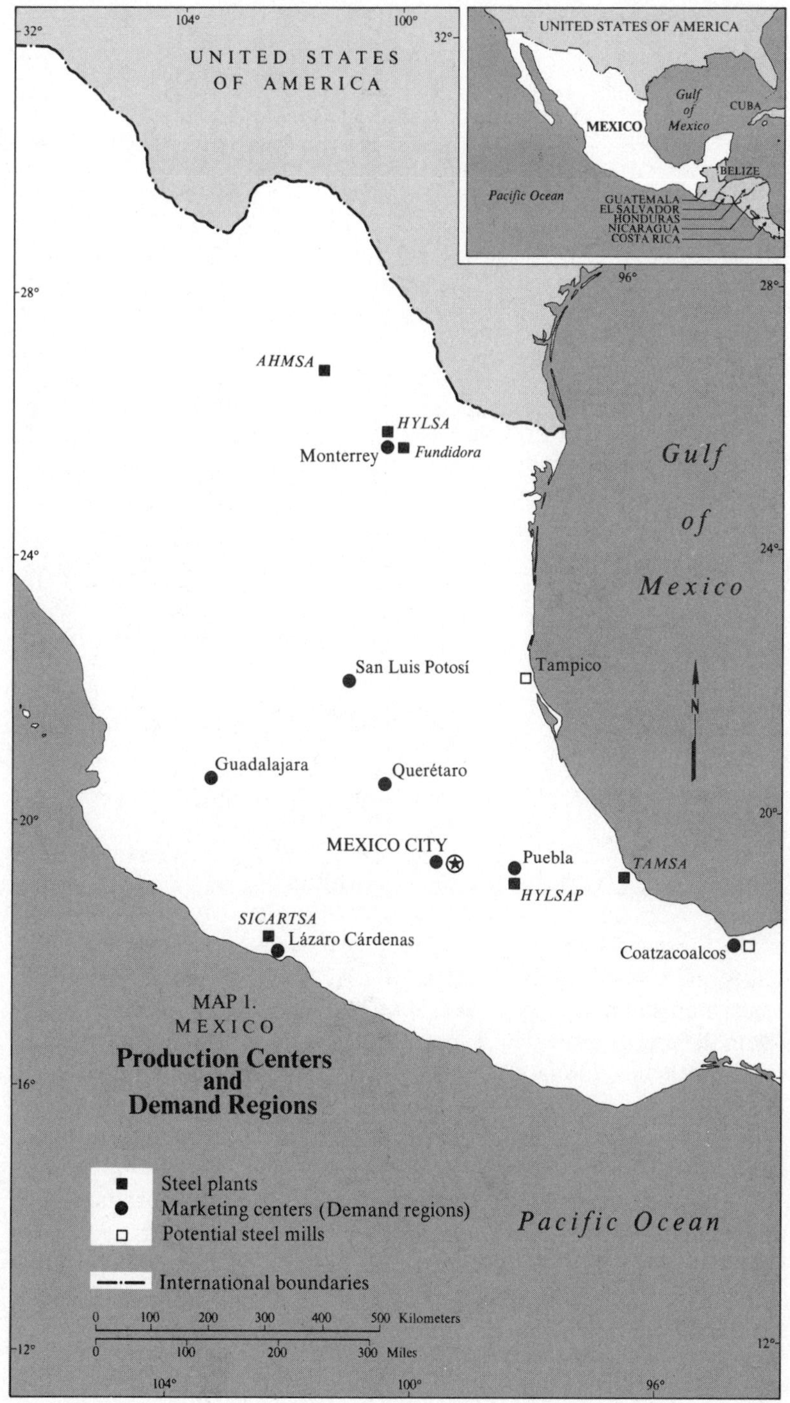

UNITED STATES OF AMERICA
UNITED STATES OF AMERICA
MEXICO
Gulf of Mexico
CUBA
BELIZE
Pacific Ocean
GUATEMALA
EL SALVADOR
HONDURAS
NICARAGUA
COSTA RICA
AHMSA
HYLSA
Monterrey
Fundidora
Gulf of Mexico
San Luis Potosí
Tampico
N
Guadalajara
Querétaro
MEXICO CITY
Puebla
HYLSAP
TAMSA
SICARTSA
Lázaro Cárdenas
Coatzacoalcos
Pacific Ocean
Steel plants
Marketing centers (Demand regions)
Potential steel mills
International boundaries
0 100 200 300 400 500 Kilometers
0 100 200 300 Miles
32°
28°
24°
20°
16°
12°
104°
100°
96°

MAP 1.
MEXICO
Production Centers and Demand Regions

	Percent
Flat products	
Steel plates	14
Hot strip sheets	11
Cold strip sheets	20
Tin mill products	6
Subtotal	51
Nonflat products	
Heavy shapes	4
Light shapes	5
Bars	5
Reinforcing rods	19
Wire	9
Rails	2
Subtotal	44
Seamless pipes	5

Nine demand regions have been identified (see map 1) and are expected to have the following shares of total demand:

	Percent		Percent
Mexico City	40	Puebla	4
Monterrey	26	Querétaro	3
Guadalajara	8	Toluca	14
Coatzacoalcos	2	San Luis Potosi	2
Lázaro Cárdenas	1		

Domestic Supply of Steel Products

In Mexico there are three types of steel producers: integrated, semi-integrated, and nonintegrated plants. As discussed earlier, integrated steel plants include all processes in steelmaking. Their operation begins with the preparation of basic raw material such as iron ore and coal and ends with the rolling process of finished products. Integrated plants usually achieve large economies of scale above a certain plant size, are complex to operate, require highly skilled labor, and produce both flat and nonflat products.

Semi-integrated steel plants do not reduce iron ore to produce steel. Their main input is steel in the form of scrap, and their first operation consists of melting the scrap in electric furnaces to obtain intermediate products such as blooms or billets. This type of plant usually specializes in the production of nonflat light products, such as bars and wire rods, which do not require large rolling mills. Flat products are not produced

Table 4-2. *Production of Raw Steel by Plant*, 1978–79
(thousand metric tons)

Plant	*1978*	*1979*
Altos Hornos de México S.A. (AHMSA)[a]	2,447	2,541
Fundidora de Monterrey S.A. (FMSA)[a]	949	888
Siderurgia Lázaro Cárdenas–Las Truchas S.A. (SICARTSA)[a]	586	646
Hojalata y Lámina S.A. Monterrey (HYLSA) Hojalata y Lámina S.A. Puebla (HYLSAP)	1,431	1,548
Tubos de Acero de México S.A. (TAMSA)	420	420
Total integrated plants	5,833	6,043
Semi-integrated plants	942	1,051
Total	6,775	7,094

a. Publicly owned companies.

by semi-integrated plants, since they require larger-scale iron and steel production and rolling units.

Nonintegrated steel plants also reroll steel products. They do not have to be large to be efficient, and their main input is scrap.

There were six integrated steel plants in Mexico in 1978–79, which accounted for 85 percent of total production. Three of these plants were controlled by the government. Table 4-2 shows the production of raw steel in 1978 and 1979.

Altos Hornos de México S.A. (AHMSA)

AHMSA was established in 1941 with the Mexican government as majority shareholder and private investors as minor participants. The steel mill was built in Monclova, Coahuila, a city in a desert region in the north of Mexico, which had no previous industrial infrastructure. The plant was originally projected to produce 100,000 tons a year of finished flat products, and it was built with second-hand equipment and a small initial investment.

In recent years, the company's expansion policy has been to preserve about 40 percent of the market share. As a result, AHMSA is the largest steel producer in Mexico, supplying almost every type of finished product. AHMSA has the concession for exploiting several iron ore mines in the northern states of Mexico. The largest mine, La Perla in the state of Chihuahua, has 49 million tons of positive reserves with 58 percent iron content. AHMSA also controls more than 530 million tons of medium quality coal in Coahuila, near the city of Monclova.

A successful operation of the mines and intensive exploration for new reserves are essential conditions for an efficient development of the company. Since it is not located near port facilities, it depends mainly on the extraction of its own coal and iron ore. The plant itself is a combination of old and new equipment. It reflects the pattern of additions to capacity that old plants usually follow, trying to keep pace with technological improvements. The older part of the steel complex, known as Steel Mill No. 1, is a mixture of steel technologies; as proficiency was being achieved in some of the traditional processes (such as open hearth furnaces), improvements were being made in the use of modern equipment (such as basic oxygen furnaces). Steel Mill No. 2 has been constructed recently.

AHMSA, as its name indicates (*altos hornos* in Spanish translates as "blast furnaces"), uses blast furnace technology for the reduction of iron ore. The metallic charge was traditionally a blend of sinter and iron ore chunks. The company has the only sintering plant in Mexico and a pelletizing plant at the iron ore mine of La Perla in Chihuahua. The installed capacity for each productive unit is given in table 4-3.

Steel Mill No. 1 has four blast furnaces of different capacities, ranging from 250,000 to 550,000 tons a year. In steelmaking, the plant has eight open hearth furnaces and two basic oxygen furnaces for a total steelmaking capacity of 2.75 million tons a year. Casting is done by pouring molten steel into ingots. The first rolling operation consists of passing the steel ingots through a primary roughing mill to obtain slabs

Table 4-3. *AHMSA: Capacity of Some Productive Units, 1979*
(thousand metric tons)

Productive unit	*Steel Mill No. 1*	*Steel Mill No. 2*
Sinter plant	1,500	0
Pellet plant[a]	600	0
Coke ovens	1,000	1,100
Blast furnace	1,800	1,500
Open hearth furnace	1,500	0
Basic oxygen furnace	1,250	820
Continuous casting unit	0	710
Roughing mill	1,850	0
Hot rolling mill	1,600	0
Cold rolling mill	700	800
Shapes rolling mill	200	0
Wire rolling mill	270	0

a. In the iron ore mine at La Perla, Chihuahua.

and blooms. The finishing section consists of hot and cold rolling mills with a total capacity of 1.6 million tons a year of flat products. The production of nonflat products plays a lesser role in the company output since the rolling capacity for nonflat is only 0.65 million tons a year.

Steel Mill No. 2 began operation in 1976. It is a fully integrated plant that operates independently of Mill No. 1, even though shipments of some intermediate products between the two mills occur. The main productive units in the plant are a set of coking batteries, a large blast furnace, a basic oxygen furnace, a continuous casting unit, a pickling line, and a cold rolling mill.

AHMSA also has a small steelmaking plant in the border town of Piedras Negras, Coahuila, north of Monclova. This plant includes a blast furnace and three open hearth furnaces that account for a small installed capacity of 0.15 million tons of steel ingots a year. The production of this plant is sent to the rolling facilities in Monclova to be processed into finished products.

Fundidora de Monterrey S.A.

Fundidora, as it is commonly known, is located in the city of Monterrey and was founded in 1900. It was the first integrated steel mill in Latin America, originally designed to produce rails for the railroad companies and shapes for the construction industry. For half a century it was the leading steel plant in Latin America, but in recent years decreases in productivity because of aging equipment have reduced its relative importance.

For years, some of the best iron ore mines in Mexico were under the control of Fundidora. Cerro del Mercado in the state of Durango and Hercules in Coahuila provided the company with high-grade ore, and, even though these mines are becoming exhausted, the relative position of Fundidora with respect to reserves is fairly good. The same cannot be asserted for coal, since total reserves are close to 100 million tons, about a fifth as much as the coal reserves of AHMSA.

The main iron-bearing material used by Fundidora in the past to feed its blast furnaces was lump ore. This was possible owing to the high quality of the ore. The declining grade of the remaining mineral in the mines, however, and the accumulation of ore fines (residue too fine to be charged directly) have generated the need for a pelletizing plant.

The two blast furnaces and eight open hearth furnaces that Fundidora has in operation are fairly old. In an effort to maintain efficiency, the blast furnaces have been modified and a BOF shop with two furnaces has

Table 4-4. *Fundidora: Capacity of Some Productive Units, 1979*
(thousand metric tons)

Productive Unit	*Capacity*
Pellet plant	750
Blast furnace	1,400
Open hearth furnace	850
Basic oxygen furnace	1,500
Roughing mill	1,450
Hot rolling mill	870
Cold rolling mill	500

been installed. Forming of semifinished products is done by ingot casting and roughing mills. A variety of hot and cold rolled sheet and commercial shapes is produced by the rolling mills. Table 4-4 gives the capacity of the main productive units of Fundidora in 1979.

The main problems the company has faced in the past decade have been labor strikes and decreasing productivity that developed into a crisis in 1976. Until that year, Fundidora had been under the control of private investors, but its mounting problems made it necessary for NAFINSA, a government credit institution, to intervene and Fundidora became a government-controlled steel mill.

Siderurgia Lázaro Cárdenas–Las Truchas S.A. (SICARTSA)

SICARTSA is the newest steel mill in Mexico. The decision to construct the new plant on the coast of Guerrero was made by the government in 1971. It was originally designed to be constructed in four stages, the first to be completed in 1976. SICARTSA was to have been operating at full capacity by 1980 and producing 1 million tons a year of nonflat products.

The plant was located in accordance with the iron ore reserves assigned to SICARTSA for its exploitation. More than 100 million tons of iron ore reserves of medium grade are located near the plant, and the mineral is transported from the mine to the pelletizing unit in a slurry pipe. Another important determinant of the seashore location of the plant is the need to import coal (mainly from Australia), since domestic reserves are located in the north of Mexico and have a high level of volatile material. (The high volatility of Mexican coal means that input-output coefficients are very high—2.2 tons of coal are required to obtain a ton of coke—and it is therefore inefficient to transport.) Reduction and

Table 4-5. *SICARTSA: Capacity of Some Productive Units, 1979*
(thousand metric tons)

Productive unit	*Capacity*
Pellet plant	1,850
Coke ovens	660
Blast furnace	1,100
Basic oxygen furnace	1,300
Continuous casting unit	1,300
Light section mill	600
Rod and bar mill	600

refining of steel is done by blast furnace and BOF units, and a continuous casting unit that is designed to produce over a million tons a year provides billets to be used in the merchant bar and wire rod mills. The first stage of SICARTSA was designed to produce 0.5 million tons of commercial shapes and 0.5 million tons of wire and wire rod. The capacity of the key productive units is given in table 4-5.

Hojalata y Lámina S.A. (HYLSA and HYLSAP)

Hojalata y Lámina was the only private integrated steel company competing with government-owned companies in Mexico in 1979. It was created in 1942 in the city of Monterrey as a subsidiary of a large brewery to provide the tin plate for beer cans.

By 1957, the company had developed the HYL process to reduce pellets to sponge iron by direct reduction with natural gas. This technological development supported the growth of the company, and by the mid-1960s the plant had become an important producer of flat products. In recent years, the HYL process has gained international recognition, and the company has increased considerably the export of its technology to countries such as Venezuela and Iran that produce natural gas.

In addition to the plant in Monterrey, which will be identified as HYLSA, the company established in the 1960s a new plant near the city of Puebla to produce nonflat steel products. This plant, known as HYLSAMEX and identified in this study as HYLSAP, is not near the iron ore mines, but rather near the most important market for its final products: the metropolitan area of Mexico City.

The company has control over iron ore reserves in the states of Jalisco, Michoacán, and Colima for a total of 70 million and 210 million tons of positive and possible reserves, respectively. The pellets required by both

Table 4-6. *HYLSA and HYLSAP: Capacity of Some Productive Units, 1979*
(thousand metric tons)

Productive unit	*HYLSA*	*HYLSAP*
Direct reduction unit	660	1,000
Electric furnace	1,000	560
Continuous casting unit	0	560
Roughing mill	1,000	0
Hot strip mill	900	0
Cold strip mill	600	0
Bar mill	0	430
Wire rolling mill	0	200

HYLSA and HYLSAP are concentrated in a pelletizing plant in the state of Colima, with an annual production of 1.5 million tons of pellets.

HYLSA (MONTERREY). The HYLSA plant had three direct reduction units, independent from one another, and a steel shop of seven electric furnaces that gave it a total capacity of 0.77 million tons of raw steel in 1979. The rolling processes include a primary and a secondary roughing mill, a pickle line, a cold rolling mill, and a tinning line. Recent modifications in the hot rolling mill, together with the addition of another electric furnace in the steel shop, have increased total capacity to 1.2 million tons of raw steel.

The location of the plant within the city of Monterrey limits considerably its expansion possibilities. Future expansion seems likely to take place either in HYLSAP near Puebla or in some other new location.

HYLSAP (PUEBLA). The HYLSAP plant in Xoxtla, very close to the city of Puebla, was designed to produce nonflat products, and it has been doing so since 1969. It consists of a direct reduction unit with four reactors, a steel shop with three electric furnaces, a continuous casting unit, and the finishing mills for reinforced bars and wire rod. Total installed capacity for the production of nonflat products added up to 0.45 million tons in 1979. The breakdown for both plants is given in table 4-6.

Tubos de Acero de México S.A. (TAMSA)

Tubos de Acero de México, commonly known as TAMSA, is near the city of Veracruz on the Gulf of Mexico. It was founded in 1952 as a nonintegrated steel plant, where imported steel ingots were to be

Table 4-7. *TAMSA: Capacity of Some Productive Units, 1979*
(thousand metric tons)

Productive unit	*Capacity*
Direct reduction unit	270
Electric furnace	450
Extrusion mill	280
Seamless pipe mill	280
Bar mill	80

transformed into seamless steel pipe. With the addition of a steel shop, TAMSA became a semi-integrated plant. Nevertheless, difficulties in the supply of steel scrap and substantial instability in the price of this input encouraged the firm to become the fourth integrated steel plant in Mexico in the mid-1960s. The plant was installed near its principal market, the oil fields of Poza Rica, Veracruz, and it was conceived as a supplier of seamless pipe for the oil industry.

TAMSA has control over a small deposit of iron ore but has not, in the past, engaged in mining activities. Most of its pellets have been purchased directly from HYLSA and other sources. It also maintains a close relation with HYLSA with respect to steelmaking technology, since it uses the HYL process for direct reduction of the pellets. The steel shop consists of four electric furnaces with a total capacity of 0.58 million tons of raw steel. In the finishing section, besides a hot extrusion mill with a capacity of 0.28 million tons of seamless pipe, TAMSA has a bar mill with a capacity of 0.25 million tons of steel bars. Table 4-7 gives a capacity breakdown.

Domestic Inputs and Raw Material

The main inputs in steelmaking are iron ore, coal, scrap, natural gas, and electricity. Of these, only iron ore and coal are mined independently by the steel companies. Scrap is either purchased in local and foreign markets or obtained by recycling processes in the rolling mills of each plant. Natural gas and electricity are provided by government monopolies in oil and gas (PEMEX) and electricity production (CFE).

Mining of Raw Material

As indicated above, mining of raw material is done individually by each company, and the permits to exploit each resource are granted by the Mexican government. By law, the mineral resources are part of the national reserve and are considered national property. Nevertheless, when considered applicable, the government gives concessions for the exploitation of some of the reserves to private companies.

A common classification of mineral reserves is that of positive, probable, and possible. Measured reserves are those that have been surveyed in detail to determine the shape and mineral content of the deposit; estimated and actual values of the reserves could differ by more than 20 percent. Indicated reserves are those that have been partially specified by sampling methods. Inferred reserves are those that have been estimated by using geological studies of the field. Surveys and measurements are rarely made of inferred reserves.

Iron Ore Mining

Table 4-8 shows the amount of iron ore reserves under the control of each company. The figures include the participation of each firm in a mining consortium created in 1974 with the participation of all steel companies except SICARTSA.

The iron ore mining consortium called Consorcio Minero Benito Juarez–Peña Colorado, commonly known as Peña Colorado, is in the state of Colima. It has a low-grade ore with 45 to 48 percent iron content that requires beneficiation methods to be of any use for the steel mills. Not far away from the mining site there is a pelletizing plant with an annual capacity of 3 million tons. The production is distributed between the steel companies. Total positive and probable reserves of the field are 104 million and 6 million tons respectively. The ownership of the reserves and the production of the pelletizing plant are distributed

Table 4-8. *Reserves of Iron Ore in Mexico, 1979*
(thousand metric tons)

Company	*Measured*	*Indicated*	*Inferred*
AHMSA	113,450	17,600	23,000
Fundidora	77,820	46,460	60,820
HYLSA	71,310	22,570	210,600
SICARTSA	105,600	11,600	0
TAMSA	17,140	1,020	0
Other reserves	41,172	37,024	26,148
Total reserves	426,492	136,274	320,668

Source : La Industria Siderurgia, vol. i, p. 45.

among the participating companies as follows: AHMSA, 50 percent; FUNDIDORA, 5 percent; HYLSA, 28.5 percent; and TAMSA, 16.5 percent. This type of organization has achieved great efficiency in distribution and operations, and because of the economies of scale in large pelletizing units, it could be the organizational mode for future mining expansions.

Coal Mining

Coal fields are concentrated in the northern part of the state of Coahuila, not far from AHMSA. Because Mexican coal has high volatility, transportation of coal would be much more inefficient than that of iron ore. This is probably the main reason that the first steel mills established in Mexico were closer to the coal mines than to the iron ore mines.

Mining of coking coal has traditionally been done by AHMSA and Fundidora. The only other steel company that consumes coal as a primary input is SICARTSA, but most of its coal is imported.

The concessions to develop coal mines are obtained by private companies in the same way as those for iron ore. The government grants permits to exploit a certain coal field, but only to Mexican companies. Table 4-9 shows total positive, probable, and possible reserves, and the concession under which such reserves are being exploited.

Most of Mexico's coal is mined underground. Because of the thinness of the seams (a maximum of 1.5 meters), the extraction of coal is limited to a maximum of 300 meters in depth. This is severe constraint on the availability of new coal reserves and on the technology to exploit them.

Steel Scrap

Steel scrap is an important input to the steel industry, regardless of the technology used in the reduction process—BOF, open hearth, or electric

Table 4-9. *Reserves of Coking Coal in Mexico, 1979*
(thousand metric tons)

Company	*Measured*	*Indicated*	*Inferred*
AHMSA	532,400	20,800	5,000
Fundidora	66,290	21,660	8,820
Carbonífera de San Patricio S.A.	15,000	0	0
Industrial Minera México S.A.	32,400	0	0
Other reserves	0	60,358	1,431,000
Total reserves	646,090	102,818	1,444,820

Table 4-10. *Origin and Use of Steel Scrap in Integrated Steel Mills, 1974–75*
(thousand metric tons)

Plant and origin of scrap	*1974*	*1975*
AHMSA		
Recycled	653	590
Domestic purchase	64	75
Imported purchase	96	222
Total	813	887
Fundidora		
Recycled	238	315
Domestic purchase	0	8
Imported purchase	40	1
Total	278	324
HYLSA		
Recycled	147	167
Domestic purchase	244	183
Imported purchase	203	337
Total	594	687
TAMSA		
Recycled	91	106
Domestic purchase	44	57
Imported purchase	0	24
Total	135	187

Table 4-11. *Imports and Exports of Raw Material and Steel Products, 1974–79*
(thousand metric tons)

Raw material and steel products	*1974*	*1975*	*1976*	*1977*	*1978*	*1979*
Imports						
Coal	369	461	94	631	391	582
Scrap	796	1,192	524	351	318	491
Steel slabs and billets	130	154	50	27	39	87
Flat products	305	294	202	309	459	476
Nonflat products	138	179	141	76	128	251
Pipes	54	48	61	825	568	601
Exports						
Flat products	8	2	15	32	14	13
Nonflat products	38	5	23	82	250	156
Pipes	71	60	96	104	84	73

furnace. Although used intensively in the integrated steel mills, scrap is even more important for the semi-integrated and nonintegrated steel plants. They depend solely on purchases of steel scrap, and since the local market experiences shortages in supply, imported steel scrap plays a major role.

Integrated steel plants satisfy their need for steel scrap either by domestic or imported purchases or by their own production. The latter is obtained with the cutting and finishing operations in the rolling mill section. This kind of first-grade scrap is called "recycled." Table 4-10 shows the use of different types of scrap by plant between 1974 and 1975.

Imports and Exports of Raw Material and Steel Products

In the early 1970s Mexico was self-sufficient in basic steel products. Most of its imports were special steel products, for which demand was not large enough to encourage domestic production. After 1974, however, excess demand for both flat and nonflat products considerably increased the need to import basic steel.

In 1979 the excess demand for steel products was due not only to the increase in consumption, but also to a decline in the production of flat products by Fundidora. In spite of the increase in the price of imported steel because of a major devaluation of the Mexican currency in 1976, there was an increase in imports of nonflat products and pipe in 1977.

Imports and exports by product types are given in table 4-11.

5
A Small Static Model

THIS CHAPTER, WHICH DRAWS in part on the study of Alatorre (1976), presents a primer on the planning of industrial programs in the steel industry, through the development of a small static model of the Mexican steel industry. First, the sets of steel mills and markets for steel products in Mexico are defined. This section overlaps slightly with the previous chapter but contains only the information required for the model. This is followed by the presentation of the small model of the industry, a listing of the data used in the model, and a discussion of the solution to the model. Later chapters in this book will use considerably more complicated models.

Recapitulation of Data on the Mexican Steel Industry

Map 2 presents an overview of the integrated steel industry in Mexico. Five of the six major steel mills in the country are included in the model; TAMSA is excluded because most of its production is for a single final product, seamless pipe. The ingot steel production capacity (in millions of metric tons) of the five plants in 1979 was:

Altos Hornos (AHMSA), Monclova, Coahuila	3.57
Fundidora, Monterrey, Nuevo León	2.35
SICARTSA, Lázaro Cárdenas, Michoacán	1.30
HYLSA, Monterrey, Nuevo León	1.13
HYLSAP, Puebla, Puebla	0.56
Total	8.91

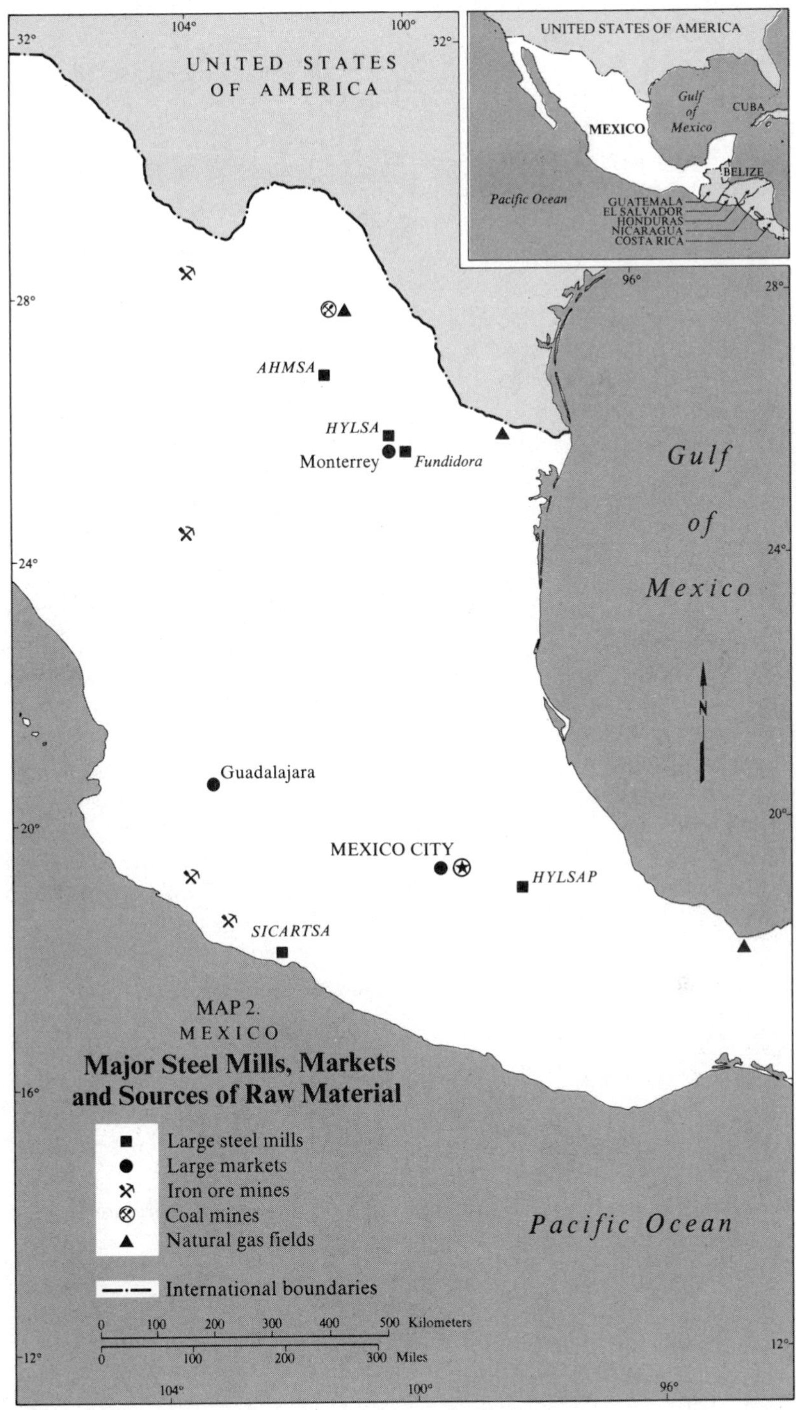

MAP 2.
MEXICO
Major Steel Mills, Markets and Sources of Raw Material

Briefly, the Altos Hornos plant is near coal and iron ore deposits, the Fundidora and HYLSA plants in Monterrey are in an important market area and not far from coal and iron ore deposits, the HYLSAP plant in Puebla is near the large Mexico City market area, and the SICARTSA plant is at a good port near iron ore deposits and not too far from the major market in Mexico City and a lesser market in Guadalajara.

A rough estimate of the size of the market for steel products was obtained by using the demand projections of the Coordinating Commission for the Steel Industry for final products of 5.209 million tons and multiplying this figure by 1.4 to convert it to ingot tons: (5.209) (1.4) = 7.296. It was assumed that 55 percent of the total market requirement was in Mexico City, 30 percent in Monterrey, and 15 percent in Guadalajara. The estimated requirement (in millions of metric tons of ingot steel) in 1979 was:

Mexico City	4.01
Monterrey	2.19
Guadalajara	1.09
Total	7.29

The capacity shown above of about 9 million tons and a market requirement of roughly 7 million tons overstate the excess capacity in 1979. The new plant at SICARTSA was not operating at full capacity at the beginning of that year, and 1.5 million tons of ingot steel capacity at Altos Hornos and 0.85 million tons of capacity at Fundidora were in the older and less efficient open hearth furnaces rather than in the newer and more efficient basic oxygen furnaces (BOF). For the purposes of this demonstration, however, we will not adjust the capacity figures downward but will leave them as they are. This will cause the model solution to show somewhat larger exports than was actually the case.

The technology employed differs from plant to plant. Altos Hornos, Fundidora, and SICARTSA have blast furnaces that use coke and iron ore pellets to produce pig iron, which is subsequently refined to steel by reduction in either open hearth furnaces or basic oxygen furnaces. HYLSA and HYLSAP employ a direct reduction technique in which iron ore pellets are first reduced by natural gas to sponge iron pellets, which are then further reduced in electric arc furnaces. Figure 5-1 provides a schematic of these processes in the simplified manner in which they are used in this small static model. For a more detailed description of the technology, see chapter 2.

Table 5-1 provides the input-output coefficients for the technologies used by the plants. The rows show the *commodities* used in the model.

Figure 5-1. *Schematic of Technologies*

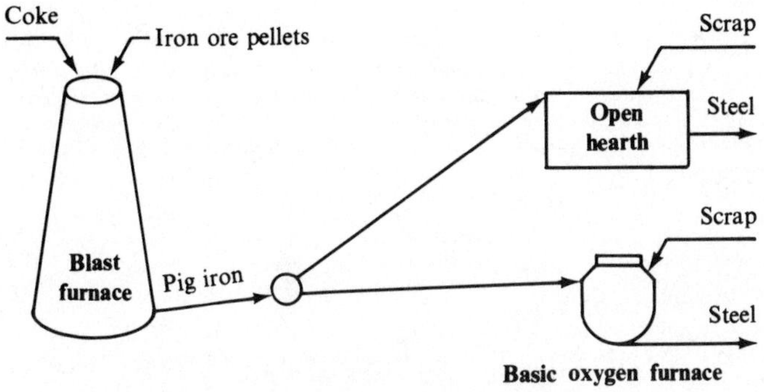

AHMSA, Fundidora, and SICARTSA

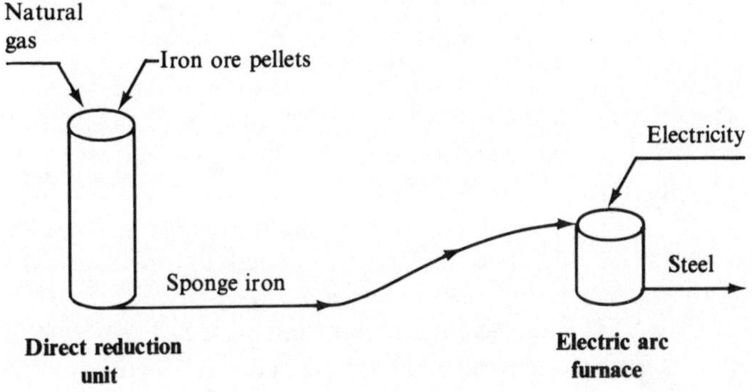

HYLSA and HYLSAP

For convenience, these commodities are divided into three groups. The first group is raw material that enters the tables only with negative coefficients; that is, the commodities are used only as inputs: iron ore pellets, coke, natural gas, electricity, and scrap. The second group enters some columns of the table with positive coefficients and others with negative coefficients; that is, the commodities are produced by some processes and consumed by others. They are called intermediate products and include pig iron and sponge iron. The third group enters

Table 5-1. *Input and Output Coefficients*

	AHMSA, *Fundidora, and* SICARTSA			HYLSA *and* HYLSAP	
Commodity	*Pig iron production*	*Steel production in open hearths*	*Steel production in* BOF	*Sponge iron pro-duction*	*Steel production in electric arc furnaces*
Iron ore pellets (tons)	– 1.58	—	—	– 1.38	—
Coke (tons)	– 0.63	—	—	—	—
Scrap (tons)	—	– 0.33	– 0.12	—	—
Pig iron (tons)	1.00	– 0.77	– 0.95	—	—
Natural gas (1,000 cubic meters)	—	—	—	– 0.57	—
Sponge iron (tons)	—	—	—	1.00	– 1.09
Electricity (megawatt-hours)	—	—	—	—	– 0.58
Steel (tons)	—	1.00	1.00	—	1.00

—Not applicable.

the tables with only positive coefficients. These commodities are called final products. In this model, there is only one final product, steel.

The columns in table 5-1 represent the *processes* used in the industry. Thus, three processes are used in the first group of plants and two processes are used in the second. Closely related to processes are *productive units.* In fact, in this model there is a one-to-one relationship between processes and productive units, shown in table 5-2. A "1" in the table indicates that the process in the column uses the productive unit in

Table 5-2. *Relation between Productive Units and Processes*

	Process				
Productive unit	*Pig iron pro-duction*	*Steel production in open hearth*	*Steel produc-tion in* BOF	*Sponge iron produc-tion*	*Steel produc-tion in electric arc*
Blast furnace	1	—	—	—	—
Open hearth	—	1	—	—	—
BOF	—	—	1	—	—
Direct reduction	—	—	—	1	—
Electric arc	—	—	—	—	1

—Not applicable.

the corresponding row. The models discussed later in this book will have alternative processes that use the same productive unit. For example, the electric arc furnaces can be charged either with relatively high amounts of sponge iron and small amounts of scrap or with the reverse of these proportions.

From the information given above one can begin to construct a small model of the industry to analyze the relative efficiency of the five different plants in meeting the product requirements for ingot steel in the three market areas. The model can also be used to identify the major bottlenecks that constrain production in the system of plants. The model will be structured to find the pattern of production levels in the steel mills and shipments from the mills to the markets that will meet the market requirements at the least cost.

The purpose of this model is not to show which steel producer in Mexico is the most efficient, but rather to illustrate how a linear programming model can be used to study the steel industry.

The Model

Sets

As discussed in chapter 3, it is convenient in modeling an industry to think in terms of sets of plants, markets, productive units, processes, and commodities. One can describe these sets in a formal manner, which will later aid in the construction of a computer model. For example, let the index i be an element of the set I of steel plants or, more formally,

$$i \in I = \{\text{Altos Hornos, Fundidora, SICARTSA, HYLSA, HYLSAP}\}.$$

This reads "i belongs to the set I of steel mills which includes Altos Hornos, Fundidora, etc."

Thus, all the sets used in the model are defined as follows:

$$\begin{aligned} i \in I &= \text{plants} \\ j \in J &= \text{markets} \\ m \in M &= \text{productive units} \\ p \in P &= \text{processes} \\ c \in C &= \text{commodities} \end{aligned}$$

where $I = \{\text{Altos Hornos, Fundidora, SICARTSA, HYLSA, HYLSAP}\}$

$J = \{\text{Mexico City, Monterrey, Guadalajara}\}$

M = {blast furnaces, open hearth furnaces, basic oxygen furnaces, direct reduction units, and electric arc furnaces}
P = {pig iron production, steel production in open hearths, steel production in BOF, sponge iron production, and steel production in electric arc furnaces}
C = {iron ore pellets, coke, natural gas, electricity, scrap, pig iron, sponge iron, and steel}

The last set, C, can be further divided into three groups in order to simplify the specification of the mathematical model. This separation may be written verbally as C consists of the three subsets CF (final products), CI (intermediate products), and CR (raw material), and mathematically as

$$C = CF \cup CI \cup CR$$

where $\cup$ = indicates the union of sets
CF = final products
CI = intermediate products
CR = raw material

with CF = {steel}
CI = {pig iron, sponge iron}
CR = {iron ore pellets, coke, natural gas, electricity, and scrap}

Variables

The variables which relate all these sets to one another represent production, shipments, exports, imports, and domestic purchases of raw material. Consider first the production (or process-level) variables:

$$z_{pi} = \text{process level for process } p \text{ in plant } i.$$

For example, if pig iron production at Altos Hornos were 3 million tons a year, one could write

$$z_{\text{pig iron production, Altos Hornos}} = 3.$$

Since it is clumsy to write out these long subscripts, the production levels will usually be described mathematically as

$$z_{pi} \quad \text{for} \quad p \in P_i, i \in I;$$

that is, as the process levels for all the processes p belonging to the set P_i

which are available at plant i, and this for all the plants i in the set I. For example, the set P_i for Altos Hornos can be written (see table 5-1):

$$P_{\text{Altos Hornos}} = \{\text{pig iron production, steel production in open hearths, and steel production in BOF}\}.$$

The variables for shipment levels represent the shipment of final products from plants to markets for each of the final commodities and are written as

$$x_{cij} = \text{shipment of commodity } c \text{ from plant } i \text{ to market } j.$$

These variables are defined for all plants and markets but are not for all commodities—only for final products. Therefore, they may be written as

$$x_{cij} \quad \text{for} \quad c \in CF, i \in I, j \in J.$$

For example, the shipment of 800 thousand tons of steel from SICARTSA to Mexico City would be written as

$$x_{\text{Steel, SICARTSA, Mexico City}} = 0.8$$

since the units used in the model are millions of metric tons.

Briefly, the other variables used in the model are

e_{ci} = exports of commodity c from plant i
v_{cj} = imports of final product c to market j
u_{ci} = purchases of domestic raw material c by plant i.

The model also includes variables for total cost and for certain subcategories of cost:

ξ = total production and shipment cost
ϕ_{ψ} = raw material cost
ϕ_{λ} = transport cost
ϕ_{π} = import cost
ϕ_{ε} = export revenues

In summary, the variables of the model are

z = process levels (production)
x = shipments of products to markets
e = exports of final products
v = imports of final products
u = domestic purchases of raw materials
ξ = total cost
ϕ = cost groups

ϕ_ψ = raw material cost
ϕ_λ = transport cost
ϕ_π = import cost
ϕ_ε = export revenues

Parameters

Only one more set of definitions—those of the parameters of the model—is required before the mathematical model can be stated. Parameters are required for input-output coefficients, capacity utilization, market requirements, prices, and transport cost.

The input-output coefficients given in table 5-1 relate commodities to processes. They are defined mathematically as

a_{cp} = input ($-$) or output ($+$) of commodity c by process p when it is operated at the unit level.

For example, from table 5-1

$$a_{\text{iron ore pellets, pig iron production}} = -1.58$$
$$a_{\text{coke, pig iron production}} = -0.63$$
$$a_{\text{pig iron, pig iron production}} = 1.00.$$

That is, 1.58 tons of pig iron pellets and 0.63 ton of coke are needed as inputs to the blast furnace to produce 1.00 ton of pig iron.

Second, the capacity utilization coefficients given in table 5-2 are represented mathematically as

$$b_{mp} = \begin{cases} 1 \text{ if productive unit } m \text{ is used by process } p \\ 0 \text{ if productive unit } m \text{ is not used by process } p. \end{cases}$$

For example,

$$b_{\text{open hearth furnace, steel production in open hearths}} = 1$$

and

$$b_{\text{open hearth furnace, steel production in BOF}} = 0.$$

Capacity parameters must be defined for each productive unit in each plant:

k_{mi} = capacity of productive unit m in plant i in metric tons per year.

These parameters values are given in table 5-3 where the rows represent productive units and the columns represent plants.

Table 5-3. *Capacity of Productive Units, 1979*
(million metric tons)

Productive unit	AHMSA	*Fundidora*	SICARTSA	HYLSA	HYLSAP
Blast furnace	3.25	1.40	1.10	—	—
Open hearth	1.50	0.85	—	—	—
BOF	2.07	1.50	1.30	—	—
Direct reduction	—	—	—	0.98	1.00
Electric arc	—	—	—	1.13	0.56

—Not applicable.

The notation for market requirements is

d_{cj} = market requirement for final product c at market j in million tons per year.

For example,

$$d_{\text{steel, Mexico City}} = 4.01 \text{ million tons.}$$

Prices require a somewhat more disaggregated treatment. A distinction will be made between the prices paid by the steel mills for domestic raw materials, the prices paid by the market areas for imported final products, and the prices received by steel companies for final products which they export. The notation for these parameters is

p_c^d = price paid for domestic purchases
p_c^v = price paid in market areas for imported final products
p_c^e = price received by steel mills for exported final products.

Table 5-4. *Prices in the Small Static Model*
(dollars per unit)

Commodity	*Domestic price*	*Import price*	*Export price*
Iron ore pellets (metric tons)	18.70	—	—
Coke (metric tons)	52.17	—	—
Natural gas (1,000 cubic meters)[a]	14.00	—	—
Electricity (megawatt-hours)	24.00	—	—
Scrap (metric tons)	105.00	—	—
Steel (metric tons)	—	150.00	140.00

—Not applicable.
a. There are 0.0283 cubic meters per cubic foot. So ($14 per thousand cubic meters) (0.0283 cubic meters per cubic foot) = $0.396 or 39.6 cents per thousand cubic feet. The 1979 world price of $3.60 per thousand cubic feet was therefore equal to $127 per thousand cubic meters.

The prices used in the model are given in table 5-4. It has been assumed that the import price of the final product steel is higher than the export price. This is ordinarily the case since freight, insurance, and other costs separate the two prices. If export prices are greater than import prices the model might have an unbounded solution since money can be made by importing and immediately reexporting.

The last set of parameters is the unit transport cost for shipping final products from plants to markets. These parameters are represented by the notation

μ^f_{ij} = unit transport cost for shipping final products from plant i to market j.

These parameters are computed from a table of distances (table 5-5) and from a cost per ton mile with the expression

$$\mu^f_{ij} = \alpha + \beta\delta^f_{ij}$$

where δ^f_{ij} = distance between plant i and market j in kilometers
α = constant term
β = proportional term.

For the model at hand, $\alpha = \$2.48$ per ton and $\beta = \$0.0084$ per ton kilometer. The resulting transport costs are given in table 5-5.

In a similar manner, the unit transport cost for shipping exports from steel mills to the nearest port is

μ^e_i = unit transport cost for shipping final products from steel mill i to the nearest port.

with

$$\mu^e_i = \alpha + \beta\delta^e_i$$

Table 5-5. *Rail Distances and Transport Costs between Plants and Markets*

	Mexico City		*Monterrey*		*Guadalajara*	
Plant	*Kilometers*	*Cost*[a]	*Kilometers*	*Cost*[a]	*Kilometers*	*Cost*[a]
AHMSA	1,204	12.59	218	4.31	1,125	11.93
Fundidora	1,017	11.02	0	2.48	1,030	11.13
SICARTSA	819	9.36	1,305	13.44	704	8.39
HYLSA	1,017	11.02	0	2.48	1,030	11.13
HYLSAP	185	4.03	1,085	11.59	760	9.50

a. Dollars per metric ton.

Table 5-6. *Distances and Transport Costs from Plants and from Markets to Nearest Port*

Plant and market	*Distance (kilometers)*	*Transport cost (dollars per metric ton)*
Plant		
AHMSA	739	8.69
Fundidora	521	6.86
SICARTSA	0	2.48
HYLSA	521	6.86
HYLSAP	315	5.13
Market		
Mexico City	428	6.08
Monterrey	521	6.86
Guadalajara	300	5.00

where the parameter δ_i^e and the transport cost μ_i^e are given in table 5-6, and the parameters α and β are 2.48 and 0.0084 respectively. Also, the import transport cost are

μ_j^v = unit transport cost for shipping final products from the nearest port to market j

with
$$\mu_j^v = \alpha + \beta\delta_j^v$$

and the δ_j^v and transport cost μ_j^v are given in table 5-6.

In summary, then, the parameters of the model are

a = process inputs ($-$) or outputs ($+$)
b = capacity utilization
k = initial capacity
d = market requirements
p^d = prices of domestic raw materials
p^v = prices of imports of final products
p^e = prices of exports of final products
μ^f = transport cost of final products
μ^e = transport cost of exports
μ^v = transport cost of imports

The mathematical model can now be stated using the notation and data discussed above.

Constraints

The constraints of the model require that (1) no more final products be shipped to domestic markets and to other countries than are produced, (2) no more intermediate products be used than are produced, (3) no more raw material be used than is purchased, (4) no more capacity be used than is available, (5) the demand requirements of each market be satisfied, and (6) exports be less than a reasonable upper bound. Each constraint is discussed in turn.

MATERIAL BALANCE CONSTRAINTS ON FINAL PRODUCTS

$$\sum_{p \in P_i} a_{cp} z_{pi} \geq \sum_{j \in J} x_{cij} + e_{ci} \qquad c \in CF \quad i \in I \tag{5.1}$$

$$\begin{bmatrix} \textit{Production of} \\ \textit{final products} \end{bmatrix} \geq \begin{bmatrix} \textit{Shipment of final} \\ \textit{products to domestic} \\ \textit{markets} \end{bmatrix} + \begin{bmatrix} \textit{Exports of} \\ \textit{final} \\ \textit{products} \end{bmatrix}$$

The symbols on the right margin of this inequality, $c \in CF$ and $i \in I$, indicate that there will be an inequality like this in the model for each combination of final products in the set CF and plants in the set I. Since there is only one final product, steel (ST), and there are five plants, there will be five such inequalities in the model.

The symbols on the left-hand side of inequality (5.1), that is,

$$\sum_{p \in P_i} a_{cp} z_{pi} \qquad c \in CF \quad i \in I \tag{5.1a}$$

then reads: "the summation over all the processes p in plant i of the coefficient a times the process level z." Consider, for example, the inequality for the plant Altos Hornos (AH). Since there are three production processes at this plant (table 5-1),

$P_{AH} =$ {pig iron production (PIP), steel production in open hearths (SOH), and steel production in BOF (SBF)}.

So the coefficients a_{cp} of interest for Altos Hornos are those in table 5-1 for the row "steel" and the columns in the set P_{AH} above.

Thus the terms in equation (5.1a) may be written as

$$a_{ST,PIP} z_{PIP,AH} + a_{ST,SOH} z_{SOH,AH} + a_{ST,SBF} z_{SBF,AH}. \tag{5.1b}$$

However, from table 5-1 these coefficients are

$$a_{ST,PIP} = 0$$
$$a_{ST,SOH} = 1$$
$$a_{ST,SBF} = 1;$$

that is, no steel is either used by or produced by the pig iron production process. One unit of steel is produced by both the steel–open hearth and the steel–BOF processes. So the entire expression (5.1) for $c =$ steel and $i =$ Altos Hornos can be written

$$z_{SOH,AH} + z_{SBF,AH} \geq \sum_{j \in J} x_{ST,AH,j} + e_{ST,AH}. \tag{5.1c}$$

$$\begin{bmatrix} \textit{Production of steel in} \\ \textit{open hearths and BOF} \\ \textit{at Altos Hornos} \end{bmatrix} \geq \begin{bmatrix} \textit{Shipments of steel} \\ \textit{to all markets } j \\ \textit{from Altos Hornos} \end{bmatrix} + \begin{bmatrix} \textit{Exports of} \\ \textit{steel from} \\ \textit{Altos Hornos} \end{bmatrix}$$

Thus inequality (5.1) requires that the total production of each final product in each plant must exceed the shipments to domestic markets and the exports.

MATERIAL BALANCE CONSTRAINTS ON INTERMEDIATE PRODUCTS

$$\sum_{p \in P_i} a_{cp} z_{pi} \geq 0 \qquad c \in CI_i \quad i \in I \tag{5.2}$$

$$\begin{bmatrix} \textit{Net production of} \\ \textit{intermediate prod-} \\ \textit{ucts} \end{bmatrix} \geq 0$$

Some processes will produce intermediate products—that is, have positive elements a_{cp}—and other processes will use those intermediate products—that is, have negative elements a_{cp} (recall table 5-1). This constraint then requires that at least as much of the intermediate product must be produced as is used.

For example, consider the Altos Hornos plant and the intermediate product pig iron, PI. Since the summation in equation (5.2) runs across the elements of the set of processes at Altos Hornos (P_{AH}), this inequality may be written as

$$a_{PI,PIP} z_{PIP,AH} + a_{PI,SOH} z_{SOH,AH} + a_{PI,SBF} z_{SBF,AH} \geq 0, \tag{5.2a}$$

and from table 5-1

$$a_{PI,PIP} = 1.00$$
$$a_{PI,SOH} = -0.77$$
$$a_{PI,SBF} = -0.95;$$

that is, pig iron is produced by the pig iron production process and used by the steel–open hearth and the steel–BOF processes. Thus, equation (5.2a) can be written as

$$(5.2b) \qquad 1.00 z_{PIP,AH} + (-0.77 z_{SOH,AH}) + (-0.95 z_{SBF,AH}) \geq 0.$$

That is, pig iron production in the blast furnace at Altos Hornos must exceed the pig iron used in the open hearth and BOF steelmaking processes at that plant.

MATERIAL BALANCE CONSTRAINTS ON RAW MATERIAL

$$(5.3) \qquad \sum_{p \in P_i} a_{cp} z_{pi} + u_{ci} \geq 0 \qquad \begin{matrix} c \in CR_i \\ i \in I \end{matrix}$$

$$\left[\text{Raw material used} \right] + \left[\begin{matrix} \text{Raw material} \\ \text{purchased} \end{matrix} \right] \geq 0$$

At least as much raw material must be purchased as is used. Note that the coefficients a_{cp} for raw material will be negative.

CAPACITY CONSTRAINTS

$$(5.4) \qquad \sum_{p \in P_i} b_{mp} z_{pi} \leq k_{mi} \qquad \begin{matrix} m \in M \\ i \in I \end{matrix}$$

$$\left[\begin{matrix} \text{Capacity} \\ \text{required} \end{matrix} \right] \leq \left[\begin{matrix} \text{Capacity} \\ \text{available} \end{matrix} \right]$$

No more capacity can be used than is available in each productive unit m in each plant i.

MARKET REQUIREMENTS

$$(5.5) \qquad \sum_{i \in I} x_{cij} + v_{cj} \geq d_{cj} \qquad \begin{matrix} c \in CF \\ j \in J \end{matrix}$$

$$\left[\begin{matrix} \text{Shipments from} \\ \text{plants to market} \end{matrix} \right] + \left[\begin{matrix} \text{Imports of final} \\ \text{product } c \text{ to} \\ \text{market } j \end{matrix} \right] \geq \left[\begin{matrix} \text{Requirement for} \\ \text{final product } c \\ \text{at market } j \end{matrix} \right]$$

Sufficient final products must be either produced or imported to meet market requirements.

MAXIMUM EXPORT

$$(5.5a) \qquad \sum_{i \in I} e_{ci} \leq \bar{e} \qquad c \in CF$$

$$\begin{bmatrix} \textit{Total exports of} \\ \textit{commodity } c \end{bmatrix} \leq \begin{bmatrix} \textit{Bound on exports} \\ \textit{of commodity } c \end{bmatrix}$$

An upper bound is placed on the total exports of each commodity c. This bound is the same for each of the commodities. The bound could be different for each commodity if $\bar{e}$ in (5.5a) were replaced with $\bar{e}_c$.

NONNEGATIVITY CONSTRAINTS

$$\begin{aligned} z_{pi} &\geq 0 \qquad && p \in P_i,\ i \in I \\ x_{cij} &\geq 0 && c \in CF, i \in I, j \in J \\ e_{ci} &\geq 0 && c \in CF, i \in I \\ v_{cj} &\geq 0 && c \in CF, j \in J \\ u_{ci} &\geq 0 && c \in CR, i \in I \end{aligned}$$

Objective Function

The above constraints must be satisfied while the analyst seeks to minimize the cost of production, transport, and imports less export revenues. (Note that both capital and labor costs are ignored in this model because they are considered to be fixed.)

(5.6)
$$\xi = \phi_\psi + \phi_\lambda + \phi_\pi - \phi_\varepsilon$$

$$\begin{bmatrix} \textit{Total} \\ \textit{cost} \end{bmatrix} = \begin{bmatrix} \textit{Raw} \\ \textit{material} \\ \textit{cost} \end{bmatrix} + \begin{bmatrix} \textit{Transport} \\ \textit{cost} \end{bmatrix} + \begin{bmatrix} \textit{Import} \\ \textit{cost} \end{bmatrix} - \begin{bmatrix} \textit{Export} \\ \textit{revenues} \end{bmatrix}$$

where

(5.7)
$$\phi_\psi = \sum_{c \in CR} \sum_{i \in I} p_c^d u_{ci}$$

$$\begin{bmatrix} \textit{Raw material} \\ \textit{cost} \end{bmatrix} = \begin{bmatrix} \textit{Domestic price times} \\ \textit{quantity purchased} \\ \textit{of raw material} \end{bmatrix}$$

(5.8)
$$\phi_\lambda = \sum_{c \in CF} \sum_{i \in I} \sum_{j \in J} \mu_{cij}^f x_{cij}$$

$$\begin{bmatrix} \textit{Transport} \\ \textit{cost} \end{bmatrix} = \begin{bmatrix} \textit{Cost of shipping final products} \\ \textit{from steel mills to markets} \end{bmatrix}$$

$$+ \sum_{c \in CF} \sum_{i \in I} \mu_i^e e_{ci} + \sum_{c \in CF} \sum_{j \in J} \mu_j^v v_{cj}$$

$$+ \begin{bmatrix} \textit{Cost of shipping final products} \\ \textit{from steel mills to nearest ports} \end{bmatrix} + \begin{bmatrix} \textit{Cost of shipping imported final} \\ \textit{products from ports to markets} \end{bmatrix}$$

(5.9)
$$\phi_\pi = \sum_{c\in CF} \sum_{j\in J} p_c^v v_{cj}$$

$$\begin{bmatrix} \textit{Import} \\ \textit{cost} \end{bmatrix} = \begin{bmatrix} \textit{Cost of final products} \\ \textit{imported to markets} \end{bmatrix}$$

(5.10)
$$\phi_\varepsilon = \sum_{c\in CF} \sum_{i\in I} p_c^e e_{ci}$$

$$\begin{bmatrix} \textit{Export} \\ \textit{revenues} \end{bmatrix} = \begin{bmatrix} \textit{Price times quantity} \\ \textit{of exports} \end{bmatrix}$$

Size of the Model

Computing the size of the model provides two kinds of information. First, it allows the analyst to estimate the computing time required to solve the problem and thus to decide on a set specification which is disaggregated enough to capture the essential elements of the problem and aggregated enough to be readily solved. Second, the computations help the analyst to check that the model specified in the equations or in the input to the matrix generator is actually the model being solved by the linear programming code.

The size of the small model is determined by the number of constraints and variables. For this section only, the notational convention is adopted that the symbols for sets represent not the set but rather the number of elements in the set. For example, *CF* is used to represent the number of final products rather than the set of final products in the model. With this convention the number of elements in the model can be written as:

CONSTRAINTS

Equation	*Number*
(5.1)	$CF \cdot I$
(5.2)	$CI \cdot I$
(5.3)	$CR \cdot I$
(5.4)	$M \cdot I$
(5.5)	$CF \cdot J$
(5.5a)	CF
(5.6)	1
(5.7)	1
(5.8)	1
(5.9)	1
(5.10)	1

$$\text{Total} = (CF + CI + CR + M)\cdot I + CF\cdot(1 + J) + 5$$

VARIABLES

Variable	*Number*
z_{pi}	$P \cdot I$
x_{cij}	$CF \cdot I \cdot J$
e_{ci}	$CF \cdot I$
v_{cj}	$CF \cdot J$
u_{ci}	$CR \cdot I$
$\xi, \phi_\psi, \phi_\lambda, \phi_\pi, \phi_\varepsilon$	5

$$\text{Total} = (P + CF \cdot J + CF + CR) \cdot I + CF \cdot J + 5$$

For the problem at hand,

$$P = 5 \qquad I = 5$$
$$M = 5 \qquad J = 3$$
$$C = 8$$
$$CF = 1$$
$$CI = 2$$
$$CR = 5$$

Therefore the number of constraints is:

$$\begin{aligned} \text{Constraints} &= (CF + CI + CR + M) \cdot I + CF \cdot (1 + J) + 5 \\ &= (1 + 2 + 5 + 5)(5) + (1)(4) + 5 \\ &= (13)5 + 9 = 74 \end{aligned}$$

and the number of variables is:

$$\begin{aligned} \text{Variables} &= (P + CF \cdot J + CF + CR) \cdot I + CF \cdot J + 5 \\ &= (5 + (1)(3) + 1 + 5)(5) + (1)(3) + 5 \\ &= (14)(5) + 3 + 5 = 70 + 8 = 78. \end{aligned}$$

In summary, the small model has 74 constraints and 78 variables. Many of these constraints and variables are not necessary, but the model has not been reduced to eliminate activities that cannot occur because plants lack the necessary productive units.

Results

Two different categories of results are presented here. First are the preliminary results achieved by using the data to do some simple comparative cost calculations. These results can be obtained quickly and easily and provide insight into the results in the second category—namely, the solutions to the linear programming model.

Preliminary Results

The small model discussed in this chapter has a structure that simplifies the calculation of comparative cost. This structure lies in the fact that (1) the sets *CR*, *CI*, and *CF* partition the entire set of commodities *C* into three sets with null intersections (that is, the subsets are nonoverlapping and cover the entire set); (2) the production technology does not include alternative processes for producing the same commodity (with one exception—the production of the final commodity steel by three alternative processes); and (3) there are no alternative processes in the model for using domestic or imported raw material and intermediate commodities.

First, it is useful to divide the set of processes into those that produce intermediate products (*PI*) and those that produce final products (*PF*). For the model at hand.

PI = {pig iron production, sponge iron production}
PF = {steel production in open hearths, steel production in BOF, and steel production in electric arc furnaces}.

Then let

ζ^n_{cp} = cost of production for intermediate commodities $c \in CI$ by processes $p \in PI$,

so that

(5.11) $$\zeta^n_{cp} = \sum_{c \in CR} a_{cp} p^d_c. \qquad c \in CI \quad p \in PI$$

$$= \left[\begin{array}{c} \textit{Unit input of raw material } c \in CR \\ \textit{per unit of output of intermediate product} \\ c \in CI \textit{ times the domestic prices of raw} \\ \textit{material } c \in CR \end{array} \right]$$

Also let

ζ^f_{cp} = cost of production for final product $c \in CF$ by process $p \in PF$

so that

(5.12) $$\zeta^f_{cp} = \sum_{c' \in CR_c} a_{c'p} p^d_{c'} + \sum_{c' \in CI_c} a_{c'p} \zeta^n_{c'p} \qquad c \in CF \quad p \in PF$$

where CR_c = set of raw materials used in producing commodity c

CI_c = set of intermediate commodities used in producing commodity c.

For example, consider the cost of production for the intermediate product pig iron. Then using the input-output data from table 5-1 and the price data from table 5-4 one can calculate intermediate cost:

$\zeta^n_{\text{pig iron, pig iron production}}$ = (1.58 tons of pellets per ton of pig iron) (\$18.70 per ton of pellets) + (0.63 ton of coke per ton of pig iron) (\$52.17 per ton of coke).
= \$29.54 + \$32.87
= \$62.41 per ton of pig iron.

Then the final cost of steel produced in the open hearths can be calculated as

$\zeta^f_{\text{steel, steel production in open hearths}}$ = (0.33 ton of scrap per ton of steel) (\$105 per ton of scrap) + (0.77 ton of pig iron per ton of steel) (\$62.41 per ton of pig iron)
= \$34.65 + \$48.05
= \$82.70 per ton of steel produced in open hearths.

Steel can also be produced in BOFS, so

$\zeta^f_{\text{steel, steel production in BOFS}}$ = (0.12 ton of scrap per ton of steel) (\$105 per ton of scrap) + (0.95 ton of pig iron per ton of steel) (\$62.41 per ton of pig iron)
= \$12.60 + \$59.28
= \$71.88 per ton of steel produced in BOFS.

Similar calculations can be made for

$$\zeta^n_{\text{sponge iron, sponge iron production}} = (1.38)(\$18.70) + (0.57)(\$14) = \$33.79$$

and

$$\zeta^f_{\text{steel, steel production in electric arc furnaces}} = (0.58)(\$24) + (1.09)(\$33.79) = \$50.75.$$

A summary of these production costs (in dollars per metric ton) shows that steel produced by the sponge iron–electric arc furnace method is less expensive than BOF steel, which in turn is less expensive than open hearth steel for the particular input prices used here:

	Pig iron production	Sponge iron production	Steel production: Open hearth	BOF	Electric arc
Pig iron	62.41	—	—	—	—
Sponge iron	—	33.79	—	—	—
Steel	—	—	82.70	71.88	50.75

The sensitivity of these results to energy cost are shown by repeating the calculations with a natural gas price of $70 per thousand cubic meters, equivalent to roughly $2 per thousand cubic feet [($70 per thousand cubic meters) (0.0283 cubic meters per cubic foot) = $1.98 per thousand cubic feet] and with an electricity price of $50 per megawatt-hour ($.05 per kilowatt-hour). The cost of steel produced by the sponge iron–electric arc furnace method then goes from $50.75 per metric ton to $100.62 per metric ton. This is greater than the cost of steel produced by the open hearth or the BOF.

In problems of industrial location one is interested not only in the cost of producing goods but also in the cost of delivering them to the markets. To set up these calculations, let

ζ^d_{cpij} = cost of making final product c by process p at plant i and delivering it to market j

$$= \zeta^f_{cpi} + \zeta^t_{ij},$$

$$= \begin{bmatrix}\textit{Production cost} \\ \textit{at plant } i\end{bmatrix} + \begin{bmatrix}\textit{Transport cost} \\ \textit{from plant } i \textit{ to} \\ \textit{market } j\end{bmatrix}$$

Table 5-7. *Delivered Cost at Market*
(dollars per metric ton)

Plant	*Mexico City*	*Monterrey*	*Guadalajara*
AHMSA	84.47	76.19	83.81
Fundidora	82.90	74.36	83.01
SICARTSA	81.24	85.32	80.27
HYLSA	61.77	53.23	61.88
HYLSAP	54.78	62.78	60.25

Note: Table 5-7 shows the delivered price of steel produced in the BOF process rather than the open hearth process for Altos Hornos and Fundidora since this is the least expensive of the two processes. These delivered costs reflect only the cost of raw material and not the costs of capital, labor, administration, and marketing.

The production costs are given above and the transport costs in table 5-5. The resulting production plus transport cost is given in table 5-7.

The most striking result of table 5-7 is the low delivered cost of steel from the sponge iron–electric arc furnace process at HYLSA and HYLSAP. With prices of natural gas and electricity nearer current world market levels this advantage changes to the blast furnace–BOF process.

Second, the table shows that SICARTSA has a transport cost advantage over both Altos Hornos and Fundidora in serving the Mexico City and Guadalajara markets. Fundidora has a transport cost advantage over Altos Hornos in all three markets.

Since it is not absolute but rather comparative cost advantage that counts in determining which plants will serve which markets, it seems likely that the Monterrey market will receive steel from Fundidora and HYLSA, the Mexico City market will be served by some combination of HYLSAP, Altos Hornos, and SICARTSA, and the Guadalajara market will be served by Altos Hornos or SICARTSA.

Linear Programming Results

The shipment pattern results from the linear programming are shown in table 5-8. (Several solutions to this problem have the same cost because the shipment costs from Fundidora and HYLSA to the markets are identical.) Fundidora and HYLSA serve the Monterrey market and Altos Hornos and HYLSAP serve the Mexico City market. SICARTSA sends steel not to Mexico City, but rather to Guadalajara and then exports the rest of its product. SICARTSA has a relative advantage as an exporter because it is located at a port, while the other plants are some

Table 5-8. *Shipment Pattern in the First Linear Programming Solution*
(million metric tons)

Plant	*Mexico City*	*Monterrey*	*Guadalajara*	*Exports*	*Total*
AHMSA	3.105	0	0.465	0	3.570
Fundidora	0	1.634	0	0	1.634
SICARTSA	0	0	0.629	0.529	1.158
HYLSA	0.346	0.553	0	0	0.899
HYLSAP	0.560	0	0	0	0.560
Total	4.011	2.187	1.094	0.529	7.821

Table 5-9. *Slack (Unused) Capacity in the First Linear Programming Solution*
(million metric tons)

Productive unit	AHMSA	*Fundidora*	SICARTSA	HYLSA	HYLSAP
Blast Furnace	0.129	0	0	0	0
Open Hearth	0	0	0	0	0
BOF	0	0.715	0.142	0	0
Direct reduction	0	0	0	0	0.390
Electric arc	0	0	0	0.231	0

distance from ports and thus incur higher transport charges if they are to export. There are no imports in the solution.

One curious aspect of the solution was confusing at first and resulted in the conclusion that there was an error in the input data. This is shown in table 5-9 which displays the slack or unused capacity in the solution for each plant. Fundidora has both open hearth furnaces and BOFS. Since the BOFS are newer and more efficient one would expect them to be used fully and the slack capacity to appear in the open hearths. As shown in table 5-9, however, the solution gives the reverse answer. This kind of check against intuition is one of the best ways to debug a linear program. A search was therefore made for an error in the inputs or in the specification of the model which would produce this strange result. A close check of the data revealed no errors, but, the problem was discovered while checking the specification of the model.

Table 5-1 provides the following input-output coefficients for the open hearth and BOF processes.

	Open Hearth	*BOF*
Scrap	– 0.33	– 0.12
Pig iron	– 0.77	– 0.95
Steel	1.00	1.00

This shows that the BOF process is the more pig iron intensive of the two processes. Furthermore, table 5-9 reveals that the blast furnaces at Fundidora are fully utilized, and thus they act as a bottleneck on production. For this reason the total cost of production and shipping in the country is minimized by using the relatively less efficient open hearth process to produce a larger amount of steel at Fundidora than would be possible with the use of the BOFS.

In fact, BOFS can be charged with a higher percentage of scrap than is used in this particular production activity. BOFS can utilize an upper limit of 30 to 40 percent of the charge as cold metal (scrap) while open hearths can utilize much higher percentages of cold metal charges—even up to 100 percent scrap. This kind of result could thus occur in reality in a steel plant.

Two possibilities offered themselves as ways of modifying the small model in the face of this problem. A new BOF activity was introduced with the following input-output coefficients:

	Old BOF activity	*New BOF activity*
Scrap	−0.12	−0.25
Pig iron	−0.95	−0.82
Steel	1.00	1.00

One possibility was to add the new activity to the model and the other was to use it to replace the old activity. It was decided to replace the old activity to keep the model as simple as possible.

One other change was also made before the model was run again. The natural gas price was increased from $14 per thousand cubic meters (equivalent to $0.40 per thousand cubic feet) to $70 per thousand cubic meters (equivalent to approximately $2 per thousand cubic feet) to make this price closer to the 1979 world market price.

The model was then solved again, and the resulting pattern of shipments is shown in table 5-10. A comparison of this solution with the first solution in table 5-8 shows that exactly the same set of shipping activities is employed. Minor changes in magnitude, however, reflect, in part, the fact that more steel can be produced in the system with the new activity since blast furnace capacity at Fundidora is no longer a bottleneck. In addition, the BOFs are now fully utilized at Fundidora, and there is excess capacity in the open hearths. This result is shown in table 5-11.

Table 5-10. *Shipment Pattern in the Second Linear Programming Solution, with Higher Natural Gas Price and New BOF Activity*
(million metric tons)

Plant	*Mexico City*	*Monter-rey*	*Guadala-jara*	*Exports*	*Total*
AHMSA	3.020	0	0.550	0	3.570
Fundidora	0	1.721	0	0	1.721
SICARTSA	0	0	0.540	0.760	1.300
HYLSA	0.430	0.469	0	0	0.899
HYLSAP	0.560	0	0	0	0.560
Total	4.010	2.190	1.090	0.760	8.050

Table 5-11. *Slack (Unused) Capacity in the Second Linear Programming Solution*
(million metric tons)

Productive unit	AHMSA	*Fundidora*	SICARTSA	HYLSA	HYLSAP
Blast furnace	0.398	0	0.034	0	0
Open hearth	0	0.629	0	0	0
BOF	0	0	0	0	0
Direct reduction	0	0	0	0	0.390
Electric arc	0	0	0	0.231	0
Total	0.398	0.629	0.034	0.231	0.390

A third solution to the linear programming was obtained by limiting total exports from the country to be less than 0.2 million metric tons per year. The resulting shipment pattern is shown in table 5-12. A comparison of total output in tables 5-10 and 5-12 (second and third solutions) shows that all plants except HYLSA produce at the same level as before. With the higher natural gas prices, HYLSA and HYLSAP are more expensive producers than the other three plants. (Of course, this balance might be changed again if higher coke prices were used.) The result is that when SICARTSA cuts back its exports from 0.76 million metric tons in the second solution to 0.20 million tons in the third solution, it uses the remaining 0.56 million tons to drive Altos Hornos out of the Guadalajara market completely. Altos Hornos in turn drives HYLSA out of the Mexico City market and HYLSA suffers a loss in production.

As mentioned above, the purpose of this discussion is not to determine the most efficient producer of steel in Mexico but rather to illustrate how a linear programming model is set up, debugged, and used to study the steel industry. In fact, when building large models of an industry that

Table 5-12. *Shipment Pattern in the Third Linear Programming Solution, with Export Bound, Higher Natural Gas Price, and New BOF Activity*
(million metric tons)

Plants	*Mexico City*	*Monterrey*	*Guadalajara*	*Exports*	*Total*
AHMSA	3.440	0	0	0	3.440
Fundidora	0	1.721	0	0	1.721
SICARTSA	0.010	0	1.090	0.200	1.300
HYLSA	0	0.469	0	0	0.469
HYLSAP	0.560	0	0	0	0.560
Total	4.010	2.190	1.090	0.200	7.490

include thousands of constraints and variables, it is useful to begin the study with a small model of this sort.

Appendix A contains a table of equivalencies between the mathematical notation and the GAMS notation, and appendix B provides a listing of the GAMS input.

Appendix A. Notational Equivalence

Inequalities

	Mathematical	*GAMS*
Material balance constraints on final products	(5.1)	MBF
Material balance constraints on intermediate products	(5.2)	MBI
Material balance constraints on raw material	(5.3)	MBR
Capacity constraints	(5.4)	CC
Market requirements	(5.5)	MR
Maximum export	(5.5a)	ME

Variables

Mathematical	*GAMS*
z	Z
x	X
e	E
v	V
u	U

Parameters

Mathematical	*GAMS*
a	A
b	B
k	K
d	D
p^d	PD
p^v	PV
p^e	PE
μ^f	MUF
μ^e	MUE
μ^v	MUV

Constraints: Some Examples

Math: (5.1) $$\sum_{p\in P} a_{cp}z_{pi} \geq \sum_{j\in J} x_{cij} + e_{ci} \qquad c\in CF,\; i\in I$$

GAMS′: MBF(CF, I)..
SUM(P, A(CF, P)*Z(P, I) = G = SUM(J, X(CF, I, J)) + E(CF, I)

Math: (5.2) $$\sum_{p\in P} a_{cp}z_{pi} \geq 0 \qquad c\in CI,\; i\in I$$

GAMS: MBI(CI, I).. SUM(P, A(CI, P)*Z(P, I)) = G = 0

Appendix B. GAMS Statement of the Small Static Model

The GAMS statement is divided into nine sections as follows:

1. Sets
2. Parameters
3. Variables
4. Equations
5. Reference map
6. Equation listing (only the first three equations of each type)
7. Column listing (only the first three columns of each type)
8. Matrix generation summary
9. Solution report
   a. Objective function
   b. Dual solution
   c. Primal solution

In the primal section of the solution report one can observe that there are constraint rows for capacity units which do not exist, such as direction reduction units at AHMSA (see page 16 of the following GAMS listing). There are also activities for processes that do not exist, such as sponge iron production at SICARTSA (GAMS listing, page 18). These activities cause no harm, but they could be eliminated by model reduction of the kind discussed in Kendrick and Meeraus (1981). In large models it is important to employ model reduction procedures.

```
GAMS 1.0  M E X I C O  -  MINI STEEL MODEL                                      01/13/83    13.33.48.    PAGE   1
          SET DEFINITIONS

                                                                                          NEW MARGIN = 002-120
          SET I     STEEL PLANTS              / AHMSA       ALTOS HORNOS - MONCLOVA
                                                FUNDIDORA  MONTERREY
                                                SICARTSA    LAZARO CARDENAS
                                                HYLSA       MONTERREY
                                                HYLSAP      PUEBLA
                                                                                      /


              J     MARKETS                   / MEXICO-DF, MONTERREY, GUADALAJA /

              C     COMMODITIES               / PELLETS     IRON ORE PELLETS - TONS
                                                COKE        TONS
                                                NAT-GAS     NATURAL GAS - 1000 N CUBIC METERS
                                                ELECTRIC    ELECTRICITY - MWH
                                                SCRAP       TONS
                                                PIG-IRON    MOLTEN PIG IRON - TONS
                                                SPONGE      SPONGE IRON - TONS
                                                STEEL       TONS                    /

              CF(C) FINAL PRODUCTS            / STEEL /


              CI(C) INTERMEDIATE PRODUCTS     / SPONGE, PIG-IRON /

              CR(C) RAW MATERIALS             / PELLETS, COKE, NAT-GAS, ELECTRIC, SCRAP /

              P     PROCESSES                 / PIG-IRON    PIG IRON PRODUCTION FROM PELLETS
                                                SPONGE      SPONGE IRON PRODUCTION
                                                STEEL-OH    STEEL PRODUCTION: OPEN HEARTH
                                                STEEL-EL    STEEL PRODUCTION: ELECTRIC FURNACE
                                                STEEL-BOF   STEEL PRODUCTION: BOF   /

              M     PRODUCTIVE UNITS          / BLAST-FURN BLAST FURNACES
                                                OPENHEARTH OPEN HEARTH FURNACES
                                                BOF        BASIC OXYGEN CONVERTERS
                                                DIRECT-RED DIRECT REDUCTION UNITS
                                                ELEC-ARC   ELECTRIC ARC FURNACES    /

```

```
GAMS 1.0  M E X I C O  -  MINI STEEL MODEL                                    01/13/83    13.33.48.    PAGE   2
          MODEL PARAMETERS

                TABLE  A(C,P)  INPUT-OUTPUT COEFFICIENTS

                   PIG-IRON  SPONGE  STEEL-OH  STEEL-EL  STEEL-BOF

          PELLETS     -1.58     -1.38
          COKE         -.63
          NAT-GAS                 -.57
          ELECTRIC                                  -.58
          SCRAP                           -.33                -.12
          PIG-IRON     1.0                -.77                -.95
          SPONGE                  1.0              -1.09
          STEEL                           1.0       1.0       1.0


                TABLE  B(M,P)  CAPACITY UTILIZATION

                   PIG-IRON  SPONGE  STEEL-OH  STEEL-EL  STEEL-BOF

          BLAST-FURN    1.0
          OPENHEARTH                       1.0
          BOF                                                  1.0
          DIRECT-RED              1.0
          ELEC-ARC                                    1.0


                TABLE  K(M,I)   CAPACITIES OF PRODUCTIVE UNITS (MILL TPY)

                   AHMSA  FUNDIDORA  SICARTSA  HYLSA  HYLSAP

          BLAST-FURN   3.25    1.40        1.10
          OPENHEARTH   1.50     .85
          BOF          2.07    1.50        1.30
          DIRECT-RED                               .98    1.00
          ELEC-ARC                                1.13     .56

            SCALARS      DT       TOTAL DEMAND FOR FINAL GOODS IN 1979 (MILLION TONS) /  5.209 /
                         RSE      RAW STEEL EQUIVALENCE (PERCENT)                     / 40     /
            PARAMETERS  D(C,J)    DEMAND FOR STEEL IN 1979 (MILL TPY)
                        DD(J)     DISTRIBUTION OF DEMAND / MEXICO-DF   55, MONTERREY   30, GUADALAJA   15 /;

            D("STEEL",J) = DT * (1 + RSE/100) * DD(J)/100;
```

```
        TABLE  RD(*,*)    RAIL DISTANCES FROM PLANTS TO MARKETS (KM)

             MEXICO-DF  MONTERREY  GUADALAJA     EXPORT

AHMSA           1204       218        1125          739
FUNDIDORA       1017                  1030          521
SICARTSA         819      1305         704
HYLSA           1017                  1030          521
HYLSAP           185      1085         760          315
IMPORT           428       521         300


  PARAMETER  MUF(I,J)  TRANSPORT RATE: FINAL PRODUCTS(US$ PER TON)
             MUV(J)    TRANSPORT RATE: IMPORTS       (US$ PER TON)
             MUE(I)    TRANSPORT RATE: EXPORTS       (US$ PER TON) ;


      MUF(I,J) = ( 2.48 + .0084*RD(I,J))       $RD(I,J);
      MUV(J)   = ( 2.48 + .0084*RD("IMPORT",J))$RD("IMPORT",J);
      MUE(I)   = ( 2.48 + .0084*RD(I,"EXPORT"))$RD(I,"EXPORT");



         TABLE PRICES(C,*)  PRODUCT PRICES (US$ PER UNIT)

            DOMESTIC  IMPORT  EXPORT

PELLETS        18.7
COKE           52.17
NAT-GAS        14.0
ELECTRIC       24.0
SCRAP         105.0
STEEL                   150.   140.



  PARAMETERS  PD(C)   DOMESTIC PRICES(US$ PER UNIT)
              PV(C)   IMPORT PRICES  (US$ PER UNIT)
              PE(C)   EXPORT PRICES  (US$ PER UNIT)
              EB      EXPORT BOUND   (MILL TPY) ;

     PD(C) = PRICES(C,"DOMESTIC");
     PV(C) = PRICES(C,"IMPORT");
     PE(C) = PRICES(C,"EXPORT");
     EB    = 1.0;
```

```
VARIABLES  Z(P,I)          PROCESS LEVEL                                (MILL TPY)
           X(C,I,J)        SHIPMENT OF FINAL PRODUCTS                   (MILL TPY)
           U(C,I)          PURCHASE OF DOMESTIC MATERIALS (MILL UNITS PER YEAR)
           V(C,J)          IMPORTS                                      (MILL TPY)
           E(C,I)          EXPORTS                                      (MILL TPY)
           PHI             TOTAL COST                                   (MILL US$)
           PHIPSI          RAW MATERIAL COST                            (MILL US$)
           PHILAM          TRANSPORT COST                               (MILL US$)
           PHIPI           IMPORT COST                                  (MILL US$)
           PHIEPS          EXPORT REVENUE                               (MILL US$)

POSITIVE VARIABLES Z, X, U, V, E

EQUATIONS  MBF(C,I)        MATERIAL BALANCES: FINAL PRODUCTS            (MILL TPY)
           MBI(C,I)        MATERIAL BALANCES: INTERMEDIATES             (MILL TPY)
           MBR(C,I)        MATERIAL BALANCES: RAW MATERIALS             (MILL TPY)
           CC(M,I)         CAPACITY CONSTRAINT                          (MILL TPY)
           MR(C,J)         MARKET REQUIREMENTS                          (MILL TPY)
           ME(C)           MAXIMUM EXPORT                               (MILL TPY)
           OBJ             ACCOUNTING: TOTAL COST                       (MILL US$)
           APSI            ACCOUNTING: RAW MATERIAL COST                (MILL US$)
           ALAM            ACCOUNTING: TRANSPORT COST                   (MILL US$)
           API             ACCOUNTING: IMPORT COST                      (MILL US$)
           AEPS            ACCOUNTING: EXPORT COST                      (MILL US$);

  MBF(CF,I)..  SUM(P, A(CF,P)*Z(P,I)) =G= SUM(J, X(CF,I,J)) + E(CF,I);

  MBI(CI,I)..  SUM(P, A(CI,P)*Z(P,I)) =G= 0 ;

  MBR(CR,I)..  SUM(P, A(CR,P)*Z(P,I)) + U(CR,I) =G= 0 ;

  CC(M,I)..    SUM(P, B(M,P)*Z(P,I)) =L= K(M,I);

  MR(CF,J)..   SUM(I, X(CF,I,J)) + V(CF,J) =G= D(CF,J);

  ME(CF)..     SUM(I, E(CF,I)) =L= EB ;

  OBJ..        PHI      =E= PHIPSI + PHILAM + PHIPI - PHIEPS ;

  APSI..       PHIPSI   =E= SUM((CR,I), PD(CR)*U(CR,I)) ;

  ALAM..       PHILAM   =E= SUM((CF,I,J), MUF(I,J)*X(CF,I,J))
                          + SUM((CF,J),   MUV(J)*V(CF,J))
                          + SUM((CF,I),   MUE(I)*E(CF,I))      ;

  API..        PHIPI    =E= SUM((CF,J), PV(CF)*V(CF,J)) ;

  AEPS..       PHIEPS   =E= SUM((CF,I), PE(CF)*E(CF,I)) ;

MODEL MEXSS  SMALL STATIC PROBLEM / ALL / ;

SOLVE MEXSS USING LP MINIMIZING PHI ;
```

```
          REFERENCE MAP OF VARIABLES


VARIABLES    TYPE    REFERENCES

A            PARAM          REF       159       161       163   DEFINED        43       DCL        43
AEPS         EQU        DEFINED       181       DCL       157
ALAM         EQU        DEFINED       175       DCL       155
API          EQU        DEFINED       179       DCL       156
APSI         EQU        DEFINED       173       DCL       154
B            PARAM          REF       165   DEFINED        57       DCL        57
C            SET            REF        23        26        28        43        81       110       123       124       125
                            128       129       130       135       136       137       138       147       148       149
                            151       152   DEFINED        14   CONTROL       128       129       130       DCL        14
CC           EQU        DEFINED       165       DCL       150
CF           SET            REF     3*159     3*167       169       175       176       177     2*179     2*181   DEFINED
                             23   CONTROL       159       167       169       175       176       177       179       181
                            DCL        23
CI           SET            REF       161   DEFINED        26   CONTROL       161       DCL        26
CR           SET            REF     2*163     2*173   DEFINED        28   CONTROL       163       173       DCL        28
D            PARAM          REF       167   DEFINED        84       DCL        81
DD           PARAM          REF        84   DEFINED        82       DCL        82
DT           PARAM          REF        84   DEFINED        79       DCL        79
E            VAR            REF       145       159       169       177       181       DCL       138
EB           PARAM          REF       169   DEFINED       131       DCL       126
I            SET            REF        68        99       101     2*104     2*106       134       135       136       138
                            147       148       149       150     3*159       161     2*163     2*165       167       169
                            173     2*175     2*177       181   DEFINED         4   CONTROL       104       106       159
                            161       163       165       167       169       173       175       177       181       DCL
                              4
J            SET            REF        81        82        84        99       100     2*104     2*105       135       137
                            151       159     3*167     2*175     2*176       179   DEFINED        12   CONTROL        84
                            104       105       159       167       175       176       179       DCL        12
K            PARAM          REF       165   DEFINED        68       DCL        68
M            SET            REF        57        68       150     2*165   DEFINED        36   CONTROL       165       DCL
                             36
MBF          EQU        DEFINED       159       DCL       147
MBI          EQU        DEFINED       161       DCL       148
MBR          EQU        DEFINED       163       DCL       149
ME           EQU        DEFINED       169       DCL       152
MEXSS        MODEL          REF       185   DEFINED       183       DCL       183
MR           EQU        DEFINED       167       DCL       151
MUE          PARAM          REF       177   DEFINED       106       DCL       101
MUF          PARAM          REF       175   DEFINED       104       DCL        99
MUV          PARAM          REF       176   DEFINED       105       DCL       100
OBJ          EQU        DEFINED       171       DCL       153
P            SET            REF        43        57       134     2*159     2*161     2*163     2*165   DEFINED        30
                        CONTROL       159       161       163       165       DCL        30
PD           PARAM          REF       173   DEFINED       128       DCL       123
PE           PARAM          REF       181   DEFINED       130       DCL       125
PHI          VAR            REF       171       185       DCL       139
PHIEPS       VAR            REF       171       181       DCL       143
PHILAM       VAR            REF       171       175       DCL       141
PHIPI        VAR            REF       171       179       DCL       142
PHIPSI       VAR            REF       171       173       DCL       140
```

```
GAMS 1.0  M E X I C O  -  MINI STEEL MODEL                                     01/13/83    13.33.48.    PAGE   6
          REFERENCE MAP OF VARIABLES

VARIABLES   TYPE    REFERENCES

PRICES      PARAM         REF       128       129       130  DEFINED      110       DCL       110
PV          PARAM         REF       179   DEFINED       129      DCL      124
RD          PARAM         REF     2*104     2*105     2*106  DEFINED       87       DCL        87
RSE         PARAM         REF        84   DEFINED        80      DCL       80
U           VAR           REF       145       163       173      DCL      136
V           VAR           REF       145       167       176      179      DCL       137
X           VAR           REF       145       159       167      175      DCL       135
Z           VAR           REF       145       159       161      163      165       DCL       134

SETS

  C          COMMODITIES
  CF         FINAL PRODUCTS
  CI         INTERPLANT
  CR         RAW/MATERIALS
  I          STEEL PLANTS
  J          MARKETS
  M          PRODUCTIVE UNITS
  P          PROCESSES

PARAMETERS

  A          INPUT-OUTPUT COEFFICIENTS
  B          CAPACITY UTILIZATION
  D          DEMAND FOR STEEL IN 1979 (MILL TPY)
  DD         DISTRIBUTION OF DEMAND
  DT         TOTAL DEMAND FOR FINAL GOODS IN 1979 (MILLION TONS)
  EB         EXPORT BOUND   (MILL TPY)
  K          CAPACITIES OF PRODUCTIVE UNITS (MILL TPY)
  MUE        TRANSPORT RATE: EXPORTS       (US$ PER TON)
  MUF        TRANSPORT RATE: FINAL PRODUCTS(US$ PER TON)
  MUV        TRANSPORT RATE: IMPORTS       (US$ PER TON)
  PD         DOMESTIC PRICES(US$ PER UNIT)
  PE         EXPORT PRICES  (US$ PER UNIT)
  PRICES     PRODUCT PRICES (US$ PER UNIT)
  PV         IMPORT PRICES  (US$ PER UNIT)
  RD         RAIL DISTANCES FROM PLANTS TO MARKETS (KM)
  RSE        RAW STEEL EQUIVALENCE (PERCENT)

VARIABLES

  E          EXPORTS                                    (MILL TPY)
  PHI        TOTAL COST                                 (MILL US$)
  PHIEPS     EXPORT REVENUE                             (MILL US$)
  PHILAM     TRANSPORT COST                             (MILL US$)
  PHIPI      IMPORT COST                                (MILL US$)
  PHIPSI     RAW MATERIAL COST                          (MILL US$)
  U          PURCHASE OF DOMESTIC MATERIALS (MILL UNITS PER YEAR)
  V          IMPORTS                                    (MILL TPY)
  X          SHIPMENT OF FINAL PRODUCTS                 (MILL TPY)
```

```
GAMS 1.0  M E X I C O  -  MINI STEEL MODEL                                01/13/83     13.33.48.     PAGE   7
          REFERENCE MAP OF VARIABLES

VARIABLES

  Z           PROCESS LEVEL                              (MILL TPY)

EQUATIONS

  AEPS        ACCOUNTING: EXPORT COST                    (MILL US$)
  ALAM        ACCOUNTING: TRANSPORT COST                 (MILL US$)
  API         ACCOUNTING: IMPORT COST                    (MILL US$)
  APSI        ACCOUNTING: RAW MATERIAL COST              (MILL US$)
  CC          CAPACITY CONSTRAINT                        (MILL TPY)
  MBF         MATERIAL BALANCES: FINAL PRODUCTS          (MILL TPY)
  MBI         MATERIAL BALANCES: INTERMEDIATES           (MILL TPY)
  MBR         MATERIAL BALANCES: RAW MATERIALS           (MILL TPY)
  ME          MAXIMUM EXPORT                             (MILL TPY)
  MR          MARKET REQUIREMENTS                        (MILL TPY)
  OBJ         ACCOUNTING: TOTAL COST                     (MILL US$)

MODELS

  MEXSS       SMALL STATIC PROBLEM
```

```
---- OBJ         =N= OBJECTIVE FUNCTION

OBJ..   PHI =N= 0 ;


---- MBF         =G= MATERIAL BALANCES: FINAL PRODUCTS         (MILL TPY)

MBF(STEEL,AHMSA)..   Z(STEEL-OH,AHMSA) + Z(STEEL-EL,AHMSA) + Z(STEEL-BOF,AHMSA) - X(STEEL,AHMSA,MEXICO-DF)
   - X(STEEL,AHMSA,MONTERREY) - X(STEEL,AHMSA,GUADALAJA) - E(STEEL,AHMSA) =G= 0 ;
MBF(STEEL,FUNDIDORA)..   Z(STEEL-OH,FUNDIDORA) + Z(STEEL-EL,FUNDIDORA) + Z(STEEL-BOF,FUNDIDORA) - X(STEEL,FUNDIDORA,MEXICO-DF)
   - X(STEEL,FUNDIDORA,MONTERREY) - X(STEEL,FUNDIDORA,GUADALAJA) - E(STEEL,FUNDIDORA) =G= 0 ;
MBF(STEEL,SICARTSA)..   Z(STEEL-OH,SICARTSA) + Z(STEEL-EL,SICARTSA) + Z(STEEL-BOF,SICARTSA) - X(STEEL,SICARTSA,MEXICO-DF)
   - X(STEEL,SICARTSA,MONTERREY) - X(STEEL,SICARTSA,GUADALAJA) - E(STEEL,SICARTSA) =G= 0 ;


---- MBI         =G= MATERIAL BALANCES: INTERMEDIATES          (MILL TPY)

MBI(PIG-IRON,AHMSA)..   Z(PIG-IRON,AHMSA) - .77*Z(STEEL-OH,AHMSA) - .95*Z(STEEL-BOF,AHMSA) =G= 0 ;
MBI(PIG-IRON,FUNDIDORA)..   Z(PIG-IRON,FUNDIDORA) - .77*Z(STEEL-OH,FUNDIDORA) - .95*Z(STEEL-BOF,FUNDIDORA) =G= 0 ;
MBI(PIG-IRON,SICARTSA)..   Z(PIG-IRON,SICARTSA) - .77*Z(STEEL-OH,SICARTSA) - .95*Z(STEEL-BOF,SICARTSA) =G= 0 ;


---- MBR         =G= MATERIAL BALANCES: RAW MATERIALS          (MILL TPY)

MBR(PELLETS,AHMSA).. - 1.58*Z(PIG-IRON,AHMSA) - 1.38*Z(SPONGE,AHMSA) + U(PELLETS,AHMSA) =G= 0 ;
MBR(PELLETS,FUNDIDORA).. - 1.58*Z(PIG-IRON,FUNDIDORA) - 1.38*Z(SPONGE,FUNDIDORA) + U(PELLETS,FUNDIDORA) =G= 0 ;
MBR(PELLETS,SICARTSA).. - 1.58*Z(PIG-IRON,SICARTSA) - 1.38*Z(SPONGE,SICARTSA) + U(PELLETS,SICARTSA) =G= 0 ;
```

```
---- CC          =L= CAPACITY CONSTRAINT                    (MILL TPY)

CC(BLAST-FURN,AHMSA)..   Z(PIG-IRON,AHMSA) =L= 3.25 ;

CC(BLAST-FURN,FUNDIDORA)..   Z(PIG-IRON,FUNDIDORA) =L= 1.4 ;

CC(BLAST-FURN,SICARTSA)..   Z(PIG-IRON,SICARTSA) =L= 1.1 ;


---- MR          =G= MARKET REQUIREMENTS                    (MILL TPY)

MR(STEEL,MEXICO-DF)..   X(STEEL,AHMSA,MEXICO-DF) + X(STEEL,FUNDIDORA,MEXICO-DF) + X(STEEL,SICARTSA,MEXICO-DF)

   + X(STEEL,HYLSA,MEXICO-DF) + X(STEEL,HYLSAP,MEXICO-DF) + V(STEEL,MEXICO-DF) =G= 4.01093 ;

MR(STEEL,MONTERREY)..   X(STEEL,AHMSA,MONTERREY) + X(STEEL,FUNDIDORA,MONTERREY) + X(STEEL,SICARTSA,MONTERREY)

   + X(STEEL,HYLSA,MONTERREY) + X(STEEL,HYLSAP,MONTERREY) + V(STEEL,MONTERREY) =G= 2.18778 ;

MR(STEEL,GUADALAJA)..   X(STEEL,AHMSA,GUADALAJA) + X(STEEL,FUNDIDORA,GUADALAJA) + X(STEEL,SICARTSA,GUADALAJA)

   + X(STEEL,HYLSA,GUADALAJA) + X(STEEL,HYLSAP,GUADALAJA) + V(STEEL,GUADALAJA) =G= 1.09389 ;


---- ME          =L= MAXIMUM EXPORT                         (MILL TPY)

ME(STEEL)..   E(STEEL,AHMSA) + E(STEEL,FUNDIDORA) + E(STEEL,SICARTSA) + E(STEEL,HYLSA) + E(STEEL,HYLSAP) =L= 1 ;


---- OBJ         =E= ACCOUNTING: TOTAL COST                 (MILL US$)

OBJ..   PHI - PHIPSI - PHILAM - PHIPI + PHIEPS =E= 0 ;


---- APSI        =E= ACCOUNTING: RAW MATERIAL COST          (MILL US$)

APSI..   PHIPSI - 18.7*U(PELLETS,AHMSA) - 18.7*U(PELLETS,FUNDIDORA) - 18.7*U(PELLETS,SICARTSA) - 18.7*U(PELLETS,HYLSA)

   - 18.7*U(PELLETS,HYLSAP) - 52.17*U(COKE,AHMSA) - 52.17*U(COKE,FUNDIDORA) - 52.17*U(COKE,SICARTSA) - 52.17*U(COKE,HYLSA)
```

```
GAMS 1.0  M E X I C O  -  MINI STEEL MODEL                                    01/13/83    13.34.08.    PAGE  10
          EQUATION LISTING

     APSI       =E= ACCOUNTING: RAW MATERIAL COST              (MILL US$)

   - 52.17*U(COKE,HYLSAP) - 14*U(NAT-GAS,AHMSA) - 14*U(NAT-GAS,FUNDIDORA) - 14*U(NAT-GAS,SICARTSA) - 14*U(NAT-GAS,HYLSA)

   - 14*U(NAT-GAS,HYLSAP) - 24*U(ELECTRIC,AHMSA) - 24*U(ELECTRIC,FUNDIDORA) - 24*U(ELECTRIC,SICARTSA) - 24*U(ELECTRIC,HYLSA)

   - 24*U(ELECTRIC,HYLSAP) - 105*U(SCRAP,AHMSA) - 105*U(SCRAP,FUNDIDORA) - 105*U(SCRAP,SICARTSA) - 105*U(SCRAP,HYLSA)

   - 105*U(SCRAP,HYLSAP) =E= 0 ;


---- ALAM       =E= ACCOUNTING: TRANSPORT COST                 (MILL US$)

ALAM..   PHILAM - 12.5936*X(STEEL,AHMSA,MEXICO-DF) - 4.3112*X(STEEL,AHMSA,MONTERREY) - 11.93*X(STEEL,AHMSA,GUADALAJA)

   - 11.0228*X(STEEL,FUNDIDORA,MEXICO-DF) - 11.132*X(STEEL,FUNDIDORA,GUADALAJA) - 9.3596*X(STEEL,SICARTSA,MEXICO-DF)

   - 13.442*X(STEEL,SICARTSA,MONTERREY) - 8.3936*X(STEEL,SICARTSA,GUADALAJA) - 11.0228*X(STEEL,HYLSA,MEXICO-DF)

   - 11.132*X(STEEL,HYLSA,GUADALAJA) - 4.034*X(STEEL,HYLSAP,MEXICO-DF) - 11.594*X(STEEL,HYLSAP,MONTERREY)

   - 8.864*X(STEEL,HYLSAP,GUADALAJA) - 6.0752*V(STEEL,MEXICO-DF) - 6.8564*V(STEEL,MONTERREY) - 5*V(STEEL,GUADALAJA)

   - 8.6876*E(STEEL,AHMSA) - 6.8564*E(STEEL,FUNDIDORA) - 6.8564*E(STEEL,HYLSA) - 5.126*E(STEEL,HYLSAP) =E= 0 ;


---- API        =E= ACCOUNTING: IMPORT COST                    (MILL US$)

API..   PHIPI - 150*V(STEEL,MEXICO-DF) - 150*V(STEEL,MONTERREY) - 150*V(STEEL,GUADALAJA) =E= 0 ;


---- AEPS       =E= ACCOUNTING: EXPORT COST                    (MILL US$)

AEPS..   PHIEPS - 140*E(STEEL,AHMSA) - 140*E(STEEL,FUNDIDORA) - 140*E(STEEL,SICARTSA) - 140*E(STEEL,HYLSA) - 140*E(STEEL,HYLSAP)

   =E= 0 ;


    75 ROWS AND    231 ENTRIES PROCESSED.     22 ROWS AND    128 ENTRIES PRINTED.
```

```
          COLUMN LISTING

---- Z          *PL* PROCESS LEVEL                        (MILL TPY)

                      Z(PIG-IRON,AHMSA)
           1.           MBI(PIG-IRON,AHMSA)
          -1.58         MBR(PELLETS,AHMSA)
           -.63         MBR(COKE,AHMSA)
           1.           CC(BLAST-FURN,AHMSA)

                      Z(SPONGE,AHMSA)
           1.           MBI(SPONGE,AHMSA)
          -1.38         MBR(PELLETS,AHMSA)
           -.57         MBR(NAT-GAS,AHMSA)
           1.           CC(DIRECT-RED,AHMSA)

                      Z(STEEL-OH,AHMSA)
           1.           MBF(STEEL,AHMSA)
           -.77         MBI(PIG-IRON,AHMSA)
           -.33         MBR(SCRAP,AHMSA)
           1.           CC(OPENHEARTH,AHMSA)


---- X          *PL* SHIPMENT OF FINAL PRODUCTS           (MILL TPY)

                      X(STEEL,AHMSA,MEXICO-DF)
          -1.           MBF(STEEL,AHMSA)
           1.           MR(STEEL,MEXICO-DF)
         -12.5936       ALAM

                      X(STEEL,FUNDIDORA,MEXICO-DF)
          -1.           MBF(STEEL,FUNDIDORA)
           1.           MR(STEEL,MEXICO-DF)
         -11.0228       ALAM

                      X(STEEL,SICARTSA,MEXICO-DF)
          -1.           MBF(STEEL,SICARTSA)
           1.           MR(STEEL,MEXICO-DF)
          -9.3596       ALAM


---- E          *PL* EXPORTS                              (MILL TPY)

                      E(STEEL,AHMSA)
          -1.           MBF(STEEL,AHMSA)
           1.           ME(STEEL)
          -8.6876       ALAM
        -140.           AEPS
```

```
     E          *PL* EXPORTS                                  (MILL TPY)


                    E(STEEL,FUNDIDORA)
       -1.            MBF(STEEL,FUNDIDORA)
        1.            ME(STEEL)
       -6.8564        ALAM
     -140.            AEPS

                    E(STEEL,SICARTSA)
       -1.            MBF(STEEL,SICARTSA)
        1.            ME(STEEL)
     -140.            AEPS


---- U          *PL* PURCHASE OF DOMESTIC MATERIALS (MILL UNITS PER YEAR)


                    U(PELLETS,AHMSA)
        1.            MBR(PELLETS,AHMSA)
      -18.7           APSI

                    U(COKE,AHMSA)
        1.            MBR(COKE,AHMSA)
      -52.17          APSI

                    U(NAT-GAS,AHMSA)
        1.            MBR(NAT-GAS,AHMSA)
      -14.            APSI


---- V          *PL* IMPORTS                                  (MILL TPY)


                    V(STEEL,MEXICO-DF)
        1.            MR(STEEL,MEXICO-DF)
       -6.0752        ALAM
     -150.            API

                    V(STEEL,MONTERREY)
        1.            MR(STEEL,MONTERREY)
       -6.8564        ALAM
     -150.            API

                    V(STEEL,GUADALAJA)
        1.            MR(STEEL,GUADALAJA)
       -5.            ALAM
     -150.            API
```

```
         COLUMN LISTING

---- PHI         *FR* TOTAL COST                       (MILL US$)

                      PHI
           1.           OBJ
           1.           OBJ

---- PHIPSI      *FR* RAW MATERIAL COST                (MILL US$)

                      PHIPSI
          -1.           OBJ
           1.           APSI

---- PHILAM      *FR* TRANSPORT COST                   (MILL US$)

                      PHILAM
          -1.           OBJ
           1.           ALAM

---- PHIPI       *FR* IMPORT COST                      (MILL US$)

                      PHIPI
          -1.           OBJ
           1.           API

---- PHIEPS      *FR* EXPORT REVENUE                   (MILL US$)

                      PHIEPS
           1.           OBJ
           1.           AEPS

   78 COLS AND   231 ENTRIES PROCESSED.   20 COLS AND   57 ENTRIES PRINTED.
```

```
GAMS 1.0  M E X I C O  -  MINI STEEL MODEL                                   01/13/83     13.34.08.     PAGE  14
          MPS GENERATION


    MATRIX GENERATION SUMMARY

EQUATIONS                 VARIABLES                  MPS MATRIX                 MPS BASIS

TYPE     NUMBER           TYPE       NUMBER          SECTION   NUMBER           STATUS  ROWS  COLUMNS
 FREE         1            FREE           5           ROWS         75            LOWER     0       78
 EQUAL        5            POSITIVE      73           COLUMNS     231            UPPER     0        0
 GREATER     43            NEGATIVE       0           RHS          16            BASIC    75        0
 LESS        26            FIXED          0           BOUNDS        5            USED      0        0
 RANGED       0            BINARY         0           RANGES        0
  TOTAL      75            INTEGER        0            TOTAL      327
                            TOTAL        78


FIELD LENGTH OR WORKSPACE REQUESTED =  16758  040566B
MAXIMUM FIELDLENGTH                 = 130560  377000B
WORK OPTION REQUESTED               =      0  000000B
```

```
GAMS 1.0  M E X I C O  -  MINI STEEL MODEL                                              01/13/83     13.34.21.     PAGE  15
          SOLUTION REPORT

                                  A P E X - I    C O N T R O L    P R O G R A M        APEX-I 1.014   FIELD LENGTH 040600 OCTAL

 EQUATIONS                        VARIABLES                        NON-ZEROS                          MISC.TOTALS
 TYPE       NUMBER                 NAME           NUMBER           NAME            NUMBER
 EQ (E)          5                 COLUMNS            78           AIJS (COL)         231             MINOR ERRORS          0
 LE (L)         26                 RHS                 1           AIJS (RHS)          16             DENSITY 0/0       3.949
 GE (G)         43                   TOTAL            79             TOTAL            247             UNIQUE VALUES        51
 FR (N)          1                MIN FL(8)       035000           AVER NZ/CO        2.96             INDIRECT NAMES        0
  TOTAL         75                REC FL(8)       035000           AVER NZ/RO        3.08              TOTAL VALUES        51


 *****  COUNT OF PRIMAL INFEASIBILITY  :               0          *****
 *****  COUNT OF MAJOR ITERATIONS      :              48          *****
 *****  COUNT OF MINOR ITERATIONS      :             100          *****

 *****  TERMINATION STATUS  :            1  OPTIMAL SOLUTION            TOTAL UTILIZATION :          .590 *****


VALUE OF OBJECTIVE FUNCTION =      538.81


---- MBF         MATERIAL BALANCES: FINAL PRODUCTS         (MILL TPY)

                                 RHS LOWER    ROW ACTIVITY     RHS UPPER       MARGINAL

 STEEL      .AHMSA                   .             .             +INF       -136.46360   GE
 STEEL      .FUNDIDORA               .             .             +INF       -138.03440   GE
 STEEL      .SICARTSA                .             .             +INF       -140.00000   GE
 STEEL      .HYLSA                   .             .             +INF       -138.03440   GE
 STEEL      .HYLSAP                  .             .             +INF       -145.02320   GE


---- MBI         MATERIAL BALANCES: INTERMEDIATES          (MILL TPY)

                                 RHS LOWER    ROW ACTIVITY     RHS UPPER       MARGINAL

 PIG-IRON   .AHMSA                   .             .             +INF        -62.41310   GE
 SPONGE     .AHMSA                   .             .             +INF        -33.78600   GE
 PIG-IRON   .FUNDIDORA               .             .             +INF       -132.03621   GE
 SPONGE     .FUNDIDORA               .             .             +INF        -33.78600   GE
 PIG-IRON   .SICARTSA                .             .             +INF       -134.10526   GE
 SPONGE     .SICARTSA                .             .             +INF        -33.78600   GE
 PIG-IRON   .HYLSA                   .             .             +INF        -62.41310   GE
 SPONGE     .HYLSA                   .             .             +INF       -113.86642   GE
 PIG-IRON   .HYLSAP                  .             .             +INF        -62.41310   GE
 SPONGE     .HYLSAP                  .             .             +INF        -33.78600   GE
```

GAMS 1.0 M E X I C O - MINI STEEL MODEL 01/13/83 13.34.21. PAGE 16
SOLUTION REPORT

---- MBR MATERIAL BALANCES: RAW MATERIALS (MILL TPY)

	RHS LOWER	ROW ACTIVITY	RHS UPPER	MARGINAL	
PELLETS .AHMSA	.	.	+INF	-18.70000	GE
COKE .AHMSA	.	.	+INF	-52.17000	GE
NAT-GAS .AHMSA	.	.	+INF	-14.00000	GE
ELECTRIC .AHMSA	.	.	+INF	-24.00000	GE
SCRAP .AHMSA	.	.	+INF	-105.00000	GE
PELLETS .FUNDIDORA	.	.	+INF	-18.70000	GE
COKE .FUNDIDORA	.	.	+INF	-52.17000	GE
NAT-GAS .FUNDIDORA	.	.	+INF	-14.00000	GE
ELECTRIC .FUNDIDORA	.	.	+INF	-24.00000	GE
SCRAP .FUNDIDORA	.	.	+INF	-105.00000	GE
PELLETS .SICARTSA	.	.	+INF	-18.70000	GE
COKE .SICARTSA	.	.	+INF	-52.17000	GE
NAT-GAS .SICARTSA	.	.	+INF	-14.00000	GE
ELECTRIC .SICARTSA	.	.	+INF	-24.00000	GE
SCRAP .SICARTSA	.	.	+INF	-105.00000	GE
PELLETS .HYLSA	.	.	+INF	-18.70000	GE
COKE .HYLSA	.	.	+INF	-52.17000	GE
NAT-GAS .HYLSA	.	.	+INF	-14.00000	GE
ELECTRIC .HYLSA	.	.	+INF	-24.00000	GE
SCRAP .HYLSA	.	.	+INF	-105.00000	GE
PELLETS .HYLSAP	.	.	+INF	-18.70000	GE
COKE .HYLSAP	.	.	+INF	-52.17000	GE
NAT-GAS .HYLSAP	.	.	+INF	-14.00000	GE
ELECTRIC .HYLSAP	.	.	+INF	-24.00000	GE
SCRAP .HYLSAP	.	.	+INF	-105.00000	GE

---- CC CAPACITY CONSTRAINT (MILL TPY)

	RHS LOWER	ROW ACTIVITY	RHS UPPER	MARGINAL	
BLAST-FURN.AHMSA	-INF	3.12150	3.25000	.	BLE
OPENHEARTH.AHMSA	-INF	1.50000	1.50000	53.75551	LE
BOF .AHMSA	-INF	2.07000	2.07000	64.57116	LE
DIRECT-RED.AHMSA	-INF	.	.	.	BLE
ELEC-ARC .AHMSA	-INF	.	.	85.71686	LE
BLAST-FURN.FUNDIDORA	-INF	1.40000	1.40000	69.62311	LE
OPENHEARTH.FUNDIDORA	-INF	.85000	.85000	1.71652	LE
BOF .FUNDIDORA	-INF	.78474	1.50000	.	BLE
DIRECT-RED.FUNDIDORA	-INF	.	.	.	BLE
ELEC-ARC .FUNDIDORA	-INF	.	.	87.28766	LE
BLAST-FURN.SICARTSA	-INF	1.10000	1.10000	71.69216	LE
OPENHEARTH.SICARTSA	-INF	.	.	2.08895	LE
BOF .SICARTSA	-INF	1.15789	1.30000	.	BLE
DIRECT-RED.SICARTSA	-INF	.	.	.	BLE
ELEC-ARC .SICARTSA	-INF	.	.	89.25326	LE
BLAST-FURN.HYLSA	-INF	.	.	.	BLE

```
GAMS 1.0  M E X I C O  -  MINI STEEL MODEL                                                 01/13/83     13.34.21.     PAGE  17
          SOLUTION REPORT


     CC          CAPACITY CONSTRAINT                       (MILL TPY)

                                  RHS LOWER   ROW ACTIVITY      RHS UPPER       MARGINAL

OPENHEARTH.HYLSA                    -INF           .               .           55.32631  LE
BOF       .HYLSA                    -INF           .               .           66.14196  LE
DIRECT-RED.HYLSA                    -INF         .98000          .98000        80.08042  LE
ELEC-ARC  .HYLSA                    -INF         .89908         1.13000            .     BLE
BLAST-FURN.HYLSAP                   -INF           .               .               .     BLE
OPENHEARTH.HYLSAP                   -INF           .               .           62.31511  LE
BOF       .HYLSAP                   -INF           .               .           73.13076  LE
DIRECT-RED.HYLSAP                   -INF         .61040         1.00000            .     BLE
ELEC-ARC  .HYLSAP                   -INF         .56000          .56000        94.27646  LE


---- MR          MARKET REQUIREMENTS                       (MILL TPY)

                                  RHS LOWER   ROW ACTIVITY      RHS UPPER       MARGINAL

STEEL     .MEXICO-DF              4.01093        4.01093          +INF        -149.05720  GE
STEEL     .MONTERREY              2.18778        2.18778          +INF        -138.03440  GE
STEEL     .GUADALAJA              1.09389        1.09389          +INF        -148.39360  GE


---- ME          MAXIMUM EXPORT                            (MILL TPY)

                 RHS LOWER   ROW ACTIVITY      RHS UPPER       MARGINAL

STEEL              -INF           .52911        1.00000            .       BLE


                     RHS LOWER   ROW ACTIVITY      RHS UPPER       MARGINAL
---- OBJ                 .             .               .           -1.00000  EQ        ACCOUNTING: TOTAL COST
---- APSI                .             .               .           -1.00000  EQ        ACCOUNTING: RAW MATERIAL COST
---- ALAM                .             .               .           -1.00000  EQ        ACCOUNTING: TRANSPORT COST
---- API                 .             .               .            -.95596  EQ        ACCOUNTING: IMPORT COST
---- AEPS                .             .               .            1.00000  EQ        ACCOUNTING: EXPORT COST


---- Z           PROCESS LEVEL                             (MILL TPY)

                                  COL LOWER   COL ACTIVITY      COL UPPER       MARGINAL

PIG-IRON  .AHMSA                      .          3.12150          +INF             .     BPL
SPONGE    .AHMSA                      .             .             +INF             .     BPL
STEEL-OH  .AHMSA                      .          1.50000          +INF             .     BPL
STEEL-EL  .AHMSA                      .             .             +INF             .     BPL
STEEL-BOF .AHMSA                      .          2.07000          +INF             .     BPL
PIG-IRON  .FUNDIDORA                  .          1.40000          +INF             .     BPL
SPONGE    .FUNDIDORA                  .             .             +INF             .     BPL
```

Z PROCESS LEVEL (MILL TPY)

		COL LOWER	COL ACTIVITY	COL UPPER	MARGINAL	
STEEL-OH	.FUNDIDORA	.	.85000	+INF	.	BPL
STEEL-EL	.FUNDIDORA	.	.	+INF	.	BPL
STEEL-BOF	.FUNDIDORA	.	.78474	+INF	.	BPL
PIG-IRON	.SICARTSA	.	1.10000	+INF	.	BPL
SPONGE	.SICARTSA	.	.	+INF	.	BPL
STEEL-OH	.SICARTSA	.	.	+INF	.	BPL
STEEL-EL	.SICARTSA	.	.	+INF	.	BPL
STEEL-BOF	.SICARTSA	.	1.15789	+INF	.	BPL
PIG-IRON	.HYLSA	.	.	+INF	.	BPL
SPONGE	.HYLSA	.	.98000	+INF	.	BPL
STEEL-OH	.HYLSA	.	.	+INF	.	BPL
STEEL-EL	.HYLSA	.	.89908	+INF	.	BPL
STEEL-BOF	.HYLSA	.	.	+INF	.	BPL
PIG-IRON	.HYLSAP	.	.	+INF	.	BPL
SPONGE	.HYLSAP	.	.61040	+INF	.	BPL
STEEL-OH	.HYLSAP	.	.	+INF	.	BPL
STEEL-EL	.HYLSAP	.	.56000	+INF	.	BPL
STEEL-BOF	.HYLSAP	.	.	+INF	.	BPL

---- X SHIPMENT OF FINAL PRODUCTS (MILL TPY)

			COL LOWER	COL ACTIVITY	COL UPPER	MARGINAL	
STEEL	.AHMSA	.MEXICO-DF	.	3.10489	+INF	.	BPL
STEEL	.FUNDIDORA	.MEXICO-DF	.	.	+INF	.	*PL
STEEL	.SICARTSA	.MEXICO-DF	.	.	+INF	.30240	PL
STEEL	.HYLSA	.MEXICO-DF	.	.34604	+INF	.	BPL
STEEL	.HYLSAP	.MEXICO-DF	.	.56000	+INF	.	BPL
STEEL	.AHMSA	.MONTERREY	.	.	+INF	2.74040	PL
STEEL	.FUNDIDORA	.MONTERREY	.	1.63474	+INF	.	BPL
STEEL	.SICARTSA	.MONTERREY	.	.	+INF	15.40760	PL
STEEL	.HYLSA	.MONTERREY	.	.55304	+INF	.	BPL
STEEL	.HYLSAP	.MONTERREY	.	.	+INF	18.58280	PL
STEEL	.AHMSA	.GUADALAJA	.	.46511	+INF	.	BPL
STEEL	.FUNDIDORA	.GUADALAJA	.	.	+INF	.77280	PL
STEEL	.SICARTSA	.GUADALAJA	.	.62878	+INF	.	BPL
STEEL	.HYLSA	.GUADALAJA	.	.	+INF	.77280	PL
STEEL	.HYLSAP	.GUADALAJA	.	.	+INF	5.49360	PL

SOLUTION REPORT

---- E EXPORTS (MILL TPY)

		COL LOWER	COL ACTIVITY	COL UPPER	MARGINAL	
STEEL	.AHMSA	.	.	+INF	5.15120	PL
STEEL	.FUNDIDORA	.	.	+INF	4.89080	PL
STEEL	.SICARTSA	.	.52911	+INF	.	BPL
STEEL	.HYLSA	.	.	+INF	4.89080	PL
STEEL	.HYLSAP	.	.	+INF	10.14920	PL

---- U PURCHASE OF DOMESTIC MATERIALS (MILL UNITS PER YEAR)

		COL LOWER	COL ACTIVITY	COL UPPER	MARGINAL	
PELLETS	.AHMSA	.	4.93197	+INF	.	BPL
COKE	.AHMSA	.	1.96655	+INF	.	BPL
NAT-GAS	.AHMSA	.	.	+INF	.	BPL
ELECTRIC	.AHMSA	.	.	+INF	.	BPL
SCRAP	.AHMSA	.	.74340	+INF	.	BPL
PELLETS	.FUNDIDORA	.	2.21200	+INF	.	BPL
COKE	.FUNDIDORA	.	.88200	+INF	.	BPL
NAT-GAS	.FUNDIDORA	.	.	+INF	.	BPL
ELECTRIC	.FUNDIDORA	.	.	+INF	.	BPL
SCRAP	.FUNDIDORA	.	.37467	+INF	.	BPL
PELLETS	.SICARTSA	.	1.73800	+INF	.	BPL
COKE	.SICARTSA	.	.69300	+INF	.	BPL
NAT-GAS	.SICARTSA	.	.	+INF	.	BPL
ELECTRIC	.SICARTSA	.	.	+INF	.	BPL
SCRAP	.SICARTSA	.	.13895	+INF	.	BPL
PELLETS	.HYLSA	.	1.35240	+INF	.	BPL
COKE	.HYLSA	.	.	+INF	.	BPL
NAT-GAS	.HYLSA	.	.55860	+INF	.	BPL
ELECTRIC	.HYLSA	.	.52147	+INF	.	BPL
SCRAP	.HYLSA	.	.	+INF	.	BPL
PELLETS	.HYLSAP	.	.84235	+INF	.	BPL
COKE	.HYLSAP	.	.	+INF	.	BPL
NAT-GAS	.HYLSAP	.	.34793	+INF	.	BPL
ELECTRIC	.HYLSAP	.	.32480	+INF	.	BPL
SCRAP	.HYLSAP	.	.	+INF	.	BPL

```
GAMS 1.0  M E X I C O  -  MINI STEEL MODEL                          01/13/83    13.34.21.    PAGE  20
          SOLUTION REPORT


---- V            IMPORTS                         (MILL TPY)

                          COL LOWER   COL ACTIVITY    COL UPPER      MARGINAL

 STEEL      .MEXICO-DF        .            .             +INF          .41160  PL
 STEEL      .MONTERREY        .            .             +INF        12.21560  PL
 STEEL      .GUADALAJA        .            .             +INF           .      BPL


                      COL LOWER   COL ACTIVITY    COL UPPER      MARGINAL
---- PHI                -INF       538.81120        +INF            .       BFR         TOTAL COST
---- PHIPSI             -INF       556.88558        +INF            .       BFR         RAW MATERIAL COST
---- PHILAM             -INF        56.00160        +INF            .       BFR         TRANSPORT COST
---- PHIPI              -INF          .             +INF            .       BFR         IMPORT COST
---- PHIEPS             -INF        74.07598        +INF            .       BFR         EXPORT REVENUE
```

6
A Large Static Model

ALTHOUGH A SMALL MODEL like the one described in the previous chapter may provide many insights, it may be asked whether those insights are robust to increases in the detail of the model. One way to check this is to construct a larger, more disaggregated model and use the results of the small model to guide the disaggregation into more plant sites, markets, productive units, productive processes, and commodities. More complete disaggregation is done in areas of interest indicated by the economics of the small model. Of course, it is not always true that more disaggregated models provide better solutions. In particular, if the disaggregated model has lower-quality data, it may produce inferior results. For the case at hand, however, the disaggregated data is of high quality.

The description of the model in this chapter is divided into sections on sets, variables, constraints, the objective function, and parameters. This is followed by a section on the size of the model. The results are presented in chapter 7.

Sets

The sets considered here are basically the same as for the small model, except that more subsets are used. Of the five primary sets used in the small model—plants, markets, productive units, processes, and commodities—only the markets are not separated into several subsets.

Plants

In the small model (also called the minimodel), the only plants were steel mills. That model is expanded here to include iron ore and coal mines. Furthermore, a separate set is added for the pelletizing plants near three of the iron ore mines and a coking plant near some of the coal mines. Thus, the set of plants is now organized into three subsets as follows:

$$I = IM \cup IR \cup IS \tag{6.1}$$

where I = all plants and mines
IM = iron ore mines and coal mines
IR = raw material processing plants
IS = steel mills.

The first subset of plants is the iron ore mines and coal mines, IM. The principal iron ore mines are shown on map 3. The older mines are in the north: La Perla near Camargo in Chihuahua, Hercules near Sierra Jojada in Coahuila, and Cerro de Mercado in Durango. The newer mines are on the Pacific coast west and south of Mexico City. The largest group, near Colima on the border of the states of Colima and Jalisco, includes two pelletizing plants at Alzada and at Peña Colorado. The mine at Las Truchas is only a few kilometers from SICARTSA, the new steel mill at Lázaro Cárdenas.

As map 4 shows, the major mines that provide coking coals are in a small area northwest of Monterrey, where there are a number of mines and a coking plant near the town of Sabinas in Coahuila. The map also shows the large natural gas fields near Reynosa in the north and near Coatzacoalcos in the south. Though the location of these gas fields is not explicitly used in this model, it is used implicitly in the small dynamic version of the model.

In summary, then, the set of iron ore and coal mines used in this version of the model is

IM = iron ore and coal mines
= {Peña Colorado, Las Truchas, La Perla, Cerro de Mercado, Hercules, La Chula, El Violin, El Encino, Coahuila coal mines}.

The next subset of plants is the pelletizing plants and coking furnaces located at mines rather than at steel mills. These are called raw material processing plants. The pelletizing plants are at Peña Colorado and

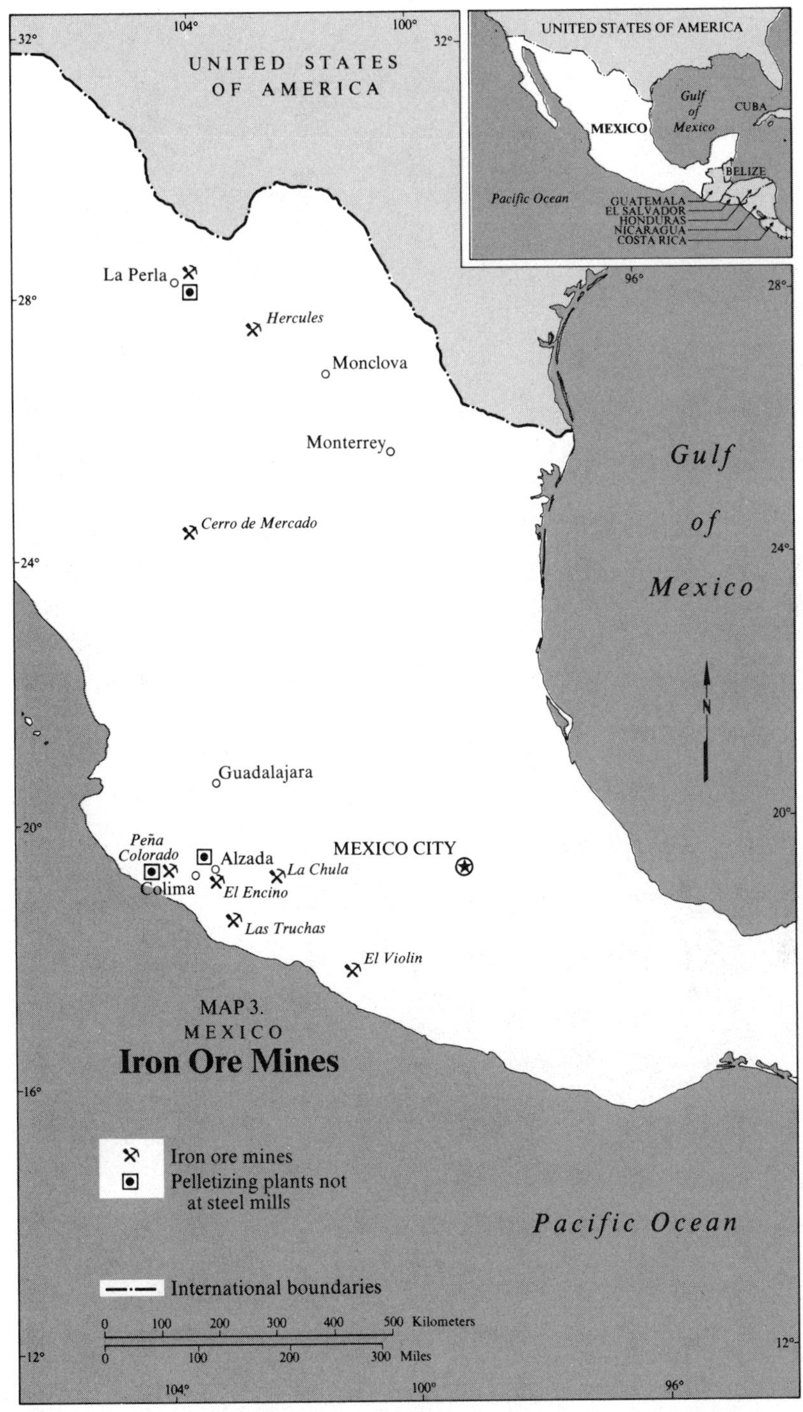
UNITED STATES OF AMERICA
UNITED STATES OF AMERICA
MEXICO
Gulf of Mexico
CUBA
BELIZE
Pacific Ocean
GUATEMALA
EL SALVADOR
HONDURAS
NICARAGUA
COSTA RICA
104°
100°
96°
32°
28°
24°
20°
16°
12°
La Perla
Hercules
Monclova
Monterrey
Cerro de Mercado
Gulf of Mexico
N
Guadalajara
Peña Colorado
Alzada
MEXICO CITY
Colima
La Chula
El Encino
Las Truchas
El Violin
Pacific Ocean
Iron ore mines
Pelletizing plants not at steel mills
International boundaries
0 100 200 300 400 500 Kilometers
0 100 200 300 Miles

MAP 3.
MEXICO
Iron Ore Mines

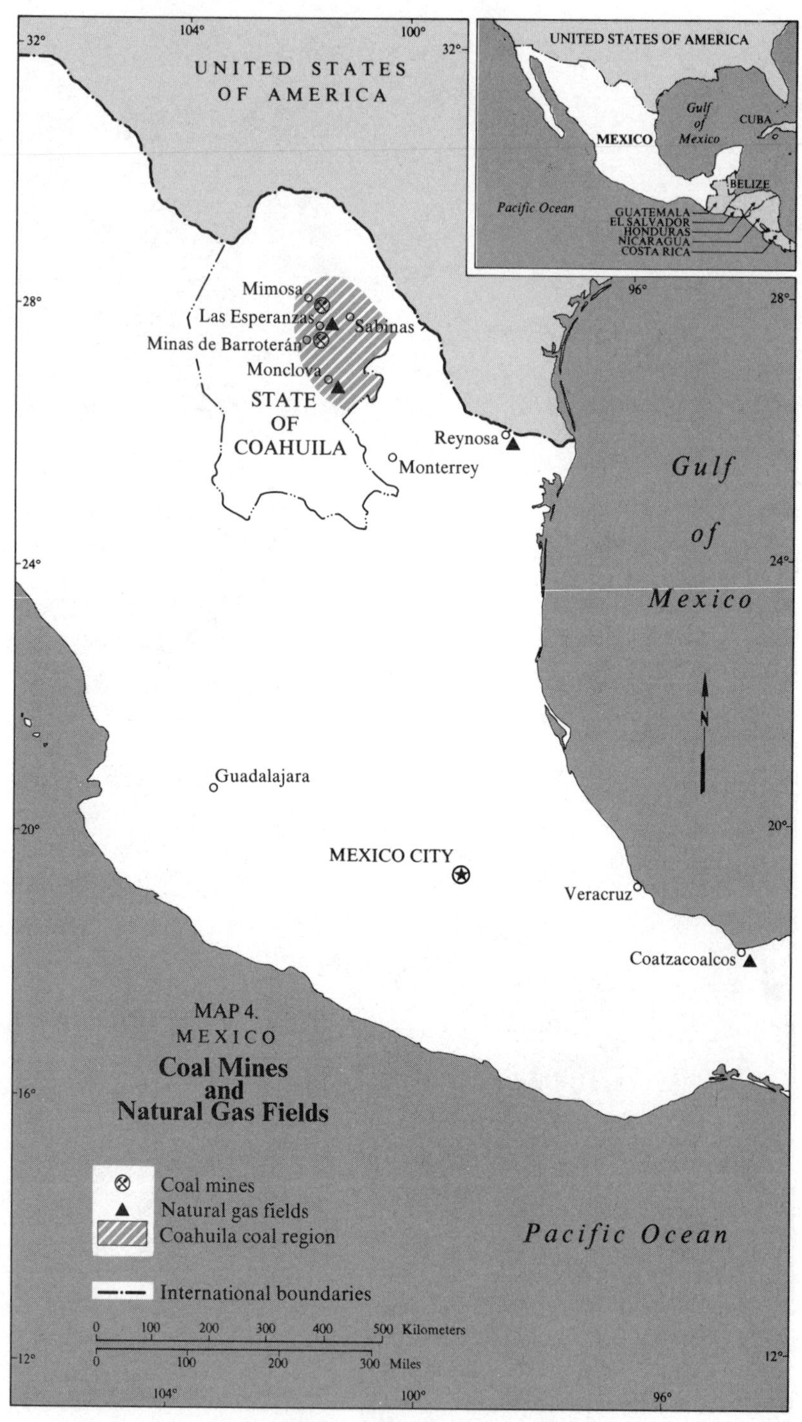
UNITED STATES OF AMERICA
UNITED STATES OF AMERICA
MEXICO
Gulf of Mexico
CUBA
BELIZE
Pacific Ocean
GUATEMALA
EL SALVADOR
HONDURAS
NICARAGUA
COSTA RICA
Mimosa
Las Esperanzas
Sabinas
Minas de Barroterán
Monclova
STATE OF COAHUILA
Reynosa
Monterrey
Gulf of Mexico
Guadalajara
MEXICO CITY
Veracruz
Coatzacoalcos
Pacific Ocean
Coal mines
Natural gas fields
Coahuila coal region
International boundaries
0 100 200 300 400 500 Kilometers
0 100 200 300 Miles
32°
28°
24°
20°
16°
12°
104°
100°
96°
N

MAP 4.
MEXICO
Coal Mines and Natural Gas Fields

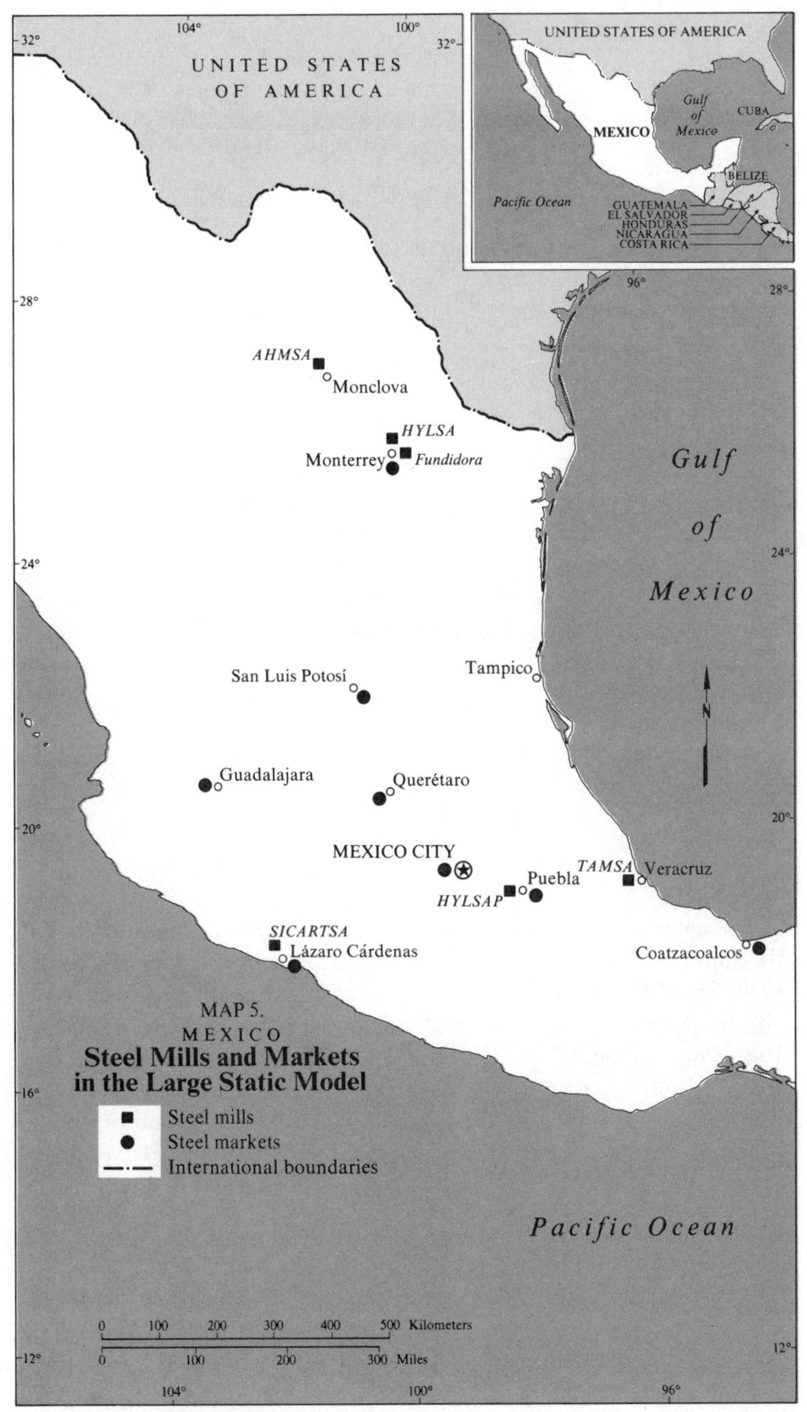

MAP 5.
MEXICO
Steel Mills and Markets in the Large Static Model

Alzada west of Mexico City and at La Perla in the north near Camargo, Chihuahua; the coking furnaces are near the coal mines in the north at Las Esperanzas (see map 4). The set is

IR = raw material plants
= {Peña Colorado, La Perla, Alzada, Las Esperanzas}.

Next is the set IS of steel mills. In the minimodel this set had five of the six existing integrated plants. Here we add the sixth integrated plant, TAMSA, the seamless pipe mill at Veracruz (see map 5). The set of steel mills shown in that figure is

IS = steel mills
= {SICARTSA, AHMSA, Fundidora, HYLSA, HYLSAP, TAMSA}.

As indicated in the discussion of the minimodel, in 1979 three of the existing plants were owned by the government (SICARTSA, AHMSA, and Fundidora) and three were privately owned (HYLSA, HYLSAP, and TAMSA). The new SICARTSA plant at Lázaro Cárdenas is near iron ore deposits and at a good port. The AHMSA and Fundidora plants are at Monclova and Monterrey, respectively, near the iron ore and coal deposits in the north of Mexico. All three of the government-owned plants use blast furnaces and basic oxygen furnaces to produce steel. In contrast, the privately owned companies use direct reduction of ores with natural gas to produce sponge iron and then produce steel from the sponge iron in electric arc furnaces.

Domestic Markets

The next set to be considered is the set J of domestic market areas. In the minimodel this set included the three largest cities in Mexico (Mexico City, Guadalajara, and Monterrey); now it is expanded to include five additional cities: Querétaro and Puebla near Mexico City; San Luis Potosí near Guadalajara; Lázaro Cárdenas near the SICARTSA steel mill, to include the possibility of a substantial market at this port; and Coatzacoalcos, to pick up the regional demand for pipe and other steel products which the oil and gas boom is causing (see map 5). In summary, the set is

J = domestic market areas
= {Mexico City, Puebla, Querétaro, San Luis Potosí, Monterrey, Guadalajara, Lázaro Cárdenas, Coatzacoalcos}.

Export Markets

In addition to domestic market areas, it is useful to represent export markets in the model. Because of transport costs, two separate export directions are considered, one via the Gulf coast and the other via the Pacific coast. Thus a new major set L is created:

$$L = \text{export markets} = \{\text{Gulf, Pacific}\}.$$

The set is not directly used in the algebraic statement of the model, but the distance from each plant to a port is given as the shorter of the distances to export points for these two markets.

Productive Units

The set of productive units M is disaggregated in this model into three subsets: productive units at the mines (MM), at the raw material plants (MR), and at the steel mills (MS). Relative to the minimodel a substantial disaggregation is made. The minimodel included five productive units

Table 6-1. *Subsets of Productive Units in the Large Static Model*

Productive units in mines (MM)	*Productive units in steel mills (contd)*
Mining equipment for coal mines	Continuous casting unit for billets
Mining equipment for iron ore mines: trucks and crushers	Ingot casting
Magnetic concentrator	Primary mill and soaking pits: flat products
Flotation concentrator	Primary mill and soaking pits: nonflat products
Productive units in raw material processing plants (MR)	Plate mills
Pellet plants	Hot strip mills
Coke oven and by-product units	Pickling lines
Productive units in steel mills (MS)	Cold strip mills
Pellet plants	Annealing units
Sinter plants	Temper mills
Coke ovens and by-product units	Tinning lines
Blast furnaces	Billet mills
Direct reduction units	Heavy shapes mills
Open hearth furnaces	Integrated bar mills
Basic oxygen converters	Integrated wire mills
Electric arc furnaces	Seamless pipe mills
Continuous casting unit for slabs	

that cover the range of processes from pig iron production to liquid steel production. The present model does not add productive units within this range of processes but rather extends the range from iron ore and coal mining to the production of final products such as hot and cold sheet, bar, and wire. The result is a model with four productive units in the mines, two in the raw material plants, and twenty-six in the steel mills (see table 6-1).

Processes

The next group of sets is of production processes. Since alternative processes for producing commodities are frequently used in a given productive unit, models of this type usually have more processes than productive units. The present model is no exception to this rule. There are thirty productive units and fifty processes. Most of the alternative processes are in the mining and concentration of different kinds of ore and in the production of pig iron and steel with different mixes of inputs.

The complete set of processes is listed in table 6-2. They may be divided into three groups: processes at mines, raw material processing plants, and steel mills.

Two characteristics of the iron ores in Mexico are captured in the manner in which the mining and concentration processes are constructed.[1] First, the ores in the north consist of roughly 25 percent magnetite ores and 75 percent hematite ores, while those in the south have the reverse of this concentration. This is an important difference because magnetite ores can be separated by magnetic means while hematite ores must be separated by flotation. The yield of concentrated ore is about 10 percent greater from magnetic separation than from flotation. A second characteristic considered here is the percentage of iron in the ore. The content is about 5 percent lower in the ore from Las Truchas than that from the other mines. The result of these two characteristics is that mining activities are separated into (1) mining in the north, (2) mining in the south (except at Las Truchas), and (3) mining at Las Truchas. It is necessary to use only two activities for magnetic and flotation concentration, however, since the yield of the northern and southern ores (except Las Truchas) is roughly the same.

Among the activities for ore preparation and coke production only the two for coke production require any special discussion. The AHMSA and

1. We are indebted to Alejandro Reyes of SIDERMEX for suggesting this specification of mining and concentration activities.

Table 6-2. *Subsets of Production Processes in the Large Static Model*

Processes at mines (PM)
- Mining unwashed coal
- Washing coal
- Mining in northern mines
- Mining in southern mines
- Mining at Las Truchas
- Concentration of northern ores
- Concentration of southern ores
- Concentration of Las Truchas ores

Processes at raw material processing plants (PR)
- Pellet production with concentrated ore
- Coke production with domestic coal

Processes at steel mills (PS)
- Pellet production using concentrated ore
- Sinter production
- Coke production with domestic coal
- Coke production with high input of imported coal

- Pig iron production with lump ore
- Pig iron production with high sinter charge
- Pig iron production with high pellets charge
- Pig iron production with coke from imported coal
- Sponge iron production

- Steel production in open hearths with high pig iron
- Steel production in open hearths with high scrap charge
- Steel production in open hearths with highest scrap charge

Processes at steel mills (PS) (contd)
- Steel production in BOFS with high pig iron charge
- Steel production in BOFS with high scrap charge
- Steel production in electric furnace with high sponge iron charge
- Steel production in electric furnace with high scrap charge

- Slabs production by continuous casting
- Billet production by continuous casting
- Ingot casting

- Slab production by rolling
- Rolling of blooms from ingots
- Billet production by rolling blooms

- Plate production from slabs
- Hot rolled coil production
- Pickled coil production
- Cold rolled coil production
- Annealed coil production
- Tempered coil production
- Tin production

- Rolling of heavy shapes
- Rolling of light shapes
- Roughing mill for nonflat products
- Rolling of bars
- Rolling of large-diameter reinforcing rods and bars
- Rolling of small-diameter reinforcing rods and bars
- Rolling of wire rods
- Rolling of seamless pipes

Fundidora plants near the coal mines in the northern part of Mexico use only domestic coal. In contrast, the SICARTSA plant on the Pacific coast uses imported coal for coke production. In fact, coke is frequently produced from a mix of several types of coal, some domestic and some imported. Furthermore, the mix of inputs changes as the relative prices and availability of different types of coal change. This model captures only a small part of this complexity by using the two different activities for producing coke.

The model includes six different activities for pig iron production and only one for sponge iron production. The explanation is that the national steel company, SIDERMEX, which owned all three of the plants using blast furnaces, was more actively involved in this study at an early stage than were the private companies which owned the plants using sponge iron production methods. Two of the six alternative activities for pig iron production reflect experimental efforts to use different mixes of sponge iron and sinter to produce pig iron at AHMSA. The other four activities reflect different mixes of lump ore, sinter, and pellets in the metal charge and different types of coke. Not all of these activities are used in the model at each plant. For example, AHMSA has a sinter plant but the other steel mills do not, so the activity for pig iron production using sinter as a part of the charge is included at AHMSA but not at SICARTSA or Fundidora. This will become clearer later when the production activity matrices are displayed.

The production activities for steel may be divided into three groups according to the type of furnace used: open hearths, basic oxygen furnaces (BOFs), and electric arc furnaces. For each type of furnace there are two or three alternative activities reflecting different percentages of scrap in the charge. The open hearths and electric arc furnaces can operate efficiently with a wider variation in the percentage of scrap in the total metal charge than can the BOFs.

A large group of activities in steel production are those for ingot casting and alternatively for slab and billet production by continuous casting methods. AHMSA, Fundidora, and HYLSA still use ingot casting, but this method is increasingly giving way to continuous casting both within these plants and in the newer plants, which use continuous casting exclusively.

Among the rolling activities, the first three are used in plants that do ingot casting. Either slabs or blooms can be rolled from ingots and the blooms can in turn be rolled into billets. The rest of the flat product rolling activities may be thought of as a continuous stream of activities with various products leaving the stream along the way: slabs to hot rolled coils to cold rolled coils to tin.

The rolling of shapes is rather more complicated. There is a profusion of different mills for rolling shapes. For large structural shapes, blooms are rolled into heavy shapes. For lighter shapes, billets are used as the input to the rolling processes. At SICARTSA billets are the input to different rolling mills to produce either large-diameter or small-diameter reinforcing rods and bars. At the HYLSA plant in Puebla bar and wire rolling mills also use billets as the input, and at TAMSA in Veracruz there is a mill used for rolling seamless pipe.

Commodities

The last major set to be considered is commodities. Although there were only eight commodities with three subsets (raw material, intermediate products, and final products) in the small model, there are fifty commodities with eleven subsets in this more disaggregated static model. Furthermore, the subset of commodities in the small model provided a partition of the set (each commodity in one and only one subset), but the subsets in this larger model do not provide a partition.

The set of commodities used in steel mills is the most comprehensive. These commodities are listed in table 6-3 with raw material first, intermediate products in the middle, and final products near the end.

Table 6-3. *Sets of All Commodities (CS) Used at Steel Mills*

Iron ore from the north, high in sulphur and phosphorus, 59 percent iron
Iron ore from the south, no phosphorus, 60 percent iron
Iron ore from Las Truchas, no phosphorus, 55 percent iron
Iron ore, concentrated
Pellets
Sinter

Coal, raw unwashed
Coal, washed domestic
Coal, imported
Coke produced with domestic coal
Coke produced with imported coal

Fuel oil
Limestone
Pig iron (hot metal)
Natural gas

Sponge iron
Steel scrap
Ferroalloys
Refractories
Dolomite
Lime
Electrodes

Liquid steel
Ingot steel
Slabs
Plates

Hot strip and sheet
Pickled strip and sheet
Cold strip and sheet
Annealed strip and sheet
Tempered strip and sheet
Tin

Blooms
Billets
Heavy shapes
Light shapes

Bars
Large-diameter reinforcing rods
Small-diameter reinforcing rods
Wire rods
Seamless pipes

Electricity
Water

Rails
Steel blooms for seamless pipes

However, this is only a rough breakdown. For example, hot strip and sheet is both a final product that can be shipped to markets and an intermediate product used to produce another intermediate product, pickled strip. For this reason, a subset of intermediate products is defined, not explicitly, but rather implicitly by the input-output matrices.

There are several new subsets in table 6-4 that did not appear in the small model. The first of these, *CRAW*, is the subset of raw material used in the plants. The next two subsets, *CM* and *CR*, commodities at the mines and at the raw material processing plants, are defined to complement the set of production processes at these sites. A relatively small subset, *CRV*, includes raw material and intermediate products that are likely to be imported. The next four sets are all for shipments of intermediate material: from mines to raw material processing plants (*CMR*), from

Table 6-4. *Subsets of Commodities in the Large Static Model*

CRAW	= domestic raw material = {fuel oil, limestone, natural gas, scrap, ferroalloys, refractories, dolomite, lime, electrodes, water, electricity}
CM	= commodities at mines = {iron ore from the north, iron ore from the south, iron ore from Las Truchas, raw unwashed coal, domestic washed coal, concentrated iron ore}
CR	= commodities at raw material processing plants = {iron ore from the north, iron ore from the south, iron ore from Las Truchas, raw unwashed coal, domestic washed coal, concentrated iron ore, pellets, coke produced with domestic ores, electricity}
CRV	= imported raw material and intermediate products = {imported coal, pellets, steel scrap, coke}
CMR	= commodities shipped from mines to raw material sites = {concentrated iron ore, washed domestic coal}
CMS	= commodities shipped from mines to steel plants = {iron ore from the north, iron ore from the south, iron ore from Las Truchas, concentrated iron ore, washed domestic coal}
CRS	= commodities shipped from raw material sites to steel mills = {pellets, coke produced with domestic coal}
CSS	= commodities for interplant shipment between steel mills = {sponge iron, pellets, coke produced with domestic coal}
CF	= final products = {plate, hot strip and sheet, tempered strip and sheet, tin, heavy shapes, light shapes, bars, large-diameter reinforcing rods, small-diameter reinforcing rods, wire rod, seamless pipe, rails}
CE	= commodities for export = *CF*
CFV	= imported final products = *CF*

mines to steel mills (CMS), from raw material processing plants to steel mills (CRS), and from steel mills to steel mills (CSS).

The subset of final products, CF, can be divided into two groups: flat and nonflat products. Flat products include plate, hot sheet and strip, tempered sheet and strip, and tin. Nonflat products include shapes such as I beams and angles which are included in CF as heavy shapes and light shapes, depending on size. Next among nonflat products come bars, reinforcing rods and wire rods, and special shapes such as seamless pipe and rails.

Two other subsets specified in table 6-4 are exported commodities and imports of final products. For the present version of the model, exports are restricted to final products only. For other versions, it might be useful to permit the export of selected intermediate products, perhaps those in the subsets of commodities which can be shipped between plants.

Three subsets are used to specify ownership constraints. These constraints arise because two of the pellet plants are owned by consortia of the plants, and fixed percentages of the capacity of these plants are assigned to each set of owners. These relationships are specified in the model with the following three subsets:

O = owner numbers
= {1, 2, 3, 4, 5}
OWN = owner groups
= {1 (SICARTSA), 2 (AHMSA), 3 (Fundidora), 4 (HYLSA, HYLSAP), 5 (TAMSA)}
$ISEX$ = companies excluded from shipments from Alzada
= {SICARTSA, AHMSA, Fundidora, TAMSA}

Because of an error in typing, the HYLSA name read "HYLS" in the owner groups of the GAMS input, which thus permitted shipment of pellets from Peña Colorado to HYLSAP but not to HYLSA. When the error was discovered the base solution was recomputed with the correction. Only one minor change in raw material flows occurred, however, and this was not deemed large enough to merit resolving all the runs.

The domain-checking procedures added to the GAMS language after the solutions of this model would have caught this error. This is yet another argument for the use of modeling languages in general and in particular for the implementation of domain-checking capabilities in those languages. For example, in the present case the modeling language would have given an error message to indicate that HYLS was being used in the set of plants when it had not been included in the original set at the top of the GAMS listing.

The GAMS listing at the end of the chapter shows the corrected input. If one wishes to replicate the solution reported in the next chapter, the spelling of HYLSA in line 310 of the GAMS input should be changed to HYLS.

A large part of the total modeling effort must be devoted to set specification. In fact, the choice of sets and elements of the sets are the key decisions in determining the usefulness of the model. A model should be disaggregated enough to capture the central economic problems of the industry and aggregated enough to permit a relatively quick and cheap solution. Once the sets are selected the next step is to choose the variables.

Variables

The principal variables for this model are the same as for the small model:

z = process levels (production levels)
x = shipments
u = domestic purchases
e = exports
v = imports.

Superscripts are added to some of these basic variables, however, to specialize them for use in this more disaggregated model. For example, the process levels are now specified as:

z^m = process levels in mines
z^r = process levels at raw material preparation plants
z^s = process levels at steel mills.

In addition, the shipment activities are separated into four groups:

x^m = shipments of intermediate products from mines
x^r = shipments of intermediate products from raw material preparation plants
x^s = shipments of intermediate products between steel mills
x^f = shipments of final products.

Similarly, domestic purchases are separated into two groups:

u^r = purchases of domestic products at raw material plants
u^s = purchases of domestic products at steel mills.

Exports are in one group of products, but imports are separated into two groups to allow imports of intermediate as well as final products:

e = exports
v^s = imports of raw material and intermediate products to steel mills
v^f = imports of final products to markets

Finally, there is a group of variables used to define total cost and its various components:

ξ = total cost less domestic by-product revenues and export revenues
ϕ = cost groups
ϕ_ψ = recurrent cost
ϕ_λ = transport cost
ϕ_π = import cost
ϕ_ε = export revenues.

Constraints

The constraints for the model are divided into five principal groups: material balance constraints, capacity constraints, market requirement constraints, export bounds, and ownership constraints. Basically, these five sets of constraints require that (1) no more material can be used than is purchased or produced, (2) production cannot exceed capacity, (3) market requirements must be met, (4) export upper bounds cannot be exceeded, and (5) ownership constraints on pellet shipments cannot be violated. The detailed specification of the constraints follows.

MATERIAL BALANCE CONSTRAINTS FOR MINES

$$\sum_{p \in PM} a^m_{cp} z^m_{pi} \geq \sum_{i' \in IR} x^m_{cii'}\Big|_{c \in CMR} + \sum_{i' \in IS} x^m_{cii'}\Big|_{c \in CMS} \qquad \begin{matrix} c \in CM \\ i \in IM \end{matrix} \tag{6.1}$$

[Use of ores and output of intermediate products at mine i] $\geq$ [Shipment of intermediate products from mine i to raw material preparation plants $i' \in IR$] + [Shipments of intermediate products from mine i to steel mills $i' \in IS$]

This constraint requires that the ores which are mined must exceed their use in the concentration process and that the concentrated ores produced at each mine must exceed the shipment of those ores to raw material plants and to steel mills. It also requires that coal production and usage be balanced.

The notation of the type

$$x^m_{cii'}\Big|_{c \in CMR}$$

is unusual and deserves comment. Consider the simpler case of the use of the variable x_{cij} to represent the shipment of commodity c from plant i to market j. It may be desirable to restrict the model so that only a subset of commodities (say, CS) can be shipped from i to j while the equation holds for all intermediate commodities CI. This could be written then as

$$x_{cij}\Big|_{c \in CS} \qquad c \in CI$$

For example, both coke and hot metal (molten pig iron) might be intermediate products in the set CI. Hot metal cannot be shipped since it will cool, but coke can be; therefore the shipment activity will be restricted to the subset of commodities CS, which includes coke but not hot metal. Now consider the particular case at hand, the variable

$$x^m_{cii'}\Big|_{c \in CMR}. \qquad c \in CM$$

The set CM contains ores, but the pellet plants in the set IR use only concentrate and not lump ore. The shipments from the mines to raw material plants should therefore be only for the commodities that can be supplied by the mines and used by the raw material plants. In this case, it is the set CMR (concentrated iron ore and washed domestic coal) that can be shipped from mines to raw material plants.

This undoubtedly seems like a very elaborate notational procedure, but its use can greatly reduce the number of variables in the model through the simple device of proper set specification.

MATERIAL BALANCE CONSTRAINTS FOR RAW MATERIAL PROCESSING PLANTS

$$\text{(6.2)} \qquad \sum_{p \in PR} a^r_{cp} z^r_{pi} + \sum_{i' \in IM} x^m_{ci'i}\Big|_{c \in CMR}$$

$$\begin{bmatrix} \textit{Use and production of} \\ \textit{commodity } c \textit{ at raw} \\ \textit{material processing} \\ \textit{plant } i \end{bmatrix} + \begin{bmatrix} \textit{Receipts from all} \\ \textit{mines of commodity } c \\ \textit{at raw material pro-} \\ \textit{cessing plant } i \end{bmatrix}$$

$$+ u^r_{ci}\Big|_{c \in CRAW} \geq \sum_{i' \in IS} x^r_{cii'}\Big|_{c \in CRS} \qquad \begin{matrix} c \in CR \\ i \in IR \end{matrix}$$

$$+\begin{bmatrix}\textit{Purchases of raw material}\\ \textit{of type c at raw material}\\ \textit{processing plant i}\end{bmatrix} \geq \begin{bmatrix}\textit{Shipment of inter-}\\ \textit{mediate product c}\\ \textit{from raw material}\\ \textit{processing plant i}\\ \textit{to all steel mills}\end{bmatrix}$$

This constraint requires that the amount of each commodity used or produced plus the amount received from mines plus the amount purchased must exceed the amount shipped to steel mills.

MATERIAL BALANCE CONSTRAINTS FOR STEEL MILLS

(6.3)
$$\sum_{p\in PS} a^s_{cpi} z^s_{pi} + \sum_{i'\in IM} x^m_{ci'i}\Big|_{c\in CMS}$$

$$\begin{bmatrix}\textit{Use of domestic raw material}\\ \textit{and labor and output of inter-}\\ \textit{mediate and final products at}\\ \textit{steel mill i}\end{bmatrix} + \begin{bmatrix}\textit{Shipment of intermediate}\\ \textit{products from all mines to}\\ \textit{steel mill i}\end{bmatrix}$$

$$+ \lambda_c \sum_{i'\in IR} x^r_{ci'i}\Big|_{c\in CRS} + \lambda_c \sum_{i'\in IS} x^s_{ci'i}\Big|_{c\in CSS}$$

$$+\begin{bmatrix}\textit{Shipment of intermediate}\\ \textit{products from all raw}\\ \textit{material processing}\\ \textit{plants to steel mill i}\end{bmatrix} + \begin{bmatrix}\textit{Shipment of intermediate}\\ \textit{products from all other}\\ \textit{steel mills to steel}\\ \textit{mill i}\end{bmatrix}$$

$$+ u^s_{ci}\Big|_{c\in CRAW} + v^s_{ci}\Big|_{c\in CRV}$$

$$+\begin{bmatrix}\textit{Purchase of local raw}\\ \textit{material}\end{bmatrix} + \begin{bmatrix}\textit{Purchase of imported}\\ \textit{raw material and}\\ \textit{intermediate products}\end{bmatrix}$$

$$\geq \sum_{i'\in IS} x^s_{cii'}\Big|_{c\in CSS} + \sum_{j\in J} x^f_{cij}\Big|_{c\in CF} + e_{ci}\Big|_{c\in CE} \qquad \begin{matrix} c\in CS \\ i\in IS \end{matrix}$$

$$\geq \begin{bmatrix}\textit{Shipment of inter-}\\ \textit{mediate products}\\ \textit{from steel mill i}\\ \textit{to all other steel}\\ \textit{mills}\end{bmatrix} + \begin{bmatrix}\textit{Shipment of final}\\ \textit{products from}\\ \textit{plant i to}\\ \textit{market j}\end{bmatrix} + \begin{bmatrix}\textit{Exports of}\\ \textit{products from}\\ \textit{plant i}\end{bmatrix}$$

This constraint requires that for each commodity c and each steel mill i the production and receipt of material must exceed the uses and shipments. Production and use are both in the first term of the inequality since the a^s_{cpi} coefficients can be either negative or positive depending on whether the commodity c is an input or is produced as an output. Receipts come from five sources: mines, raw material plants, other steel mills, local purchases, and imports. Shipments go out to other steel mills, markets, and exports.

The factor λ represents the fact that coke tends to crumble somewhat during transport so that there is some product loss. Thus, λ is the percentage of the shipment that arrives at the receiving steel mill.

CAPACITY CONSTRAINTS FOR MINES

(6.4)
$$\sum_{p \in PM} b^{m}_{mp} z^{m}_{pi} \leq k^{m}_{mi} \qquad m \in MM \quad i \in IM$$

$$\left[\textit{Capacity required} \right] \leq \left[\begin{matrix} \textit{Initial capacity} \\ \textit{at mine } i \end{matrix} \right]$$

Note that m is used both as a superscript and a subscript here and has different meanings in the two positions. As a superscript, it denotes mines and as a subscript it denotes machines.

CAPACITY CONSTRAINTS FOR RAW MATERIAL PROCESSING PLANTS

(6.5)
$$\sum_{p \in PR} b^{r}_{mp} z^{r}_{pi} \leq k^{r}_{mi} \qquad m \in MR \quad i \in IR$$

$$\left[\textit{Capacity required} \right] \leq \left[\begin{matrix} \textit{Initial capacity at} \\ \textit{raw material plant } i \end{matrix} \right]$$

CAPACITY CONSTRAINTS FOR STEEL MILLS

(6.6)
$$\sum_{p \in PS} b^{s}_{mp} z^{s}_{pi} \leq k^{s}_{mi} \qquad m \in MS \quad i \in IS$$

$$\left[\textit{Capacity required} \right] \leq \left[\begin{matrix} \textit{Initial capaicty} \\ \textit{in plant } i \end{matrix} \right]$$

MARKET REQUIREMENTS

(6.7)
$$\sum_{i \in IS} x^{f}_{cij} + v^{f}_{cj} \geq d_{cj} \qquad c \in CF \quad j \in J$$

$$\left[\begin{matrix} \textit{Shipment of final} \\ \textit{product c from} \\ \textit{all steel mills} \\ \textit{to market } j \end{matrix} \right] + \left[\begin{matrix} \textit{Imports of} \\ \textit{final prod-} \\ \textit{uct c to} \\ \textit{market } j \end{matrix} \right] \geq \left[\begin{matrix} \textit{Requirements} \\ \textit{for product} \\ \textit{c at market } j \end{matrix} \right]$$

EXPORT CONSTRAINTS ON COMMODITIES

(6.8) $$\sum_{i \in IS} e_{ci} \leq \bar{e}_c \qquad c \in CE$$

TOTAL EXPORTS CONSTRAINT

(6.8a) $$\sum_{c \in CE} \sum_{i \in IS} e_{ci} \leq 250$$

OWNERSHIP CONSTRAINTS ON PELLET SHIPMENTS

(6.9) $$\sum_{i' \in OWN_o} x^r_{cii'} \leq \zeta_o k^r_{ci} \qquad \begin{array}{l} c \in \{\text{pellets}\} \\ o \in O \\ i \in \{\text{Peña Colorado}\} \end{array}$$

$$\begin{bmatrix} \textit{Shipment of pellets} \\ \textit{from Peña Colorado} \\ \textit{to all steel mills} \\ \textit{in ownership group } o \end{bmatrix} \leq \begin{bmatrix} \textit{Share of ownership} \\ \textit{group } o \end{bmatrix}$$

This constraint requires that the total amount of pellets shipped from the Peña Colorado raw material plant to the steel mills in each ownership group must be less than or equal to the percentage ownership by group *o* times the capacity of the Peña Colorado pellet plant.

(6.10) $$\sum_{i' \in ISEX} x^r_{cii'} = 0 \qquad \begin{array}{l} c \in \{\textit{Pellets}\} \\ i \in \{\textit{Alzada}\} \end{array}$$

$$\begin{bmatrix} \textit{Shipments of pellets} \\ \textit{to plants} \\ \textit{not in the HYLSA} \\ \textit{group} \end{bmatrix} = 0$$

This ownership constraint requires that none of the pellets from the Alzada plant should be shipped to AHMSA, Fundidora, SICARTSA, and TAMSA, the plants that are not in the HYLSA group. Or specified in a positive way, it requires that all the pellets from the Alzada raw material plant be shipped to HYLSA or HYLSAP.

NONNEGATIVITY CONSTRAINTS

$$z^m_{pi} \geq 0 \qquad p \in PM,\ i \in IM$$

$$z^r_{pi} \geq 0 \qquad p \in PR,\ i \in IR$$

$$z^s_{pi} \geq 0 \qquad p \in PS,\ i \in IS$$

$$x^m_{ci'i} \geq 0 \qquad c \in CM,\ I' \in IM,\ i \in IS \cup IR$$

$$x^r_{ci'i} \geq 0 \qquad c \in CRS,\ i' \in IR,\ i \in IS$$

$$x^s_{cii'} \geq 0 \qquad c \in CSS,\ i \in IS,\ i' \in IS, \text{ with } i \neq i'$$
$$x^f_{cij} \geq 0 \qquad c \in CF,\ i \in IS,\ j \in J$$
$$u^r_{ci} \geq 0 \qquad c \in CR,\ i \in IR$$
$$u^s_{ci} \geq 0 \qquad c \in CRAW,\ i \in IS$$
$$e_{ci} \geq 0 \qquad c \in CE,\ i \in IS$$
$$v^s_{ci} \geq 0 \qquad c \in CRV,\ i \in IS$$
$$v^f_{cj} \geq 0 \qquad c \in CF,\ j \in J$$

Objective Function

The constraints above must be satisfied while the analyst seeks to minimize the sum of production cost, transport cost, and import cost less revenues from exports and by-products.

(6.11)
$$\xi = \phi_\psi + \phi_\lambda + \rho(\phi_\pi - \phi_\varepsilon)$$

$$\begin{bmatrix} \textit{Total} \\ \textit{cost} \end{bmatrix} = \begin{bmatrix} \textit{Recurrent cost of} \\ \textit{raw material} \\ \textit{and labor} \end{bmatrix} + \begin{bmatrix} \textit{Transport} \\ \textit{cost} \end{bmatrix}$$
$$+ \begin{bmatrix} \textit{Exchange} \\ \textit{rate} \end{bmatrix} \left(\begin{bmatrix} \textit{Import} \\ \textit{cost} \end{bmatrix} - \begin{bmatrix} \textit{Export} \\ \textit{revenues} \end{bmatrix} \right)$$

where

(6.12)
$$\phi_\psi = \sum_{p \in PM} \sum_{i \in IM} m^c_p z^m_{pi} + \sum_{c \in CRAW} \sum_{i \in IR} p^d_c u^r_{ci}$$

$$\begin{bmatrix} \textit{Recurrent cost of} \\ \textit{raw material} \\ \textit{and labor} \end{bmatrix} = \begin{bmatrix} \textit{Cost of mining} \\ \textit{operations} \end{bmatrix} + \begin{bmatrix} \textit{Price times quantity} \\ \textit{purchased at} \\ \textit{raw material plants} \end{bmatrix}$$
$$+ \sum_{c \in CRAW} \sum_{i \in IS} p^d_c u^s_{ci}$$
$$+ \begin{bmatrix} \textit{Domestic price times quantity} \\ \textit{purchased of raw material} \\ \textit{and labor at steel mills} \end{bmatrix}$$

(6.13)
$$\phi_\lambda = \sum_{c \in CMR} \sum_{i \in IM} \sum_{i' \in IR} \mu^{mr}_{ii'} x^m_{cii'}$$

$$\begin{bmatrix} \textit{Transport} \\ \textit{cost} \end{bmatrix} = \begin{bmatrix} \textit{Cost of shipping intermediate} \\ \textit{products between mines} \\ \textit{and raw material processing} \\ \textit{plants} \end{bmatrix}$$

$$+ \sum_{c \in CMS} \sum_{i \in IM} \sum_{i' \in IS} \mu_{ii'}^{ms} x_{cii'}^{m} + \sum_{c \in CRS} \sum_{i \in IR} \sum_{i' \in IS} \mu_{ii'}^{rs} x_{cii'}^{r}$$

+ [Cost of shipping intermediate products from all mines to all steel mills] + [Cost of shipping intermediate products from all raw material processing plants to all steel mills]

$$+ \sum_{c \in CSS} \sum_{i \in IS} \sum_{i' \in IS} \mu_{ii'}^{ss} x_{cii'}^{s} + \sum_{c \in CF} \sum_{i \in IS} \sum_{j \in J} \mu_{ij}^{sj} x_{cij}^{f}$$

+ [Cost of shipping intermediate products between steel mills] + [Cost of shipping final products from steel plants to markets]

$$+ \sum_{c \in CE} \sum_{i \in IS} \mu_{i}^{spf} e_{ci} + \sum_{c \in CRV} \sum_{i \in IS} \mu_{i}^{psr} v_{ci}^{s}$$

+ [Cost of shipping final products for export from steel mills to nearest port] + [Cost of shipping imported intermediate products from nearest port to steel mills]

$$+ \sum_{c \in CF} \sum_{j \in J} \mu_{j}^{pj} v_{cj}^{f}$$

+ [Cost of shipping imported final products from nearest port to markets]

(6.14) $$\phi_{\pi} = \sum_{c \in CRV} \sum_{i \in IS} p_{c}^{v} v_{ci}^{s}$$

[Import cost] = [Cost of intermediate products imported to steel mills]

$$+ \sum_{c \in CFV} \sum_{j \in J} p_{c}^{v} v_{cj}^{f}$$

+ [Cost of final products imported to markets]

(6.15) $$\phi_{\varepsilon} = \sum_{c \in CE} \sum_{i \in IS} p_{c}^{e} e_{ci}$$

[Export revenues] = [Price times quantity of exports]

Parameters

Table 6-5 provides a summary of the parameters used in the model. They are separated into five groups: production, capacity, demand,

Table 6-5. *Parameters in the Large Static Model*

Production	
a^m	Process inputs ($-$) or outputs ($+$) at mines
a^r	Process inputs ($-$) or outputs ($+$) at raw material plants
a^s	Process inputs ($-$) or outputs ($+$) at steel mills
b^m	Capacity utilization in mines
b^r	Capacity utilization in raw material plants
b^s	Capacity utilization in steel mills
Capacity	
k^m	Capacity at mines
k^r	Capacity at raw material plants
k^s	Capacity at steel mills
Demand	
d	Market requirements
$\bar{e}$	Export upper bound
Prices and cost	
ρ	Exchange rate (pesos per dollar)
m^c	Cost of production of mines
p^d	Prices at raw material plants and steel mills
p^e	Prices of exports
p^v	Prices of imports
Unit transport cost	
μ^{mr}	Intermediate products shipped from mines to raw material plants
μ^{ms}	Intermediate products shipped from mines to steel mills
μ^{rs}	Intermediate products shipped from raw material plants to steel mills
μ^{ss}	Intermediate products shipped between steel mills
μ^{psr}	Imports shipped from ports to steel mills of raw material
μ^{sj}	Final products shipped from steel mills to markets
μ^{spf}	Exports of final products shipped from steel mills to ports
μ^{pj}	Imports shipped from ports to markets

prices, and unit transport cost. Since all the parameters are contained in the GAMS listing in appendix **B** to this chapter, this section will not list every parameter, but a selection will illustrate the method employed and help the reader interpret the data in the GAMS listing.

Production

The principal set of production parameters are the input-output coefficients a^m for the mines, a^r for the raw material plants, and a^s for the steel mills. As an example, consider a^s by looking at the input-output table for a single plant, SICARTSA. Table 6-6 gives a portion of such a table, the input-output matrix for processes for producing pellets, coke, and pig iron. In the pellet production process, 0.99 metric ton of concentrated ore is used to produce a ton of pellets. In the coke process, 1.38 tons of

Table 6-6. *Input-Output Matrix for SICARTSA: Pellets to Pig Iron*
(metric tons unless otherwise specified)

Inputs and outputs	*Pellets*	*Coke*	*Pig Iron*
Ore, Las Truchas	—	—	– 0.2
Ore, concentrated	– 0.99	—	—
Pellets	1.0	—	– 1.384
Coal, imported	—	– 1.38	– 0.6
Coke from imported coal	—	1.0	—
Fuel oil (1,000 liters)	—	—	– 0.045
Limestone	—	—	– 0.081
Dolomite	—	—	– 0.049
Electricity (megawatt-hours)	—	—	– 0.090
Pig iron	—	—	1.0

—Not applicable.

imported coal are used to produce 1.0 ton of coke. Finally, 0.2 ton of lump ore from the Las Truchas mine and 1.384 tons of pellets are combined with 0.6 ton of coke, 45 liters of fuel oil, 0.081 ton of limestone, 0.049 ton of dolomite, and 90 kilowatt-hours (kwh) of electricity to produce a ton of pig iron. One of the reasons that both lump ore and pellets are charged to the blast furnace is that the Las Truchas mines near SICARTSA yield both magnetite and hematite ores. The magnetite ores are separated magnetically and then shipped to the SICARTSA plant in a slurry pipeline. The hematite ores would require a flotation process if they were

Table 6-7. *Input-Output Matrix for SICARTSA: Steel and Billets*
(metric tons unless otherwise specified)

Inputs and outputs	*Steel in BOF with high pig iron*	*Steel in BOF with high scrap*	*Billets, continuous casting*
Pig iron	– 0.944	– 0.833	—
Scrap	– 0.166	– 0.180	0.04
Ferroalloys	– 0.033	– 0.033	—
Refractories	– 0.006	– 0.006	—
Dolomite	– 0.06	– 0.06	—
Lime	– 0.09	– 0.09	—
Electricity (megawatt-hours)	– 0.068	– 0.068	—
Steel	1.0	1.0	– 1.05
Billets	—	—	1.00

—Not applicable.

to be concentrated, but since that process is not available at Las Truchas, they are charged directly to the blast furnace.

Table 6-7 continues the illustration of the production processes by displaying those for steel and billet production. Two alternative processes for steel production in the BOF furnaces at SICARTSA are shown. One has a relatively high pig iron charge and the other has a relatively high scrap iron charge: the first process uses 0.944 metric ton of pig iron and 0.166 ton of scrap to produce a ton of steel, while the second uses 0.833 ton of pig iron and 0.180 ton of scrap. Which process is used in the model solution will depend on the relative cost and availability of pig iron and scrap at SICARTSA.

The billet production process in table 6-7 shows a case in which a single input (steel) is used to produce two outputs (scrap and billets). The scrap is then recycled and used as an input to the BOFs.

Table 6-8 gives the input-output information for the rolling of shapes at SICARTSA. Light shapes are typically angles and tees an inch or two in width. Reinforcing rods are used to reinforce concrete in structures. The four activities are very similar. The input in every case is billets, and the product is rolled to completion without becoming a named intermediate product. This pattern contrasts with the rolling of flat products, which can be sold as final products at several stages or treated as intermediate products and rolled into a different final product. This is illustrated in table 6-9 which shows a portion of the input-output matrix for AHMSA.

Table 6-8. *Input-Output Matrix for SICARTSA: Shapes*
(metric tons unless otherwise specified)

Inputs and outputs	*Light shapes*	*Reinforcing rods*		*Wire*
		Large-diameter	*Small-diameter*	
Scrap	0.03	0.03	0.03	0.02
Billets	– 1.06	– 1.06	– 1.06	– 1.05
Light shapes	1.0	—	—	—
Reinforcing rods				
Large-diameter	—	1.0	—	—
Small-diameter	—	—	1.0	—
Wire	—	—	—	1.0
Electricity (megawatt-hours)	– 0.08	– 0.08	– 0.08	– 0.08
Water (1,000 cubic meters)	– 0.01	– 0.01	– 0.01	– 0.01

—Not applicable.

Table 6-9. *Input-Output Matrix for AHMSA: Some Flat Products*
(metric tons)

Inputs and outputs	*Continuous casting of slabs*	*Plate*	*Hot strip and sheet*	*Pickled strip and sheet*
Scrap	0.02	0.02	0.03	—
Steel, liquid	– 1.04	—	—	—
Slabs	1.0	– 1.04	– 1.05	—
Plate	—	1.0	—	—
Hot strip	—	—	1.0	– 1.0
Pickled strip	—	—	—	1.0
	Cold strip and sheet	*Annealed*	*Tempered*	*Tin*
Scrap	0.13	—	—	—
Pickled strip	– 1.17	—	—	—
Cold strip	1.0	– 1.0	—	—
Annealed strip	—	1.0	– 1.0	—
Tempered strip	—	—	1.0	– 1.02
Tin	—	—	—	1.0

—Not applicable.

The input-output structure for flat products in table 6-9 has a stair-step shape. This is caused by the fact that hot strip is used to produce pickled strip which is used to produce cold strip, and so on. There are normally electricity inputs for these processes, but these data were not obtained for AHMSA.

The capital inputs are not included in the production relationships in the input-output matrices, but are contained separately in the capital utilization matrix, which provides a relationship between productive units and processes. An entry of "1" indicates that the productive unit is used by a particular process, and a blank entry indicates that it is not used. A portion of the capital utilization matrix is shown below:

	Coke from domestic coal	*Coke from imported coal*	*Pig iron from ore*	*Pig iron from sinter*	*Pig iron from pellets*
Coke oven	1	1	—	—	—
Blast furnace	—	—	1	1	0.96

Each of the alternative processes for producing coke uses the coke ovens but not the blast furnaces, so there are entries of 1 in the coke oven row and blanks in the blast furnace row. A similar structure for three alternative ways of producing pig iron in blast furnaces is also shown in the table. The last process illustrates that the entries in the capital utilization matrix need not always be blank or 1. The capacity of the blast furnace in this case was determined with a lump ore charge. When pellets are used in the charge, however, the capacity of the furnace rises to 104 percent of the original capacity, and therefore only $1/1.04 = 0.96$ as much capacity is required per ton of pig iron produced.

Capacity

The capacity of the iron ore mines in 1979 is shown in table 6-10. It is divided into three types of productive units: (1) trucks, draglines, drills, and crushers; (2) magnetic concentrators for magnetite ores; and (3) flotation concentrators for hematite ores. According to the availability of magnetite and hematite ores, magnetic concentrators are located in the southern mines (Peña Colorado, Las Truchas, and El Encino), and flotation concentrators are located at the northern mines (La Perla and Cerro Mercado; see map 3).

Two kinds of productive units, pellet plants and coke ovens, are footloose, in the sense that they are sometimes located near mines and sometimes located at steel mills. The advantage of locating them near mines is that there is some weight loss in this process. The disadvantage is that coke, and to a lesser extent pellets, may crumble somewhat while being transported. In Mexico three of the pellet plants and one of the coke plants are located at the mines. The capacity of the productive units at these plants (in thousands of tons a year) is:

	Peña Colorado	*La Perla*	*Alzada*	*Las Esperanzas*
Pellet plant	3,000	600	1,500	—
Coke ovens	—	—	—	684

The capacity of the productive units in the steel mills in 1979 is shown in table 6-11. The structure of capacity in the Mexican steel industry in that year is apparent. The three government-owned plants which belonged to SIDERMEX (SICARTSA, AHMSA, and Fundidora) used blast furnaces, open hearths, and basic oxygen furnaces to produce pig iron and steel; the three private plants (HYLSA in Monterrey, HYLSAP in Puebla, and TAMSA in Veracruz) employed direct reduction and electric arc furnaces to produce sponge iron and steel.

Table 6-10. *Capacity of Iron Ore Mines and Coal Mines*
(thousand tons a year)

Productive unit	*Peña Colorado*	*Las Truchas*	*La Perla*	*Cerro de Mercado*	*Hercules*	*La Chula*	*El Encino*	*Coahuila*
Mining equipment for iron ore								
Trucks and crushers	4,000	2,700	1,000	3,000	1,000	500	3,000	—
Magnetic concentrator	4,000	1,500	—	—	—	—	3,000	—
Flotation concentrator	—	—	1,000	3,000	—	—	—	—
Mining equipment for coal mines	—	—	—	—	—	—	—	7,000

—Not applicable.

Table 6-11. *Capacity of Productive Units in Steel Mills,* 1979
(thousand metric tons a year)

Productive unit	SICARTSA	AHMSA	*Fundidora*	HYLSA	HYLSAP	TAMSA
Pellet plant	1,850	—	750	—	—	—
Sinter plant	—	1,500	—	—	—	—
Coke oven	660	2,100	—	—	—	—
Blast furnace	1,100	3,247	1,400	—	—	—
Direct reduction	—	—	—	660	1,000	270
Open hearth	—	1,500	850	—	—	—
Basic oxygen furnace	1,300	2,070	1,500	—	—	—
Electric arc furnace	—	—	—	1,000	560	450
Continuous caster of slabs	—	710	—	—	—	—
Continuous caster of billets	1,300	—	—	—	560	—
Ingot casting	—	2,600	2,000	1,000	—	420
Primary mill for flats	—	1,850	1,450	1,000	—	—
Primary mill for nonflats	—	1,200	—	—	—	—
Plate mill	—	960	250	—	—	—
Hot strip mill	—	1,600	870	900	—	—
Pickling line	—	1,600	575	650	—	—
Cold strip mill	—	1,495	500	600	—	—
Annealing furnaces	—	1,348	420	450	—	—
Temper mill	—	1,225	520	450	—	—
Tinning line	—	315	—	70	—	—
Billet mill	—	1,000	200	—	—	—
Heavy shapes mill	—	200	—	—	—	—
Bar mill	600	135	—	—	430	80
Wire mill	600	270	—	—	200	—
Seamless pipe mill	—	—	—	—	—	280

—Not applicable.

In contrast, the separation in rolling mills was divided not along government and private lines but along plant lines. One government plant (SICARTSA) produced shapes, one (Fundidora) produced primarily flat products, and one (AHMSA) produced both shapes and flat products. Similarly, one private plant (HYLSAP) produced shapes and one (HYLSA) produced flat products. Finally, a private plant (TAMSA) produced almost exclusively seamless pipe.

Table 6-11 also shows some of the imbalances in capacity which result from economies of scale and technology changes in some productive units. Fundidora had excess capacity in steel production in its open hearths (850,000 tons) and basic oxygen furnaces (1.5 million tons) relative to its pig iron producing capacity (1.4 million tons) in the blast furnaces. HYLSAP had a sponge iron producing capacity of 1 million tons in its direct reduction units while its continuous caster had a capacity of only 560,000 tons. These imbalances presented interesting opportunities for interplant shipments of intermediate products. Some of these opportunities are exploited in the solutions presented in chapter 7.

Demand

Two components of demand, domestic and export, are treated in the model. Domestic demand is considered first.

The demand projections used in this study are from a study by the Coordinating Commission for the Steel Industry (1978), which is located in Mexico City and has responsibility for overseeing the entire Mexican steel industry, both private and public. In this version of the static model an attempt was made to replicate the situation in the industry for 1979. The projections for that year are shown in table 6-12.

These projections include the demand for some shapes that is satisfied by the small-scale rerolling industry. To obtain the demand for products produced by the integrated steel plants, which are the focus of this study, it is therefore necessary to subtract the part of demand met by the semi-integrated companies and the rerollers. In 1979 it was estimated that this

Table 6-12. *Domestic Demand Projections for 1979*
(thousand metric tons)

Product	*Total*	*Semi-integrated*[a]	*Net*
Plate	1,050	—	1,050
Hot sheet and strip	600	—	600
Cold sheet and strip (tempered)	1,250	—	1,250
Tin	400	—	400
Heavy shapes	300	130	170
Light shapes	310	160	150
Bars	340	155	185
Reinforcing rods	1,150	395	755
Wire rod	600	190	410
Seamless pipe	800	—	800
Rails	110	—	110

—Not applicable

a. We are indebted to Alejandro Reyes for these estimates.

Source: Based on results in Coordinating Commission for the Steel Industry (1978).

Table 6-13. *Demand for Steel Products from Integrated Steel Mills, 1979*
(thousand metric tons)

Steel product	*Demand*
Plate	1,050
Hot sheet and strip	600
Cold sheet and strip (tempered)	1,250
Tin	400
Heavy shapes	170
Light shapes	150
Bars	185
Reinforcing rods, large-diameter	453
Reinforcing rods, small-diameter	302
Wire rod	410
Seamless pipe	800
Rails	110

part of the industry supplied the amounts listed under semi-integrated in table 6-12. These figures are subtracted from the total figures to obtain the net domestic demand used in the model. One other modification of the data is necessary. Since some of the plants use different productive units for different sizes of reinforcing rods, demand for large-diameter is separated from that for small-diameter reinforcing rods. It is assumed that six-tenths of the demand for reinforcing rods is for large-diameter rods and the remaining four-tenths is for small-diameter rods. Thus, the demand for large-diameter reinforcing rods is (0.6) (755) = 453, and the demand for small-diameter reinforcing rods is (0.4) (755) = 302. After these changes, the demand for steel products from the integrated steel mills is as shown in table 6-13.

Next, it is necessary to distribute the demand for steel products among the nine regional markets used in the study (see table 6-14). For example, it is assumed that 87.6 percent of the total demand for tin is in Mexico City but only 10.5 percent of the demand for seamless pipes. Coatzacoalcos, in the center of the new gas fields, has a negligible percentage of the demand for tin but 39 percent of the demand for seamless pipe.

The results of multiplying the national demand times the regional percentages is given in table 6-15. This gives the demand in eight regional market centers for twelve categories of final products of the integrated steel industry in 1979 as projected from data available through 1977.

Table 6-14. *Percentage of Demand for Steel Products in Each Market Area, 1979*

Product	Mexico City	Puebla	Queré-taro	San Luis Potosí	Monterrey	Guadala-jara	Lázaro Cárdenas	Coatza-coalcos
Plate	63.5	0.2	0.3	0.3	31.0	4.5	0.1	0.1
Hot strip	41.9	2.8	1.6	2.8	36.2	12.6	0.5	1.6
Tempered strip	45.1	2.5	4.5	1.1	41.7	4.3	0.4	0.4
Tin	87.6	0.3	0	0	9.4	2.7	0	0
Heavy shapes	36.6	2.2	3.2	0.8	12.9	42.6	1.4	0.3
Light shapes	74.4	2.5	1.9	1.8	8.1	8.9	1.6	0.8
Bars	46.6	4.2	23.5	2.2	11.2	11.8	0.4	0.1
Reinforcing rods								
Large-diameter	46.7	10.3	4.0	3.4	12.8	11.8	6.1	4.9
Small-diameter	46.7	10.3	4.0	3.4	12.8	11.8	6.1	4.9
Wire rod	61.2	5.3	3.9	3.7	12.2	9.8	1.9	2.0
Seamless pipe	10.5	28.0	0.4	0.2	18.4	1.8	1.7	39.0
Rails	40.0	5.0	5.0	10.0	20.0	10.0	5.0	5.0

Table 6-15. *Regional Demand for Final Products from the Integrated Steel Industry, 1979*
(thousand metric tons)

Product	*Mexico City*	*Puebla*	*Queré-taro*	*San Luis Potosí*	*Monterrey*	*Guadala-jara*	*Lázaro Cárdenas*	*Coatza-coalcos*	*Total*
Plate	667	2	3	3	325	47	1	1	1,050
Hot strip	251	17	10	17	217	76	3	10	600
Tempered strip	564	31	56	14	521	54	5	5	1,250
Tin	350	0	1	0	38	11	0	0	400
Heavy shapes	62	4	5	1	22	72	2	1	170
Light shapes	111	4	3	3	12	13	2	1	150
Bars	86	8	44	4	21	22	1	0	185
Reinforcing rods									
Large-diameter	211	47	18	15	57	53	27	22	453
Small-diameter	141	31	12	10	38	35	18	15	302
Wire rod	250	22	16	15	50	40	8	8	410
Seamless pipe	84	224	3	2	147	14	14	312	800
Rails	44	6	6	11	22	11	6	6	110
Total	2,823	394	176	95	1,472	450	87	380	5,880

Note: Row and column totals may be off slightly because of rounding errors.

Prices

The prices used in the model are shown in table 6-16. Domestic prices are in 1979 pesos and international prices are in 1979 dollars. The exchange rate used in the model is 25 pesos per dollar. One set of cost terms and three sets of prices play a role in the model:

m^c = cost of production at mines
p^d = prices at raw material plants and steel mills
p^e = prices of exports
p^v = prices of imports.

Each of these sets of costs and prices will be discussed in turn.

The domestic costs at mines used in the model are 250 pesos a ton for raw, unwashed coal and 100 pesos a ton for ore. This price for ore applies to the three types used in the model: northern, southern, and Las Truchas ores.

Domestic prices at raw material plants and steel mills are given in the first column of table 6-16. The prices of natural gas, electricity, and coal have been changing very rapidly in recent years and are important in determining the relative efficiency of direct reduction–electric arc processes and blast furnace–BOF processes.

The price given in table 6-16 for natural gas is 322 pesos per thousand cubic meters, equivalent to \$0.36 per thousand cubic feet.[2] Similarly, the international price for natural gas given in table 6-16 is \$152 per thousand cubic meters which is equal to \$4.30 per thousand cubic feet.[3] There is therefore a large disparity between the domestic and the international price. This is an accurate description of the situation in 1979. Natural gas was sold in Mexico for a substantially lower price than in other countries.

Electricity is priced in the model at 552 pesos per thousand kilowatt-hours, equivalent to roughly 2 cents per kilowatt-hour, which can be compared to prices in the United States in 1979 of 4 to 5 cents per kilowatt-hour.

The prices for imports of final products are shown in the second

2. There are 0.0283 cubic meters per cubic foot and 25 pesos per dollar so 0.36 per thousand cubic feet = (322 pesos per thousand cubic meters) (0.0283 cubic meters per cubic foot) (1/25 dollars per peso).

3. \$4.30 per thousand cubic feet = (\$152 per thousand cubic meters) (0.0283 cubic meters per cubic foot).

Table 6-16. *Domestic and International Prices Used in the Large Static Model*
(pesos or dollars per metric ton unless otherwise noted)

Commodity	*Domestic price (1979 pesos)*	*International price (1979 dollars)*
Ore, concentrated	—	28
Pellets	430	45
Coal, domestic	880	—
Coal, imported	—	63
Coke	1,200	100
Fuel Oil (1,000 liters)	1,000	—
Limestone	120	—
Natural gas (1,000 cubic meters)	322	152
Scrap	3,050	120
Ferroalloys	16,000	—
Refractories	50,000	—
Dolomite	800	—
Lime	690	—
Electrodes	48,000	—
Electricity (megawatt-hours)	552	—
Plate	—	347
Hot sheet and strip	—	393
Cold sheet and strip (tempered)	—	373
Tin	—	393
Billets	—	300
Heavy shapes	—	338
Light shapes	—	364
Bars	—	350
Reinforcing rods, large-diameter	—	347
Reinforcing rods, small-diameter	—	368
Wire rods	—	434
Seamless pipes	—	455
Rails	—	345

—Not applicable.

column of table 6-16. These prices are assumed to hold at the port of entry. Additional costs are incurred in the model in transporting the imported raw material from the ports to the plants and the imported final products from the ports to the markets.

Export prices are assumed to be only 80 percent of the international price. This is a relatively arbitrary estimate of the difference between f.o.b. and c.i.f. prices for products in the steel industry.

Transport Cost

Transport costs are differentiated in the model according to the kind of commodities being shipped. This difference is embodied in the relationship used to calculate unit transport cost. The expressions used for calculating transport cost are:

$$\mu_{ii'}^{mr} = \alpha^r + \beta^r \delta_{ii'}^{mr} \qquad i \in IM, i' \in IR$$
$$\mu_{ii'}^{ms} = \alpha^r + \beta^r \delta_{ii'}^{ms} \qquad i \in IM, i' \in IS$$
$$\mu_{ii'}^{rs} = \alpha^r + \beta^r \delta_{ii'}^{rs} \qquad i \in IR, i' \in IS$$
$$\mu_{ii'}^{ss} = \alpha^r + \beta^r \delta_{ii'}^{ss} \qquad i \in IS, i' \in IS$$
$$\mu_{i}^{psr} = \alpha^r + \beta^r \delta_{i}^{ps} \qquad i \in IS$$
$$\mu_{ij}^{sj} = \alpha^r + \beta^f \delta_{ij}^{sj} \qquad i \in IS, j \in J$$
$$\mu_{i}^{spf} = \alpha^f + \beta^f \delta_{i}^{ps} \qquad i \in IS$$
$$\mu_{j}^{pj} = \alpha^f + \beta^f \delta_{j}^{pj} \qquad j \in J$$

where α^r = loading and unloading cost per ton for raw material

β^r = proportional cost per ton-kilometer for raw material

α^f = loading and unloading cost per ton for final products

β^f = proportional cost per ton kilometer for final products

δ^{mr} = distance in kilometers from mines to raw material plants.

All other distances are similarly defined with the superscripts defined as:

m = mines
r = raw material plants
s = steel mills
p = ports
j = markets.

For this model the parameter values used are:

$$\alpha^r = 30 \qquad \alpha^f = 60$$
$$\beta^r = 0.11 \qquad \beta^f = 0.19$$

The distances δ are given in the GAMS statement of the model in appendix B to this chapter.

The final parameter used in the model is a transport loss function for coke. It is used to represent the fact that coke tends to crumble somewhat when transported. It is assumed here that there is a 10 percent loss rate so this factor was set at 0.9 for coke and at 1.0 for all other commodities:

$$\lambda_c = 0.9 \qquad \text{for } c \in \{\text{coke}\}$$
$$\lambda_c = 1.0 \qquad \text{for all other } c \in CS$$

Appendix A. Notational Equivalence

This appendix contains a list of equivalences between the mathematical and GAMS terms. For a discussion of the model size and of the procedures used to reduce the model size, see Meeraus and Kendrick (1982). That paper provides a motivation for the use of the productive unit, process, and commodity possibility sets such as *MMPOS*, *PMPOS*, and *CMPOSN*. These sets are used to do the model reduction and can be ignored on a first reading of the GAMS statement for the large static model.

The notational equivalence between the mathematical and the GAMS versions of the large static Mexican steel model follows.

Equations

	Mathematical	*GAMS*
Material balance constraints for mines	(6.1)	MBM
Material balance constraints for raw material processing plants	(6.2)	MBR
Material balance constraints for steel mills	(6.3)	MBS
Capacity constraints for mines	(6.4)	CCM
Capacity constraints for raw material processing plants	(6.5)	CCR
Capacity constraints for steel mills	(6.6)	CCS
Market requirements	(6.7)	MREQ

Export constraints on commodities	(6.8)	ME
Total exports constraint	(6.8a)	ME2
Ownership constraints on pellet shipments	(6.9) and (6.10)	PELPC and PELAL
Accounting cost, total	(6.11)	ACOST
Accounting cost, recurrent	(6.12)	AREC
Accounting cost, transport	(6.13)	ATRANS
Accounting cost, imports	(6.14)	AIMP
Accounting revenues, exports	(6.15)	AEXP

Sets

The mathematical and GAMS notations are identical.

Variables

Mathematical	*GAMS*	*Mathematical*	*GAMS*
z^m	ZM	v^f	VF
z^r	ZR	v^s	VS
z^s	ZS	u^r	UR
x^m	XM	u^s	US
x^r	XR	ξ	COST
x^s	XS	ϕ_ψ	RECURRENT
x^f	XF	ϕ_λ	TRANSPORT
e	E	ϕ_π	IMPORT
		ϕ_ε	EXPORT

Parameters

Mathematical	*GAMS*	*Mathematical*	*GAMS*
a^m	AM	k^s	KS
a^r	AR	$\bar{e}$	EMAX
a^s	AS	d	D
b^m	BM	p^d	PD
b^r	BR	p^m	PM
b^s	BS	p^v	PV
k^m	KM	p^e	PE
k^r	KR	μ^{mr}	MUMR

(*continued*)

Parameters (continued)

Mathematical	*GAMS*	*Mathematical*	*GAMS*
μ^{ms}	MUMS	μ^{psr}	MUPSR
μ^{rs}	MURS	μ^{pj}	MUPJ
μ^{ss}	MUSS	m^c	MC
μ^{sj}	MUSJ	ρ	SH
μ^{spf}	MUSPF	ζ	PCT

A sampling of terms is given here to display the equivalence between mathematical notation and GAMS notation.

Mathematical		*GAMS*
$\sum_{p \in PM} a^m_{cp} z^m_{pi}$ [Use of domestic raw material and labor and output of intermediate products at mine i]	$c \in CM$ $i \in IM$	SUM(PM, AM(CM, PM)*ZM(PM, IM))
$u^s_{ci}\big\vert_{c \in CRAW}$ [Purchase of local raw material and labor]	$c \in CS$ $i \in IS$	US(CS, IS)$CRAW(CS)

The variable u_{ci} enters a set of equations defined over CS and IS but u^s_{ci} enters only a subset $CRAW$ of the set CS of commodity equations.

Appendix B. GAMS Statement of the Large Static Model

A GAMS statement of the large static model including the sets, data, equations, and reference map begins on the following page.

```
                                                                      NEW MARGIN = 002-120
*    REFERENCES
*    ----------
*
*    1.  SICARTSA, DESCRIPCION DE LOS PROCESOS QUE SE REALIZAN EN LAS
*        PLANTAS  DEL COMPLEJO SIDERURGICO SICARTSA, 1978
*
*    2.  ALTOS HOROS, INFORMATION GENERAL (BLUEPRINT), 1974
*
*    3.  ALTOS HORNOS, DIAGRAMA DE FLUJO  3.75 MMT/A AND 4.25 MMT/A
*        (BLUEPRINTS), 1978
*
*    4.  CCIS, SITUATION ACTUAL Y CRECIMIENTO FUTORO DE LA INDUSTRIA
*        SIDERURGICA, 1978
*
*    5.  CCIS, REPORTE DE LA PRUEBA DEL EMPLEO DE FIERRO ESPONJA
*        HYL EN EL ALTO HORNO 2, 1978
*
*    6.  CCIS, ESTUDIO DE PRE-FACTIBILIDAD PARA UNA PLANTA DE FIERRO
*        ESPONJA PARA EXPORTACION CONVENIO MEXICO-BRASIL, 1978
*
*    7.  CCIS, LAS MATERIAS PRIMAS Y OTROS INSUMOS EN LA INDUSTRIA
*        SIDERURGICA, 1977
*
*    8.  RUSSEL AND VAUGHAN, STEEL PRODUCTION, 1976
*
*    9.  SECRETARIA DE LA PRECIDENCIA, LA INDUSTRIA SIDERURGICA
*        INTEGRADA DE MEXICO  (VOL I AND II), 1976
*
*   10.  AHMSA, CAPACITY SHEET, 1978
*
*   11.  AHMSA, CAPACITY EXPANSION 1979 - 1982, 1978
*
*   12.  FUNDIDORA, LA MODERNA FUNDIDORA ...., 197..
*
*   13.  SICARTSA, PRODUCTION Y CONSUMO
*
*   14.  SICARTSA, INSUMOS PRINCIPALES, PECIOS DE PRESUPUESTO, 1979
*
*   15.  HYLSA, THE HYL IRON ORE DIRECT REDUCTION PROCESS, 1973
*
*   16.  FUNDIDORA, COMPUTER DATA BANK, 1978
*
*   17.  FUNDIDORA, OFERTA Y DEMANDA, JOINT INDUSTRY PROJECTIONS, 1978
*
*   18.  CCIS, TRANSPORT COST AND DISTANCES FOR MINERAL COAL
*
*   19.  CCIS, TRANSPORT COST AND DISTANCES FOR IRON ORE
*
*   20.  CCIS, SHORTEST RAILROAD DISTANCES BETWEEN MAJOR CITIES
*
*   21.  CCIS, TRANSPORT COST AND DISTANCES FOR SOME STEEL PRODUCTS
```

```
*
*  22.  IBRD, SICARTSA II, 1975
*
*  23.  CAPITAL COST. SICARTSA FIRST STAGE. 1973. REPORT BY
*       INDUSTRIAL DEPARTMENT. IBRD.
*
*  24.  PLAN DE DESARROLLO DE LA INDUSTRIA SIDERURGICA PARAESTATAL
*       1979-1990. SIDERMEX. CONFIDENTIAL DOCUMENT. NOT PUBLISHED YET

```

SET DEFINITIONS

```
SET IM       IRON ORE AND COAL MINES /

             P-COLORADA   PENA COLORADA COLIMA
             LASTRUCHAS   LAZARO CARDENAS MICHOACAN
             LA-PERLA     CAMARGO CHIHUAHUA
             CERRO-MER    CERRO DE MERCADO DURANGO
             HERCULES     SIERRA MOJADA COAHUILA

             LA-CHULA     MINATITLAN COLIMA
             EL-ENCINO    PIHUAMO JALISCO
             COAHUILA     COAL MINING REGION    /

    IR       RAW MATERIAL PLANTS /

             PENACOL      PENA COLORADA COLIMA
             LAPERLA      CAMARGO CHIHUAHUA
             ALZADA       COLIMA
             ESPERANZAS   COAHUILA             /

    IS       STEEL MILLS /

             SICARTSA     LAS TRUCHAS
             AHMSA        MONCLOVA
             FUNDIDORA    MONTERREY
             HYLSA        MONTERREY
             HYLSAP       PUEBLA
             TAMSA        VERACRUZ /

    J        DOMESTIC MARKET AREAS /

             MEXICO-DF    MEXICO D.F.
             PUEBLA       PUEBLA
             QUERETARO    QUERETARO
             SAN-LUIS     SAN LUIS POTOSI
             MONTERREY    NUEVO LEON

             GUADALAJA    GUADALAJARA JALISCO
             L-CARDENAS   MICHOACAN
             COATZACOAL   VERACRUZ  /

    L        EXPORT POINTS /

             GULF
             PACIFIC  /

    MM       PRODUCTIVE UNITS AT MINES /

             MINE-CO      MINING EQUIPMENT FOR COAL MINES
             MINE-EQ      MINING EQUIPMENT: TRUCKS AND CRUSHERS
             CONC-MAG     MAGNETIC CONCENTRATOR
             CONC-FLOT    FLOTATION CONCENTRATOR  /
```

SET DEFINITIONS

```
      MR       PRODUCTIVE UNITS AT RAW MATERIAL PLANTS /

               PELLET       PELLET PLANT
               COKE-OVEN    COKE OVEN AND BYPRODUCT UNITS  /

      MS       PRODUCTIVE UNITS AT STEEL MILLS /

               PELLET       PELLET PLANT
               SINTER       SINTER PLANT
               COKE-OVEN    COKE OVENS AND BY-PRODUCT UNITS
               BLAST-FURN   BLAST FURNACES
               DIRECT-RED   DIRECT REDUCTION UNITS

               OPENHEARTH   OPEN HEARTH FURNACES
               BOF          BASIC OXYGEN CONVERTERS
               ELEC-ARC     ELECTRIC ARC FURNACES
               CONCAS-SL    CONTINUOUS CASTING UNIT FOR SLABS
               CONCAS-BI    CONTINUOUS CASTING UNIT FOR BILLETS

               INGOT-CAST   INGOT CASTING
               PRIMARY-FL   PRIMARY MILL AND SOAKING PITS - FLAT PRODUCTS
               PRIMARY-NF   PRIMARY MILLS AND SOAKING PITS - NON FLAT
               PLATE-MILL   PLATE MILL
               HOT-MILL     HOT STRIP MILL

               PICKLELINE   PICKLING LINE
               COLD-MILL    COLD STRIP MILL
               ANNEAL       ANNEALING UNITS
               TEMPERMILL   TEMPER MILL
               TIN-LINE     TINNING LINE

               BILLET       BILLET MILL
               HEAVYSMILL   HEAVY SHAPES MILL
               BAR-MILL     INTEGRATED BAR MILL
               WIRE-MILL    INTEGRATED WIRE MILL
               SEAML-MILL   SEAMLESS PIPE MILL /

      PM       PRODUCTION PROCESSES AT MINES /

               MIN-CO       MINING UNWASHED COAL
               WAS-CO       WASHING OF COAL
               MIN-N        MINING IN THE NORTHERN MINES
               MIN-S        MINING IN THE SOUTHERN MINES
               MIN-TR       MINING IN LAS TRUCHAS MINE

               CONC-N       CONCENTRATION OF NORTHERN ORE
               CONC-S       CONCENTRATION OF SOUTHERN ORE
               CONC-TR      CONCENTRATION OF TRUCHAS ORE  /

      PR       PRODUCTION PROCESSES AT RAW MATERIAL PLANTS /

               PELT-C        PELLET PRODUCTION USING CONC ORE
```

```
                COKE-HD       COKE PRODUCTION WITH  DOMESTIC COAL /

         PS     PRODUCTION PROCESSES AT STEEL MILLS /

                PELT-C        PELLET PRODUCTION USING CONCENTRATED ORE
                SINTER        SINTER PRODUCTION
                COKE-HD       COKE PRODUCTION WITH HIGH DOMESTIC COAL INPUT
                COKE-HI       COKE PRODUCTION WITH HIGH IMPORT COAL INPUT
                PIG-ORE       PIG IRON ORE PRODUCTION WITH LUMP ORE

                PIG-SIN       PIG IRON PRODUCTION WITH HIGH SINTER CHARGE
                PIG-PEL       PIG IRON PRODUCTION WITH HIGH PELLETS CHARGE
                PIG-PEL-M     PIG IRON PRODUCTION WITH COKE FROM IMPORTED COAL
                SPONGE        SPONGE IRON PRODUCTION
                STL-OH-P      STEEL PRODUCTION IN OPEN HEARTHS WITH HIGH PIG IRO

                STL-OH-S      STEEL PRODUCTION IN OPEN HEARTHS WITH HIGH SCRAP CHARGE
                STL-OH-S2     STEEL PRODUCTION IN OPEN HEARTHS WITH HIGHEST SCRAP CHARGE
                STL-BOF-P     STEEL PRODUCTION IN BOF WITH HIGH PIG IRON CHARGE
                STL-BOF-S     STEEL PRODUCTION IN BOF WITH HIGH SCRAP CHARGE
                STL-EAF-SP    STEEL PRODUCTION IN ELECTRIC FUR. WITH HIGH SPONGE

                STL-EAF-S     STEEL PRODUCTION IN ELECTRIC FURNACE WITH HIGH SCRAP
                SLABS-CC      SLABS PRODUCTION BY CONTINUOUS CASTING
                BILLETS-CC    BILLET PRODUCTION BY CONTINUOUS CASTING
                INGOT         INGOT CASTING
                SLAB-ROLL     SLAB PRODUCTION BY ROLLING

                BLOOM-ROLL    ROLLING OF BLOOMS FROM INGOTS
                BILLET-ROL    BILLET PRODUCTION BY ROLLING BLOOMS
                PLATE         PLATE PRODUCTION FROM SLABS
                HOT-SHEET     HOT ROLLED COIL PRODUCTION
                PICKLED       PICKLED COIL PRODUCTION

                COLD-SHEET    COLD ROLL COIL PRODUCTION
                ANNEALED      ANNEALED COIL PRODUCTION
                TEMPERED      TEMPERED COIL PRODUCTION
                TINNING       TIN PRODUCTION
                HEAVYSHAPE    HEAVY SHAPE ROLLING

                LIGHTSHAPE    ROLLING OF LIGHT SHAPES
                ROUGH-NF      ROUGHING MILL FOR NON-FLAT PRODUCTS
                BAR-ROLL      ROLLING OF BARS
                REBARS-LD     ROLLING OF LARGE DIAMETER RE-RODS AND BARS
                REBARS-SD     ROLLING OF SMALL DIAMETER RE-RODS AND BARS

                WIRE ROD      ROLLING OF WIRE ROD
                SEAM-ROL      ROLLLING OF SEAMLESS PIPES    /

         CS     COMMODITIES AT STEEL MILLS /

                ORE-N         IRON ORE FROM NORTH. HIGH S AND P. 59% FE.
```

SET DEFINITIONS

```
                 ORE-S          IRON ORE FROM SOUTH. NO P. 60% FE.
                 ORE-TRUCHA     IRON ORE FROM SICARTSA. NO P. 55% FE.
                 ORE-CONC       IRON ORE CONCENTRATED
                 PELLETS        PELLETS

                 SINTER         SINTER
                 COAL-D         COAL-DOMESTIC: WASHED
                 COAL-I         COAL-IMPORTED: WASHED
                 COAL-R         RAW UNWASHED COAL
                 COKE           COKE PRODUCED WITH DOMESTIC COAL

                 COKE-IMP-C     COKE PRODUCED WITH IMPORTED COAL
                 FUEL-OIL       FUEL OIL IN THOUSAND LITERS
                 LIMESTONE      LIMESTONE
                 PIG-IRON       PIG IRON (HOT METAL)
                 NAT-GAS        NATURAL GAS IN 1000 M3

                 SPONGE         SPONGE IRON
                 SCRAP          STEEL SCRAP
                 FERRO-ALLO     FERROALLOYS
                 REFRAC         REFRACTORIES
                 DOLOMITE       DOLOMITE

                 LIME           LIME
                 ELECTRODES     ELECTRODES (KG)
                 STEEL-LIQ      LIQUID STEEL
                 STEEL-ING      INGOT STEEL
                 SLABS          SLABS

                 PLATE          PLATE
                 HOT-STRIP      HOT STRIP SHEET
                 PICK-STRIP     PICKLED STRIP SHEET
                 COLD-STRIP     COLD STRIP SHEET
                 ANL-STRIP      ANNEALED STRIP SHEET

                 TEMP-STRIP     TEMPERED STRIP SHEET
                 TIN            TIN SHEET
                 BLOOMS         BLOOMS
                 BILLETS        BILLETS
                 HEAVYSHAPE     HEAVY SHAPES
                 LIGHTSHAPE     LIGHT SHAPES
                 BARS           BARS
                 REBARS         REINFORCING RODS - DEMAND DATA IS AVAILABLE ONLY FOR AGGREGATE
                 REBARS-LD      LARGE DIAMETER REINFORCING RODS
                 REBARS-SD      SMALL DIAMETER REINFORCING RODS
                 WIRE           WIRE ROD

                 SEAMLESS       SEAMLESS PIPE
                 PESOS          MEXICAN CURRENCY
                 ELECTRIC       ELECTRICITY IN 1000 KWH
                 WATER          WATER IN 1000 M3
                 ING-BLOOMS     STEEL BLOOMS FOR SEAMLESS PIPE
```

```
                RAILS        RAILS - ONLY IMPORTED          /

       CRAW(CS) DOMESTIC RAW MATERIALS /

                FUEL-OIL, LIMESTONE, NAT-GAS, SCRAP, FERRO-ALLO, REFRAC
                DOLOMITE, LIME, ELECTRODES, WATER, ELECTRIC  /

       CM(CS)   COMMODITIES AT MINES /

                ORE-N, ORE-S, ORE-TRUCHA, COAL-R, COAL-D, ORE-CONC  /

       CR(CS)   COMMODITIES AT RAW MATERIAL PLANTS /

                ORE-N, ORE-S, ORE-TRUCHA, COAL-R, COAL-D, ORE-CONC, PELLETS, COKE, ELECTRIC  /

       CRV(CS)  IMPORTED RAW MATERIALS AND INTERMEDIATE PRODUCTS / COAL-I, PELLETS, SCRAP, COKE  /


       CMR(CS)  COMMODITIES SHIPPED FROM MINES TO RAW MATERIAL PLANTS / ORE-CONC, COAL-D  /


       CMS(CS)  COMMODITIES SHIPPED FROM MINES TO STEEL PLANTS / COAL-D, ORE-CONC, ORE-S, ORE-N, ORE-TRUCHA /


       CRS(CS)  COMMODITIES SHIPPED FROM RAW MATERIAL PLANTS TO STEEL MILLS / PELLETS, COKE  /


       CSS(CS)  COMMODITIES FOR INTERPLANT SHIPMENT BETWEEN STEEL MILLS / SPONGE, PELLETS, COKE  /

       CF(CS)   FINAL PRODUCTS / PLATE, HOT-STRIP, TEMP-STRIP, TIN , HEAVYSHAPE, LIGHTSHAPE
                                 BARS , REBARS-LD, REBARS-SD , WIRE, SEAMLESS  , RAILS      /

       CE(CS)   COMMODITIES FOR EXPORTS

       CFV(CS)  IMPORTED FINAL PRODUCTS

       O        OWNER NUMBERS   / 1*5  /

       OWN(O,IS) OWNER GROUPS   / 1.SICARTSA, 2.AHMSA, 3.FUNDIDORA, 4.(HYLSA,HYLSAP), 5.TAMSA /


       ISEX(IS) PLANTS EXCLUDED FROM ALZADA ORES / SICARTSA, AHMSA, FUNDIDORA, TAMSA /

       RES(CM,IM) RESERVE TYPES AT LOCATIONS     / ORE-S.P-COLORADA, ORE-TRUCHA.LASTRUCHAS, ORE-N.LA-PERLA
                                                   ORE-N.CERRO-MER , ORE-N.HERCULES       , ORE-S.LA-CHULA
                                                   ORE-S.EL-ENCINO , COAL-R.COAHUILA                     / ;

   CE(CF)  = YES    ;
   CFV(CF) = YES    ;

   ALIAS(IS,ISP)    ;
```

```
PARAMETER AS(CS,PS,IS)  INPUT OUTPUT RELATIONS FOR STEEL MILLS ;

TABLE AM(CM,PM)   A MATRIX FOR MINING PRODUCTS

            MIN-N   MIN-S   MIN-TR  CONC-N  CONC-S  CONC-TR  MIN-CO  WAS-CO

ORE-N         1.                    -1.42
ORE-S                 1.                    -1.28
ORE-TRUCHA                    1.                    -1.37
ORE-CONC                              1.      1.      1.
COAL-R                                                        1.     -2.1
COAL-D                                                                1.


TABLE AR(CS,PR)   A MATRIX FOR RAW MATERIAL PLANTS

            PELT-C  COKE-HD

FUEL-OIL     -.02
ORE-CONC     -.99
PELLETS      1.0
COAL-D               -1.50
COKE                  1.0
ELECTRIC     -.045    -.060

TABLE ASIC(CS,PS)   A MATRIX FOR SICARTSA

            PELT-C  COKE-HI  PIG-PEL-M  STL-BOF-P  STL-BOF-S

ORE-TRUCHA                    -.20
ORE-CONC     -.99
PELLETS      1.0              -1.384
COAL-I               -1.38
COKE-IMP-C            1.0      -.60
FUEL-OIL                       -.045
LIMESTONE                      -.081
PIG-IRON                       1.0        -.944      -.833
SCRAP                                     -.166      -.180
FERRO-ALLO                                -.033      -.033
REFRAC                                    -.006      -.006
DOLOMITE                       -.049      -.06       -.06
LIME                                      -.09       -.09
STEEL-LIQ                                 1.0        1.0
ELECTRIC     -.045   -.060     -.090      -.068      -.068
```

```
   +         BILLETS-CC  LIGHTSHAPE  REBARS-LD  REBARS-SD  WIRE

SCRAP              .04         .03        .03        .03      .02
STEEL-LIQ        -1.05
BILLETS           1.0        -1.06      -1.06      -1.06    -1.05
LIGHTSHAPE                    1.0
REBARS-LD                                 1.0
REBARS-SD                                            1.0
WIRE                                                          1.0
ELECTRIC                     -.08       -.08       -.08     -.08
WATER                        -.01       -.01       -.01     -.01
*
*  DATA FOR PELT-C AND COKE-HI COME FROM PLANT VISIT. DATA FOR PIG-PEL
*  AND STL-BOF-P COMES FROM (1 PAGE 83 AND 95). IDEALIZED DATA RATHER
*  THAN HISTORICAL YIELDS FOR 1978 WERE USED FOR ROLLING MILLS.


TABLE AAHM(CS,PS)   A MATRIX FOR AHMSA

            COKE-HD  SINTER  PIG-PEL  PIG-SIN

ORE-N                 -1.1             -.64
COAL-D       -1.50
SINTER                 1.0            -1.03
PELLETS                        -1.6
COKE          1.0     -.11     -.63    -.70
LIMESTONE             -.17             -.10
DOLOMITE                       -.049   -.049
PIG-IRON                       1.0     1.0
NAT-GAS                        -.05    -.05
SPONGE
ELECTRIC     -.060   -.040     -.090   -.090
FERRO-ALLO                     -.065   -.065

   +        STL-OH-S  STL-BOF-P  STL-BOF-S  INGOT  SLABS-CC  SLAB-ROLL

ORE-N                              -.02
PIG-IRON      -.77      -1.02      -.74
SCRAP         -.33       -.11      -.42      .02      .02       .13
NAT-GAS                            -.078    -.05               -.05
FUEL-OIL                           -.079
LIMESTONE     -.14
FERRO-ALLO    -.011      -.011     -.011
REFRAC        -.012      -.006     -.012
DOLOMITE      -.10       -.06
LIME                     -.09      -.14
STEEL-LIQ     1.0        1.0       1.0     -1.04    -1.04
STEEL-ING                                   1.0               -1.17
SLABS                                                1.0       1.0
ELECTRIC      -.040      -.068     -.068

   +        BLOOM-ROLL  BILLET-ROL  PLATE  HOT-SHEET  PICKLED
```

```
SCRAP            .13          .13        .02       .03
STEEL-ING     -1.17
SLABS                                  -1.04     -1.05
PLATE                                    1.0
HOT-STRIP                                          1.0       -1.0
BLOOMS          1.0         -1.17
BILLETS                       1.0
PICK-STRIP                                                    1.0

     +        COLD-SHEET  ANNEALED  TEMPERED  TINNING

SCRAP             .13
PICK-STRIP      -1.17
COLD-STRIP       1.0        -1.0
ANL-STRIP                    1.0       -1.0
TEMP-STRIP                              1.0  -1.02
TIN                                            1.0

     +      HEAVYSHAPE  LIGHTSHAPE  BAR-ROLL  REBARS-LD  REBARS-SD  WIRE
BLOOMS         -1.15
HEAVYSHAPE      1.0
BILLETS                     -1.14     -1.06     -1.06      -1.06    -1.0
LIGHTSHAPE                    1.0
BARS                                    1.0
REBARS-LD                                         1.0
REBARS-SD                                                    1.0
WIRE                                                                1.0
SCRAP             .05         .03       .04       .04        .04     .0

TABLE AFUND(CS,PS)   A MATRIX FOR FUNDIDORA

           PIG-PEL  PIG-ORE  PELT-C

ORE-N        -.29    -1.38
ORE-CONC                        -.99
PELLETS     -1.38     -.29      1.0
COKE         -.69     -.75
LIMESTONE    -.24     -.27
PIG-IRON     1.0      1.0
NAT-GAS      -.051    -.029
ELECTRIC     -.06     -.036    -.045
WATER        -.003    -.001
FERRO-ALLO   -.065    -.065

     +        STL-OH-S  STL-BOF-P  STL-BOF-S  STL-OH-S2

ORE-N           -.02                            -.02
FUEL-OIL         -.079                          -.079
PIG-IRON        -.74      -.96       -.81       -.32
NAT-GAS         -.078                           -.078
SCRAP           -.42      -.15       -.27       -.80
```

```
FERRO-ALLO      -.012      -.012       -.012      -.012
REFRAC          -.012      -.006       -.006      -.012
LIME            -.14                              -.14
STEEL-LIQ       1.0        1.0         1.0        1.0
ELECTRIC        -.072      -.068       -.068      -.072

   +         INGOT  SLAB-ROLL  PLATE  HOT-SHEET  PICKLED  COLD-SHEET

SCRAP          .01       .10       .10                          .13
STEEL-LIQ    -1.04
STEEL-ING     1.0      -1.14
SLABS                    1.0     -1.12    -1.05
PLATE                              1.0
HOT-STRIP                                  1.0      -1.0
PICK-STRIP                                           1.0      -1.17
COLD-STRIP                                                      1.0

   +         ANNEALED  TEMPERED  BLOOM-ROLL  BILLET-ROL  LIGHTSHAPE

SCRAP                                 .10                     .10
STEEL-ING                          -1.13
COLD-STRIP     -1.0
ANL-STRIP       1.0       -1.0
TEMP-STRIP                 1.0
BLOOMS                               1.0       -1.03
BILLETS                                         1.0         -1.14
LIGHTSHAPE                                                    1.0

   +         WIRE  REBARS-SD

SCRAP          .04       .04
BILLETS      -1.06     -1.06
REBARS-SD                1.0
WIRE          1.0


* DATA FOR  THE PIG-ORE AND PIG-PEL PROCESSES WERE DERIVED
* FROM BF NO. 2 AND BF NO. 3 DATA FOR 1975 AS REPORTED IN
* (9- VOL I) TABLE 3.3.6
* *  DATA FOR STL-OH-S  ARE FROM SAME SOURCE TABLE 3.4.6


TABLE  AHYL(CS,PS)   A MATRIX FOR HYLSA IN MONTERREY

             SPONGE  STL-EAF-SP  STL-EAF-S  INGOT  SLAB-ROLL

PELLETS      -1.38
NAT-GAS       -.470                                   -.05
SPONGE        1.0       -1.09       -.60
SCRAP                               -.46               .05
FERRO-ALLO              -.012       -.012
REFRAC                  -.006       -.006
```

```
ELECTRODES           -.0052       -.0052
DOLOMITE               -.009        -.009
LIME                   -.007        -.007
STEEL-LIQ              1.0          1.0        -1.02
STEEL-ING                                       1.0    -1.07
SLABS                                                   1.0
ELECTRIC      -.10     -.68        -.60

    +        HOT-SHEET  PICKLED  COLD-SHEET  ANNEALED

SCRAP          .05        .06        .02
SLABS        -1.07
PLATE
HOT-STRIP     1.0      -1.06
PICK-STRIP               1.0       -1.05
COLD-STRIP                          1.0        -1.0
ANL-STRIP                                       1.0

    +        TEMPERED  TINNING

SCRAP           .03       .01
ANL-STRIP     -1.04
TEMP-STRIP     1.0      -1.02
TIN                      1.0

*  DATA FOR EAF FROM (15), ROLLING PROCESSES FROM (9 VOL II)
*  VERIFY SCRAP GENERATION AND ELECTRICITY


TABLE AHYLP(CS,PS)   A MATRIX FOR HYLSA IN PUEBLA

             SPONGE  STL-EAF-SP  STL-EAF-S  BILLETS-CC

PELLETS       -1.38
NAT-GAS        -.420
SPONGE        1.0     -1.09
SCRAP                             -1.06
FERRO-ALLO              -.014      -.012
REFRAC                  -.006      -.006
ELECTRODES              -.0052       -.0052
DOLOMITE                -.009      -.009
LIME                    -.007      -.007
STEEL-LIQ               1.0        1.0        -1.06
BILLETS                                        1.0
ELECTRIC       -.010    -.68       -.50

    +         LIGHTSHAPE  BAR-ROLL  REBARS-LD  REBARS-SD  WIRE

SCRAP             .04        .04       .04         .03      .03
BILLETS         -1.06      -1.06     -1.06       -1.05    -1.05
LIGHTSHAPE       1.0
BARS                        1.0
```

```
REBARS-LD                              1.0
REBARS-SD                                          1.0
WIRE                                                        1.0
ELECTRIC          -.03       -.025      -.025      -.03      -.03

*   ROLLING PROCESSES FROM (9-II), SPONGE AND ST-EAF FROM PLANT VISITS
*   AND (15)


TABLE ATAM(CS,PS)    A MATRIX FOR TAMSA

              SPONGE  STL-EAF-SP  STL-EAF-S    INGOT

PELLETS        -1.38
NAT-GAS         -.50
SPONGE          1.0       -1.09
SCRAP                                -1.06
FERRO-ALLO                 -.033      -.033
REFRAC                     -.006      -.006
ELECTRODES                 -.0052       -.0052
DOLOMITE                   -.009      -.009
LIME                       -.007      -.007
STEEL-LIQ                  1.0        1.0         -1.06
ING-BLOOMS                                         1.0
ELECTRIC        -.01       -.68       -.50

    +        BILLET-ROL  LIGHTSHAPE  BAR-ROLL  SEAM-ROL

SCRAP             .01          .04        .04       .35
ING-BLOOMS      -1.03                              -1.45
BILLETS          1.0         -1.06      -1.06
LIGHTSHAPE                    1.0
BARS                                     1.0
SEAMLESS                                            1.0
                                ;

     AS(CS,PS,"SICARTSA")      = ASIC(CS,PS);
     AS(CS,PS,"AHMSA")         = AAHM(CS,PS);
     AS(CS,PS,"FUNDIDORA")     = AFUND(CS,PS);
     AS(CS,PS,"HYLSA")         = AHYL(CS,PS);
     AS(CS,PS,"HYLSAP")        = AHYLP(CS,PS);
     AS(CS,PS,"TAMSA")         = ATAM(CS,PS);


TABLE BM(MM,PM)   CAPACITY UTILIZATION MATRIX FOR MINES

              MIN-N  MIN-S  MIN-TR  CONC-S  CONC-TR CONC-N  MIN-CO

MINE-EQ         1      1      1
CONC-MAG                               1       1
CONC-FLOT                                              1
MINE-CO                                                        1
```

```
TABLE BR(MR,PR)   CAPACITY UTILIZATION FOR RAW MATERIALS PLANTS

                COKE-HD    PELT-C

COKE-OVEN          1
PELLET                         1

TABLE BS(MS,PS)   CAPACITY UTILIZATION MATRIX FOR STEEL MILLS

            COKE-HD  COKE-HI  PIG-ORE PIG-SIN PIG-PEL PIG-PEL-M

COKE-OVEN      1        1
BLAST-FURN                       1       1      .96       1

    +           SPONGE STL-OH-P STL-OH-S STL-OH-S2

BLAST-FURN
DIRECT-RED         1
OPENHEARTH                 1          1        1

    +       STL-BOF-P  STL-BOF-S  STL-EAF-SP  STL-EAF-S

BOF             1          1
ELEC-ARC                             1            1

    +       SLABS-CC  BILLETS-CC  INGOT  SLAB-ROLL  BLOOM-ROLL

CONCAS-SL       1
CONCAS-BI                1
INGOT-CAST                         1
PRIMARY-FL                                   1
PRIMARY-NF                                               1

    +       BILLET-ROL   PLATE  HOT-SHEET  PICKLED  COLD-SHEET

PLATE-MILL                 1
HOT-MILL                             1
PICKLELINE                                    1
COLD-MILL                                                1
BILLET             1

    +       ANNEALED  TEMPERED  TINNING  HEAVYSHAPE  LIGHTSHAPE

ANNEAL          1
TEMPERMILL                1
TIN-LINE                            1
HEAVYSMILL                                  1
BAR-MILL                                                 1

    +       BAR-ROLL  REBARS-LD  REBARS-SD  WIRE  SEAM-ROL

```

```
PRODUCTION

BAR-MILL          1          1
WIRE-MILL                                1         1
SEAML-MILL                                                   1

  +          PELT-C     SINTER

PELLET          1
SINTER                     1

```

```
TABLE KM(MM,IM)   INITIAL CAPACITIES FOR MINES (1000 TPY)

            P-COLORADA LASTRUCHAS LA-PERLA CERRO-MER HERCULES

MINE-EQ        4000       2700      1000     3000      1000
CONC-MAG       4000       1500
CONC-FLOT                           1000     3000


+           LA-CHULA  EL-ENCINO  COAHUILA

MINE-EQ         500       3000
CONC-MAG                  3000
MINE-CO                            7000

TABLE KR(MR,IR)   INITIAL CAPACITIES FOR RAW MATERIAL PLANTS  (1000 TPY)

            PENACOL  LAPERLA  ALZADA  ESPERANZAS

PELLET         3000     600      1500
COKE-OVEN                                684


TABLE KS(MS,IS)   INITIAL CAPACITIES FOR STEEL MILLS  (1000 TPY)

            SICARTSA  AHMSA  FUNDIDORA  HYLSA  HYLSAP  TAMSA

PELLET          1850                  750
SINTER                 1500
COKE-OVEN        660   2100
BLAST-FURN      1100   3247       1400
DIRECT-RED                                 660    1000    270
OPENHEARTH             1500        850
BOF             1300   2070       1500
ELEC-ARC                                  1000     560    450
CONCAS-SL               710
CONCAS-BI       1300                               560
INGOT-CAST             2600       2000    1000            420
PRIMARY-FL             1850       1450    1000
PRIMARY-NF             1200
PLATE-MILL              960        250
HOT-MILL               1600        870     900
PICKLELINE             1600        575     650
COLD-MILL              1495        500     600
ANNEAL                 1348        420     450
TEMPERMILL             1225        520     450
TIN-LINE                315                 70
BILLET                 1000        200
HEAVYSMILL              200
BAR-MILL         600    135                        430     80
WIRE-MILL        600    270                        200
SEAML-MILL                                                280
```

```

        ;
* SICARTSA
*
*   1. COKE-OVEN (1)  2200 T/DAY = 660 MT/A  BASED ON STATED COAL MIX
*   2. BLAST-FURN (1)  3300 T/DAY WITH 330 DAYS/YEAR = 1100 MT/A
*   3. ALL CAPACITIES FROM (1) UNLESS OTHERWISE NOTED
*
* AHMSA
*
*   1. ALL CAPACITIES FROM (10) UNLESS OTHERWISE NOTED
*
* FUNDIDORA
*
*   1. COKE PLANT IS AT THE MINE
*   2. ALL CAPACITIES FROM (12) UNLESS OTHERWISE NOTED
*   3. OPEN HEARTH CAPACITY IS FOR STEELSHOP NO. 2 FROM (9 - VOL I)
*      TABLE 3.4.3
*
* HYLSA
*
*   1. ALL CAPACITIES FROM (9 - VOL I) UNLESS OTHERWISE NOTED
*   2. ONLY ROUGH ESTIMATES FOR PICKLE, ANNEALING, AND TEMPER LINES
*   3. MONTERREY VISIT APRIL 1981
*
* HYLSAP
*
*   1. DATA OBTAINED DURING PLANT VISIT
*
* TAMSA
*
*   1. ALL CAPACITIES FROM(9 -VOL I)
*   2. MONTERREY VISIT 1981


 PARAMETER UT(IS) CAPACITY UTILIZATION / SICARTSA .5, (AHMSA,FUNDIDORA,TAMSA) .9, HYLSA 1, HYLSAP 1.1 / ;

  KM(MM,IM) = .9*KM(MM,IM);
  KR(MR,IR) = .9*KR(MR,IR);
  KS(MS,IS) = UT(IS)*KS(MS,IS);
```

```
SET DS         DEMAND DATA COMPONENTS / DEMAND, SEMI-INT, ADJ-DEM /

TABLE MROD(CS,CS) MAP FOR DISAGGREGATING DEMAND FOR REINFORCED BARS TO LARGE AND SMALL DIAMETERS

           REBARS-SD  REBARS-LD
REBARS        .4         .6


TABLE DEMDAT(CS,DS)   DEMAND AND SEMI-INTGRATED OUTPUT (1000 TPY)

              DEMAND      SEMI-INT

PLATE          1050
HOT-STRIP       600
TEMP-STRIP     1250
TIN             400
HEAVYSHAPE      300          130
LIGHTSHAPE      310          160
BARS            340          155
REBARS         1150          395
WIRE            600          190
SEAMLESS        800
RAILS           110


TABLE REGDEM(CS,J)  REGIONAL DEMAND PER PRODUCT ( % OF TOTAL )

            MEXICO-DF PUEBLA QUERETARO SAN-LUIS MONTERREY

PLATE         63.5      0.2     0.3       0.3      31.0
HOT-STRIP     41.9      2.8     1.6       2.8      36.2
TEMP-STRIP    45.1      2.5     4.5       1.1      41.7
TIN           87.6              0.3                 9.4
HEAVYSHAPE    36.6      2.2     3.2       0.8      12.9
LIGHTSHAPE    74.4      2.5     1.9       1.8       8.1
BARS          46.6      4.2    23.5       2.2      11.2
REBARS        46.7     10.3     4.0       3.4      12.8
WIRE          61.2      5.3     3.9       3.7      12.2
SEAMLESS      10.5     28.0     0.4       0.2      18.4
RAILS         40.0      5.0     5.0      10.0      20.0

+           GUADALAJA  L-CARDENAS  COATZACOAL

PLATE          4.5        0.1         0.1
HOT-STRIP     12.6        0.5         1.6
TEMP-STRIP     4.3        0.4         0.4
TIN            2.7
HEAVYSHAPE    42.6        1.4         0.3
LIGHTSHAPE     8.9        1.6         0.8
BARS          11.8        0.4         0.1
REBARS        11.8        6.1         4.9
WIRE           9.8        1.9         2.0
```

```
GAMS 1.0  M E X I C O    S T E E L    M O D E L    FOR 1979                                   01/13/83    09.02.38.    PAGE  19
          DEMAND DATA

          SEAMLESS        1.8         1.7         39.0
          RAILS          10.0         5.0          5.0
                                  ;

     *     DATA BASE ESTIMATED
     *     RAIL DISTIBUTION HAS BEEN ADDED IN WASHINGTON

           DEMDAT(CS,"ADJ-DEM") = DEMDAT(CS,"DEMAND") - DEMDAT(CS,"SEMI-INT");

           DEMDAT(CF,"ADJ-DEM")$SUM(CS, MROD(CS,CF)) = SUM(CS, MROD(CS,CF)*DEMDAT(CS,"ADJ-DEM"));

           REGDEM(CF,J)$SUM(CS, MROD(CS,CF)) = SUM(CS$MROD(CS,CF), REGDEM(CS,J));

          PARAMETER D(*,*)  ADJUSTED DEMAND FOR SEMI-INTEGR PLANTS (1000 TPY) ;

          D(CF,J) = DEMDAT(CF,"ADJ-DEM")*REGDEM(CF,J)/100;
          D("   TOTAL   ",J)  =  SUM(CF, D(CF,J))    ;
          D(CF,"   TOTAL   ") =  SUM(J, D(CF,J))     ;
          D("   TOTAL   ","   TOTAL   ") =  SUM(CF,  D(CF,"   TOTAL   "))  ;

          DISPLAY DEMDAT, REGDEM, D;


          PARAMETER EMAX(CF) EXPORT LIMIT BY PRODUCT (1000 TPY)
                    ETOT     TOTAL EXPORT LIMIT       (1000 TPY) ;

          EMAX(CF) = 500 ;  ETOT = 250 ;
```

```
SET SP  DOMESTIC AND INTERNATIONAL PRICES / DOMESTIC, INTERNAT /


PARAMETER  MC(PM)  MINING COST (PESOS PER TON) / MIN-CO 250, (MIN-S,MIN-N,MIN-TR) 100 / ;

TABLE PRICES(CS,SP)   DOMESTIC AND INTERNATIONAL PRICES OF COMMODITIES

                 DOMESTIC     INTERNAT
*               (79 PESOS)  (79 DOLLARS)
                                                                              NEW MARGIN = 002-040

ORE-CONC                       28                    TONS
PELLETS          430           45                    TONS
COAL-D           880                                 TONS
COAL-I                         63                    TONS
COKE            1200          100                    TONS
FUEL-OIL        1000                                 TONS **** 1000LITERS
LIMESTONE        120                                 TONS
NAT-GAS          322          152                    1000 M3
SCRAP           3050          120                    TONS
FERRO-ALLO     16000                                 TONS
REFRAC         50000                                 TONS
DOLOMITE         800                                 TONS
LIME             690                                 TONS
ELECTRODES     48000                                 TONS
ELECTRIC         552                                 1000 KWH
PLATE                         347                    TONS
HOT-STRIP                     393                    TONS
TEMP-STRIP                    373                    TONS
TIN                           393                    TONS
BILLETS                       300                    TONS
HEAVYSHAPE                    338                    TONS
LIGHTSHAPE                    364                    TONS
BARS                          350                    TONS
REBARS-LD                     347                    TONS
REBARS-SD                     368                    TONS
WIRE                          434                    TONS
SEAMLESS                      455                    TONS
RAILS                         345                    TONS
                                                                              NEW MARGIN = 002-120
*  DIFFERENT PRICES FOR LIMESTONE: AHMSA 90, FUNDIDORA 60, SICARTSA 120
*  PRICE OF NATURAL GAS FOR SICARTSA EXPANSIONS: 30% LOWER.


 PARAMETER   PD(CS)     PRICES OF DOMESTIC PRODUCTS  (1979 PESOS PER UNIT)
             PV(CS)     PRICES OF IMPORTS              (1979 US $ PER TON)
             PE(CS)     EXPORT PRICES                  (1979 US $ PER TON)
             SH         SHADOW EXCHANGE RATE         (1979 PESOS PER US$);

 SH            = 25.0 ;
 PD(CRAW)      = PRICES(CRAW,"DOMESTIC");
 PV(CRV)       = PRICES(CRV,"INTERNAT");
```

PRICES

```
PV(CFV)      = PRICES(CFV,"INTERNAT");
PE(CE)       = .8*PRICES(CE,"INTERNAT");
```

```
TABLE RDSJ(IS,J)  RAIL DISTANCES FROM STEEL MILLS TO MARKETS  (KM)

            MEXICO-DF PUEBLA QUERETARO SAN-LUIS MONTERREY

SICARTSA       819      995      691      875      1305
AHMSA         1204     1300      849      592       218
FUNDIDORA     1017     1159      755      498
HYLSA         1017     1159      755      498
HYLSAP         185               410      667      1085
TAMSA          428      315      650      907      1330

 +          GUADALAJA L-CARDENAS COATZACOAL

SICARTSA       704                1638
AHMSA         1125      1416      1850
FUNDIDORA     1030      1322      1756
HYLSA         1030      1322      1756
HYLSAP         760       995       671
TAMSA         1005      1239       550

*     DATA FROM (20) AND (21)
*     ONLY STEEL PLANTS INCLUDED, SINCE PELLET AND COKE PLANTS DO NOT
*     SEND FINAL PRODUCTS TO MARKETS

TABLE RDSS(IS,IS)  RAIL DISTANCES BETWEEN STEEL PLANTS

            SICARTSA AHMSA FUNDIDORA HYLSA HYLSAP TAMSA

AHMSA         1416
FUNDIDORA     1322     218
HYLSA         1322     218      10
HYLSAP         995    1300    1159    1159
TAMSA         1239    1499    1405    1405   315

TABLE RDRS(IR,IS)  RAIL DISTANCES FROM RAW MATERIAL PLANTS TO STEEL MILLS

               SICARTSA  AHMSA  FUNDIDORA  HYLSA  HYLSAP  TAMSA

PENACOL           1037    1490     1396     1396    1116    1360
LAPERLA           1797     403      621      621    1595    1703
ALZADA             920    1360     1260     1260     990    1300
ESPERANZAS        1522     122      340      340    1422    1670


*     DATA FROM (19) AND(20)

TABLE RDMS(IM,IS)  RAIL DISTANCES FROM MINES TO STEEL PLANTS

            SICARTSA AHMSA FUNDIDORA HYLSA HYLSAP TAMSA

P-COLORADA     1037   1490    1396    1396  1116   1360
LASTRUCHAS            1416    1322    1322   995   1239
```

```
LA-PERLA         1797     403      621      621  1595   1927
CERRO-MER        1275     677      636      636  1245   1489
HERCULES         1613     219      563      563  1411   1655
LA-CHULA         1044    1480     1300     1300  1112   1356
EL-ENCINO         965    1401     1307     1307  1033   1277
COAHUILA         1500     120      400      400  1420   1700

TABLE RDMR(IM,IR)  RAIL DISTANCES FROM MINES TO RAW MATERIAL PLANTS

               PENACOL  LAPERLA  ALZADA  ESPERANZAS

P-COLORADA                 1803      70
LASTRUCHAS     1037        1797     920
LA-PERLA       1803                1800
CERRO-MER      1500         400    1500
HERCULES       1616         400    1600
LA-CHULA         90        1800      60
EL-ENCINO        90        1800      40
COAHUILA                                     15

*     DATA FROM (19)
*     DATA FROM (18)
*     DISTANCES FROM COAL MINES TO PELLET PLANTS NOT INCLUDED FOR OBVIOU

TABLE RDPS(*,IS)   RAIL DISTANCES FROM NEAREST PORT TO STEEL MILL

                 SICARTSA AHMSA FUNDIDORA HYLSA HYLSAP TAMSA

GULF                 1239    739     521    521    315
PACIFIC                     1416    1322   1322    995    1239



*     DATA FROM (19) AND (20)
*     DISTANCES IN THIS TABLE ARE FROM PLANT TO NEAREST PORT.
*     FOR GULF: SICARTSA,HYLSAP,TAMSA AND NEW-MANZ PO VERACRUZ.
*               AHMSA,FUNDIDORA,HYLSA,NAW-TAMP TO TAMPICO.
*               NEW-COAT TO COATZACOALCOS.
*     FOR PACIFIC: ALL PLANTS TO LAZARO CAR@ENAS, AXCEPT FPR
*                  NEW-MANZ TO MANZANILLO



TABLE RDPJ(*,J)  RAIL DISTANCES FROM NEAREST PORT TO MARKETS

               MEXICO-DF PUEBLA QUERETARO SAN-LUIS MONTERREY

GULF              428      315      650      444      521
PACIFIC           819      995      691      875     1305

    +          GUADALAJA L-CARDENAS COATZACOAL
```

```
GULF              995        1239
PACIFIC           300                    1638


*      DATA BASE FROM (20) AND (21)
*      NEAREST PORTS FOR
*         GULF: VERACRUZ TO MEXICO-DF,PUEBLA,QUERETARO,TOLUCA,L-CARDENAS
*               TAMPICO TO SAN-LUIS,GUADALAJARA
*               MATAMOROS TO MONTERREY
*               COATZACOALCOS TO COATZACOAL
*      PACIFIC: ALL TO LAZARO CARDENAS, EXCEPT FOR MANZANILLO TO GUADALAJA

* MINES - IRON ORE AND COAL MINES
* PLANTS - RAW MATERIAL PLANTS
* MILLS - STEEL MILLS
 PARAMETER MUMR(IM,IR)  TRANSPORT COST: MINES TO PLANTS                  (US$ PER TON)
           MUMS(IM,IS)  TRANSPORT COST: MINES TO MILLS                   (US$ PER TON)
           MURS(IR,IS)  TRANSPORT COST: PLANTS TO MILLS                  (US$ PER TON)
           MUSS(IS,IS)  TRANSPORT COST: BETWEEN MILLS                    (US$ PER TON)
           MUSJ(IS,J)   TRANSPORT COST: MILLS TO MARKETS                 (US$ PER TON)
           MUPSR(IS)    TRANSPORT COST: PORTS TO MILLS - RAW MATERIAL    (US$ PER TON)
           MUSPF(IS)    TRANSPORT COST: MILLS TO PORTS - FINAL PRODUCT   ($ PER TON)
           MUPJ(J)      TRANSPORT COST: PORTS TO MARKETS                 (US$ PER TON);

      RDPS("SHORT",IS)    = MIN(RDPS("GULF",IS) ,RDPS("PACIFIC",IS) );
      RDSS(IS,ISP)        = MAX(RDSS(IS,ISP),RDSS(ISP,IS));
      RDPJ("SHORT",J)     = MIN(RDPJ("GULF",J ),RDPJ("PACIFIC",J ));

    MUMR(IM,IR)   = (35 + .11*RDMR(IM,IR))$RDMR(IM,IR);
    MUMS(IM,IS)   = (35 + .11*RDMS(IM,IS))$RDMS(IM,IS);
    MURS(IR,IS)   = (35 + .11*RDRS(IR,IS))$RDRS(IR,IS);
    MUSS(IS,ISP)  = (35 + .11*RDSS(IS,ISP))$RDSS(IS,ISP);
    MUPSR(IS)     = (35 + .11*RDPS("SHORT",IS))$RDPS("SHORT",IS);
    MUSJ(IS,J)    = (60 + .19*RDSJ(IS,J))$RDSJ(IS,J);
    MUSPF(IS)     = (60 + .19*RDPS("SHORT",IS))$RDPS("SHORT",IS);
    MUPJ(J)       = (60 + .19*RDPJ("SHORT",J))$RDPJ("SHORT",J);

*  DATA BASE FROM (19) AND (20)
*  OLD FIGURES WERE 57.16 + .194  AND   17.46 + .106
 DISPLAY MUMR, MUMS, MURS, MUSS, MUSJ, MUPSR, MUSPF, MUPJ;

 PARAMETER  LOSS(CS)  CORRECTION FACTOR FOR COKE LOSSES DURING INTERMILL SHIPMENTS OF COKE
            PCT(O)    SHARE OF PELLET SHIPMENTS FROM PENA COLARADA BY OWNERSHIP / 2 = .46, 3 = .1, 4 = .26, 5 = .18 /;

 LOSS(CS) = 1;  LOSS("COKE") = 0.9;
```

```
SET  MMPOS(MM,IM)  PRODUCTIVE UNIT POSSIBILITY: MINES
     MRPOS(MR,IR)  PRODUCTIVE UNIT POSSIBILITY: RAW MATERIAL PLANTS
     MSPOS(MS,IS)  PRODUCTIVE UNIT POSSIBILITY: STEEL MILLS

     PMPOS(PM,IM)  PROCESS POSSIBILITY: MINES
     PRPOS(PR,IR)  PROCESS POSSIBILITY: RAW MATERIAL PLANTS
     PSPOS(PS,IS)  PROCESS POSSIBILITY: STEEL MILLS

     CMPOSP(CS,IM) COMMODITY PRODUCTION POSSIBILITY: MINES
     CRPOSP(CS,IR) COMMODITY PRODUCTION POSSIBILITY: RAW MATERIAL PLANTS
     CSPOSP(CS,IS) COMMODITY PRODUCTION POSSIBILITY: STEEL MILLS

     CMPOSN(CS,IM) COMMODITY CONSUMPTION POSSIBILITY: MINES
     CRPOSN(CS,IR) COMMODITY CONSUMPTION POSSIBILITY: RAW MATERIAL PLANTS
     CSPOSN(CS,IS) COMMODITY CONSUMPTION POSSIBILITY: STEEL MILLS ;

 MMPOS(MM,IM) = KM(MM,IM);
 MRPOS(MR,IR) = KR(MR,IR);
 MSPOS(MS,IS) = KS(MS,IS);

 PMPOS(PM,IM)$SUM(CM, AM(CM,PM)$RES(CM,IM) NE 0 ) =
          SUM(MM$(NOT MMPOS(MM,IM)), BM(MM,PM) NE 0) EQ 0 ;
 PRPOS(PR,IR)$SUM(CR, AR(CR,PR) NE 0 ) =
          SUM(MR$(NOT MRPOS(MR,IR)), BR(MR,PR) NE 0) EQ 0 ;
 PSPOS(PS,IS)$SUM(CS, AS(CS,PS,IS) NE 0 ) =
          SUM(MS$(NOT MSPOS(MS,IS)), BS(MS,PS) NE 0) EQ 0 ;

 CMPOSP(CM,IM) = SUM(PM$PMPOS(PM,IM), AM(CM,PM) GT 0) ;
 CRPOSP(CR,IR) = SUM(PR$PRPOS(PR,IR), AR(CR,PR) GT 0) ;
 CSPOSP(CS,IS) = SUM(PS$PSPOS(PS,IS), AS(CS,PS,IS) GT 0) ;

 CMPOSN(CM,IM) = SUM(PM$PMPOS(PM,IM), AM(CM,PM) LT 0) ;
 CRPOSN(CR,IR) = SUM(PR$PRPOS(PR,IR), AR(CR,PR) LT 0);
 CSPOSN(CS,IS) = SUM(PS$PSPOS(PS,IS), AS(CS,PS,IS) LT 0);

DISPLAY MMPOS, MRPOS, MSPOS, PMPOS, PRPOS, PSPOS, CMPOSP, CRPOSP,
        CSPOSP, CMPOSN, CRPOSN, CSPOSN ;

SET IMRES(IM)        RESTRICTED MINES / LASTRUCHAS /
    IMFREE(IM)       FREE MINES
    XMPOS(CS,IM,*)   POSSIBLE SHIPMENTS OF MINING PRODUCTS TO RAW MAT PLANTS;

    IMFREE(IM) = YES - IMRES(IM) ;

    XMPOS("COAL-D","COAHUILA","ESPERANZAS")  = YES;
    XMPOS("ORE-CONC","P-COLORADA","PENACOL") = YES;
    XMPOS("ORE-CONC","LA-PERLA","LAPERLA")   = YES;
    XMPOS("ORE-CONC","EL-ENCINO","ALZADA")   = YES;
    XMPOS(CM,"LASTRUCHAS","SICARTSA")        = YES;
    XMPOS(CM,IMFREE,IS)                      = YES;
```

```
EQUATIONS

  MBM(CM,IM)        MATERIAL BALANCE: MINES                        (1000 TPY)
  MBR(CR,IR)        MATERIAL BALANCE: RAW MATERIAL PLANTS    (1000 UNITS TPY)
  MBS(CS,IS)        MATERIAL BALANCE: STEEL MILLS            (1000 UNITS TPY)

  CCM(MM,IM)        CAPACITY CONSTRAINT: MINES                     (1000 TPY)
  CCR(MR,IR)        CAPACITY CONSTRAINT: RAW MATERIAL PLANTS       (1000 TPY)
  CCS(MS,IS)        CAPACITY CONSTRAINT: STEEL MILLS               (1000 TPY)

  MREQ(CF,J)        MARKET REQUIREMENTS                            (1000 TPY)
  ME(CF)            EXPORT BOUNDS                                  (1000 TPY)
  ME2               TOTAL EXPORTS                                  (1000 TPY)

  PELPC(O)          PELLET SHIPMENTS FROM PENA COLARADA            (1000 TPY)
  PELAL             PELLET SHIPMENTS FROM ALZADA                   (1000 TPY)

  ACOST             ACCOUNTING: TOTAL COST                         (MILL US$)
  AREC              ACCOUNTING: RECURRENT COST                     (MILL US$)
  ATRANS            ACCOUNTING: TRANSPORT COST                     (MILL US$)
  AIMP              ACCOUNTING: IMPORT COST                        (MILL US$)
  AEXP              ACCOUNTING: EXPORT REVENUE                     (MILL US$)

VARIABLES

  ZM(PM,IM)         PROCESS LEVEL: MINES                           (1000 TPY)
  ZR(PR,IR)         PROCESS LEVEL: RAW MATERIAL PLANTS             (1000 TPY)
  ZS(PS,IS)         PROCESS LEVEL: STEEL MILLS                     (1000 TPY)

  XM(CS,IM,*)       SHIPMENTS: MINE PRODUCTS                       (1000 TPY)
  XR(CS,IR,IS)      SHIPMENTS: FROM RAW MATERIAL PLANTS            (1000 TPY)
  XS(CS,IS,ISP)     SHIPMENTS: INTERPLANT                          (1000 TPY)
  XF(CS,IS,J)       SHIPMENTS: FINAL PRODUCTS                      (1000 TPY)

  UR(CS,IR)         DOMESTIC PRODUCTS PURCHASE: RAW MAT. PLANTS  (1000 UNITS TPY)
  US(CS,IS)         DOMESTIC PRODUCTS PURCHASE: STEEL MILLS      (1000 UNITS TPY)

  E(CS,IS)          EXPORTS                                        (1000 TPY)
  VS(CS,IS)         IMPORTS TO STEEL MILLS                         (1000 TPY)
  VF(CS,J)          IMPORT OF FINAL PRODUCTS                       (1000 TPY)

  COST              TOTAL COST                                     (MILL US$)
  RECURRENT         COST                                           (MILL US$)
  TRANSPORT         COST                                           (MILL US$)
  IMPORT            COST                                           (MILL US$)
  EXPORT            COST                                           (MILL US$)

POSITIVE VARIABLES ZM, ZR, ZS, XM, XR, XS, XF, UR, US, E, VS, VF;
```

```
MBM(CM,IM).. SUM(PM$PMPOS(PM,IM), AM(CM,PM)*ZM(PM,IM))
           =G= ( SUM(IR$(XMPOS(CM,IM,IR)*CRPOSN(CM,IR)), XM(CM,IM,IR))
               + SUM(IS$(XMPOS(CM,IM,IS)*CSPOSN(CM,IS)), XM(CM,IM,IS)))$CMPOSP(CM,IM);

MBR(CR,IR).. SUM(PR$PRPOS(PR,IR), AR(CR,PR)*ZR(PR,IR))
             + ( SUM(IM$(CMPOSP(CR,IM)*XMPOS(CR,IM,IR)), XM(CR,IM,IR))$CMR(CR) + UR(CR,IR)$CRAW(CR) )$CRPOSN(CR,IR)
           =G= SUM(IS$(CRS(CR)*CRPOSP(CR,IR)*CSPOSN(CR,IS)), XR(CR,IR,IS)) ;

MBS(CS,IS).. SUM(PS$PSPOS(PS,IS), AS(CS,PS,IS)*ZS(PS,IS))
             + ( SUM(IM$(CMPOSP(CS,IM)*XMPOS(CS,IM,IS)), XM(CS,IM,IS))$CMS(CS)
               + SUM(IR$CRPOSP(CS,IR), LOSS(CS)*XR(CS,IR,IS))$CRS(CS)
               + SUM(ISP$CSPOSP(CS,ISP), LOSS(CS)*XS(CS,ISP,IS))$CSS(CS)
               + US(CS,IS)$CRAW(CS) + VS(CS,IS)$CRV(CS)        )$CSPOSN(CS,IS)
           =G= ( SUM(ISP$CSPOSN(CS,ISP), XS(CS,IS,ISP))$CSS(CS)
               + SUM(J, XF(CS,IS,J))$CF(CS) + E(CS,IS)$CE(CS)    )$CSPOSP(CS,IS) ;

CCM(MM,IM)$MMPOS(MM,IM)..  SUM(PM$PMPOS(PM,IM), BM(MM,PM)*ZM(PM,IM)) =L= KM(MM,IM);

CCR(MR,IR)$MRPOS(MR,IR)..  SUM(PR$PRPOS(PR,IR), BR(MR,PR)*ZR(PR,IR)) =L= KR(MR,IR);

CCS(MS,IS)$MSPOS(MS,IS)..  SUM(PS$PSPOS(PS,IS), BS(MS,PS)*ZS(PS,IS)) =L= KS(MS,IS);

MREQ(CF,J).. SUM(IS$CSPOSP(CF,IS), XF(CF,IS,J)) + VF(CF,J) =G= D(CF,J);

ME(CF)..     SUM(IS$CSPOSP(CF,IS), E(CF,IS)) =L= EMAX(CF);
```

```
ME2..        SUM((CF,IS)$CSPOSP(CF,IS), E(CF,IS))  =L=  ETOT  ;

PELPC(O)..   SUM(IS$(OWN(O,IS)*CSPOSN("PELLETS",IS)), XR("PELLETS","PENACOL",IS)) =L= PCT(O)*KR("PELLET","PENACOL");

PELAL..      SUM(ISEX$CSPOSN("PELLETS",ISEX), XR("PELLETS","ALZADA",ISEX)) =E= 0;

ACOST..      COST =E= RECURRENT + TRANSPORT + SH*(IMPORT-EXPORT) ;

AREC..       RECURRENT =E= ( SUM((PM,IM)$PMPOS(PM,IM), MC(PM)*ZM(PM,IM))
                           + SUM((CRAW,IR)$CRPOSN(CRAW,IR), PD(CRAW)*UR(CRAW,IR))
                           + SUM((CRAW,IS)$CSPOSN(CRAW,IS), PD(CRAW)*US(CRAW,IS)) )/1000;

ATRANS..     TRANSPORT =E= ( SUM((CMR,IM,IR)$(CMPOSP(CMR,IM)*XMPOS(CMR,IM,IR)*CRPOSN(CMR,IR)),
                                         MUMR(IM,IR)*XM(CMR,IM,IR))
                           + SUM((CMS,IM,IS)$(CMPOSP(CMS,IM)*CSPOSN(CMS,IS)*XMPOS(CMS,IM,IS)),
                                         MUMS(IM,IS)*XM(CMS,IM,IS))
                           + SUM((CRS,IR,IS)$(CRPOSP(CRS,IR)*CSPOSN(CRS,IS)), MURS(IR,IS)*XR(CRS,IR,IS))
                           + SUM((CSS,IS,ISP)$(CSPOSP(CSS,IS)*CSPOSN(CSS,ISP)), MUSS(IS,ISP)*XS(CSS,IS,ISP))
                           + SUM((CF,IS,J)$CSPOSP(CF,IS), MUSJ(IS,J)*XF(CF,IS,J))
                           + SUM((CRV,IS)$CSPOSN(CRV,IS), MUPSR(IS)*VS(CRV,IS))
                           + SUM((CF,IS)$CSPOSP(CF,IS), MUSPF(IS)*E(CF,IS)) + SUM((CF,J), MUPJ(J)*VF(CF,J)) )/1000;

AIMP..       IMPORT =E= ( SUM((CRV,IS)$CSPOSN(CRV,IS), PV(CRV)*VS(CRV,IS)) + SUM((CFV,J), PV(CFV)*VF(CFV,J)) )/1000;

AEXP..       EXPORT =E= ( SUM((CE,IS)$CSPOSP(CE,IS), PE(CE)*E(CE,IS)) )/1000;
```

```
MODEL ONE /ALL/ ;

*  DEFINE RUN 1

   VS.UP("COKE",IS) = 0; US.UP("SCRAP",IS) = 0;

   KS(MS,"AHMSA")      = KS(MS,"AHMSA")*0.9;
   KS(MS,"FUNDIDORA")  = KS(MS,"FUNDIDORA")*0.95;
 DISPLAY KS;

   SOLVE ONE MINIMIZING COST USING LP ;
```

REFERENCE MAP OF VARIABLES

```
VARIABLES  TYPE    REFERENCES

AAHM       PARAM        REF      616  DEFINED      388      DCL      388
ACOST      EQU      DEFINED     1206      DCL     1141
AEXP       EQU      DEFINED     1224      DCL     1145
AFUND      PARAM        REF      617  DEFINED      453      DCL      453
AHYL       PARAM        REF      618  DEFINED      517      DCL      517
AHYLP      PARAM        REF      619  DEFINED      556      DCL      556
AIMP       EQU      DEFINED     1222      DCL     1144
AM         PARAM        REF     1092     1099     1103     1174  DEFINED      326      DCL      326
AR         PARAM        REF     1094     1100     1104     1178  DEFINED      338      DCL      338
AREC       EQU      DEFINED     1208      DCL     1142
AS         PARAM        REF     1096     1101     1105     1182  DEFINED      615      616      617      618
                        619      620      DCL      324
ASIC       PARAM        REF      615  DEFINED      349      DCL      349
ATAM       PARAM        REF      620  DEFINED      588      DCL      588
ATRANS     EQU      DEFINED     1212      DCL     1143
BM         PARAM        REF     1093     1190  DEFINED      623      DCL      623
BR         PARAM        REF     1095     1192  DEFINED      632      DCL      632
BS         PARAM        REF     1097     1194  DEFINED      639      DCL      639
CCM        EQU      DEFINED     1190      DCL     1130
CCR        EQU      DEFINED     1192      DCL     1131
CCS        EQU      DEFINED     1194      DCL     1132
CE         SET          REF      920     1188   3*1224  DEFINED      319  CONTROL      920     1224      DCL
                        304
CF         SET          REF    2*848    2*850    2*854      855      856      857      862     1134     1135
                       1188   4*1196   3*1198   2*1200   2*1218   3*1220  DEFINED      301  CONTROL      319
                        320      848      850      854      855      856      857      865     1196     1198
                       1200     1218   2*1220      DCL      301
CFV        SET          REF      919   2*1222  DEFINED      320  CONTROL      919     1222      DCL      306
CM         SET          REF      315      326   2*1092     1099     1103     1126     1174   3*1175   4*1176
                    DEFINED      279  CONTROL     1092     1099     1103     1120     1121     1174      DCL
                        279
CMPOSN     SET          REF     1108  DEFINED     1103      DCL     1084
CMPOSP     SET          REF     1107     1176     1179     1183     1212     1214  DEFINED     1099      DCL
                       1080
CMR        SET          REF     1179   3*1212     1213  DEFINED      290  CONTROL     1212      DCL      290
CMS        SET          REF     1183   3*1214     1215  DEFINED      293  CONTROL     1214      DCL      293
COST       VAR          REF     1206     1236      DCL     1165
CR         SET          REF     1094     1100     1104     1127     1178   7*1179   4*1180  DEFINED      283
                    CONTROL     1094     1100     1104     1178      DCL      283
CRAW       SET          REF      917     1179     1186   3*1209   3*1210  DEFINED      274  CONTROL      917
                       1209     1210      DCL      274
CRPOSN     SET          REF     1108     1175     1179     1209     1212  DEFINED     1104      DCL     1085
CRPOSP     SET          REF     1107     1180     1184     1216  DEFINED     1100      DCL     1081
CRS        SET          REF     1180     1184   3*1216  DEFINED      296  CONTROL     1216      DCL      296
CRV        SET          REF      918     1186   2*1219   3*1222  DEFINED      287  CONTROL      918     1219
                       1222      DCL      287
CS         SET          REF      274      279      283      287      290      293      296      299      301
                        304      306      324      338      349      388      453      517      556      588
                        615      616      617      618      619      620    2*789      795      812    2*846
                      3*848    3*850      872      911      912      913     1067     1080     1081     1082
```

```
         REFERENCE MAP OF VARIABLES

VARIABLES    TYPE     REFERENCES

                           1084      1085      1086      1096      1101      1105      1112      1128      1153      1154
                           1155      1156      1158      1159      1161      1162      1163      1182    4*1183    4*1184
                         4*1185    5*1186    3*1187    5*1188   DEFINED       217   CONTROL       615       616       617
                            618       619       620       846     2*848     2*850      1070      1096      1101      1105
                           1182       DCL       217
CSPOSN       SET            REF      1108      1176      1180      1186      1187      1202      1204      1210      1214
                           1216      1217      1219      1222   DEFINED      1105       DCL      1086
CSPOSP       SET            REF      1108      1185      1188      1196      1198      1200      1217      1218      1220
                           1224   DEFINED      1101       DCL      1082
CSS          SET            REF      1185      1187    3*1217   DEFINED       299   CONTROL      1217       DCL       299
D            PARAM          REF       855       856       857       859      1196   DEFINED       854       855       856
                            857       DCL       852
DEMDAT       PARAM          REF     2*846       848       854       859   DEFINED       795       846       848       DCL
                            795
DS           SET            REF       795   DEFINED       787       DCL       787
E            VAR            REF      1171      1188      1198      1200      1220      1224       DCL      1161
EMAX         PARAM          REF      1198   DEFINED       865       DCL       862
ETOT         PARAM          REF      1200   DEFINED       865       DCL       863
EXPORT       VAR            REF      1206      1224       DCL      1169
IM           SET            REF       315       693       782       968       981      1041      1042    2*1054    2*1055
                           1072      1076      1080      1084      1088      1092      1093      1099      1103      1110
                           1111      1112      1114      1126      1130      1149      1153    2*1174    2*1175    3*1176
                         3*1179    3*1183    4*1190    2*1208    2*1212    2*1213    2*1214    2*1215   DEFINED        64
                        CONTROL       782      1054      1055      1088      1092      1099      1103      1114      1174
                           1179      1183      1190      1208      1212      1214       DCL        64
IMFREE       SET        DEFINED      1114   CONTROL      1121       DCL      1111
IMPORT       VAR            REF      1206      1222       DCL      1168
IMRES        SET            REF      1114   DEFINED      1110       DCL      1110
IR           SET            REF       708       783       956       981      1041      1043    2*1054    2*1056      1073
                           1077      1081      1085      1089      1095      1100      1104      1127      1131      1150
                           1154      1158    3*1175    2*1178    4*1179    2*1180    2*1184    4*1192    2*1209    2*1212
                         2*1213    3*1216   DEFINED        76   CONTROL       783      1054      1056      1089      1094
                           1100      1104      1175      1178      1184      1192      1209      1212      1216       DCL
                             76
IS           SET            REF       310       313       322       324       716       780     2*784       922     2*946
                            956       968       998      1042      1043    2*1044      1045      1046      1047    2*1050
                         2*1051    2*1055    2*1056    2*1057    2*1058    2*1059    2*1060      1074      1078      1082
                           1086      1090      1096      1097    2*1101    2*1105      1128      1132      1151      1154
                           1155      1156      1159      1161      1162    3*1176    2*1180    3*1182    2*1183      1184
                           1185    3*1186      1187    3*1188    4*1194    2*1196    2*1198    2*1200    3*1202    2*1210
                         2*1214    2*1215    3*1216    3*1217    3*1218    3*1219    3*1220    2*1222    2*1224   DEFINED
                             83   CONTROL       784      1050      1051      1055      1056      1057      1058      1059
                           1060      1090      1096      1101      1105      1121      1176      1180      1182      1194
                           1196      1198      1200      1202      1210      1214      1216      1217      1218      1219
                           1220      1222      1224    2*1230       DCL        83
ISEX         SET            REF    2*1204   DEFINED       313   CONTROL      1204       DCL       313
ISP          SET            REF    2*1051    2*1057      1155    2*1185    2*1187    3*1217   CONTROL      1051      1057
                           1185      1187      1217       DCL       322
J            SET            REF       812       850       854       855       856       922      1017      1045      1048
                         2*1052    2*1059    2*1061      1134      1156      1163      1188    3*1196    2*1218    2*1220
```

```
         REFERENCE MAP OF VARIABLES

VARIABLES  TYPE   REFERENCES

                     1222  DEFINED       92  CONTROL      850      854      855      856     1052     1059
                     1061     1188     1196     1218     1220     1222      DCL       92
KM         PARAM      REF      782     1088     1190  DEFINED      693      782      DCL      693
KR         PARAM      REF      783     1089     1192     1202  DEFINED      708      783      DCL      708
KS         PARAM      REF      784     1090     1194     1232     1233     1234  DEFINED      716      784
                     1232     1233      DCL      716
L          SET    DEFINED      104      DCL      104
LOSS       PARAM      REF     1184     1185  DEFINED   2*1070      DCL     1067
MAX        FUNCT      REF     1051
MBM        EQU    DEFINED     1174      DCL     1126
MBR        EQU    DEFINED     1178      DCL     1127
MBS        EQU    DEFINED     1182      DCL     1128
MC         PARAM      REF     1208  DEFINED      870      DCL      870
ME         EQU    DEFINED     1198      DCL     1135
ME2        EQU    DEFINED     1200      DCL     1136
MIN        FUNCT      REF     1050     1052
MM         SET        REF      623      693      782     1072     1088   2*1093     1130   3*1190  DEFINED
                      109  CONTROL      782     1088     1093     1190      DCL      109
MMPOS      SET        REF     1093     1107     1190  DEFINED     1088      DCL     1072
MR         SET        REF      632      708      783     1073     1089   2*1095     1131   3*1192  DEFINED
                      116  CONTROL      783     1089     1095     1192      DCL      116
MREQ       EQU    DEFINED     1196      DCL     1134
MROD       PARAM      REF    2*848    2*850  DEFINED      789      DCL      789
MRPOS      SET        REF     1095     1107     1192  DEFINED     1089      DCL     1073
MS         SET        REF      639      716      784     1074     1090   2*1097     1132   3*1194     1232
                     1233  DEFINED      121  CONTROL      784     1090     1097     1194     1232     1233
                      DCL      121
MSPOS      SET        REF     1097     1107     1194  DEFINED     1090      DCL     1074
MUMR       PARAM      REF     1065     1213  DEFINED     1054      DCL     1041
MUMS       PARAM      REF     1065     1215  DEFINED     1055      DCL     1042
MUPJ       PARAM      REF     1065     1220  DEFINED     1061      DCL     1048
MUPSR      PARAM      REF     1065     1219  DEFINED     1058      DCL     1046
MURS       PARAM      REF     1065     1216  DEFINED     1056      DCL     1043
MUSJ       PARAM      REF     1065     1218  DEFINED     1059      DCL     1045
MUSPF      PARAM      REF     1065     1220  DEFINED     1060      DCL     1047
MUSS       PARAM      REF     1065     1217  DEFINED     1057      DCL     1044
O          SET        REF      310     1068     1138   2*1202  DEFINED      308  CONTROL     1202      DCL
                      308
ONE        MODEL      REF     1236  DEFINED     1226      DCL     1226
OWN        SET        REF     1202  DEFINED      310      DCL      310
PCT        PARAM      REF     1202  DEFINED     1068      DCL     1068
PD         PARAM      REF     1209     1210  DEFINED      917      DCL      911
PE         PARAM      REF     1224  DEFINED      920      DCL      913
PELAL      EQU    DEFINED     1204      DCL     1139
PELPC      EQU    DEFINED     1202      DCL     1138
PM         SET        REF      326      623      870     1076     1092     1093   2*1099   2*1103     1149
                   3*1174   3*1190   3*1208  DEFINED      153  CONTROL     1092     1099     1103     1174
                     1190     1208      DCL      153
PMPOS      SET        REF     1099     1103     1107     1174     1190     1208  DEFINED     1092      DCL
                     1076
```

```
           REFERENCE MAP OF VARIABLES

VARIABLES   TYPE    REFERENCES

PR          SET         REF      338       632     1077     1094     1095   2*1100   2*1104     1150   3*1178
                     3*1192  DEFINED       165  CONTROL     1094     1100     1104     1178     1192      DCL
                        165
PRICES      PARAM       REF      917       918      919      920  DEFINED      872      DCL      872
PRPOS       SET         REF     1100      1104     1107     1178     1192  DEFINED     1094      DCL     1077
PS          SET         REF      324       349      388      453      517      556      588      615      616
                        617      618       619      620      639     1078     1096     1097   2*1101   2*1105
                       1151   3*1182    3*1194  DEFINED      170  CONTROL      615      616      617      618
                        619      620      1096     1101     1105     1182     1194      DCL      170
PSPOS       SET         REF     1101      1105     1107     1182     1194  DEFINED     1096      DCL     1078
PV          PARAM       REF   2*1222   DEFINED      918      919      DCL      912
RDMR        PARAM       REF   2*1054   DEFINED      981      DCL      981
RDMS        PARAM       REF   2*1055   DEFINED      968      DCL      968
RDPJ        PARAM       REF   2*1052    2*1061  DEFINED     1017     1052      DCL     1017
RDPS        PARAM       REF   2*1050    2*1058   2*1060  DEFINED      998     1050      DCL      998
RDRS        PARAM       REF   2*1056   DEFINED      956      DCL      956
RDSJ        PARAM       REF   2*1059   DEFINED      922      DCL      922
RDSS        PARAM       REF   2*1051    2*1057  DEFINED      946     1051      DCL      946
RECURRENT   VAR         REF     1206      1208      DCL     1166
REGDEM      PARAM       REF      850       854      859  DEFINED      812      850      DCL      812
RES         SET         REF     1092   DEFINED      315      DCL      315
SH          PARAM       REF     1206   DEFINED      916      DCL      914
SP          SET         REF      872   DEFINED      867      DCL      867
TRANSPORT   VAR         REF     1206      1212      DCL     1167
UR          VAR         REF     1171      1179     1209      DCL     1158
US          VAR         REF     1171      1186     1210  DEFINED     1230      DCL     1159
UT          PARAM       REF      784   DEFINED      780      DCL      780
VF          VAR         REF     1171      1196     1220     1222      DCL     1163
VS          VAR         REF     1171      1186     1219     1222  DEFINED     1230      DCL     1162
XF          VAR         REF     1171      1188     1196     1218      DCL     1156
XM          VAR         REF     1171      1175     1176     1179     1183     1213     1215      DCL     1153
XMPOS       SET         REF     1175      1176     1179     1183     1212     1214  DEFINED     1116     1117
                       1118     1119      1120     1121      DCL     1112
XR          VAR         REF     1171      1180     1184     1202     1204     1216      DCL     1154
XS          VAR         REF     1171      1185     1187     1217      DCL     1155
ZM          VAR         REF     1171      1174     1190     1208      DCL     1149
ZR          VAR         REF     1171      1178     1192      DCL     1150
ZS          VAR         REF     1171      1182     1194      DCL     1151

SETS

  CE          COMMODITIES FOR EXPORTS
  CF          FINAL PRODUCTS
  CFV         IMPORTED FINAL PRODUCTS
  CM          COMMODITIES AT MINES
  CMPOSN      COMMODITY CONSUMPTION POSSIBILITY: MINES
  CMPOSP      COMMODITY PRODUCTION POSSIBILITY: MINES
  CMR         COMMODITIES SHIPPED FROM MINES TO RAW MATERIAL PLANTS
  CMS         COMMODITIES SHIPPED FROM MINES TO STEEL PLANTS
  CR          COMMODITIES AT RAW MATERIAL PLANTS
```

```
         REFERENCE MAP OF VARIABLES

SETS

  CRAW       DOMESTIC RAW MATERIALS
  CRPOSN     COMMODITY CONSUMPTION POSSIBILITY: RAW MATERIAL PLANTS
  CRPOSP     COMMODITY PRODUCTION POSSIBILITY: RAW MATERIAL PLANTS
  CRS        COMMODITIES SHIPPED FROM RAW MATERIAL PLANTS TO STEEL MILLS
  CRV        IMPORTED RAW MATERIALS AND INTERMEDIATE PRODUCTS
  CS         COMMODITIES AT STEEL MILLS
  CSPOSN     COMMODITY CONSUMPTION POSSIBILITY: STEEL MILLS
  CSPOSP     COMMODITY PRODUCTION POSSIBILITY: STEEL MILLS
  CSS        COMMODITIES FOR INTERPLANT SHIPMENT BETWEEN STEEL MILLS
  DS         DEMAND DATA COMPONENTS
  IM         IRON ORE AND COAL MINES
  IMFREE     FREE MINES
  IMRES      RESTRICTED MINES
  IR         RAW MATERIAL PLANTS
  IS         STEEL MILLS
  ISEX       PLANTS EXCLUDED FROM ALZADA ORES
  ISP        ALIAS FOR IS
  J          DOMESTIC MARKET AREAS
  L          EXPORT POINTS
  MM         PRODUCTIVE UNITS AT MINES
  MMPOS      PRODUCTIVE UNIT POSSIBILITY: MINES
  MR         PRODUCTIVE UNITS AT RAW MATERIAL PLANTS
  MRPOS      PRODUCTIVE UNIT POSSIBILITY: RAW MATERIAL PLANTS
  MS         PRODUCTIVE UNITS AT STEEL MILLS
  MSPOS      PRODUCTIVE UNIT POSSIBILITY: STEEL MILLS
  O          OWNER NUMBERS
  OWN        OWNER GROUPS
  PM         PRODUCTION PROCESSES AT MINES
  PMPOS      PROCESS POSSIBILITY: MINES
  PR         PRODUCTION PROCESSES AT RAW MATERIAL PLANTS
  PRPOS      PROCESS POSSIBILITY: RAW MATERIAL PLANTS
  PS         PRODUCTION PROCESSES AT STEEL MILLS
  PSPOS      PROCESS POSSIBILITY: STEEL MILLS
  RES        RESERVE TYPES AT LOCATIONS
  SP         DOMESTIC AND INTERNATIONAL PRICES
  XMPOS      POSSIBLE SHIPMENTS OF MINING PRODUCTS TO RAW MAT PLANTS

PARAMETERS

  AAHM       A MATRIX FOR AHMSA
  AFUND      A MATRIX FOR FUNDIDORA
  AHYL       A MATRIX FOR HYLSA IN MONTERREY
  AHYLP      A MATRIX FOR HYLSA IN PUEBLA
  AM         A MATRIX FOR MINING PRODUCTS
  AR         A MATRIX FOR RAW MATERIAL PLANTS
  AS         INPUT OUTPUT RELATIONS FOR STEEL MILLS
  ASIC       A MATRIX FOR SICARTSA
  ATAM       A MATRIX FOR TAMSA
  BM         CAPACITY UTILIZATION MATRIX FOR MINES
  BR         CAPACITY UTILIZATION FOR RAW MATERIALS PLANTS
```

```
         REFERENCE MAP OF VARIABLES

PARAMETERS

  BS          CAPACITY UTILIZATION MATRIX FOR STEEL MILLS
  D           ADJUSTED DEMAND FOR SEMI-INTEGR PLANTS (1000 TPY)
  DEMDAT      DEMAND AND SEMI-INTGRATED OUTPUT (1000 TPY)
  EMAX        EXPORT LIMIT BY PRODUCT (1000 TPY)
  ETOT        TOTAL EXPORT LIMIT       (1000 TPY)
  KM          INITIAL CAPACITIES FOR MINES (1000 TPY)
  KR          INITIAL CAPACITIES FOR RAW MATERIAL PLANTS  (1000 TPY)
  KS          INITIAL CAPACITIES FOR STEEL MILLS  (1000 TPY)
  LOSS        CORRECTION FACTOR FOR COKE LOSSES DURING INTERMILL SHIPMENTS OF COKE
  MC          MINING COST (PESOS PER TON)
  MROD        MAP FOR DISAGGREGATING DEMAND FOR REINFORCED BARS TO LARGE AND SMALL DIAMETERS
  MUMR        TRANSPORT COST: MINES TO PLANTS                (US$ PER TON)
  MUMS        TRANSPORT COST: MINES TO MILLS                 (US$ PER TON)
  MUPJ        TRANSPORT COST: PORTS TO MARKETS               (US$ PER TON)
  MUPSR       TRANSPORT COST: PORTS TO MILLS - RAW MATERIAL  (US$ PER TON)
  MURS        TRANSPORT COST: PLANTS TO MILLS                (US$ PER TON)
  MUSJ        TRANSPORT COST: MILLS TO MARKETS               (US$ PER TON)
  MUSPF       TRANSPORT COST: MILLS TO PORTS - FINAL PRODUCT  ($ PER TON)
  MUSS        TRANSPORT COST: BETWEEN MILLS                  (US$ PER TON)
  PCT         SHARE OF PELLET SHIPMENTS FROM PENA COLARADA BY OWNERSHIP
  PD          PRICES OF DOMESTIC PRODUCTS  (1979 PESOS PER UNIT)
  PE          EXPORT PRICES              (1979 US $ PER TON)
  PRICES      DOMESTIC AND INTERNATIONAL PRICES OF COMMODITIES
  PV          PRICES OF IMPORTS          (1979 US $ PER TON)
  RDMR        RAIL DISTANCES FROM MINES TO RAW MATERIAL PLANTS
  RDMS        RAIL DISTANCES FROM MINES TO STEEL PLANTS
  RDPJ        RAIL DISTANCES FROM NEAREST PORT TO MARKETS
  RDPS        RAIL DISTANCES FROM NEAREST PORT TO STEEL MILL
  RDRS        RAIL DISTANCES FROM RAW MATERIAL PLANTS TO STEEL MILLS
  RDSJ        RAIL DISTANCES FROM STEEL MILLS TO MARKETS  (KM)
  RDSS        RAIL DISTANCES BETWEEN STEEL PLANTS
  REGDEM      REGIONAL DEMAND PER PRODUCT ( % OF TOTAL )
  SH          SHADOW EXCHANGE RATE        (1979 PESOS PER US$)
  UT          CAPACITY UTILIZATION

VARIABLES

  COST        TOTAL COST                                          (MILL US$)
  E           EXPORTS                                             (1000 TPY)
  EXPORT      COST                                                (MILL US$)
  IMPORT      COST                                                (MILL US$)
  RECURRENT   COST                                                (MILL US$)
  TRANSPORT   COST                                                (MILL US$)
  UR          DOMESTIC PRODUCTS PURCHASE: RAW MAT. PLANTS   (1000 UNITS TPY)
  US          DOMESTIC PRODUCTS PURCHASE: STEEL MILLS       (1000 UNITS TPY)
  VF          IMPORT OF FINAL PRODUCTS                            (1000 TPY)
  VS          IMPORTS TO STEEL MILLS                              (1000 TPY)
  XF          SHIPMENTS: FINAL PRODUCTS                           (1000 TPY)
  XM          SHIPMENTS: MINE PRODUCTS                            (1000 TPY)
  XR          SHIPMENTS: FROM RAW MATERIAL PLANTS                 (1000 TPY)
```

```
         REFERENCE MAP OF VARIABLES

VARIABLES

  XS        SHIPMENTS: INTERPLANT                            (1000 TPY)
  ZM        PROCESS LEVEL: MINES                             (1000 TPY)
  ZR        PROCESS LEVEL: RAW MATERIAL PLANTS               (1000 TPY)
  ZS        PROCESS LEVEL: STEEL MILLS                       (1000 TPY)

EQUATIONS

  ACOST     ACCOUNTING: TOTAL COST                           (MILL US$)
  AEXP      ACCOUNTING: EXPORT REVENUE                       (MILL US$)
  AIMP      ACCOUNTING: IMPORT COST                          (MILL US$)
  AREC      ACCOUNTING: RECURRENT COST                       (MILL US$)
  ATRANS    ACCOUNTING: TRANSPORT COST                       (MILL US$)
  CCM       CAPACITY CONSTRAINT: MINES                       (1000 TPY)
  CCR       CAPACITY CONSTRAINT: RAW MATERIAL PLANTS         (1000 TPY)
  CCS       CAPACITY CONSTRAINT: STEEL MILLS                 (1000 TPY)
  MBM       MATERIAL BALANCE: MINES                          (1000 TPY)
  MBR       MATERIAL BALANCE: RAW MATERIAL PLANTS      (1000 UNITS TPY)
  MBS       MATERIAL BALANCE: STEEL MILLS              (1000 UNITS TPY)
  ME        EXPORT BOUNDS                                    (1000 TPY)
  ME2       TOTAL EXPORTS                                    (1000 TPY)
  MREQ      MARKET REQUIREMENTS                              (1000 TPY)
  PELAL     PELLET SHIPMENTS FROM ALZADA                     (1000 TPY)
  PELPC     PELLET SHIPMENTS FROM PENA COLARADA              (1000 TPY)

MODELS

  ONE
```

7
Results of the Large Static Model

AN ILLUSTRATIVE SOLUTION to the static model is presented in this chapter. The purpose is not to obtain the optimal operating pattern for the Mexican steel industry but rather to characterize the solution for this kind of problem and to discuss the strong and weak points of the analysis. This solution is a logical step along the way to the small dynamic model of the industry presented in chapter 8.

Although some of the actual institutional constraints facing the industry in 1979 were imposed on the model, the solution was neither expected nor desired to be the same as the actual pattern of operation in the industry. It was hoped, however, that the solution might provide some ideas about gains in efficiency that could have been made in the industry.

Several of the institutional constraints listed below are relaxed in alternative solutions to the model presented in the last part of this chapter. The constraints are: (1) no domestic scrap purchases, (2) strikes at AHMSA and Fundidora, (3) limited exports, (4) limited interplant shipments of intermediate products, and (5) no imports of coke.

The first constraint arises from an assumption that the domestic rerollers would buy all of the domestic scrap and leave the major plants to import any scrap required above and beyond their own internally generated scrap. The second constraint comes from actual strikes in 1979 that reduced the effective capacity of AHMSA by 10 percent and that of Fundidora by 5 percent. Exports are limited by the third constraint to a total of no more than 250,000 tons of final products—roughly the magnitude of exports in 1979. The fourth constraint limits interplant shipments to coke, pellets, and sponge iron. In some of the experiments, this constraint is dropped and interplant shipments of a wide variety of intermediate products are permitted. This provides a useful means of mitigating the effects of bottlenecks at individual plants. The final constraint prohibits the importation of coke, though importation of coal is permitted. This corresponds to the national policy of using domestic raw material insofar as possible.

With all these institutional constraints in place, the results of the model correspond roughly to the actual steel production (in millions of tons) in Mexico in 1979:

	Model solution	*Actual*
Open hearth	1.94	1.47
Basic oxygen	2.70	2.61
Electric arc	2.00	2.02

The model solution will differ in many particulars from the actual situation, but these results indicate that the model is fairly close to reality in the crucial dimension of total steel production by type of technology.

First, the solution with all five constraints will be discussed in some detail to give an idea of the richness of results which can be obtained with this class of steel industry models. Then in the last part of the chapter the experiments are discussed to analyze the benefits which might have accrued to the industry from the removal of different combinations of these constraints. Each solution will be discussed briefly.

The solution of the version of the model with all the constraints is presented here by following the flow of material through the steel industry from raw material to final products. Thus, the discussion will proceed from mines, to separate pellet and coke plants, to steel mills, and finally to markets. At each step the incoming material, the processing of that material, and the outgoing material will be discussed and illustrated.

Raw Material

Coal and Coke

The flows of coal and coke between plants are shown in figure 7-1. The domestic coal mines are located in a small region near Sabinas in the state of Coahuila. In the solution of this model for 1979 the coal mines extract 6.3 million tons of raw unwashed coal. This yields 3.0 million tons of washed coal, of which 2.08 million tons are shipped from the mines to

Figure 7-1. *Flows of Coal and Coke*
(thousand metric tons a year)

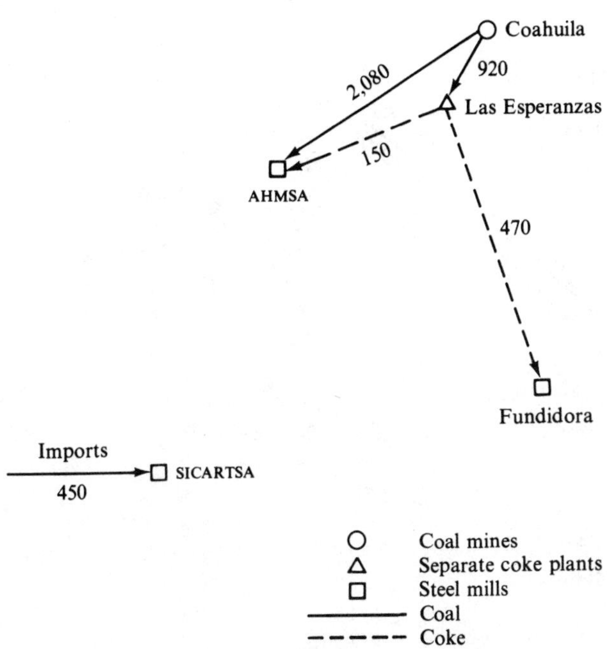

AHMSA.[1] The remaining 920 thousand tons are shipped to the nearby coking plant at Las Esperanzas where they are transformed into 620 thousand tons of coke, which are then shipped to AHMSA and Fundidora. SICARTSA imports 450 thousand tons of coal which it transforms to coke in its own ovens.

Iron Ore and Pellets

The flows of ore and pellets are shown in figure 7-2. Although there are other mines in Mexico, the six identified here are the largest and most

1. The apparent accuracy of a number such as 2.08 million tons is misleading. The actual quality of our data would justify rounding off such numbers to 2 million tons, but we have retained all the digits in this discussion to make it easier to retain the consistency of the detailed results that models of this kind typically yield.

Figure 7-2. *Flows of Ore and Pellets*
(thousand metric tons a year)

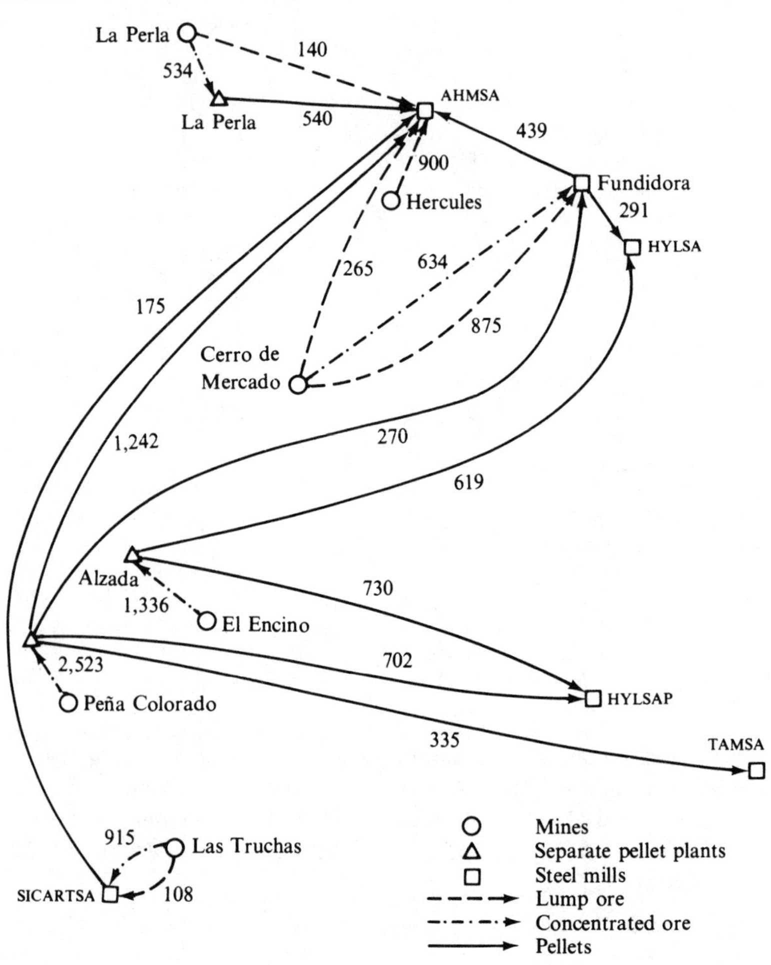

important. One other mine in the model (La Chula) does not enter the solution of this run.

To begin with the southernmost mine in the solution, Las Truchas produces 1.36 million tons of ore (see table 7-1). About 108 thousand

Table 7-1. *Extraction at Mines*
(thousand metric tons)

Mine	*Commodity*	*Production*
Peña Colorado	Southern ore	3,230
Las Truchas	Las Truchas ore	1,362
La Perla	Northern ore	900
Cerro de Mercado	Northern ore	2,041
Hercules	Northern ore	900
La Chula	Southern ore	0
El Encino	Southern ore	1,710
Coahuila	Raw unwashed coal	6,300

tons of the ore are shipped directly to SICARTSA and the remaining 1.254 million tons are passed through the magnetic separator to yield 915 thousand tons of concentrated ore which is shipped to SICARTSA in a slurry pipeline.

The mine at Peña Colorado produces 3.23 million tons of ore that is passed through a magnetic separator to yield (3.23/1.28) = 2.523 million tons of concentrated ore, which is shipped from the mine to the pellet plant at Peña Colorado. The pellets produced at Peña Colorado cannot be shipped freely to any steel mill since the shipment pattern is constrained by the ownership (see table 7-2). AHMSA owns 46 percent, TAMSA owns 18 percent, Fundidora owns 10 percent, and HYLSA and HYLSAP together own 26 percent. The model therefore includes constraints that no more than 46 percent of the pellets produced at Peña Colorado may be shipped to AHMSA. Shipments to the other plants are constrained in a similar manner. For example, the capacity of the pellet plant at Peña Colorado is given in the model as 3 million tons of pellets a year, and it is assumed that all productive units can be operated at 90 percent of rated capacity. Thus, the usable capacity is 2.7 million tons of pellets. AHMSA's share of this is (0.46)(2.7) = 1.242 million tons. The upper

Table 7-2. *Ownership Quota for Pellet Plants*
(percent)

Pellet plant	*Peña Colorado*	*Alzada*
AHMSA	46	0
TAMSA	18	0
HYLSA and HYLSAP	26	100
Fundidora	10	0

bound on shipments to TAMSA is (0.18)(2.7) = 486 thousand tons, and the bound on shipments to Fundidora is (0.10)(2.7) = 270 thousand tons. Finally, the sum of the shipments to HYLSA and HYLSAP is constrained to be less than 702 thousand tons; that is, less than 26 percent of the capacity may be used to provide shipments to HYLSA and HYLSAP [(0.26)(2.7) = 702 thousand tons].

Figure 7-2 shows that the shipments to AHMSA, Fundidora, and the HYLSA plants are bound by the ownership constraints. The shipment from Peña Colorado to AHMSA is 1.242 million tons, to Fundidora is 270 thousand tons, and to HYLSAP is 702 thousand tons. The bound on shipments to TAMSA is not tight since the bound is 486 thousand tons and the shipment level is 335 thousand tons of pellets. In the model all of the HYLSA and HYLSAP quota is shipped to HYLSAP. HYLSA then gets its pellets from the pellet plant at Alzada and from Fundidora. In effect, Fundidora sells its quota to HYLSA.

The shipments from Alzada (figure 7-2) go to HYLSA (619 thousand tons) and to HYLSAP (730 thousand tons). Table 7-2 shows that all of Alzada's product must go to these two plants.

Proceeding from the southern to the northern mines, one encounters next in figure 7-2 the Cerro de Mercado mine. This mine ships 634 thousand tons of concentrated ore and 875 thousand tons of lump ore to Fundidora in Monterrey. This mine also ships 265 thousand tons of lump ore to AHMSA.

The rest of AHMSA's requirements are satisfied in this solution by 140 thousand tons of lump ore and 540 thousand tons of pellets from La Perla. Shipments of pellets are also received from Fundidora (439 thousand tons) and from SICARTSA (175 thousand tons).

It is unlikely that Fundidora actually sold its quota of Peña Colorado pellets to HYLSA or that Fundidora and SICARTSA shipped pellets to AHMSA in 1979. The model solution suggests, however, that this alternative might be explored in the future as a means of increasing the output of the industry without additional investment. Of course, this assumes that the railroad system has the capacity to carry those quantities of raw material. This assumption has been of questionable validity in some years.

Steel Mills

Each steel mill in Mexico has a different capacity configuration. For example, some have rolling mills for flat products, others for nonflat products, and one has both types of capacity. As a result of this pattern, each mill has a comparative advantage in producing certain products.

In this section, material flow charts for each plant illustrate the flow of commodities through the plants—from inputs of pellets, coke, and natural gas to the final product. No attempt is made to be comprehensive by showing all the inputs, outputs, processes, and productive units used in the model. Rather, the flow charts illustrate the key commodity flows and productive units in each plant.

Each of the six plants will be discussed in turn. In the SICARTSA plant, shown in figure 7-3, coke and pellets are used in a blast furnace to

Figure 7-3. *Commodity Flows at SICARTSA*
(thousand metric tons a year)

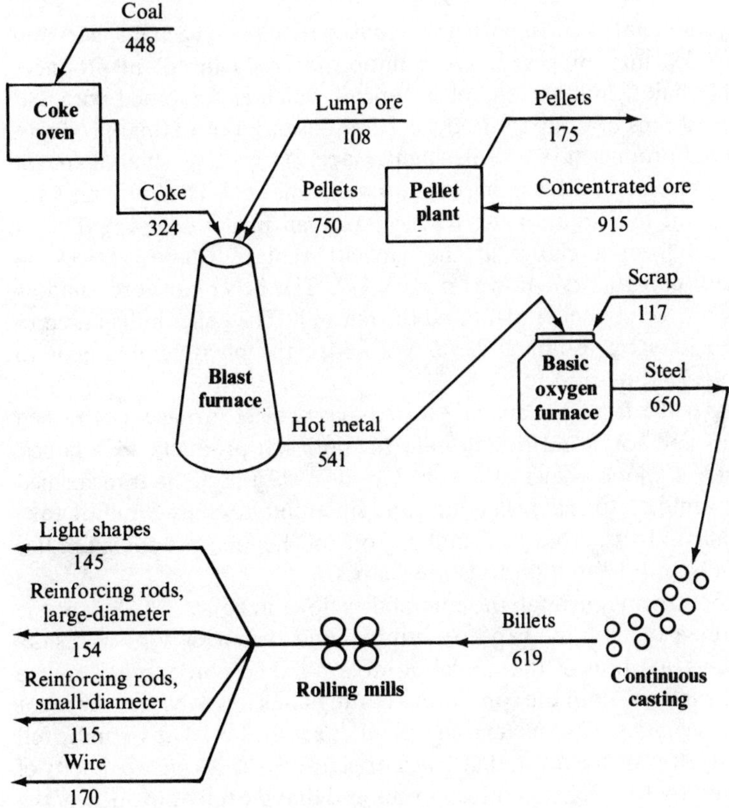

Table 7-3. *Capacity and Shadow Prices at SICARTSA*
(capacity in thousand metric tons)

Productive unit	*Capacity*		*Shadow price (thousand pesos per ton)*
	Available	*Utilized*	
Pellet plant	925	925	0.38
Coke oven	330	324	0
Blast furnace	550	541	0
BOFS	650	650	4.49
Continuous casting of billets	650	619	0
Bar mill	300	300	0.02
Wire mill	300	285	0

make hot metal (pig iron), which is reduced in basic oxygen furnaces and then rolled into shapes. In this solution for 1979 the plant produces roughly half a million tons of hot metal which is combined with 117 thousand tons of scrap to produce 584 thousand tons of final products. The final product mix includes light shapes, large- and small-diameter reinforcing rods, and wire in roughly equal amounts. The bottleneck for SICARTSA in this solution is the basic oxygen furnaces (BOFS). This is apparent from a glance at the capacity rentals (shadow prices on capacity constraints) shown in table 7-3. The other nonzero shadow prices are for the pellet plant and the bar mill. The pellet mill is used to full capacity by shipping the excess above the plant requirement to AHMSA (175 thousand tons).

AHMSA, the largest plant in Mexico, has a blast furnace, both open hearths and BOFS, and rolling mills for both flat products and shapes. Figure 7-4 shows that in the solution for 1979 the plant transformed about 4 million tons of pellets, ore, and sinter into roughly 2 million tons of final products. About 1.7 million tons of the final products are flat products and 0.3 million tons are shapes.

Before tracing through the commodity flows in figure 7-4, look at the available capacity, the capacity utilized, and the shadow price results from this solution of the model in table 7-4. The bottleneck is in the casting units —both the continuous casting units for slabs and the ingot casting facilities. The steelmaking facilities are also used at virtually full capacity. Recall, however, that a strike decreased the effective capacity of the plant by 10 percent in this solution, and that the full utilization of the

Figure 7-4. *Commodity Flows at AHMSA*
(thousand metric tons a year)

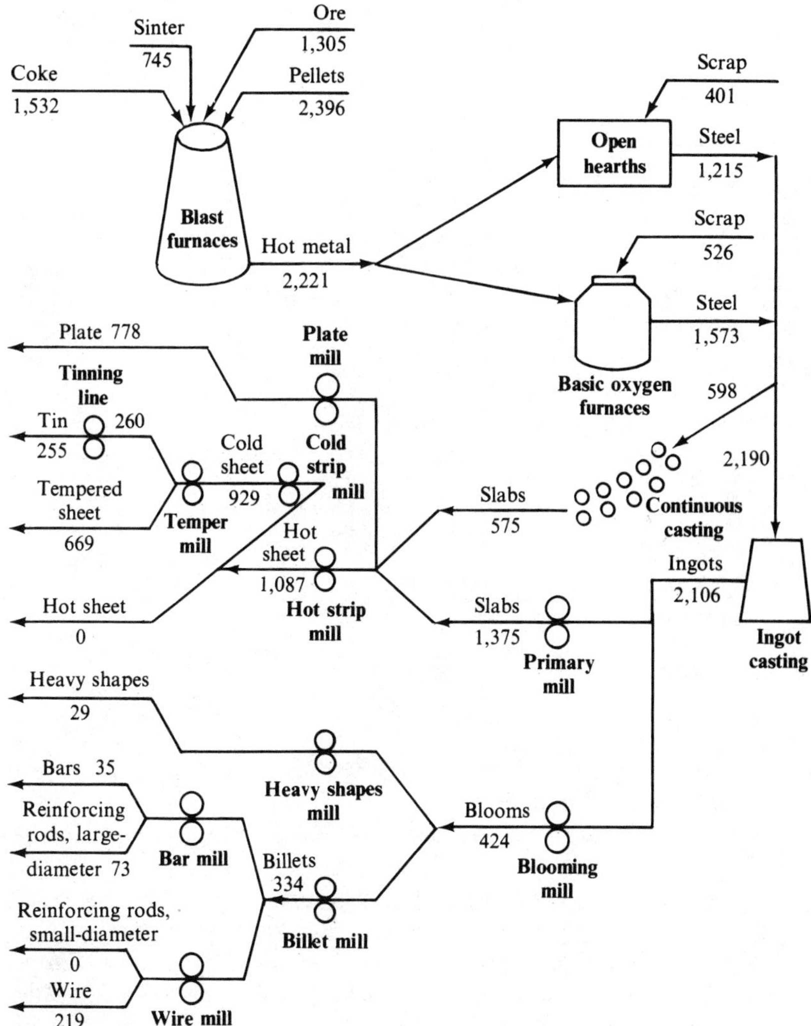

Table 7-4. *Capacity and Shadow Prices at AHMSA*
(capacity in thousand metric tons)

Productive unit	*Capacity*		*Shadow price (thousand pesos per ton)*
	Available	*Utilized*	
Sinter plant	1,215	745	0
Coke ovens	1,701	1,384	0
Blast furnaces	2,630	2,071	0
Open hearths	1,215	1,215	0.258
BOFS	1,676	1,573	0
Continuous casting of slabs	575	575	1.273
Ingot casting	2,106	2,106	0.578
Primary mill for flats	1,498	1,375	0
Primary mill for shapes	972	424	0
Plate mill	777	777	0.924
Hot mill	1,296	1,087	0
Pickling line	1,296	1,087	0
Cold mill	1,210	929	0
Annealing	1,091	929	0
Temper mill	992	929	0.966
Tinning mill	255	255	0
Billet mill	810	334	0
Heavy shapes mill	162	28	0
Bar mill	109	109	0.067
Wire mill	218	218	0.257

plant is abetted by the receipt of 175 thousand tons of pellets from SICARTSA and 439 thousand tons of pellets from Fundidora.

Table 7-4 gives one result that seems to be incorrect: the open hearths at AHMSA are used to full capacity and the BOFs have excess capacity in this solution. This is akin to one of the results in the small static model. Perhaps this result is due to the fact that the BOFs require relatively higher charges of hot metal and lower charges of scrap than the open hearths. A higher scrap price might therefore reverse this utilization pattern. Since capital costs are treated as sunk costs in this static model, the fact that the BOFs require less capital per ton of steel than do the open hearths plays no role in the decision about which of the existing furnaces to use.

The shadow prices in table 7-4 give the amount by which the objective function could be reduced if capacity were to be expanded by 1,000 tons. Of course, this is only true for small changes, in the sense that expanding the capacity by 1,000 tons might decrease the cost, but expanding it by 2,000 tons could shift the bottleneck to some other productive unit. The shadow prices on the new bottleneck unit would become larger. Even with these limitations there is useful information in the shadow prices. For example, table 7-4 shows that the open hearths, the continuous casting unit for slabs, the ingot casting plant, and the plate, temper, bar, and wire mills are the effective constraints on production at AHMSA in this solution.

In figure 7-4 some of the hot metal flows go to the BOFs and some to the open hearths. Most steel goes to ingot casting, and 598 thousand tons is used in the continuous casting unit for slabs. The continuous caster is used at full capacity. The rest of the slabs are produced by the primary

Figure 7-5. *Receipt of Raw Material by Fundidora*
(thousand metric tons a year)

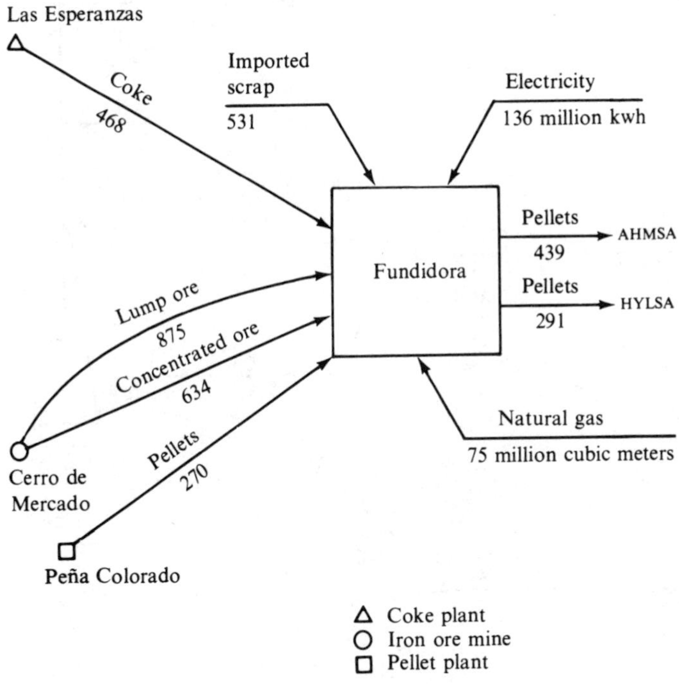

mill for flats. The blooming mill (primary mill for shapes) plays a similar role for nonflat products.

For the last of the three government-owned plants, Fundidora in Monterrey, figure 7-5 shows the receipt of raw material and the shipment of pellets from the plant. Since there is no coking plant at

Figure 7-6. *Commodity Flows at Fundidora*
(thousand metric tons a year)

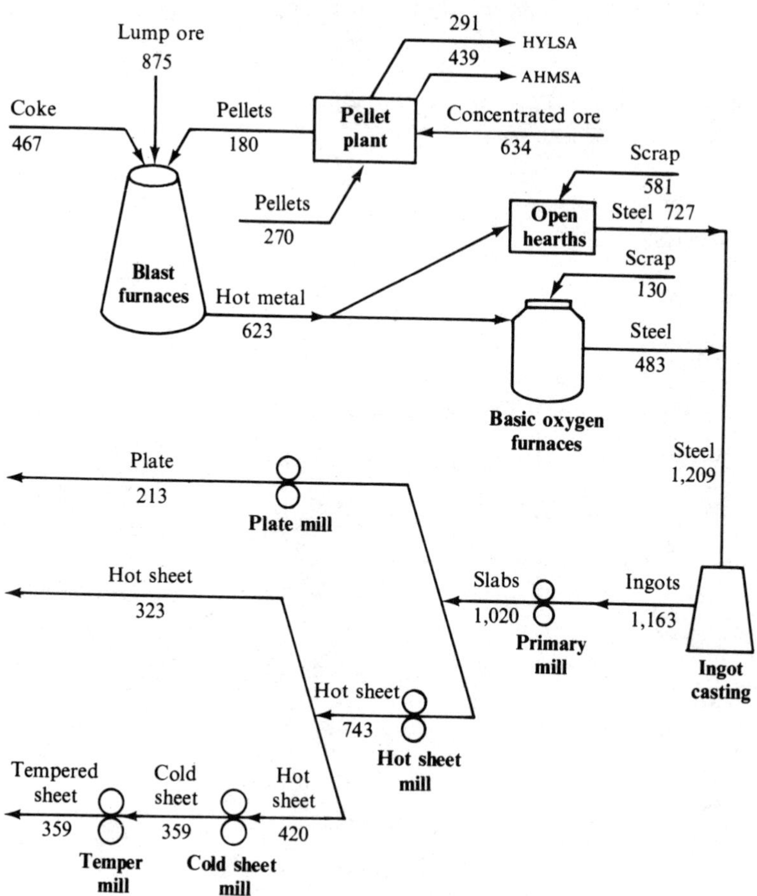

Fundidora, 468 thousand tons of coke are brought in by train from Las Esperanzas. Fundidora has three sources of iron ore in this solution: 875 thousand tons of lump ore from Cerro de Mercado are charged directly to the blast furnace, and 634 thousand tons of concentrated ore from Cerro de Mercado are converted to pellets in the pellet plant. Fundidora also receives 270 thousand tons of pellets from Peña Colorado. This gives Fundidora an excess of pellets, so 291 thousand tons are sold to HYLSA and 439 thousand tons are sold to AHMSA. Fundidora purchases 531 thousand tons of scrap, 136 million kilowatt-hours of electricity, and 75 million cubic meters of natural gas.

This raw material is processed into final products as shown in figure 7-6. Fundidora has a blast furnace, BOFS, and flat product mills as well as some older open hearths. In this solution, the plant produced roughly 1.2 million tons of steel from 623 thousand tons of hot metal and 711 thousand tons of scrap. The steel was then cast into ingots and rolled into 895 thousand tons of flat products. Table 7-5 shows some unused capacity at Fundidora in this solution, mainly because HYLSA and HYLSAP are the least-cost producers with the natural gas and electricity prices used in this solution.

As in the solution for AHMSA, the open hearths are more fully utilized at Fundidora than are the BOFS. This occurs in spite of the fact that the

Table 7-5. *Capacity and Shadow Prices at Fundidora*
(capacity in thousand metric tons)

	Capacity		*Shadow prices (thousand pesos per ton)*
Productive unit	*Available*	*Utilized*	
Pellet plant	641	641	0.402
Blast furnaces	1,197	623	0
Open hearths	726	726	0.114
BOFS	1,282	483	0
Ingot casting	1,710	1,163	0
Primary mill for flats	1,239	1,020	0
Plate mill	213	213	2.552
Hot mill	743	743	1.565
Pickling line	491	420	0
Cold mill	427	359	0
Annealing	359	359	0.143
Temper mill	444	359	0
Billet mill	171	0	0

Table 7-6. *Steel Production Technologies at AHMSA and Fundidora*
(tons per ton of steel)

Input	*STL-OH-S*	*STL-OH-S2*	*STL-BOF-P*	*STL-BOF-S*
AHMSA				
Pig iron	– 0.77	—	– 1.02	– 0.74
Scrap	– 0.33	—	– 0.11	– 0.42
Fundidora				
Pig iron	– 0.74	– 0.32	– 0.96	– 0.81
Scrap	– 0.42	– 0.80	– 0.15	– 0.27

—Not applicable.
Note:
STL-OH-S = Steel production in open hearths with average scrap charge.
STL-OH-S2 = Steel production in open hearths with high scrap charge.
STL-BOF-P = Steel production in BOFS with high pig iron charge.
STL-BOF-S = Steel production in BOFS with high scrap iron charge.

model includes an alternative technology for steel production in the BOFS at Fundidora and AHMSA (see table 7-6). The available technologies include a high-scrap-charge open hearth process (ST-OH-S2), which is not in the model for AHMSA but is the process used at Fundidora. Given the relative price of scrap and cost of hot metal (pig iron), this high-scrap-charge open hearth process is apparently very efficient.

The commodity flows in the HYLSA plant at Monterrey are shown in figure 7-7. The plant produces 660 thousand tons of sponge iron by direct reduction of 910 thousand tons of pellets using 356 million cubic meters of natural gas. It also receives about 300 thousand tons of sponge iron from the HYLSAP plant. The sponge iron is then complemented with 123 thousand tons of scrap iron to produce 1 million tons of steel in electric arc furnaces. The steel is then rolled into 800 thousand tons of flat products.

Table 7-7 shows that the bottlenecks at the plant are the direct reduction units and the electric arc furnaces. The direct reduction units alone cannot be a bottleneck because there are two alternative processes in the model for producing steel (see the A matrix for HYLSA in the GAMS statement of the large static model in chapter 6, appendix B). One process uses sponge iron and the other uses scrap to produce steel. If there is a shortage of sponge iron, more scrap can be purchased to produce more steel. Thus, the capacity of the electric arc furnaces is the most important constraint on total steel production at HYLSA.

The result of these constraints on steel production is to leave

Figure 7-7. ***Commodity Flows at HYLSA***
(thousand metric tons a year)

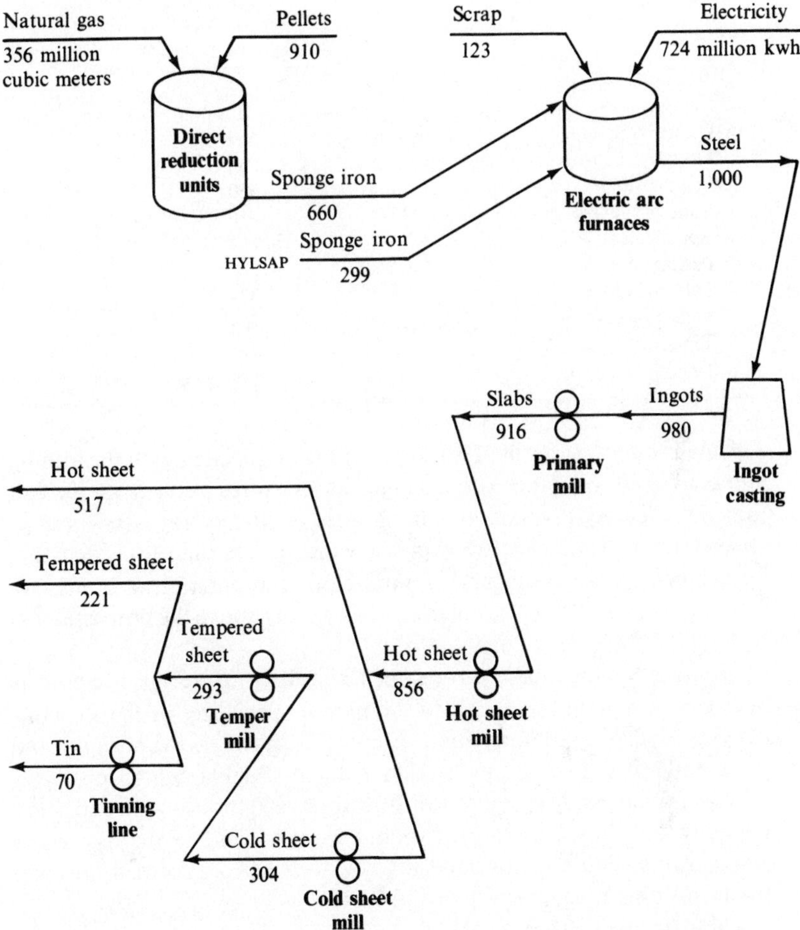

substantial unused capacity in the rolling mills at HYLSA as shown in table 7-7. This raises the possibility that interplant shipments of hot strip could be used to increase the overall efficiency of the industry. This type of shipment is not permitted in this particular solution of the model but will be permitted in some other solutions discussed later in this chapter.

Table 7-7. *Capacity and Shadow Prices at HYLSA*
(capacity in thousand metric tons)

Productive unit	*Capacity*		*Shadow price (thousand pesos per ton)*
	Available	*Utilized*	
Direct reduction	660	660	0.056
Electric arc furnaces	1,000	1,000	4.099
Ingot casting	1,000	980	0
Primary mill for flats	1,000	916	0
Hot strip mill	900	856	0
Pickling line	650	320	0
Cold strip mill	600	304	0
Annealing furnaces	450	304	0
Temper mill	450	293	0
Tinning line	70	70	0.979

A high shadow price of 979 pesos per ton is associated with the tinning line at HYLSA (see table 7-7). This high shadow price stems from the fact that the capacity of the two tinning lines in Mexico (at HYLSA and at AHMSA) have a total effective capacity which is less than total demand. Consequently, it is necessary to import tin at an international price of $393 a ton (see table 6-16), which is substantially above the domestic cost of production.

The HYLSAP plant employs the same technology for steel production as does its sister plant, HYLSA. However, HYLSAP specializes in shapes while HYLSA specializes in flat products. Figure 7-8 shows the technology and the commodity flows of the HYLSAP plant in Puebla, which produces about 1 million tons of sponge iron and about 600 thousand tons of steel. Roughly 400 thousand tons of sponge iron are sent to the HYLSA and TAMSA plants. The 600 thousand tons of steel are transformed into 550 thousand tons of shapes.

Table 7-8 shows that the shadow price on the electric arc furnaces at HYLSAP is high since this is the effective bottleneck on production in that plant, as it is at HYLSA in Monterrey.

One of the shortcomings of the model is shown by the structure of the flow chart for the rolling mills in figure 7-8. In the figure billets can be processed either through the bar mill into light shapes, bars, and large-diameter reinforcing rods, or through the wire mill into small-diameter reinforcing rods or wire. In fact, the two rolling mills act in tandem rather than in parallel. That structure has not yet been fully captured in the

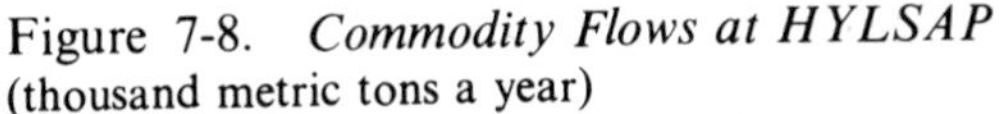

Figure 7-8. *Commodity Flows at HYLSAP*
(thousand metric tons a year)

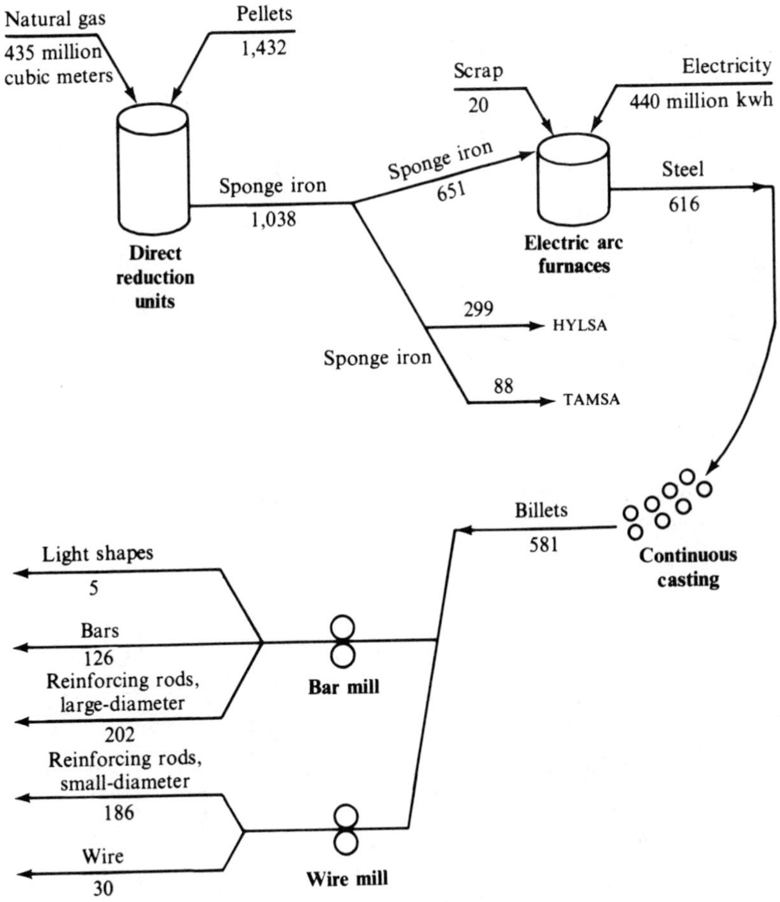

model, however, because it required adding additional types of rolling mills and substantially increasing the size of the model.

The final plant to consider is TAMSA (figure 7-9), which produces 252 thousand tons of seamless pipe from steel which is in turn produced from sponge iron. Table 7-9 shows that the bottleneck at TAMSA is the seamless pipe mill.

Table 7-8. *Capacity and Shadow Prices at HYLSAP*
(capacity in thousand metric tons)

Productive unit	*Capacity*		*Shadow price (thousand pesos per ton)*
	Available	*Utilized*	
Direct reduction	1,100	1,038	0
Electric arc furnaces	616	616	5.458
Continuous casting of billets	616	581	0
Bar mill	473	333	0
Wire mill	220	216	0

Figure 7-9. *Commodity Flows at TAMSA*
(thousand metric tons a year)

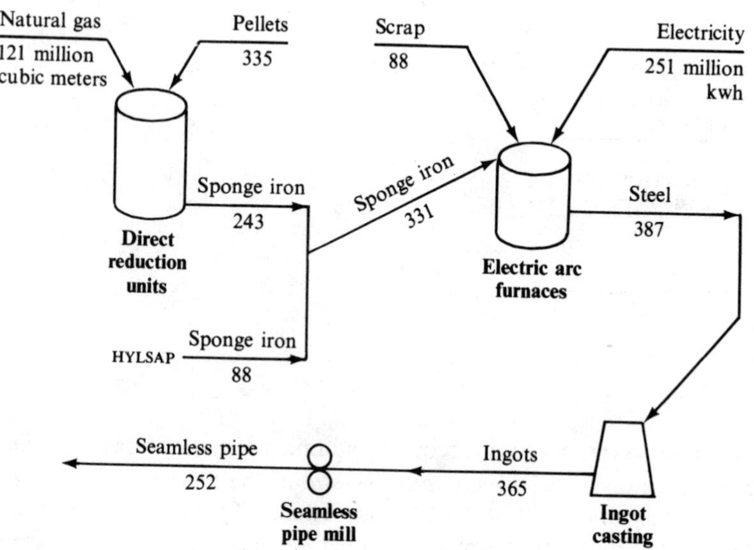

Table 7-9. *Capacity and Shadow Prices at TAMSA*
(capacity in thousand metric tons)

Productive unit	*Capacity*		*Shadow price (thousand pesos per ton)*
	Available	*Utilized*	
Direct reduction	243	243	0.515
Electric arc furnaces	405	387	0
Ingot casting	378	365	0
Bar mill	72	0	0
Seamless pipe mill	252	252	7.649

Markets

There are two aspects to the solution of the problem with regard to markets. The first is the flow of final products (1) from plants to domestic markets and to exports and (2) from imports to domestic markets. The second aspect relates to the shadow prices on final products at each market.

Total Product Shipments

The variable of interest here is x^f_{cij}, the shipment of final product c from plant i to market j. Since there are 12 final products, 6 plants, and 8 markets, more than 500 numbers are required to fully specify this part of the solution. Only a small percentage of these numbers will be presented—those representing the largest product flows.

The aggregate product flows from plants to markets, the variables x^f_{ij}, are defined as

$$x^f_{ij} = \sum_{c \in CF} x^f_{cij},$$

that is, the total flow of all final products from plant i to market j. The largest of these flows is shown in figure 7-10. Basically AHMSA and HYLSA serve both Monterrey and Mexico City, Fundidora serves Monterrey, HYLSAP serves Mexico City, and SICARTSA serves Guadalajara and Mexico City. This aggregated shipment pattern is similar to the solution to the small static model shown in table 5-8. AHMSA and HYLSAP serve Mexico City, and HYLSA and Fundidora serve Monterrey in both. The solutions differ, however, in that SICARTSA serves Mexico City in the large but not in

Figure 7-10. *Selected Product Flows*
(thousand metric tons a year)

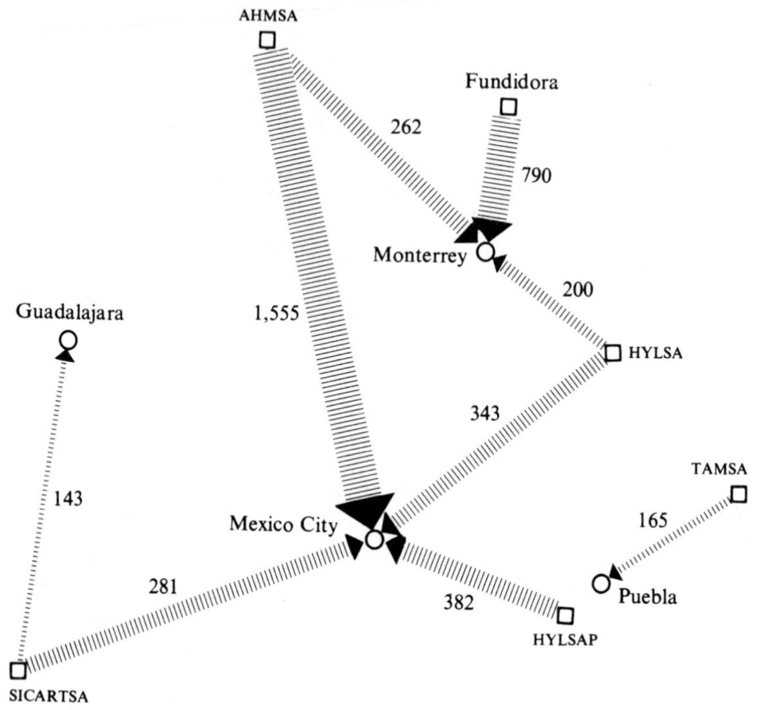

the small static model solution. Since figure 7-10 shows only aggregate product flows greater than 140 thousand tons, the smaller markets are excluded.

A slightly different picture of total product flows is given by figure 7-11, which shows the shipments from the five largest steel mills to each of the three largest market areas. Most of the mills have at least small shipments of some type of final product to each of the three largest market areas. For example, SICARTSA sends products to Mexico City, Monterrey, and Guadalajara. This of course differs from the small static model solution since that model does not have any final product disaggregation.

Figure 7-11. *Product Flows between Major Mills and Markets*
(thousand metric tons a year)

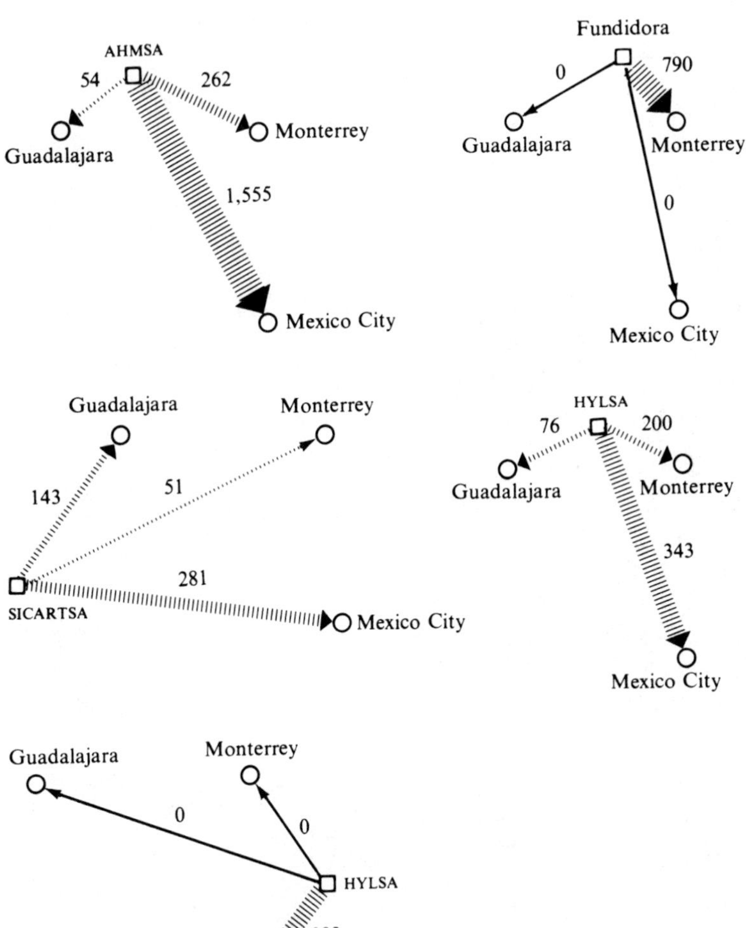

Table 7-10. *Shipments of Final Products*
(thousand metric tons)

Market	SICARTSA	AHMSA	*Fundi-dora*	HYLSA	HYLSAP	TAMSA	*Imports*	*Total*
Mexico City	281	1,555	0	343	382	84	177	2,823
Puebla	0	31	0	17	111	165	71	394
Querétaro	33	93	0	10	32	3	5	177
San Luis Potosí	13	53	0	17	0	0	13	95
Monterrey	51	262	790	200	0	0	169	1,472
Guadalajara	143	54	0	76	0	0	178	450
Lázaro Cárdenas	56	5	0	3	0	0	24	88
Coatzacoalcos	0	5	10	10	24	0	341	380
Exports	9	0	97	144	0	0	0	250
Total	586	2,059	896	809	550	252	978	6,129

Note: Row and column totals may be off slightly because of rounding errors.

The details of the total product flows for 1979, including domestic shipments, exports, and imports, are shown in table 7-10. A breakdown of products that are imported is shown in table 7-11. There is greater demand for each of those products than there is domestic capacity to meet that demand. Just as in the small model solutions, the imports are used to satisfy demand at markets in or near ports, such as Lázaro Cárdenas and Coatzacoalcos. Guadalajara is the receiving market for many imported products because it is relatively near the ocean.

Table 7-11. *Imports of Final Products*
(thousand metric tons)

Market	*Plate*	*Tin*	*Heavy shapes*	*Seamless pipe*	*Rebars*[a]	*Rails*	*Bars*	*Total*
Mexico City	7	64	62	0	0	44	0	177
Puebla	2	0	4	59	0	6	0	71
Querétaro	0	0	0	0	0	6	0	6
San Luis Potosí	0	0	0	2	0	11	0	13
Monterrey	0	0	0	147	0	22	0	169
Guadalajara	47	11	72	14	0	11	22	177
Lázaro Cárdenas	1	0	2	14	0	6	1	24
Coatzacoalcos	1	0	1	312	22	6	0	342
Total	58	75	141	548	22	112	23	979

a. Large-diameter reinforcing rods.

Figure 7-12. *Shipments of Hot Sheet*
(thousand metric tons a year)

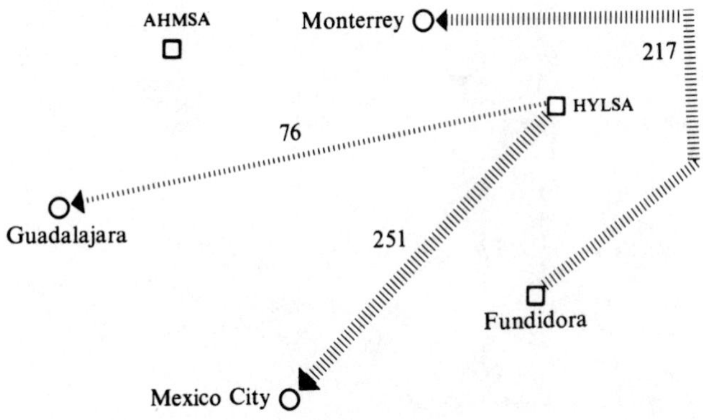

Figure 7-13. *Shipments of Tempered (Cold) Sheet*
(thousand metric tons a year)

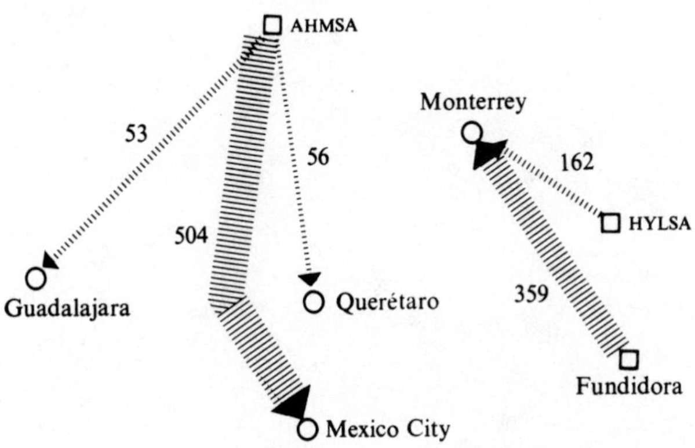

Figure 7-14. *Shipments of Large-diameter Reinforcing Rods* (thousand metric tons a year)

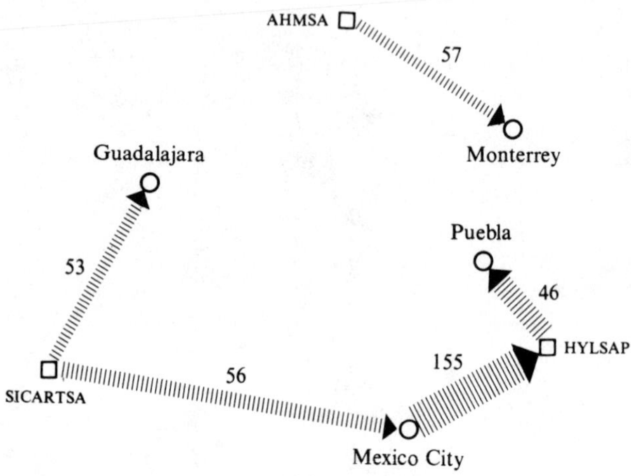

Figure 7-15. *Shipments of Small-diameter Reinforcing Rods* (thousand metric tons a year)

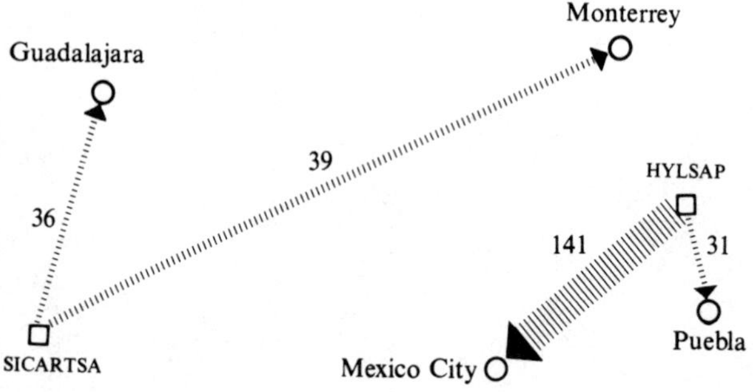

Specific Product Shipments

Next, the shipment of specific final products, such as hot strip, reinforcing rods, and seamless pipe is discussed. Since the plants have different structures of rolling mill capacity and the markets require different types of final product, these shipment breakdowns should show the comparative advantage of the various plants. Our results indicate that the optimal pattern of final product shipments can vary considerably without changes in the total cost of the solution. This is not true for production but is true for shipment patterns.

Figure 7-12 shows the shipments of hot sheet, and figure 7-13 shows the flows of tempered (cold) sheet. Only shipments greater than 35 thousand tons are shown in order to simplify the figures. Of the six plants, only AHMSA, Fundidora, and HYLSA have capacity to produce both hot and cold sheet. Even though AHMSA has the capacity to sell hot sheet, it uses that capacity instead to provide intermediate products which are

Figure 7-16. *Shipments of Seamless Pipe*
(thousand metric tons a year)

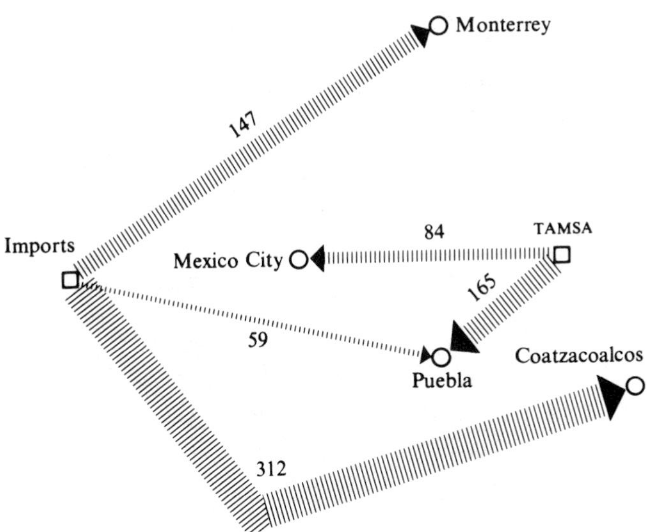

further processed into tempered sheets. Thus, in these figures, AHMSA ships no hot sheet but more than 600 thousand tons of tempered sheets.

One undesirable characteristic of linear programming solutions appears in figures 7-12 and 7-13, which show most cities served by only one plant. In fact, several plants probably serve each city. The product breakdown used in this model is not disaggregated enough to show this, however, nor does the model capture important institutional arrangements between buyers and sellers of steel products.

Figures 7-14 and 7-15 show shipments of large-diameter reinforcing rods of more than 25 thousand tons, and shipments of small-diameter reinforcing rods of more than 20 thousand tons. Once again, only three of the plants—SICARTSA, AHMSA, and HYLSAP—can produce these shapes. HYLSAP takes the largest share in both markets.

The product shipment pattern for all four products discussed above was determined in large part by the capacity structure in the plants. In contrast, the shipment pattern for seamless pipe is determined largely by the geographic distribution of demand. Figure 7-16 shows the pattern of shipments of more than 80 thousand tons. TAMSA is the only plant that produces seamless pipe. The market for this product is concentrated not in Mexico City but rather in Puebla, Coatzacoalcos, and Monterrey, which receive imported pipe in this solution.

Shadow Prices of Products

Table 7-12 gives the shadow prices of the final products in three of the market areas. These prices differ from the actual prices in Mexico

Table 7-12. *Shadow Prices on Final Products*
(thousand pesos per ton)

Product	*Mexico City*	*Monterrey*	*Guadalajara*
Plate	8.81	8.63	8.79
Hot sheet	7.80	7.55	7.80
Tempered sheet	8.83	8.58	8.81
Tin	9.96	9.71	9.94
Heavy shapes	8.59	8.40	8.56
Light shapes	8.81	8.90	8.79
Bars	8.82	8.73	8.67
Reinforcing rods			
Large-diameter	8.82	8.73	8.79
Small-diameter	8.75	8.89	8.78
Wire	8.75	8.56	8.72
Seamless pipe	11.52	11.53	11.49
Rails	8.76	8.78	8.74

because the cost of labor, capital, and marketing is not included in this version of the model. The differences in the shadow prices in the table reflect primarily differences in raw material processing and transport cost. For example, tempered sheet is more expensive than hot sheet because it requires relatively more raw material and processing. The differences in shadow prices also reflect the fact that some products must be at least partially imported. For example, the price of tin in Mexico City of 9,960 pesos per ton reflects the fact that some tin has to be imported.

The prices for products also differ across markets because of the availability of nearby capacity. For example, hot sheet is cheaper in Monterrey (7,550 pesos per ton) than in Mexico City (7,800) or Guadalajara (7,800). In contrast, light shapes are less expensive in Mexico City (8,810) than in Monterrey (8,900).

Experimental Runs

So far this chapter has provided a discussion of the main results from one solution to the large static model. As such, these results provide a rich fabric that interweaves the cost and availability of raw material, production capacity and cost in steel mills, transport cost, and market requirements. The results are best used in comparisons of several solutions rather than in discussion of a single solution.

Five experimental runs of the model were made. The runs involved the progressive release of the five institutional constraints mentioned at the

Table 7-13. *Experimental Runs and Cost Differences*

	Run				
Constraint	*1*	*2*	*3*	*4*	*5*
1. No coke imports	*				
2. Limited exports	*	*			
3. Limited interplant shipments	*	*	*		
4. Strikes	*	*	*	*	
5. No domestic scrap	*	*	*	*	
Objective function value (billion pesos)	27.2	26.6	26.5	25.4	24.0
Difference between runs					
Billion pesos		0.6	0.1	1.1	1.4
Million dollars		25	4	44	56

* Indicates that the constraint was used in the run.

beginning of this chapter. The constraints and the run numbers are given in table 7-13. The asterisks in that table indicate that the constraint was active. Thus, the first run was constrained as follows:

1. There were no imports of coke.
2. Exports were limited to a total of 250 thousand tons of final products.
3. Interplant shipments were limited to coke, pellets, and sponge iron.
4. A strike reduced effective capacity of AHMSA by 10 percent and of Fundidora by 5 percent.
5. Domestic scrap was all purchased by rerollers so the integrated mills had to import their scrap.

The objective function value in table 7-13 is the total cost of production and shipping to meet the market requirements in 1979. Since this figure excludes the cost of capital and labor it is considerably lower than the actual cost of operating the industry. The objective value is a net cost term since export revenues are subtracted from the total cost.

Table 7-13 shows that the objective value declines as one progresses from Run 1 to Run 5. That is, as fewer institutional constraints are imposed, the cost of operating the industry declines. Thus, the difference in cost between Run 1 and Run 5 is (27.2 – 24.0) = 3.2 billion pesos or $139 million. Even though labor and capital costs are excluded from the objective function value, this may be a fairly good estimate of the cost difference because both capital and labor costs are fixed and do not change much with variations in output levels. In contrast, the raw material cost included in the objective function value is extremely responsive to changes in output levels.

The differences in cost between the various runs are shown at the bottom of table 7-13 in both billions of pesos and millions of dollars. The only difference between Runs 1 and 2 is that coke imports are allowed in Run 2 but not in Run 1. This makes a difference in cost of 0.6 billion pesos, or $25 million, that arises entirely because in Run 2 Fundidora imports roughly 500 thousand tons of coke. This permits the whole industry to readjust in such a fashion that substantial cost savings are realized. Compare the steel output levels (in millions of metric tons) by process for Runs 1 and 2:

	Run 1	*Run 2*
Open hearth	1.9	1.1
Basic oxygen	2.7	3.5
Electric arc	2.0	2.0

The coke imports permit greater use of the basic oxygen furnaces and less use of the open hearths. This occurs because the coke constraint limits hot metal production. Therefore, it is necessary to import scrap to provide enough iron to meet market requirements. In Run 1 roughly 1 million tons of scrap are imported but no coke. In Run 2, 265 thousand tons of scrap and 559 thousand tons of coke are imported, so substantial savings are achieved. The comparison of these two runs illustrates how import restrictions interact with operating decisions in steel mills to affect the economics of the industry.

Next, compare Runs 2 and 3 in table 7-13. Total exports of final products are constrained to be less than 250 thousand tons in Run 2 but are effectively unconstrained in Run 3. (There is a constraint that the exports of *each* final product should be less than 500 thousand tons, but this constraint is not binding.) The result is only a small change in exports from a total of 250 thousand tons to 335 thousand tons. This occurs because the industry is operating at close to full capacity in Run 2.

The next comparison is of Runs 3 and 4, where the change is to permit more interplant shipments of intermediate products. In Run 3 only coke, pellets, and sponge iron are permitted to be shipped between plants. In Run 4 steel ingots, slabs, hot sheet, blooms, and billets may also be

Table 7-14. *Capacity Utilization with and without Interplant Shipments of Ingots and Slabs*
(percent)

	Interplant shipments	
Productive unit and plant	*Constrained (Run 3)*	*Permitted (Run 4)*
Ingot casting unit		
AHMSA	100	100
Fundidora	68	100
HYLSA	98	98
Primary mill for flats		
AHMSA	97	89
Fundidora	82	100
HYLSA	91	100
Hot strip mill		
AHMSA	89	100
Fundidora	100	100
HYLSA	95	100

shipped between plants. Table 7-13 shows that these additional interplant shipments permit a decrease in total cost of 1.1 billion pesos ($44 million). The reason for this can be partially seen in table 7-14, which shows capacity utilization percentages in selected productive units when interplant shipments of rolled products are included and when they are excluded from the model. In Run 3, when interplant shipments of ingots and slabs are excluded, Fundidora has capacity utilization in its ingot casting shop of 68 percent and in its primary mill for flats of 82 percent. HYLSA has capacity utilization in its primary mill for flats of 91 percent, and both AHMSA and HYLSA have less than full capacity utilization in their hot strip mills. Thus, production efficiency in the system can be improved with the interplant shipments shown in figure 7-17. In Run 4, 90 thousand tons of ingots are shipped from Fundidora to HYLSA. This permits full utilization of HYLSA's primary mill for flats by an increased

Figure 7-17. *Selected Interplant Shipments of Ingots and Slabs in Run 4*
(thousand metric tons a year)

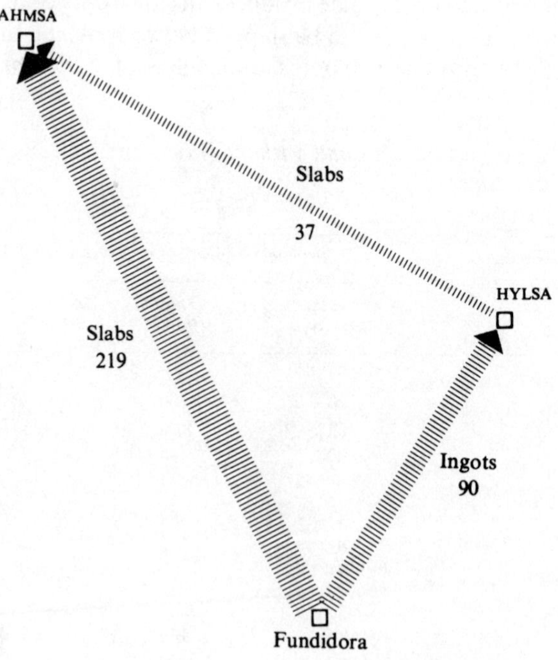

Table 7-15. *Capacity Utilization with and without Interplant Shipments of Ingots, Blooms, and Billets*
(percent)

Productive unit and plant	Interplant shipments: Constrained (Run 3)	Interplant shipments: Permitted (Run 4)
Ingot casting unit		
AHMSA	100	100
Fundidora	68	100
Primary mill for nonflats		
AHMSA	36	65
Billet mill		
AHMSA	34	29
Fundidora	0	100
Bar mill		
AHMSA	51	100
HYLSAP	69	83

production of slabs. Part of these slabs are then sent to AHMSA to permit fuller utilization of the hot strip mill there. In addition, 219 thousand tons of slabs are shipped from Fundidora to AHMSA. This increases capacity utilization in Fundidora's primary mill from 82 to 100 percent and in AHMSA's hot strip mill from 89 to 100 percent.

A similar situation occurs for interplant shipments of ingots, blooms, and billets for shapes. As shown in table 7-15, in Run 3 without interplant shipments AHMSA operates its ingot casting facility at full capacity but Fundidora uses its facility at only 68 percent of capacity. Furthermore, AHMSA has excess capacity for making blooms in its primary mill for nonflats, both plants have excess capacity in their billet mills, and AHMSA and HYLSAP have excess capacity in their bar mills. Under Run 4 in table 7-15 it is shown that interplant shipments permit much more complete utilization of these facilities. This is accomplished as shown in figure 7-18. Fundidora ships ingots to AHMSA, which transforms them to blooms and ships them back to Fundidora. Then Fundidora rolls the blooms into billets and sends them back to AHMSA and also to HYLSAP.

All of these cross shipments are complicated, but they permit a more efficient use of the capacity in the industry that saves 1.1 billion pesos ($44 million) per year.

Figure 7-18. *Selected Interplant Shipments of Ingots, Blooms, and Billets in Run* 4
(thousand metric tons a year)

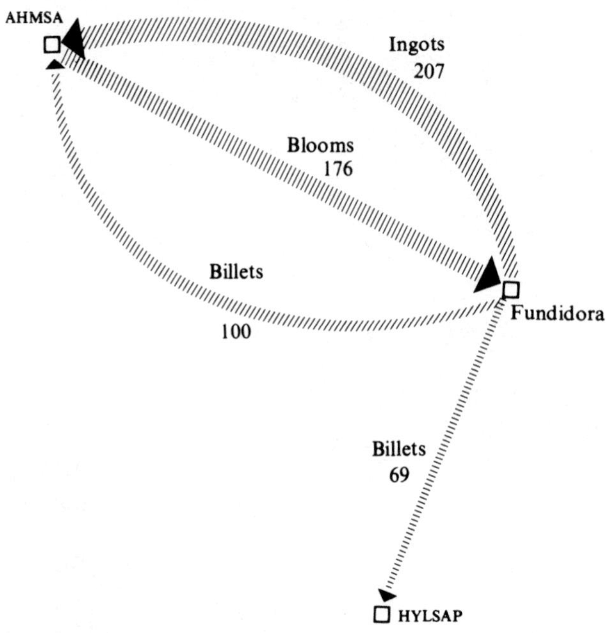

In the last set of comparisons in table 7-13, Runs 4 and 5, two changes are made. The first asks the question of the effective cost of the strike against AHMSA and Fundidora. The second change lowered the domestic price of scrap in the model so that the integrated mills could purchase it instead of having to import it. Although it would have been better to make these changes separately, so that the two effects could be untangled, the result does at least indicate that the strike cost no more than the 1.4 billion pesos ($56 million) indicated in table 7-13.

This chapter has shown what a rich level of detail can be developed and studied in a static model that is still small enough to be solved at reasonable cost. It has also shown how the model can be used in searching for more efficient operational procedures such as interplant shipments. These kinds of result might be even more interesting in dynamic models that include investment. Therefore, the next chapter discusses a small dynamic model.

8
A Small Dynamic Model

MODEL BUILDING IS BEST done in stages. On a typical project one does not simply build a single large model and solve it, but rather builds up from simpler to more complex models. Thus, one can gain experience with the problem while working with smaller, less complicated models that can be solved in less time and at less expense. It is also possible to learn about the problem a little bit at a time. In fact, this procedure is basic to our modeling work. The purpose of modeling is not to find an optimal solution, but rather to enhance understanding of the problem at hand.

Another reason for building multiple models is that each model has a comparative advantage. Since small models are easier to understand and less costly to solve, one can solve the model repeatedly while attempting to gain a better understanding of the industry. In contrast, large models provide more detailed specification that allows one to analyze certain problems of interest and to check the validity of the solutions to the small models. Also, static models have a comparative advantage in studying problems of operation, and dynamic models have a comparative advantage in analyzing investment problems.

This chapter returns to the small static model of chapter 5 and enriches it by making it dynamic and by adding exhaustible resources. Only the new elements are explained; then the entire model is stated in summary form.

Sets

The small static model had five plants (AHMSA, Fundidora, SICARTSA, HYLSA, and HYLSAP), the largest existing steel mills. TAMSA is not included in this model because it specializes in a single product, seamless pipe. It is possible that all expansion in the period covered by the dynamic model will be accomplished by constructing additional productive units at these five plants. It is useful, however, to consider the possibility that one or more entirely new plants will be constructed on "green field" sites.

Two green field sites, Tampico and Coatzacoalcos, are considered in this small dynamic model (see map 1, p. 41). Coatzacoalcos was chosen because it is near the large natural gas fields discovered recently. If direct reduction methods are used in the future and if domestic ores are depleted to the point that importation of pellets is necessary, then Coatzacoalcos might be an attractive site for a new steel mill. Tampico was chosen as a potential site for similar reasons. First, it is a port. Second, it is in the vicinity of gas fields and near the existing natural gas pipeline that goes from Coatzacoalcos to the Texas border. Third, it is closer to the existing coal and northern ores than is Coatzacoalcos. Thus, a plant established there could use existing northern ores and coal until they are depleted and then could switch to imported pellets and coke.

This model also has a set of mines that is not considered in the small static model. The mines are included so that the model can be used to analyze the effect of declining ore grades and coal quality. Although there are many different ore mines in Mexico, in this small dynamic model they are represented by only two sites, one in the northern part of the country and one in the southern part. All of the reserves of iron ore are assumed to be concentrated at one or the other of these two sites. In contrast, there is really only one large coal mining area, and this can be satisfactorily represented in the model as a single coal mine in Coahuila.

A subset of the plants is used in the model to identify locations that are permitted to purchase natural gas and electricity at subsidized prices. This set is:

IE = plants that qualify for subsidized energy prices
= {Coatzacoalcos, SICARTSA, Tampico}.

In summary, then, the sets of plants and mines in the model are:

IM = Mines
= {Coahuila coal mines, northern iron ore mines, southern iron ore mines}

I = Plants
= {AHMSA, Fundidora, SICARTSA, HYLSA, HYLSAP, Tampico, Coatzacoalcos}.

The set of markets remains the same as in the small static model:

$J = \{$Mexico City, Monterrey, Guadalajara$\}$.

The set of productive units is also the same as in the small static model:

$M = \{$Blast furnace, open hearth furnace, basic oxygen furnace, direct reduction furnace, electric arc furnace$\}$.

The set of processes is the same as in the small static model with one exception: a process for production in BOFs with a high scrap charge was added to the original small static model to correct an inaccuracy in that model. The change was reflected in the second linear programming solution, which was discussed in chapter 5. Thus, the set of processes is:

$P = \{$pig iron production, sponge iron production, steel production in open hearths, steel production in electric arc furnaces, steel production in BOFs, steel production in BOFs with high scrap$\}$.

The set of commodities is the same for this model as for the small static model, but the subsets are treated in a slightly different manner. The set of commodities is:

$C = \{$pellets, coke, natural gas, electricity, scrap, pig iron, sponge iron, steel$\}$.

The subsets of C are:

CR = raw material
= {natural gas, electricity, scrap}
CV = imported raw material
= {coke, pellets}
CM = mining products
= {coke, pellets}
CI = interplant shipment commodities
= {sponge iron}
CF = final products
= {steel}
CE = exported commodities
= {steel}
$CENR$ = subsidized energy commodities
= {natural gas, electricity}.

The set CM is used differently here than in the small static model. There, it defines the set of intermediate products. In the small dynamic model, however, the input-output matrix defines implicitly the set of intermediate products, and the set CM is used for the commodities (coke and pellets) that are shipped from mines to plants. In fact, most of the productive units that convert coal to coke and some of the units that convert iron ore to pellets are located at plants rather than at mines, but this abstraction serves a useful purpose in this small model.

Three sets not used in the small static model are necessary in the dynamic model: the sets of expansion units, of time periods, and of expansion periods.

The expansion units are the productive units considered in the expansion plans. As discussed in chapter 3, in some cases this set will be identical to the set of productive units. Some productive units may be unlikely candidates for investment, however, and are therefore excluded from the set of expansion units. Open hearth furnaces, for example, are in the set of productive units but not in the set of expansion units since they are dominated as investment choices by basic oxygen furnaces. Some new technologies that are not in the existing plants may also be considered in the set of expansion units. In summary, the set of expansion units is:

$$ME = \{\text{blast furnace, basic oxygen furnace, direct reduction furnace, electric arc furnace}\}.$$

The set of time periods covers the time horizon from 1981 to 1995 in three-year intervals. Thus, there are five time periods of three years each:

$$\begin{aligned} T &= \text{time periods} \\ &= \{1981\text{–}83, 1984\text{–}86, 1987\text{–}89, 1990\text{–}92, 1993\text{–}95\}. \end{aligned}$$

There is also a subset of time periods during which capacity can be expanded. This is used to represent the long lags in construction times. Thus, new capacity which comes on-line in the first time period (1981–83) must already be under construction and should be exogenously added to the model. Therefore, the following set is used:

$$\begin{aligned} TE &= \text{time periods during which capacity can be expanded} \\ &= \{1984\text{–}86, 1987\text{–}89, 1990\text{–}92, 1993\text{–}95\}. \end{aligned}$$

This model uses a set of quality levels (Q) for coal and iron ore, but since those commodities are not in this small model, Q actually refers to coke and pellets. The quality levels are used to model the declining quality (and rising cost of mining) of both coal and iron ore as the present reserves in Mexico are exploited. With level 1 as the best quality and level 5 as the worst, this set is:

$$\begin{aligned} Q &= \text{quality levels for coal and iron ore} \\ &= \{1, 2, 3, 4, 5\}. \end{aligned}$$

Another new set, G, is used for the grid points of the investment cost function. The set is simply the integers from 1 to 4 to represent the four grid points used in approximating the investment cost functions:

G = grid points for the investment cost function approximation
$= \{1, 2, 3, 4\}$.

In summary, the sets are:

IM = mines
I = plants
J = markets
M = productive units
ME = productive units for expansion
P = processes
C = commodities
CR = raw material
CV = imported raw material
CM = mining products
CI = interplant shipment commodities
CF = final products
CE = exported commodities
$CENR$ = subsidized energy commodities
T = time periods
TE = expansion time periods
TS = set of time period pairs for the investment equations
Q = quality levels for coal and iron ore
G = grid points for investment function approximation

Variables

Table 8-1 lists the variables in the small dynamic model. The process levels z, shipments x, domestic purchases u, imports v, and exports e are familiar from the small static model. And the specification of the shipment variables x^f for final products, x^n for intermediate product shipment between plants, and x^m for raw material shipments from mines to plants are familiar from the large static model. The notation for the process-level variables w at the mines is new. The cost category variables are all familiar except for the capital cost variables ϕ_κ. Thus, the new variables in the small dynamic model which were not in the small static

Table 8-1. *Variables in the Small Dynamic Model*

w_{cqit}	Production of commodity c of quality level q at mine i in time period t
z_{pit}	Process level of process p at plant i in time period t
x^f_{cijt}	Shipment of final product c from plant i to market j in time period t
$x^n_{ci'it}$	Shipment of intermediate product c from plant i' to plant i in time period t
$x^m_{xi'it}$	Shipment of commodities from mine i' to plant i in time period t
u_{cit}	Purchases of raw material c at plant i in time period t
v^r_{cit}	Imports of raw material c to plant i in time period t
v_{cjt}	Imports of final product c to market j in time period t
e_{cit}	Exports of commodity c from plant i in time period t
h_{mit}	Expansion of productive unit m at plant i in time period t
s_{mit}	Auxiliary variable for investment in productive unit m at plant i in time period t
y_{mit}	Zero-one variable for investment in productive unit m at plant i in time period t
ϕ	Total discounted cost less discounted export revenues
$\phi_{\kappa t}$	Capital cost in time period t
$\phi_{\psi t}$	Recurrent raw material and labor cost in time period t
$\phi_{\lambda t}$	Transport cost in time period t
$\phi_{\pi t}$	Import cost in time period t
$\phi_{\epsilon t}$	Export revenues in time period t

model are: the investment variables h, s, and y and the associated investment cost variables ϕ_κ; the shipment variables x^m; and the mine process-level variables w.

The only change to the familiar variables is that they now have a subscript for time period t. Thus, the variable z_{pit} for

$$z_{\text{pig iron production, Altos Hornos, 1981–83}} = 1.25$$

means that average annual production of pig iron at Altos Hornos in the three-year interval 1981–83 would be 1.25 million metric tons. The variable does not represent the total production in the three-year interval but rather the average annual production level. It is assumed that the process level will be different in the three years in the 1981–83 interval, and the model solution will be the average annual production level in the interval.

The same treatment of time holds for the other variables w, x, u, v, and e. That is, they all represent average annual activity levels within the time interval.

In contrast, the investment variables do *not* represent the average amount of capacity added in each year of the time interval, but rather the total amount of new capacity that comes on-line at the beginning of the time interval. To see this, consider the investment variables introduced in this chapter: h, y, and s. Of these, the h variables are the simplest to interpret. They are the expansion of productive unit m at plant i in time period t. For example, h_{mit} for

$$h_{\text{blast furnace, Altos Hornos, 1984–86}} = 1.5$$

means that a new blast furnace with a capacity of 1.5 million metric tons per year would be put into production at Altos Hornos at the beginning of 1984.

The y_{mit} variables are the zero-one variables associated with the expansion of productive unit m at plant i in time period t. In the continuous solutions to the problem the y variables take on a value in the interval from zero to one, and in the mixed integer programming (MIP) solutions they take on either the value zero *or* the value one. In the MIP solutions the y variables indicate whether there is any expansion of the productive unit in the particular plant and time period. Thus, the y's indicate yes or no and the h's indicate the amount of capacity expansion when the y's are one.

The s variables are used in the approximation of the investment cost function as shown in figure 8-1. That figure shows four grid points on the horizontal axis for the size of the additions to capacity: $\bar{h}_1, \bar{h}_2, \bar{h}_3$, and $\bar{h}_4$. The first of these points is set to zero:

$$\bar{h}_1 = 0. \tag{8.1}$$

The second is chosen as the size at which economies of scale are exhausted, $\hat{h}$:

$$\bar{h}_2 = \hat{h}. \tag{8.2}$$

For example, if economies of scale for basic oxygen furnaces (BOFs) are exhausted at a furnace size of 1.5 million tons, then $\bar{h}_2 = 1.5$ million tons. That is, $\bar{h}_2$ is the size at which capacity is expanded by replicating units rather than by increasing the size of individual units. In a BOF shop there may thus be several furnaces, each with a capacity no larger than 1.5 million tons per year. (Theoretically, economies of scale may not be exhausted at the point of the largest size of productive unit observed, but this notion is accurate enough for purposes of the approximation used here.)

Next, the grid point variable $\bar{h}_3$ is chosen to be a multiple of the size $\hat{h}$:

$$\bar{h}_3 = n_{\text{const}} \hat{h}. \tag{8.3}$$

It is the multiple at which diseconomies of scale are expected. In this study n_{const} is chosen to be 3; that is, it is assumed that after the unit is replicated three times diseconomies of scale begin to occur. In the case of

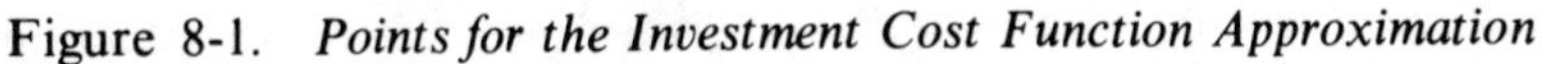

Figure 8-1. *Points for the Investment Cost Function Approximation*

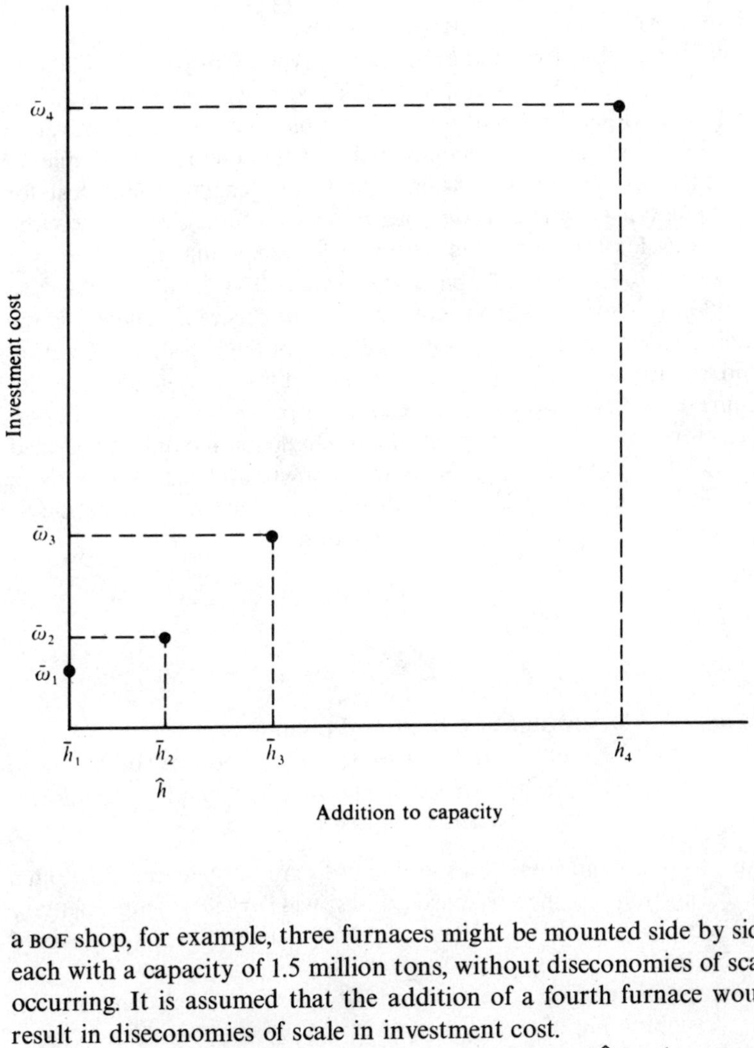

a BOF shop, for example, three furnaces might be mounted side by side, each with a capacity of 1.5 million tons, without diseconomies of scale occurring. It is assumed that the addition of a fourth furnace would result in diseconomies of scale in investment cost.

Finally, the grid point $\bar{h}_4$ is chosen to be a multiple of $\hat{h}$ that is an upper bound on the capacity of a set of productive units which would be installed at a single point in time:

$$\bar{h}_4 = n_{max}\hat{h}. \quad (8.4)$$

For this study, n_{max} is set at 6; that is, it is assumed that no more than six identical units of a size at which economies of scale are exhausted would be installed at a single plant in a particular time period. Thus, for the BOF example, the restriction in the model is that no more than six BOFs of 1.5 million tons would be installed at one time.

This is the first use of this particular type of investment function approximation in this series of books, so there is relatively little experience with it and caution in its use is appropriate. However, it embodies the old idea from economic theory that there are economies of scale in investment cost for small plant sizes, constant unit cost for intermediate sizes, and diseconomies of scale for large sizes. It therefore seems a useful approximation with which to experiment.

Figure 8-1 also shows the parameter values $\bar{\omega}_g$. It is sufficient here to say that $\bar{\omega}_g$ is the investment cost for a plant of size $\bar{h}_g$ where g is the running index for the grid points (1, 2, 3, 4) of the investment function approximation. A full discussion of how these parameters are determined is deferred to the next section on parameters.

The investment function approximation used in this study is obtained graphically by connecting the points shown in figure 8-1. This is displayed with the dark line in figure 8-2. This approximation is represented mathematically by the function

(8.5) $$\phi_\kappa = \sum_{g \in G} \bar{\omega}_g s_g$$

(8.6) $$\sum_{g \in G} s_g = 1$$

where $\bar{\omega}_g$ = investment cost at grid point g

s_g = a set of variables used to obtain a convex combination of the approximation points $(\bar{\omega}_g, \bar{h}_g)$ for the investment cost function.

Thus, to represent points on the line in figure 8-2 between the points $(\bar{\omega}_1, \bar{h}_1)$ and $(\bar{\omega}_2, \bar{h}_2)$, the variables s_1 and s_2 will vary in a complementary way between zero and one. That is, a point relatively near $(\bar{\omega}_2, \bar{h}_2)$ would be obtained by setting $s_1 = 0.2$, $s_2 = 0.8$, $s_3 = 0$, and $s_4 = 0$.

Finally, the amount of capacity added is also a convex combination, but a combination of the $\bar{h}$'s instead of the $\bar{\omega}$'s:

(8.7) $$h = \sum_{g \in G} \bar{h}_g s_g.$$

The discussion above has been simplified by ignoring most of the subscripts on the investment variables h and s. When those subscripts are

Figure 8-2. *Three-Segment Investment Cost Approximation*

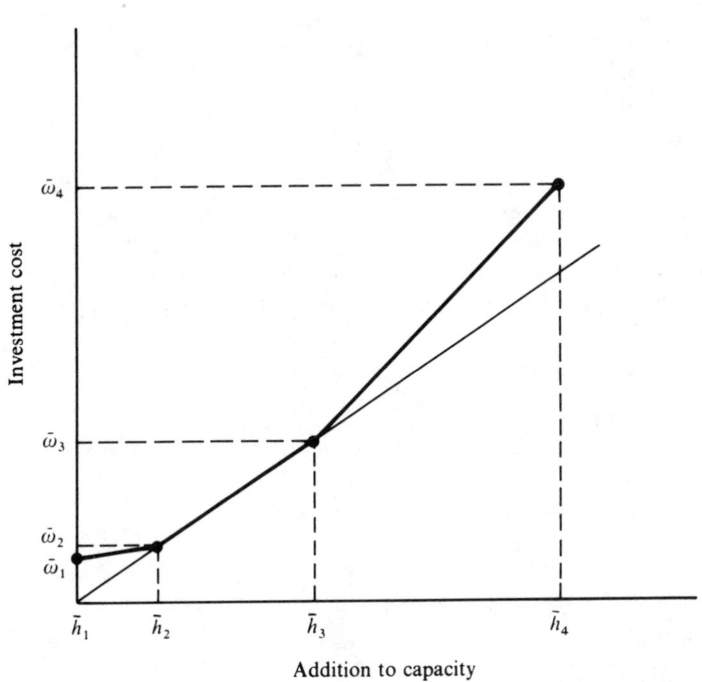

added back into the variables they become

h_{mit} = expansion of productive unit m at plant i in time period t
s_{gmit} = level of convex combination variable at grid point g for productive unit m at plant i in time period t.

Two other new variables, the shipment variables x^m and the mine process variables w, need to be discussed. The shipment variables $x^m_{ci'i}$ are added to the model to represent the shipment from mines to steel mills of raw material. The production of this raw material at the mines is represented with the mine process variables w_{cqit}. It is assumed that the raw material is available in deposits of varying quality. The quality index $q = 1$ represents the highest quality ores and larger values of q represent ores of lower quality.

Parameters

Table 8-2 lists the parameters in this model. Only the parameters which differ from those of the small static model will be discussed in detail.

The first three parameters in the table—the input-output coefficients a, the capacity utilization coefficients b, and the initial capacity parameters k—are identical to those in the small static model. In contrast, the demand parameters d have been changed from d_{cj} to d_{cjt}; that is, a time subscript has been added. This represents the demand projections in the model.

Recall that demand in the small static model is treated in the following fashion:

$$d_{cj} = d_j^p (1.4)(5.2) \tag{8.8}$$

Table 8-2. *Parameters in the Small Dynamic Model*

a_{cp}	Input (−) or output (+) of commodity c per unit level of operation of process p
b_{mp}	$\begin{cases} 1 \text{ if productive unit } m \text{ is used by process } p \\ 0 \text{ if productive unit } m \text{ is not used by process } p \end{cases}$
k_{mi}	Initial capacity of productive unit m at plant i
θ	Years per time period
γ_t	Midyear for time period t
d_{cjt}	Demand for commodity c at market j in time period t
e_t^u	Upper bound on exports of all commodities from all plants in time period t
$\bar{\omega}_{mgi}$	Capital cost at grid point g for productive unit m at plant i
$\bar{h}_{mg}$	Plant size for productive unit m at grid point g
δ_t	Discount term for time period t
σ	Capital recovery factor
p_{cqi}^w	Price of commodity c produced from coal or ores of quality q at mine i
p_{cit}^d	Domestic price of commodity c delivered to plant i in time period t
p_c^v	Import price of commodity c at the port
p_c^e	Export price commodity c at the port
μ_{ij}^f	Unit cost of transporting final products from plant i to market j
μ_{ij}^v	Unit cost of transporting final products from the port to market j
μ_i^e	Unit cost of transporting final products from plant i to nearest port
$\mu_{ii'}^n$	Unit cost of transporting intermediate products from plant i to plant i'
$\mu_{i'i}^m$	Unit cost of transporting commodities from mine i' to plant i
$\bar{w}_{cqi}$	Reserves of each quality level q of commodity c at mine i

where d_{cj} = demand for final product c in market j in 1979
d_j^p = the percentage of the total national demand which is located in market area j
1.4 = tons of ingot steel required per ton of final products
5.2 = million metric tons of final products consumed in 1979.

In this small dynamic model the demand projections are made with the expression:

(8.9) $$d_{cjt} = (d_{c,j,1979})(1.10)^{(\gamma_t - 1979)}$$

d_{cjt} = demand for final product c in market area j in time period t
$d_{c,j,1979} = d_{cj}$ = demand for final product c in market area j in 1979
1.10 = 1 plus the annual growth rate of the demand for final products, in this case 10 percent
γ_t = the midyear of time period t.

The parameter γ_t is the only unusual part of the expression (8.9). Since each time period consist of three years and the time periods are 1981–83, 1984–86, and so on, the parameter γ_t can be defined as

(8.10) $$\gamma_t = 1979 + \theta t$$

where θ = years per time period = 3
t = the time period number (1, 2, 3,...)

As an example, consider the demand for steel in Mexico City in the time period 1981–83. From (8.9),

(8.11) $$d_{\text{steel, Mexico City, 1981-83}} = (d_{\text{steel, Mexico City, 1979}})(1.10)^{(\gamma_{1981\text{-}83} - 1979)},$$

then from (8.8)

(8.12) $$d_{\text{steel, Mexico City, 1979}} = (d^p_{\text{Mexico City}})(1.4)(5.2) = (0.55)(1.4)(5.2) = 4.004,$$

and from (8.10)

(8.13) $$\gamma_{1981\text{-}83} = 1979 + 3(1) = 1982.$$ since 1981–83 is the first time period

Then substitution of (8.12) and (8.13) into (8.11) yields

(8.14) $$d_{\text{steel, Mexico City, 1981-83}} = (4.004)(1.10)^{(1982-1979)} = (4.004)(1.1)^3 = (4.004)(1.331) = 5.329.$$

Table 8-3. *Demand Projections for the Small Dynamic Model*
(million metric tons of steel per year)

Time period	*Mexico City*	*Monterrey*	*Guadalajara*	*Total*
1981–83	5.329	2.907	1.453	9.689
1984–86	7.093	3.869	1.935	12.897
1987–89	9.441	5.150	2.575	17.166
1990–92	12.566	6.854	3.427	22.847
1993–95	16.726	9.123	4.562	30.411

This number and the remaining demand projections are shown in table 8-3. The numbers in this table are the demand for (ingot) steel in each year of the three-year period covered by each time interval.

The next parameter in table 8-2 is e^u_t, the upper bound on exports of all products from all markets in period t. Though it would be interesting to experiment with the effects of an upper bound which changes across time periods, it has been assumed here that this bound is constant across time periods:

$$e^u_t = 0.2. \qquad t \in T \tag{8.15}$$

Thus, the bound is set at 200 thousand tons of steel products.

The next new parameters in table 8-2 are the capital cost parameters $\bar{\omega}_{mgi}$. These parameters were discussed above along with the description of the capital cost variables h, s, and y. They were shown graphically in figures 8-1 and 8-2. In that discussion, four grid points for investment cost were selected:

Grid point g	*Investment size h*
1	Zero
2	Size at which economies of scale are exhausted
3	Size at which diseconomies of scale begin
4	Maximum size

The capital costs which correspond to each of these grid points are:

$$\omega_{m1} = \hat{\omega}_m(0.5^{\beta_m - 1} - 1) \tag{8.16}$$

$$\omega_{m2} = \hat{\omega}_m \tag{8.17}$$

$$\omega_{m3} = n_{\text{const}}\hat{\omega}_m \tag{8.18}$$

$$\omega_{m4} = n_{\max}(1.25)\,\hat{\omega}_m \tag{8.19}$$

where $\hat{\omega}$ = capital cost for an investment of size $\hat{h}$
$\hat{h}$ = size at which economies of scale are exhausted

Table 8-4. *Investment Cost Parameters*

Productive unit	*Size* ($\hat{h}$) (*million metric tons a year*)	*Cost* ($\hat{\omega}$) (*million dollars*)	*Scale* (β)
Blast furnace	1.5	250	0.6
BOF	1.5	120	0.6
Direct reduction	0.8	100	0.6
Electric arc	0.5	42	0.6

Note: The cost parameters in this table were provided by HYLSA officials, who indicated that the data were taken from an article by R. T. Kuhl in the June 1979 issue of *Steel Times International.*

$n_{const} = 3 =$ multiple of size $\hat{h}$ at which diseconomies of scale begin

$n_{max} = 6 =$ multiple of $\hat{h}$ representing the maximum amount of equipment which can be installed in a single time period.

Since $\hat{\omega}$, n_{const}, and n_{max} are given data, only the cost ω_1 is difficult to obtain. The derivation of the expression (8.16) is relatively long and is therefore relegated to appendix C to this chapter. The parameters $\hat{h}_m$, $\hat{\omega}_m$, and β_m are given in table 8-4.

The expressions (8.16)–(8.19) embody the assumption that capital costs are the same at all plant locations. That is frequently not the case in investment planning problems and is not the case for the problem at hand. Rather the investment costs at each plant location are adjusted by a site factor, π_i. Thus, the expressions (8.16)–(8.19) become

$$\omega_{m1i} = \pi_i \hat{\omega}_m (0.5^{\beta_m - 1} - 1) \tag{8.20}$$

$$\omega_{m2i} = \pi_i \hat{\omega}_m \tag{8.21}$$

$$\omega_{m3i} = \pi_i n_{const} \hat{\omega}_m \tag{8.22}$$

$$\omega_{m4i} = \pi_i n_{max} (1.25) \hat{\omega}_m. \tag{8.23}$$

The values for the parameters π_i are given in table 8-5. The site factors for Fundidora and HYLSA are set slightly higher because both are in the midst of the city of Monterrey and land costs are relatively high. The factors for Tampico and Coatzacoalcos are set relatively high because both are green field sites, and all the required infrastructure would have to be installed.

The next two parameters in table 8-2 are the discount term δ_t and the capital recovery factor σ. The expression for the discount term is

$$\delta_t = (1 + \rho)^{1979 - \gamma_t} \tag{8.24}$$

Table 8-5. *Site Construction Cost Factors*

Site (i)	*Factor* (π_i)
AHMSA	1.0
Fundidora	1.1
SICARTSA	1.0
HYLSA	1.1
HYLSAP	1.0
Tampico	1.2
Coatzacoalcos	1.2

where $\rho =$ discount rate $= 10$ percent

$\gamma_t =$ midyear of period t.

For example,

$$\delta_{1984\text{-}86} = (1.10)^{1979-1985} = (1.10)^{-6} = 0.564. \quad (8.25)$$

The capital recovery factor is defined by the expression

$$\sigma = \frac{\rho(1+\rho)^{\zeta}}{(1+\rho)^{\zeta} - 1} \quad (8.26)$$

where $\zeta =$ equipment life in years.

This expression is derived in Kendrick and Stoutjesdijk (1978, pp. 47–49). For example, in the case at hand $\rho = 0.1$ and $\zeta = 20$ years, so

$$\sigma = \frac{(0.1)(1.1)^{20}}{(1.1)^{20} - 1} = 0.117. \quad (8.27)$$

The price parameters p are the next set in table 8-2. There are four sets of prices in the model: prices of mining products p^w, domestic prices of other raw material p^d, import prices p^v, and export prices p^e.

Consider first the prices of mining products. One of the most important economic realities for the Mexican steel industry is the likely increase in mining cost per ton for coal and iron ore as the known reserves are exhausted. Of course, it is possible that new and richer coal and iron ore deposits will be discovered. More likely, however, is a slow but sure increase in the cost of mining coal and iron ore with the depletion of existing reserves. Therefore, the model includes prices for coke (as a proxy for coal) and for pellets (as a proxy for iron ore) that are equated with production costs and rise as the existing reserves are used up in the coming years. This is done by assuming there are five qualities of reserves for both coal and iron ore, from $q = 1$ for the best quality to $q = 5$ for the worst quality. Coke produced from the highest quality coal is assumed to sell at the 1979 domestic price of \$52 per metric ton, and coke produced from the lowest quality coal is assumed to cost \$100 per metric ton. Similarly, it is assumed that pellets produced from the highest quality ores sell at the 1979 domestic price level of \$18.70 per metric ton and that pellets produced from the lowest quality ores will cost \$38 per metric ton. Then the price, or production cost, for coke and pellets produced from the intermediate quality levels of coal and iron ore respectively are assumed to be determined by the following exponential function:

$$p^{w}_{cqi} = p^{\text{low}}_{ci} + (p^{\text{high}}_{ci} - p^{\text{low}}_{ci})\left(\frac{\text{ord}(q) - 1}{\text{card}(Q) - 1}\right)^{\alpha} \qquad \begin{matrix} c \in CM \\ q \in Q \\ i \in IM \end{matrix} \tag{8.28}$$

where p^{w}_{cqi} = price of commodity c produced from coal or ores of quality q at mine i

p^{low}_{ci} = the domestic price in 1979 (a relatively low price) of commodity c at plant i

p^{high}_{ci} = the projected domestic price (a relatively high price) of commodity c in the future when it is produced with the lowest quality of ores

$\text{ord}(q)$ = the ordinal number associated with the quality level q: $\text{ord}(1) = 1$, $\text{ord}(2) = 2$, and so on

$\text{card}(Q)$ = the cardinal number associated with the number of elements in the set Q; that is, the number of different quality levels of coal and ore used in the model

$\alpha = 1.3$ = an exponential parameter representing the fact that the quality of coal and ores will decline slowly at first and then rapidly as the reserves are exhausted.

For example, the price of pellets produced from ores of the third quality level at the northern mines is estimated to be

$$\begin{aligned} p_{\text{pellets, 3, northern ore mines}} &= 18.7 + (38 - 18.7)\left(\frac{3-1}{5-1}\right)^{1.3} \\ &= 18.7 + 19.3\,(0.5)^{1.3} \\ &= \$26.5 \text{ per metric ton.} \end{aligned}$$

Table 8-6. *Prices of Commodities Produced at Mines*
(dollars per metric ton)

Quality level (q)	*Coke at Coahuila*	*Pellets from northern mines*	*Pellets from southern mines*
1	52.0	18.7	18.7
2	59.9	21.9	21.9
3	71.5	26.5	26.5
4	85.0	32.0	32.0
5	100.0	38.0	38.0

The prices of coke and pellets which result from these transformations are shown in table 8-6.

Consider next the prices of other domestic raw material in the model: electricity, scrap, and natural gas. The price of natural gas is discussed first since it is the most complicated of the three.

The domestic price of natural gas in Mexico in 1979 was $14 per thousand cubic meters (roughly 40 cents per thousand cubic feet—using 0.0283 cubic meters per cubic foot). In contrast, the international price of natural gas (as represented by the contract price between Mexico and the United States) was $128 per thousand cubic meters ($3.62 per thousand cubic feet).

It has been assumed in this model that the Mexican government will gradually let the domestic price of natural gas rise to the level of the international price. This has been represented in the model with the following relationship:

(8.29) $$p^d_{ct} = p^l_c + \left(\frac{p^u_c - p^t_c}{\text{steps}}\right)(\text{ord}(t) - 1) \qquad c = \text{natural gas} \quad t \in T$$

where p^d_{ct} = domestic price of commodity c in time period t
p^l_c = lower (or initial) price
p^h_c = higher (or international) price
steps = number of steps taken in changing the price from the lower to the higher level
ord(t) = the ordinal number associated with t: ord (1981–83) = 1, and ord (1984–86) = 2.

For example, with

p^l_{ng} = $14 per thousand cubic meters (lower natural gas price)

Table 8-7. *Domestic Price of Natural Gas*

	Domestic price	
Time period	*Dollars per thousand cubic meters*	*Dollars per thousand cubic feet*
1981–83	14.0	0.40
1984–86	42.5	1.20
1987–89	71.0	2.00
1990–92	99.5	2.81
1993–95	128.0	3.62

p^u_{ng} = \$128 per thousand cubic meters (international natural gas price)

steps = 4; that is, the price would be changed from the low to the high level in 4 steps.

Then the price of natural gas in the 1984–86 time period could be

$$p_{ng,1984\text{–}86} = 14 + \frac{128 - 14}{4}\ (2 - 1)$$

$$= 14 + 28.5 = \$42.50 \text{ per thousand cubic meters.}$$

The resulting time path for natural gas prices is shown in table 8-7.

Natural gas and electricity prices in Mexico are further complicated because some plants are close to natural gas supplies and some are distant, and the government has introduced an energy pricing scheme to promote industrialization at some locations. In an attempt to capture both phenomena, this version of the model employs site factors for natural gas prices. With these factors the natural gas and electricity prices are computed with the relationship

(8.30) $$p^d_{cit} = p^d_{ct}(1 - \pi^g_i). \qquad i \in I,\ c \in CENR,\ t \in T$$

The values for the location factor (π^g_i) are given in table 8-8. The base run in this case represents government policy rather than the real cost of resources. Thus, the fact that some plants are closer to natural gas supplies than others is ignored, and natural gas is priced in such a way as to encourage decentralization of industry. The sites for the older plants

Table 8-8. *Location Factor and Price of Natural Gas*
(dollars per thousand cubic meters)

Plant	*Location factor*	*1981–83*	*1984–86*	*1987–89*	*1990–92*	*1993–95*
AHMSA	1.00	14.0	42.5	71.0	99.5	128.0
Fundidora	1.00	14.0	42.5	71.0	99.5	128.0
SICARTSA	0.70	9.8	29.7	49.7	69.5	89.6
HYLSA	1.00	14.0	42.5	71.0	99.5	128.0
HYLSAP	1.00	14.0	42.5	71.0	99.5	128.0
Tampico	0.70	9.8	29.7	49.7	69.5	89.6
Coatzacoalcos	0.70	9.8	29.7	49.7	69.5	89.6

(AHMSA, Fundidora, HYLSA, and HYLSAP) are assigned factors of 1.0, and those for the newer plant at SICARTSA and the potential sites at Tampico and Coatzacoalcos are assigned factors of 0.7. Thus, there is a 30 percent reduction in actual gas and electricity prices to the plants at SICARTSA, Tampico, and Coatzacoalcos. After all these transformations, the resulting prices of natural gas used in the model are shown in table 8-8. Since the electricity price calculations are less complicated they are not shown explicitly.

Next consider the domestic prices of the other raw material, scrap steel. The model is developed in a manner that permits price projections over time, as was done with natural gas. Locational factors could also be used. However, neither of these modeling capabilities has yet been exploited, and it is assumed that this price remains constant over time and is the same at all plant locations.

(8.31) $$p^d_{cit} = \bar{p}^d_c \qquad c = \text{scrap steel},\; i \in I,\; t \in T$$

where p^d_{cit} = the domestic price of raw material c at plant i in time period t

$\bar{p}^d_c$ = the 1979 domestic price of commodity c

with $\bar{p}^d_{\text{scrap steel}}$ = \$105 per metric ton.

This leaves only two groups of prices to be discussed: import prices p^v, and export prices p^e. It is assumed that two raw materials and one final product can be imported and that one final product can be exported. The prices used for those imports and exports (in dollars per metric ton) are:

Table 8-9. *Interplant Rail Distances*
(kilometers)

	AHMSA	*Fundidora*	SICARTSA	HYLSA	HYLSAP	*Tampico*
Fundidora	218					
SICARTSA	1,416	1,322				
HYLSA	218	10	1,327			
HYLSAP	1,300	1,159	995	1,159		
Tampico	739	521	1,319	521	1,111	
Coatzacoalcos	1,850	1,756	1,638	1,756	671	1,702

	Import price	*Export price*
Coke	60	—
Pellets	40	—
Steel	150	140

The next set of parameters in table 8-2 is the transport costs. These costs are the same as for the small static model with two exceptions: the new sets of terms for the costs of interplant shipments and of shipments from mines to plants. The interplant shipment costs are:

$$\mu^n_{ii'} = \alpha^\mu + \beta^\mu \delta^p_{ii'} \tag{8.32}$$

where
$\mu^n_{ii'}$ = cost per metric ton for transporting intermediate products from plant i to plant i'
α^μ = loading and unloading cost per metric ton = \$2.48 per ton
β^μ = cost per ton mile = \$0.0084 per ton mile
$\delta^p_{ii'}$ = distance from plant i to plant i'

The interplant distances are given in table 8-9.

The mine-to-plant shipment costs are:

$$\mu^m_{i'i} = \alpha^\mu + \beta^\mu \delta^m_{i'i} \tag{8.33}$$

where
$\mu^m_{i'i}$ = cost per metric ton for transporting commodities from the mine i' to plant i
α^μ = loading and unloading cost per metric ton = \$2.48 per ton
β^μ = cost per ton mile = \$0.0084 per ton mile
$\delta^m_{i'i}$ = distance from mine i' to plant i

The distances from mines to plants are given in table 8-10.

Table 8-10. *Rail Distances from Mines to Plants*
(kilometers)

Plant	*Coahuila coal mines*	*Northern ore mines*	*Southern ore mines*
AHMSA	120	219	1,490
Fundidora	400	563	1,396
SICARTSA	1,500	1,613	0
HYLSA	400	563	1,396
HYLSAP	1,420	1,411	1,116
Tampico	900	1,048	1,338
Coatzacoalcos	2,100	2,195	1,500

The last set of parameters in table 8-2 is the reserves of mining products:

$\bar{w}_{cqi}$ = the reserves of quality level q of commodity c at mine i.

The commodities are coke and pellets. Obviously, there are no reserves of coke and pellets at the mines but rather of coal and iron ore. Therefore, it is necessary to obtain the data on coal and iron ore reserves and to transform those figures into the equivalent figures for reserves of coke and pellets. This is a slightly roundabout procedure. It would have been more straightforward to have added the commodities coal and iron ore to the model and to have introduced production activities for transforming the coal into coke and the iron ore into pellets. To keep the model as small as possible, however, this was not done. It is therefore necessary to think of the reserve figures as the amount of coke which could be produced by the existing coal reserves and the amount of pellets which could be produced with the existing iron ore reserves.

These reserves were computed by beginning with the measured, indicated, and inferred reserves of each mine as shown in table 8-11. There are 650 million tons of unwashed coal reserves at Coahuila. Since about 2 tons of unwashed coal are required to produce a ton of washed coal, the reserves may be thought of as 325 million tons of washed coal. And about 1.4 tons of washed coal are required to produce a ton of coke, so the positive coal reserves would be equivalent to 232 million tons of coke.

As discussed earlier, to keep the model small, the existing iron ore mines are aggregated into two mines, one in the north and one in the south. The iron ore reserves at La Perla, Cerro de Mercado, and

Table 8-11. *Coal and Iron Ore Reserves*
(million metric tons)

Mine	*Measured*	*Indicated*	*Inferred*
Coal			
Coahuila	650	40	15
Iron ore			
Peña Colorado	103.9	6.2	0.0
Las Truchas	105.6	11.6	0.0
La Perla	49.0	8.1	0.0
Cerro de Mercado	20.6	2.7	0.0
Hercules	61.0	5.4	25.0
La Chula	4.6	28.2	0.0
El Encino	14.7	0.0	0.0
El Violin	20.0	10.0	10.0
Total iron ore	379.4	72.2	35.0

Hercules were grouped together to provide a northern mine with 130.6 million tons of measured reserves. The reserves at Peña Colorado, Las Truchas, La Chula, El Encino, and El Violin were grouped together to form a southern mine with 248.8 million tons of measured reserves.

It was assumed that only 70 percent of the total measured reserves should be used during the time horizon covered by the model. Thus, 30 percent of the measured reserves would be set aside for use by the steel industry in the years after the period covered by the model. In the north $(130.6)(0.7) = 91$ million tons and in the south $(248.8)(0.7) = 174$ million tons of measured reserves would be available for use during the period covered by the model. Using a ratio of 1.5 tons of ore per ton of pellets provides roughly 60 million tons in the north and 115 million tons in the south of pellet-equivalent reserves for use during the time horizon covered by the model.

One final step was necessary in preparing the data for the model. It is assumed that there are several grades of ore in each mine and that the grades are exhausted one by one, moving from superior to inferior quality. This is modeled by using the set Q of quality levels. These quality levels are the integers 1 to 5, and the size (cardinality) of the set gives the number of grades used in the model. It is then assumed that the available reserves are evenly distributed among the grades so that

$$\bar{w}_{ci} = w_{ci}^{\text{res}}/\text{card}(Q) \tag{8.34}$$

where $\bar{w}_{ci}$ = reserves of each quality level of commodity c at plant i

w_{ci}^{res} = reserves of all quality levels at mine i
card (Q) = cardinality of the set Q, that is, the number of quality levels.

Constraints

All of the constraints for the small dynamic model will be displayed in this section, but only those aspects that differ substantially from the small static model will be discussed in detail.

The first set of constraints are material balance inequalities for the mines. They require that no more material be shipped from the mines than is produced. They are written as

MATERIAL BALANCE CONSTRAINTS FOR MINES

(8.35)
$$\sum_{q \in Q} w_{cqit} \geq \sum_{i' \in I} x_{cii't}^{m} \qquad \begin{array}{l} c \in CM \\ i \in IM \\ t \in T \end{array}$$

$$\begin{bmatrix} \textit{Production of all} \\ \textit{quality grades of} \\ \textit{commodity c at} \\ \textit{mine i in} \\ \textit{period t} \end{bmatrix} \geq \begin{bmatrix} \textit{Shipment of product} \\ \textit{c from mine i} \\ \textit{to all plants in} \\ \textit{period t} \end{bmatrix}$$

The material balance constraints for plants in this model differ substantially from those in the small static model—not because of the difference between static and dynamic models, but because of a different procedure for disaggregating commodities. In the small static model there are separate sets of contraints for final products, intermediate products, and raw material. This treatment was possible because the three sets are disjoint; that is, no commodity belonged to two different sets. If the sets had not been disjoint, a given commodity (say, sponge iron) might be both a final product and an intermediate product. Thus, it would be necessary to write constraints for final products, intermediate products, and products that are both final and intermediate. When other commodity sets, such as exported products or products shipped between plants, are added to the model the situation becomes even more complicated. It may be necessary to write six or eight types of material balance constraints.

An alternative approach is used here. A single set of material balance constraints for plants is used. Then it is left to the pattern of entries in the input-output matrix to determine which commodities are final products, intermediate products, raw material, and a combination of these. Restrictions are introduced on the summation signs as was done on the large static model in chapter 6. For example, the term in the material balance constraint which relates to interplant shipments is restricted to apply only to products that can be shipped between plants.

MATERIAL BALANCE CONSTRAINTS FOR STEEL MILLS

(8.36)

$$\sum_{p \in P} a_{cp} z_{pit} + u_{cit}\Big|_{c \in CR}$$

$$\begin{bmatrix} \textit{Inputs and outputs} \\ \textit{of commodity } c \textit{ at} \\ \textit{plant } i \end{bmatrix} + \begin{bmatrix} \textit{Domestic purchases} \\ \textit{of raw material } c \\ \textit{at plant } i \end{bmatrix}$$

$$+ \sum_{i' \in IM} x^{m}_{ci'it}\Big|_{c \in CM} + v^{r}_{cit}\Big|_{c \in CV}$$

$$+ \begin{bmatrix} \textit{Shipments from all mines to} \\ \textit{steel mill } i \textit{ of mine} \\ \textit{product } c \end{bmatrix} + \begin{bmatrix} \textit{Imports of commodity } c \\ \textit{to steel mill } i \end{bmatrix}$$

$$+ \sum_{i' \in I} x^{n}_{ci'it}\Big|_{c \in CI} \geq \sum_{i' \in I} x^{n}_{cii't}\Big|_{c \in CI}$$

$$+ \begin{bmatrix} \textit{Interplant shipments} \\ \textit{from plant } i' \textit{ to} \\ \textit{plant } i \end{bmatrix} \geq \begin{bmatrix} \textit{Interplant shipments} \\ \textit{from plant } i \textit{ to} \\ \textit{plant } i' \end{bmatrix}$$

$$+ \sum_{j \in J} x_{cijt}\Big|_{c \in CF} + e_{cit}\Big|_{c \in CE} \qquad \begin{matrix} c \in C \\ i \in I \\ t \in T \end{matrix}$$

$$+ \begin{bmatrix} \textit{Final product shipments} \\ \textit{from plant } i \textit{ to all} \\ \textit{markets} \end{bmatrix} + \begin{bmatrix} \textit{Exports from} \\ \textit{plant } i \end{bmatrix}$$

The next set of constraints is the capacity constraints. First, it is necessary to include a constraint on the total supply of each quality of mining commodities. It is assumed that there is a fixed supply of each quality of mining product. As discussed above, the mining products actually used in the model are coke and pellets, while the reserves used in the production of these commodities are coal and iron ore respectively. Therefore, the reserves of coal and iron ore are transformed into the equivalent reserves of coke and pellets and the constraints are written for coke and pellets.

CAPACITY CONSTRAINTS FOR MINING RESERVES

(8.37)
$$\theta\left(\sum_{t\in T} w_{cqit}\right) \le \bar{w}_{cqi} \qquad c\in CM,\ i\in IM,\ q\in Q$$

$$\begin{bmatrix}\textit{Number}\\ \textit{of years}\\ \textit{per time}\\ \textit{period}\end{bmatrix}\begin{bmatrix}\textit{Production of commodity}\\ \textit{c of quality level q}\\ \textit{at mine i in one year}\\ \textit{of each time period for}\\ \textit{all time periods}\end{bmatrix} \le \begin{bmatrix}\textit{Reserves of}\\ \textit{quality q}\\ \textit{of commodity}\\ \textit{c at}\\ \textit{mine i}\end{bmatrix}$$

Since the units of the w variables are average annual production in *each year* of the years in the time period, it is necessary to multiply the annual production times the number of years per time period in order to obtain the total production.

The next set of constraints is the capacity constraints for steel mills. They differ substantially from those in the small static model because they include additions to capacity.

CAPACITY CONSTRAINTS FOR STEEL MILLS

(8.38)
$$\sum_{p\in P} b_{mp} z_{pit} \le k_{mi} + \sum_{\substack{\tau\in T\\ \tau\le t}} h_{mi\tau}\Big|_{m\in ME} \qquad m\in M,\ i\in I,\ t\in T$$

$$\begin{bmatrix}\textit{Capacity}\\ \textit{utilized}\end{bmatrix} \le \begin{bmatrix}\textit{Initial}\\ \textit{capacity}\end{bmatrix} + \begin{bmatrix}\textit{Capacity added}\\ \textit{before or during}\\ \textit{time period t}\end{bmatrix}$$

The distinction between τ and t in this equation is noteworthy. As elsewhere in the model, t is the time period index. Although τ is also a time period index, it is used in (8.38) as the running index to sum over the periods prior to time period t. Thus, the summation on the right-hand side of (8.38) is over $\tau\in T$ and $\tau \le t$; that is, for the time periods before *and* including time period t. Consistent with this, the subscript on h is τ rather than t.

The next three constraints are for the investment variables h, s, and y. The first of these is like equation (8.7) discussed earlier.

DEFINITION OF h

(8.39)
$$h_{mit} = \sum_{g\in G} \bar{h}_{mg} s_{mgit} \qquad m\in ME,\ i\in I,\ t\in TE$$

$$\begin{bmatrix} \textit{Addition to} \\ \textit{capacity in} \\ \textit{expansion unit} \\ \textit{m at steel mill} \\ \textit{i in time} \\ \textit{period t} \end{bmatrix} = \begin{bmatrix} \textit{Convex combination} \\ \textit{of investment sizes} \\ \bar{h} \textit{ at grid points} \\ \textit{g for expansion} \\ \textit{unit m} \end{bmatrix}$$

Since the s variables are nonnegative and must sum to one (as indicated in the next constraint), the right-hand side of this constraint is said to be a "convex combination" of the investment-size grid points $\bar{h}$. The summation requirement on the s variables is written in combination with the zero-one requirement on the y variables to provide the constraint.

CONVEX COMBINATION CONSTRAINTS

$$(8.40) \qquad y_{mit} = \sum_{g \in G} s_{mgit} \qquad m \in ME,\ i \in I,\ t \in TE$$

In the mixed integer programming solutions to this problem the y variables are required to be either zero or one. If y is equal to one the s variables when summed over the grid points g must equal to one. This produces the convex combination. When the y variable is zero then the corresponding s variables must be zero.

When the problem was solved in the linear rather than the mixed integer form, the y variables were restricted to be less than or equal to one.

The market requirement constraint for this model is the same as for the small static model with the exception that time subscripts are added.

MARKET REQUIREMENT CONSTRAINTS

$$(8.41) \qquad \sum_{i \in I} x_{cijt} + v_{cjt} \geq d_{cjt} \qquad c \in CF,\ j \in J,\ t \in T$$

$$\begin{bmatrix} \textit{Shipment from all} \\ \textit{plants to} \\ \textit{market j} \end{bmatrix} + \begin{bmatrix} \textit{Imports to} \\ \textit{market j} \end{bmatrix} \geq \begin{bmatrix} \textit{Market} \\ \textit{requirement} \\ \textit{at market j} \end{bmatrix}$$

The next set of constraints is a set of upper bounds on total exports.

EXPORT UPPER BOUNDS

$$(8.42) \qquad \sum_{c \in CE} \sum_{i \in I} e_{cit} \leq e_t^u \qquad t \in T$$

$$\begin{bmatrix} \textit{Total exports in} \\ \textit{period } t \end{bmatrix} \leq \begin{bmatrix} \textit{Export upper} \\ \textit{bound} \end{bmatrix}$$

This constraint requires that exports of all products from all plants in each time period be less than or equal to an upper bound. It might be preferable to have an upper bound on the total exports of each type of product, but that level of detail is not used here.

Although the model includes increasing marginal cost for investment in each expansion unit of each steel mill in each time period, it does not represent the fact that since most steel mills are surrounded by oceans, mountains, and cities it is impossible to construct a steel mill of more than a certain size at each location. In this model that size was set at 30 million tons of iron (both pig iron and sponge iron). It would be desirable in future versions of the model to replace this constraint with a site-specific upper bound or an increasing investment cost when total capacity exceeds certain levels. The constraint used in this model is:

LIMIT ON IRON PRODUCTION AT EACH SITE

(8.43)
$$\sum_{p \in \{\text{pig iron, sponge iron}\}} z_{pit} \leq 30 \qquad i \in I \quad t \in T$$

NONNEGATIVITY CONSTRAINTS

(8.44)
$$w_{cqit}, z_{pit}, x^{f}_{cijt}, x^{m}_{ci'it}, x^{n}_{ci'it}, u_{cit}, v^{r}_{cit}, v_{cjt}, e_{cit}, h_{mit}, s_{mgit} \geq 0$$

BINARY VARIABLE

(8.45)
$$y_{mit} = 0 \quad \text{or} \quad 1$$

These constraints restrict the investment variables y to be zero or one.

Objective Function

The objective function of this model is identical to the function for the small static model with two exceptions: there is a summation for all time periods and an appropriate discounting procedure, and there is an additional term for investment cost.

OBJECTIVE FUNCTION

(8.46)
$$\phi = \sum_{t \in T} \delta_t \theta$$

$$\begin{bmatrix} \textit{Total} \\ \textit{cost} \end{bmatrix} = \begin{bmatrix} \textit{Discount} \\ \textit{factor} \end{bmatrix} \begin{bmatrix} \textit{Years per} \\ \textit{time period} \end{bmatrix}$$

$$(\phi_{\kappa t} + \phi_{\psi t} + \phi_{\lambda t} + \phi_{\pi t} - \phi_{\varepsilon t})$$

$$\left[\textit{Investment}\right] + \left[\begin{matrix}\textit{Raw}\\ \textit{material}\end{matrix}\right] + [\textit{Transport}] + [\textit{Imports}] - [\textit{Exports}]$$

The only unusual thing about this objective function is the θ parameter. Since the costs in all the cost component terms are on an annual basis and there are several years in each time period, it is necessary to multiply the annual cost by the number of years per time period. Of course, this arrangement embodies the assumption that the level of activity is the average for the years in the time period. This assumption is necessary to reduce the size of the model.

The investment cost term ϕ_κ is new and therefore worthy of special attention.

INVESTMENT COST

(8.47)
$$\phi_{\kappa t} = \sigma \sum_{\substack{\tau \in T \\ \tau \leq t}} \sum_{m \in ME} \sum_{g \in G} \sum_{i \in I} \bar{\omega}_{mgt} s_{mgi\tau} \qquad t \in T$$

$$\left[\begin{matrix}\textit{Investment}\\ \textit{cost}\end{matrix}\right] = \left[\begin{matrix}\textit{Capital}\\ \textit{recovery}\\ \textit{factor}\end{matrix}\right] \left[\begin{matrix}\textit{Convex combination of capital cost}\\ \textit{at grid points}\end{matrix}\right]$$

The summation for the running time index τ is over all time periods previous to and including time period t. This is required because investment costs are treated here like rental payments, and it is necessary to pay rent on all the investment done in previous periods and in the current period.

For the sake of completeness, all the other cost terms are listed here. The only changes in these terms from those in the small static model are the addition of a time subscript and the addition of one term to the raw material cost equality.

RAW MATERIAL COST

(8.48)
$$\phi_{\psi t} = \sum_{c \in CR} \sum_{i \in I} p^d_{cit} u_{cit} + \sum_{c \in CM} \sum_{q \in Q} \sum_{i \in IM} p^w_{cqi} w_{cqit} \qquad t \in T$$

$$\left[\begin{matrix}\textit{Raw}\\ \textit{material}\\ \textit{cost}\end{matrix}\right] = \left[\begin{matrix}\textit{Domestic}\\ \textit{purchases}\end{matrix}\right] + \left[\begin{matrix}\textit{Production}\\ \textit{of mining}\\ \textit{products}\end{matrix}\right]$$

TRANSPORT COST

(8.49)
$$\phi_{\lambda t} = \sum_{c \in CF} \sum_{i \in I} \sum_{j \in J} \mu^f_{ij} x_{cijt} + \sum_{c \in CF} \sum_{j \in J} \mu^v_j v_{cjt}$$

$$\begin{bmatrix}\textit{Transport}\\ \textit{cost}\end{bmatrix}=\begin{bmatrix}\textit{Final products to}\\ \textit{markets}\end{bmatrix}+\begin{bmatrix}\textit{Imports}\\ \textit{to markets}\end{bmatrix}$$

$$+\sum_{c\in CM}\sum_{i'\in IM}\sum_{i\in I}\mu^m_{i'i}x^m_{ci'it}+\sum_{c\in CE}\sum_{i\in I}\mu^e_i e_{cit}$$

$$+[\textit{Mines to steel mills}]+[\textit{Exports}]$$

$$+\sum_{c\in CI}\sum_{i\in I}\sum_{i'\in I}\mu^n_{ii'}x^n_{cii't}+\sum_{c\in CV}\sum_{i\in I}\mu^e_i v^r_{cit} \qquad t\in T$$

$$+\begin{bmatrix}\textit{Interplant shipments}\end{bmatrix}+\begin{bmatrix}\textit{Imports to}\\ \textit{plants}\end{bmatrix}$$

IMPORT COST

(8.50)

$$\phi_{\pi t}=\sum_{c\in CF}\sum_{j\in J}p^v_c v_{cjt}+\sum_{c\in CV}\sum_{i\in I}p^v_c v^r_{cit} \qquad t\in T$$

$$\begin{bmatrix}\textit{Import}\\ \textit{cost}\end{bmatrix}=\begin{bmatrix}\textit{Imports}\\ \textit{to}\\ \textit{markets}\end{bmatrix}+\begin{bmatrix}\textit{Imports}\\ \textit{to}\\ \textit{plants}\end{bmatrix}$$

EXPORT REVENUES

(8.51)

$$\phi_{et}=\sum_{c\in CE}\sum_{i\in I}p^e_c e_{cit} \qquad t\in T$$

$$\begin{bmatrix}\textit{Export}\\ \textit{revenues}\end{bmatrix}=\begin{bmatrix}\textit{Price}\\ \textit{of}\\ \textit{exports}\end{bmatrix}\begin{bmatrix}\textit{Exports}\end{bmatrix}$$

Appendix A. Notational Equivalence

Sets

	Mathematical	*GAMS*
Mines	*IM*	IM
Plants	*I*	I
Markets	*J*	J
Productive units	*M*	M
Productive units for expansion	*ME*	ME
Processes	*P*	P
Commodities	*C*	C
Raw material	*CR*	CR
Imported raw material	*CV*	CV
Mining products	*CM*	CM

Sets

	Mathematical	GAMS
Interplant shipments	CI	CI
Final products	CF	CF
Exportable commodities	CE	CE
Energy commodities	$CENR$	ENERGY
Time period	T	T
Expansion time periods	TE	TE
Quality levels	Q	Q
Grid points	G	G

Inequalities

	Mathematical	GAMS
Material balance constraints for mines	(8.35)	MBM
Material balance constraints for steel mills	(8.36)	MB
Capacity constraints for mining reserves	(8.37)	CCM
Capacity constraints for steel mills	(8.38)	CC
Definition of h	(8.39)	IH
Convex combination constraints	(8.40)	IC
Market requirement constraints	(8.41)	MR
Export upper bounds	(8.42)	EB
Limit on iron production at each site	(8.43)	ZB
Objective function	(8.46)	OBJ
Investment cost	(8.47)	AKAP
Raw material cost	(8.48)	APSI
Transport cost	(8.49)	ALAM
Import cost	(8.50)	API
Export revenues	(8.51)	AEPS

Variables

Mathematical	GAMS
z	Z
w	W
x^f	X
x^n	XN
x^m	XM
u	U
h	H
s	S
y	Y
v	V

(*continued*)

Variables (continued)

Mathematical	*GAMS*
v^r	VR
e	E
ϕ	PHI
ϕ_κ	PHIKAP
ϕ_ψ	PHIPSI
ϕ_λ	PHILAM
ϕ_π	PHIPI
ϕ_ε	PHIEPS

Appendix B. GAMS Statement of the Small Dynamic Model

A GAMS statement of the small dynamic model begins on the following page.

```
                                                                                        NEW MARGIN = 002-120
SET I     STEEL PLANTS           / AHMSA      ALTOS HORNOS - MONCLOVA
                                   FUNDIDORA  MONTERREY
                                   SICARTSA   LAZARO CARDENAS
                                   HYLSA      MONTERREY
                                   HYLSAP     PUEBLA
                                   TAMPICO    TAMPICO
                                   COATZA     COATZACOALCOS /

    IM    MINES                  / COAHUILA   COAL MINING REGION
                                   ORE-NORTH  NORTHERN IRON-ORE MINES
                                   ORE-SOUTH  SOUTHERN IRON-ORE MINES /

    J     MARKETS                / MEXICO-DF  MEXICO CITY
                                   MONTERREY  MONTERREY
                                   GUADALAJA  GUADALAJARA      /

    C     COMMODITIES            / PELLETS    IRON ORE PELLETS - TONS
                                   COKE       TONS
                                   NAT-GAS    NATURAL GAS - 1000 N CUBIC METERS
                                   ELECTRIC   ELECTRICITY - MWH
                                   SCRAP      TONS
                                   PIG-IRON   MOLTEN PIG IRON - TONS
                                   SPONGE     SPONGE IRON - TONS
                                   STEEL      TONS /

    CF(C) FINAL PRODUCTS         / STEEL /

    CE(C) EXPORT PRODUCT         / STEEL /

    CI(C) INTERMEDIATE PRODUCTS  / SPONGE /

    CR(C) RAW MATERIALS          / NAT-GAS, ELECTRIC, SCRAP /

    CM(C) MINING PRODUCTS        / COKE, PELLETS /

    CV(C) RAW MATERIALS IMPORTED / COKE, PELLETS /

    P     PROCESSES              / PIG-IRON   PIG IRON PRODUCTION FROM PELLETS
                                   SPONGE     SPONGE IRON PRODUCTION
                                   STEEL-OH   STEEL PRODUCTION IN OPEN HEARTH
                                   STEEL-EL   STEEL PRODUCTION IN ELECTRIC FURNACE
                                   STEEL-BOF  STEEL PRODUCTION IN BOF
                                   STEEL-BOFS STEEL PRODUCTION IN BOF WITH HIGH SCRAP /

    M     PRODUCTIVE UNITS       / BLAST-FURN BLAST FURNACES
                                   OPENHEARTH OPEN HEARTH FURNACES
                                   BOF        BASIC OXYGEN FURNACES
                                   DIRECT-RED DIRECT REDUCTION UNITS
                                   ELEC-ARC   ELECTRIC ARC FURNACES /

    ME(M) EXPANSION UNITS        / BLAST-FURN, BOF, DIRECT-RED, ELEC-ARC /
```

```
GAMS 1.0  M E X I C O - SMALL DYNAMIC  BASIC DEFINITIONS                     08/11/83    13.43.33.   PAGE    2
          SET DEFINITIONS


                T     TIME PERIODS           / 1981-83, 1984-86, 1987-89, 1990-92, 1993-95 /

                TE(T) EXPANSION PERIODS      / 1984-86, 1987-89, 1990-92, 1993-95 /

                ENERGY(CR)                   / NAT-GAS, ELECTRIC /

                Q     COST LEVELS            / 1*5 /

                G     INVESTMENT FUNCTION SEGMENTS / 1*4 /

                ALIAS (T,TAU),(I,IP),(TE,TAUE);

          SCALAR    BASEYEAR   BASE YEAR             / 1979 /
                    THETA      YEARS PER TIME PERIOD /    3 /
          PARAMETER MIDYEAR(T) PERIOD MID-YEARS
                    TS(T,TAU)  TIME SUMMATION MATRIX;

          MIDYEAR(T) = BASEYEAR + THETA*ORD(T) ;
          TS(TE,TAUE)$(ORD(TAUE) LE ORD(TE)) = 1 ;

          DISPLAY  MIDYEAR,TS;
```

```
        TABLE  A(C,P)  INPUT-OUTPUT COEFFICIENTS

             PIG-IRON  SPONGE  STEEL-OH  STEEL-EL  STEEL-BOF  STEEL-BOFS

 PELLETS      -1.58     -1.38
 COKE          -.63
 NAT-GAS                 -.38
 ELECTRIC                                 -.68
 SCRAP                            -.33               -.12       -.25
 PIG-IRON      1.0                -.77               -.95      -.82
 SPONGE                  1.0               -1.09
 STEEL                            1.0       1.0       1.0       1.0

* TWO IO COEFFICIENTS WERE CHANGED ACCORDING TO SUGGESTIONS BY HYLS
*
*   NAT-GAS,SPONGE   FROM -.57 TO -.38
*   ELECTRIC,STEEL-EL  FROM -.58 TO -.68
*
* THESE FIGURES CORRESPOND TO SUMMER 1980 HYLSAP PERFORMANCE


         TABLE  B(M,P)   CAPACITY UTILIZATION

             PIG-IRON  SPONGE  STEEL-OH  STEEL-EL  STEEL-BOF  STEEL-BOFS

 BLAST-FURN     1.0
 OPENHEARTH                         1.0
 BOF                                                    1.0       1.0
 DIRECT-RED               1.0
 ELEC-ARC                                    1.0


         TABLE  K(M,I)  CAPACITIES OF PRODUCTIVE UNITS (MILL TONS PER YEAR)

             AHMSA  FUNDIDORA  SICARTSA  HYLSA  HYLSAP

 BLAST-FURN   3.25    1.40       1.10
 OPENHEARTH   1.50     .85
 BOF          2.07    1.50       1.30
 DIRECT-RED                                .98    1.00
 ELEC-ARC                                 1.13     .56

                                                                    NEW MARGIN = 002-072
        TABLE KM(CM,IM,*)  MINING CAPACITY DATA

                      P-LOW     P-HIGH    WMAX     EXPO             P-LOW : LOW PRICE            (US$ PER TON)
                                                                    P-HIGH: HIGH PRICE           (US$ PER TON)
 COKE.COAHUILA          52        100      230      1.3             WMAX  : MAXIMUM MINE CAPACITY (MILLION TONS)
 PELLETS.ORE-NORTH     18.7        38       60      1.3
 PELLETS.ORE-SOUTH     18.7        38      115      1.3
                                                                    NEW MARGIN = 002-120

```

```
GAMS 1.0  M E X I C O - SMALL DYNAMIC  BASIC DEFINITIONS                          08/11/83     13.43.33.    PAGE     4
          TECHNOLOGY DATA

  PARAMETER    WBAR(CM,IM)    STOCK OF MINE PRODUCTS (MILLION TONS)
               PW(CM,Q,IM)    PURCHASE PRICE OF MINE PRODUCTS (US $ PER TON);

  WBAR(CM,IM) = KM(CM,IM,"WMAX")/CARD(Q);
  PW(CM,Q,IM)$KM(CM,IM,"WMAX") = KM(CM,IM,"P-LOW") + (KM(CM,IM,"P-HIGH")-KM(CM,IM,"P-LOW"))*
                                                   ((ORD(Q)-1)/(CARD(Q)-1))**KM(CM,IM,"EXPO");

DISPLAY WBAR,PW;

  SCALAR       DT          TOTAL DEMAND FOR FINAL GOODS IN 1979 (MILLION TONS)   /  5.2 /
               RSE         RAW STEEL EQUIVALENCE (PERCENT)                       / 40   /
               GD          ANNUAL GROWTH RATE OF DEMAND (PERCENT)                / 10   /
  PARAMETER    DD(J)       DISTRIBUTION OF DEMAND                      / MEXICO-DF .55, MONTERREY .3, GUADALAJA .15 /
               D(CF,J,T) DEMAND FOR STEEL (MILL TPY)
               EU(T)       EXPORT BOUND: UPPER ;

  D("STEEL",J,T)       = DT * (1 + RSE/100) * DD(J) * (1 + GD/100)**(MIDYEAR(T)-BASEYEAR);
  EU(T) = .2;

DISPLAY  D;
```

```
        TABLE RD(*,*)  RAIL DISTANCES FROM PLANTS TO MARKETS (KM)

                 MEXICO-DF  MONTERREY  GUADALAJA    EXPORT

AHMSA               1204        218        1125         739
FUNDIDORA           1017                   1030         521
SICARTSA             819       1305         704
HYLSA               1017                   1030         521
HYLSAP               185       1085         760         315
TAMPICO              941        521         995
COATZA               900       1756        1100
IMPORT               428        521         300


       TABLE RI(I,IP)  INTERPLANT RAIL DISTANCES (KM)

            AHMSA  FUNDIDORA  SICARTSA  HYLSA  HYLSAP  TAMPICO  COATZA

FUNDIDORA    218
SICARTSA    1416     1322
HYLSA        218       10        1327
HYLSAP      1300     1159         995    1159
TAMPICO      739      521        1319     521   1111
COATZA      1850     1756        1638    1756    671      1702


             TABLE RM(IM,I)  RAIL DISTANCES FROM MINES TO PLANTS (KM)

             AHMSA  FUNDIDORA  SICARTSA  HYLSA  HYLSAP  TAMPICO  COATZA

COAHUILA       120      400        1500    400    1420      900     2100
ORE-NORTH      219      563        1613    563    1411     1048     2195
ORE-SOUTH     1490     1396                1396    1116     1338     1500

* HERCULES USED AS THE CENTER OF THE NORHERN ORE DISTRICT
* PENA COLORADO USED AS THE CENTER FOR THE SOUTHERN ORE DISTRICT
* EXCEPT SICARTSA WHICH USES LAS TRUCHAS DISTANCES

  PARAMETER  MUF(I,J)  TRANSPORT COST: FINAL PRODUCTS       (US $ PER TON)
             MUN(I,IP) TRANSPORT COST: INTERPLANT SHIPMENTS (US $ PER TON)
             MUM(IM,I) TRANSPORT COST: MINE TO PLANT        (US $ PER TON)
             MUV(J)    TRANSPORT COST: IMPORTS              (US $ PER TON)
             MUE(I)    TRANSPORT COST: EXPORTS              (US $ PER TON);

       RI(I,IP) = MAX(RI(I,IP),RI(IP,I));
       MUF(I,J) = ( 2.48 + .0084*RD(I,J))       $RD(I,J);
       MUN(I,IP)= ( 2.48 + .0084*RI(I,IP))      $RI(I,IP);
       MUM(IM,I)= ( 2.48 + .0084*RM(IM,I))      $RM(IM,I);
       MUV(J)   = ( 2.48 + .0084*RD("IMPORT",J))$RD("IMPORT",J);
       MUE(I)   = ( 2.48 + .0084*RD(I,"EXPORT"))$RD(I,"EXPORT");

DISPLAY  MUF,MUN,MUM,MUV,MUE;
```

```
GAMS 1.0  M E X I C O - SMALL DYNAMIC  BASIC DEFINITIONS                      08/11/83    13.43.33.   PAGE    6
          INVESTMENT AND PRICE DATA

                                                                                          NEW MARGIN = 002-072
     TABLE INV(ME,*)  INVESTMENT COST TABLE

           HHAT  PHIHAT   BETA                                                    HHAT  : ECONOMIES OF SCALE SIZE (MILL TONS/YR)
                                                                                  PHIHAT: COST OF PLANT OF SIZE HHAT  (MILL US$)
BLAST-FURN  1.5    250     .6                                                     BETA  : SCALE FACTOR: PHIHAT = XX*HHAT**BETA
BOF         1.5    120     .6
DIRECT-RED   .8    100     .6                                                      ACCORDING TO R.J. KUHL, STEEL TIMES INTERN
ELEC-ARC     .5     42     .6                                                                                JUNE 1979

                                                                                          NEW MARGIN = 002-120

    PARAMETER SITE(I)        SITE FACTOR / (FUNDIDORA,HYLSA) 1.1, (SICARTSA,HYLSAP,AHMSA) 1, (TAMPICO,COATZA) 1.2 /
              OMEGA(ME,G,I) PLANT COST AT SEGMENT                (MILLION US$)
              SB(ME,G)       SEGMENT SIZE             (MILLION TONS PER YEAR)
              ZETA           LIFE OF PRODUCTIVE UNIT                      (YEARS)
              RHO            DISCOUNT RATE
              SIGMA          CAPITAL RECOVERY FACTOR
              DELTA(T)       DISCOUNT FACTOR ;

   INV(ME,"FIXED")     = INV(ME,"PHIHAT")*(.5**(INV(ME,"BETA")-1)-1);

   OMEGA(ME,"1",I)     =  INV(ME,"FIXED")*SITE(I)     ; SB(ME,"1") = 0                ;
   OMEGA(ME,"2",I)     =  INV(ME,"PHIHAT")*SITE(I)    ; SB(ME,"2") = INV(ME,"HHAT") ;
   OMEGA(ME,"3",I)     =  OMEGA(ME,"2",I)*3           ; SB(ME,"3") = SB(ME,"2")*3    ;
   OMEGA(ME,"4",I)     =  OMEGA(ME,"2",I)*6*1.25      ; SB(ME,"4") = SB(ME,"2")*6    ;

   ZETA = 20; RHO = .1; SIGMA = RHO/(1-(1+RHO)**(-ZETA));
   DELTA(T) = (1+RHO)**(BASEYEAR-MIDYEAR(T));


 SCALAR     RLEV       RESOURCE LEVEL                                   /  1 /
            IRON       IRON PRODUCTION BOUND (MILLION TONS PER YEAR)    / 30 /
 PARAMETER  PD(CR,I,T) DOMESTIC PRICES
            REGION(I)  LOCATIONS WITH ENERGY SUBSIDY                    / (COATZA,SICARTSA,TAMPICO)  .3 /
            PDB(CR)    BASE PRICE OF DOMESTIC MATERIALS (PESOS PER TON) / NAT-GAS 14, ELECTRIC 26, SCRAP 105 /
            PV(C)      IMPORT PRICES                      (US$ PER TON) / COKE    60, PELLETS  40, STEEL 150 /
            PE(CE)     EXPORT PRICES                      (US$ PER TON) / STEEL  140                          / ;

PD(CR,I,T)        = PDB(CR);
PD("NAT-GAS",I,T) = MIN(128, PDB("NAT-GAS") + (128-PDB("NAT-GAS"))/4*(ORD(T)-1));
PD(ENERGY,I,T)    = PD(ENERGY,I,T)*(1-REGION(I));

DISPLAY  OMEGA,SIGMA,DELTA,INV,SB,PD,IRON,RLEV;
```

```
VARIABLES  Z(P,I,T)          PROCESS LEVEL                              (MILL TPY)
           W(CM,Q,IM,T)      PRODUCTION OF MINING PRODUCTS              (MILL TPY)
           X(C,I,J,T)        SHIPMENT OF FINAL PRODUCTS                 (MILL TPY)
           XN(C,I,IP,T)      INTERPLANT SHIPMENTS                       (MILL TPY)
           XM(C,IM,I,T)      SHIPMENT OF MINING PRODUCTS                (MILL TPY)
           U(C,I,T)          PURCHASE OF DOMESTIC MATERIALS       (MILL UNITS PER YEAR)
           H(M,I,T)          CAPACITY EXPANSION                         (MILL TPY)
           S(ME,G,I,T)       INVESTMENT FUNCTION SEGMENT
           Y(ME,I,TE)        BINARY VARIABLE
           V(CF,J,T)         IMPORTS                                    (MILL TPY)
           VR(C,I,T)         IMPORTS OF RAW MATERIALS                   (MILL TPY)
           E(C,I,T)          EXPORTS                                    (MILL TPY)

           PHI               TOTAL COST (DISCOUNTED)                    (MILL US$)
           PHIKAP(T)         CAPITAL COST                               (MILL US$)
           PHIPSI(T)         RAW MATERIAL COST                          (MILL US$)
           PHILAM(T)         TRANSPORT COST                             (MILL US$)
           PHIPI(T)          IMPORT COST                                (MILL US$)
           PHIEPS(T)         EXPORT REVENUE                             (MILL US$)

POSITIVE VARIABLES Z,W,X,XN,XM,U,H,S,V,VR,E; BINARY VARIABLE Y;

EQUATIONS  MB(C,I,T)         MATERIAL BALANCE: STEEL PLANTS             (MILL TPY)
           MBM(CM,IM,T)      MATERIAL BALANCE: MINES                    (MILL TPY)
           CC(M,I,T)         CAPACITY CONSTRAINT: STEEL PLANTS          (MILL TPY)
           CCM(CM,Q,IM)      CAPACITY CONSTRAINT: MINES                 (MILL TPY)
           IH(ME,I,TE)       DEFINITION OF H
           IC(ME,I,TE)       CONVEX COMBINATION AND 0-1 CONSTR
           MR(CF,J,T)        MARKET REQUIREMENTS                        (MILL TPY)
           EB(T)             EXPORT BOUNDS                              (MILL TPY)
           ZB(I,T)           LIMIT ON STEEL PRODUCTION                  (MILL TPY)

           OBJ               ACCOUNTING: TOTAL DISCOUNTED COST          (MILL US$)
           AKAP(T)           ACCOUNTING: INVESTMENT COST CHARGES        (MILL US$)
           APSI(T)           ACCOUNTING: RAW MATERIALS                  (MILL US$)
           ALAM(T)           ACCOUNTING: TRANSPORT                      (MILL US$)
           API(T)            ACCOUNTING: IMPORT COST                    (MILL US$)
           AEPS(T)           ACCOUNTING: EXPORT REVENUE                 (MILL US$);
```

```
MB(C,I,T)..     SUM(P, A(C,P)*Z(P,I,T)) + U(C,I,T)$CR(C) + SUM(IM, XM(C,IM,I,T))$CM(C) + VR(C,I,T)$CV(C)
                     + SUM(IP, XN(C,IP,I,T))$CI(C) =G= SUM(IP, XN(C,I,IP,T))$CI(C) + SUM(J, X(C,I,J,T))$CF(C) + E(C,I,T)$CE(C);

MBM(CM,IM,T).. SUM(Q, W(CM,Q,IM,T)) =G= SUM(I, XM(CM,IM,I,T));

CC(M,I,T)..     SUM(P, B(M,P)*Z(P,I,T)) =L= K(M,I) + SUM(TAU$TS(T,TAU), H(M,I,TAU)$ME(M));

CCM(CM,Q,IM).. SUM(T, W(CM,Q,IM,T)) =L= RLEV*WBAR(CM,IM)/THETA;

IH(ME,I,TE)..  H(ME,I,TE) =E= SUM(G, SB(ME,G)*S(ME,G,I,TE));

IC(ME,I,TE)..  Y(ME,I,TE) =E= SUM(G, S(ME,G,I,TE));

MR(CF,J,T)..    SUM(I, X(CF,I,J,T)) + V(CF,J,T) =G= D(CF,J,T);

EB(T)..         SUM((CE,I), E(CE,I,T)) =L= EU(T);


ZB(I,T)..       Z("PIG-IRON",I,T) + Z("SPONGE",I,T) =L= IRON;

OBJ..           PHI =E= SUM(T, DELTA(T)*THETA*(PHIKAP(T) + PHIPSI(T) + PHILAM(T) + PHIPI(T) - PHIEPS(T)));

AKAP(T)..       PHIKAP(T) =E= SIGMA*SUM(TAU$TS(T,TAU), SUM((ME,G,I), OMEGA(ME,G,I)*S(ME,G,I,TAU)));

APSI(T)..       PHIPSI(T) =E= SUM((CR,I), PD(CR,I,T)*U(CR,I,T)) + SUM((CM,Q,IM), PW(CM,Q,IM)*W(CM,Q,IM,T));
```

```
ALAM(T)..       PHILAM(T) =E= SUM(CF, SUM((I,J), MUF(I,J)*X(CF,I,J,T)) + SUM(J, MUV(J)*V(CF,J,T)))
                          + SUM((CM,IM,I), MUM(IM,I)*XM(CM,IM,I,T)) + SUM((CE,I), MUE(I)*E(CE,I,T))
                          + SUM((CI,I,IP), MUN(I,IP)*XN(CI,I,IP,T)) + SUM((CV,I), MUE(I)*VR(CV,I,T));

API(T)..        PHIPI(T) =E= SUM((CF,J), PV(CF)*V(CF,J,T)) + SUM((CV,I), PV(CV)*VR(CV,I,T));

AEPS(T)..       PHIEPS(T) =E= SUM((CE,I), PE(CE)*E(CE,I,T));

MODEL MEXSD SMALL DYNAMIC STEEL PROBLEM / ALL / ;

SOLVE MEXSD MINIMIZING PHI USING RMIP;
```

```
GAMS 1.0  M E X I C O - SMALL DYNAMIC  BASIC DEFINITIONS                                    08/11/83     13.43.33.    PAGE   10
          REFERENCE MAP OF VARIABLES


VARIABLES    TYPE     REFERENCES

A            PARAM           REF        289   DEFINED        78        DCL        78
AEPS         EQU         DEFINED        321       DCL       286
AKAP         EQU         DEFINED        311       DCL       282
ALAM         EQU         DEFINED        315       DCL       284
API          EQU         DEFINED        319       DCL       285
APSI         EQU         DEFINED        313       DCL       283
B            PARAM           REF        294   DEFINED        99        DCL        99
BASEYEAR     PARAM           REF         73       146       232    DEFINED        68       DCL        68
C            SET             REF         29        31        33         35        37        39        78       240       251
                             252        253       254       259        260       271     7*289     8*290   DEFINED        20
                         CONTROL        289       DCL        20
CC           EQU         DEFINED        294       DCL       273
CCM          EQU         DEFINED        296       DCL       274
CE           SET             REF        241       290       304        316     2*321   DEFINED        31   CONTROL       304
                             316        321       DCL        31
CF           SET             REF        143       258       277        290     3*302     2*315     2*319   DEFINED        29
                         CONTROL        302       315       319        DCL        29
CI           SET             REF      2*290       317   DEFINED         33   CONTROL       317       DCL        33
CM           SET             REF        121       130       131        133     4*134       135       250       272       274
                             289      2*292     2*296     2*313        316   DEFINED        37   CONTROL       133       134
                             292        296       313       316        DCL        37
CR           SET             REF         60       237       239        243       289     2*313   DEFINED        35   CONTROL
                             243        313       DCL        35
CV           SET             REF        289       317     2*319    DEFINED        39   CONTROL       317       319       DCL
                              39
D            PARAM           REF        149       302   DEFINED        146       DCL       143
DD           PARAM           REF        146   DEFINED       142        DCL       142
DELTA        PARAM           REF        247       309   DEFINED        232       DCL       222
DT           PARAM           REF        146   DEFINED       139        DCL       139
E            VAR             REF        269       290       304        316       321       DCL       260
EB           EQU         DEFINED        304       DCL       278
ENERGY       SET             REF        245   DEFINED        60    CONTROL       245       DCL        60
EU           PARAM           REF        304   DEFINED       147        DCL       144
G            SET             REF        217       218       256      2*298       300     2*311   DEFINED        64   CONTROL
                             298        300       311       DCL         64
GD           PARAM           REF        146   DEFINED       141        DCL       141
H            VAR             REF        269       294       298        DCL       255
I            SET             REF         66       110       165        177       189       190       191       193     2*195
                           2*196      2*197     2*198     2*200        216       217       226       227       228       229
                             237        238     2*245       249        251       252       253       254       255       256
                             257        259       260       271        273       275       276       279     4*289     4*290
                             292      3*294     2*298     2*300        302       304     2*307     2*311     2*313     2*315
                           4*316      4*317       319       321    DEFINED         4   CONTROL       195       196       197
                             198        200       226       227        228       229       243       244       245       289
                             292        294       298       300        302       304       307       311       313       315
                           2*316      2*317       319       321        DCL         4
IC           EQU         DEFINED        300       DCL       276
IH           EQU         DEFINED        298       DCL       275
IM           SET             REF        121       130       131        133     4*134       135       177       191     2*198
                             250        253       272       274        289     2*292     2*296     2*313     2*316   DEFINED
```

```
VARIABLES    TYPE     REFERENCES

                            12   CONTROL       133       134       198       289       292       296       313       316
                           DCL        12
INV          PARAM         REF     2*224       226     2*227       247   DEFINED       205       224       DCL       205
IP           SET           REF       165       190     2*195     2*197       252     2*290     2*317   CONTROL       195
                           197     2*290       317       DCL        66
IRON         PARAM         REF       247       307   DEFINED       236       DCL       236
J            SET           REF       142       143       146       189       192     2*196     2*199       251       258
                           277       290     3*302     4*315       319   DEFINED        16   CONTROL       146       196
                           199       290       302     2*315       319       DCL        16
K            PARAM         REF       294   DEFINED       110       DCL       110
KM           PARAM         REF       133     4*134       135   DEFINED       121       DCL       121
M            SET           REF        54        99       110       255       273     4*294   DEFINED        48   CONTROL
                           294       DCL        48
MAX          FUNCT         REF       195
MB           EQU       DEFINED       289       DCL       271
MBM          EQU       DEFINED       292       DCL       272
ME           SET           REF       205       217       218     2*224       226     2*227     2*228     2*229       256
                           257       275       276       294     3*298     2*300     2*311   DEFINED        54   CONTROL
                           224     2*226     2*227     2*228     2*229       298       300       311       DCL        54
MEXSD        MODEL         REF       325   DEFINED       323       DCL       323
MIDYEAR      PARAM         REF        76       146       232   DEFINED        73       DCL        70
MIN          FUNCT         REF       244
MR           EQU       DEFINED       302       DCL       277
MUE          PARAM         REF       202       316       317   DEFINED       200       DCL       193
MUF          PARAM         REF       202       315   DEFINED       196       DCL       189
MUM          PARAM         REF       202       316   DEFINED       198       DCL       191
MUN          PARAM         REF       202       317   DEFINED       197       DCL       190
MUV          PARAM         REF       202       315   DEFINED       199       DCL       192
OBJ          EQU       DEFINED       309       DCL       281
OMEGA        PARAM         REF       228       229       247       311   DEFINED       226       227       228       229
                           DCL       217
P            SET           REF        78        99       249     2*289     2*294   DEFINED        41   CONTROL       289
                           294       DCL        41
PD           PARAM         REF       245       247       313   DEFINED       243       244       245       DCL       237
PDB          PARAM         REF       243     2*244   DEFINED       239       DCL       239
PE           PARAM         REF       321   DEFINED       241       DCL       241
PHI          VAR           REF       309       325       DCL       262
PHIEPS       VAR           REF       309       321       DCL       267
PHIKAP       VAR           REF       309       311       DCL       263
PHILAM       VAR           REF       309       315       DCL       265
PHIPI        VAR           REF       309       319       DCL       266
PHIPSI       VAR           REF       309       313       DCL       264
PV           PARAM         REF     2*319   DEFINED       240       DCL       240
PW           PARAM         REF       137       313   DEFINED       134       DCL       131
Q            SET           REF       131       133     2*135       250       274       292       296     2*313   DEFINED
                            62   CONTROL       134       292       296       313       DCL        62
RD           PARAM         REF     2*196     2*199     2*200   DEFINED       151       DCL       151
REGION       PARAM         REF       245   DEFINED       238       DCL       238
RHO          PARAM         REF     2*231       232   DEFINED       231       DCL       220
RI           PARAM         REF     2*195     2*197   DEFINED       165       195       DCL       165
```

```
           REFERENCE MAP OF VARIABLES

VARIABLES  TYPE    REFERENCES

RLEV       PARAM        REF      247      296  DEFINED      235      DCL      235
RM         PARAM        REF    2*198  DEFINED      177      DCL      177
RSE        PARAM        REF      146  DEFINED      140      DCL      140
S          VAR          REF      269      298      300      311      DCL      256
SB         PARAM        REF      228      229      247      298  DEFINED      226      227      228      229
                        DCL      218
SIGMA      PARAM        REF      247      311  DEFINED      231      DCL      221
SITE       PARAM        REF      226      227  DEFINED      216      DCL      216
T          SET          REF       58       66       70       71       73      143      144      146      222
                        232      237      244      245      249      250      251      252      253      254
                        255      256      258      259      260      263      264      265      266      267
                        271      272      273      277      278      279      282      283      284      285
                        286    4*289    4*290    2*292    2*294      296    3*302    2*304    2*307    6*309
                      2*311    4*313    3*315    2*316    2*317    3*319    2*321  DEFINED       56  CONTROL
                         73      146      147      232      243      244      245      289      292      294
                        296      302      304      307      309      311      313      315      319      321
                        DCL       56
TAU        SET          REF       71    2*294    2*311  CONTROL      294      311      DCL       66
TAUE       SET          REF       74  CONTROL       74      DCL       66
TE         SET          REF       66       74      257      275      276    2*298    2*300  DEFINED       58
                    CONTROL       74      298      300      DCL       58
THETA      PARAM        REF       73      296      309  DEFINED       69      DCL       69
TS         PARAM        REF       76      294      311  DEFINED       74      DCL       71
U          VAR          REF      269      289      313      DCL      254
V          VAR          REF      269      302      315      319      DCL      258
VR         VAR          REF      269      289      317      319      DCL      259
W          VAR          REF      269      292      296      313      DCL      250
WBAR       PARAM        REF      137      296  DEFINED      133      DCL      130
X          VAR          REF      269      290      302      315      DCL      251
XM         VAR          REF      269      289      292      316      DCL      253
XN         VAR          REF      269    2*290      317      DCL      252
Y          VAR          REF      269      300      DCL      257
Z          VAR          REF      269      289      294    2*307      DCL      249
ZB         EQU      DEFINED      307      DCL      279
ZETA       PARAM        REF      231  DEFINED      231      DCL      219

SETS

  C          COMMODITIES
  CE         EXPORT PRODUCT
  CF         FINAL PRODUCTS
  CI         INTERMEDIATE PRODUCTS
  CM         MINING PRODUCTS
  CR         RAW MATERIALS
  CV         RAW MATERIALS IMPORTED
  ENERGY
  G          INVESTMENT FUNCTION SEGMENTS
  I          STEEL PLANTS
  IM         MINES
  IP         ALIAS FOR I
```

```
SETS

  J          MARKETS
  M          PRODUCTIVE UNITS
  ME         EXPANSION UNITS
  P          PROCESSES
  Q          COST LEVELS
  T          TIME PERIODS
  TAU        ALIAS FOR T
  TAUE       ALIAS FOR TE
  TE         EXPANSION PERIODS

PARAMETERS

  A          INPUT-OUTPUT COEFFICIENTS
  B          CAPACITY UTILIZATION
  BASEYEAR   BASE YEAR
  D          DEMAND FOR STEEL (MILL TPY)
  DD         DISTRIBUTION OF DEMAND
  DELTA      DISCOUNT FACTOR
  DT         TOTAL DEMAND FOR FINAL GOODS IN 1979 (MILLION TONS)
  EU         EXPORT BOUND: UPPER
  GD         ANNUAL GROWTH RATE OF DEMAND (PERCENT)
  INV        INVESTMENT COST TABLE
  IRON       IRON PRODUCTION BOUND (MILLION TONS PER YEAR)
  K          CAPACITIES OF PRODUCTIVE UNITS (MILL TONS PER YEAR)
  KM         MINING CAPACITY DATA
  MIDYEAR    PERIOD MID-YEARS
  MUE        TRANSPORT COST: EXPORTS              (US $ PER TON)
  MUF        TRANSPORT COST: FINAL PRODUCTS       (US $ PER TON)
  MUM        TRANSPORT COST: MINE TO PLANT        (US $ PER TON)
  MUN        TRANSPORT COST: INTERPLANT SHIPMENTS (US $ PER TON)
  MUV        TRANSPORT COST: IMPORTS              (US $ PER TON)
  OMEGA      PLANT COST AT SEGMENT              (MILLION US$)
  PD         DOMESTIC PRICES
  PDB        BASE PRICE OF DOMESTIC MATERIALS (PESOS PER TON)
  PE         EXPORT PRICES                      (US$ PER TON)
  PV         IMPORT PRICES                      (US$ PER TON)
  PW         PURCHASE PRICE OF MINE PRODUCTS (US $ PER TON)
  RD         RAIL DISTANCES FROM PLANTS TO MARKETS (KM)
  REGION     LOCATIONS WITH ENERGY SUBSIDY
  RHO        DISCOUNT RATE
  RI         INTERPLANT RAIL DISTANCES (KM)
  RLEV       RESOURCE LEVEL
  RM         RAIL DISTANCES FROM MINES TO PLANTS (KM)
  RSE        RAW STEEL EQUIVALENCE (PERCENT)
  SB         SEGMENT SIZE              (MILLION TONS PER YEAR)
  SIGMA      CAPITAL RECOVERY FACTOR
  SITE       SITE FACTOR
  THETA      YEARS PER TIME PERIOD
  TS         TIME SUMMATION MATRIX
  WBAR       STOCK OF MINE PRODUCTS (MILLION TONS)
```

```
GAMS 1.0  M E X I C O - SMALL DYNAMIC  BASIC DEFINITIONS                08/11/83    13.43.33.   PAGE   14
          REFERENCE MAP OF VARIABLES

PARAMETERS

  ZETA        LIFE OF PRODUCTIVE UNIT                (YEARS)

VARIABLES

  E           EXPORTS                                          (MILL TPY)
  H           CAPACITY EXPANSION                               (MILL TPY)
  PHI         TOTAL COST (DISCOUNTED)                          (MILL US$)
  PHIEPS      EXPORT REVENUE                                   (MILL US$)
  PHIKAP      CAPITAL COST                                     (MILL US$)
  PHILAM      TRANSPORT COST                                   (MILL US$)
  PHIPI       IMPORT COST                                      (MILL US$)
  PHIPSI      RAW MATERIAL COST                                (MILL US$)
  S           INVESTMENT FUNCTION SEGMENT
  U           PURCHASE OF DOMESTIC MATERIALS         (MILL UNITS PER YEAR)
  V           IMPORTS                                          (MILL TPY)
  VR          IMPORTS OF RAW MATERIALS                         (MILL TPY)
  W           PRODUCTION OF MINING PRODUCTS                    (MILL TPY)
  X           SHIPMENT OF FINAL PRODUCTS                       (MILL TPY)
  XM          SHIPMENT OF MINING PRODUCTS                      (MILL TPY)
  XN          INTERPLANT SHIPMENTS                             (MILL TPY)
  Y           BINARY VARIABLE
  Z           PROCESS LEVEL                                    (MILL TPY)

EQUATIONS

  AEPS        ACCOUNTING: EXPORT REVENUE                       (MILL US$)
  AKAP        ACCOUNTING: INVESTMENT COST CHARGES              (MILL US$)
  ALAM        ACCOUNTING: TRANSPORT                            (MILL US$)
  API         ACCOUNTING: IMPORT COST                          (MILL US$)
  APSI        ACCOUNTING: RAW MATERIALS                        (MILL US$)
  CC          CAPACITY CONSTRAINT: STEEL PLANTS                (MILL TPY)
  CCM         CAPACITY CONSTRAINT: MINES                       (MILL TPY)
  EB          EXPORT BOUNDS                                    (MILL TPY)
  IC          CONVEX COMBINATION AND 0-1 CONSTR
  IH          DEFINITION OF H
  MB          MATERIAL BALANCE: STEEL PLANTS                   (MILL TPY)
  MBM         MATERIAL BALANCE: MINES                          (MILL TPY)
  MR          MARKET REQUIREMENTS                              (MILL TPY)
  OBJ         ACCOUNTING: TOTAL DISCOUNTED COST                (MILL US$)
  ZB          LIMIT ON STEEL PRODUCTION                        (MILL TPY)

MODELS

  MEXSD       SMALL DYNAMIC STEEL PROBLEM
```

Appendix C. Derivation of Part of the Investment Cost

This appendix derives the expression

$$\omega_1 = \hat{\omega}(0.5^{\beta-1} - 1),$$

which is the fixed charge portion of the capital cost approximation.

Consider first the general problem of specifying the investment cost function in industrial planning models. Frequently, the only data available from the engineers provide the analyst with a single point; for example, "the last blast furnace we built cost $250 million and had a capacity of 1.5 million tons of pig iron per year."

This kind of information is used to provide the point $(\hat{\omega}, \hat{h})$ in figure 8-3. That is, $\hat{h}$ is the size of unit at which economies of scale are exhausted, and $\hat{\omega}$ is the investment cost for a productive unit of that size. It is then assumed that the investment cost between 0 and $\hat{h}$ is a smooth

Figure 8-3. *Investment Cost Approximation*

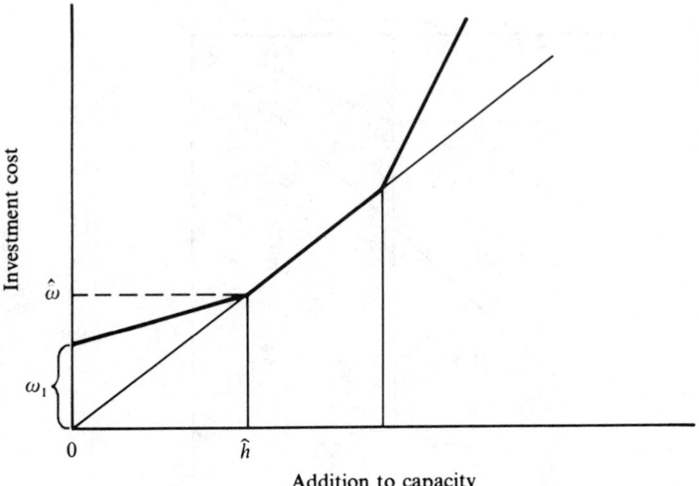

Figure 8-4. *Nonlinear Investment Cost Approximation*

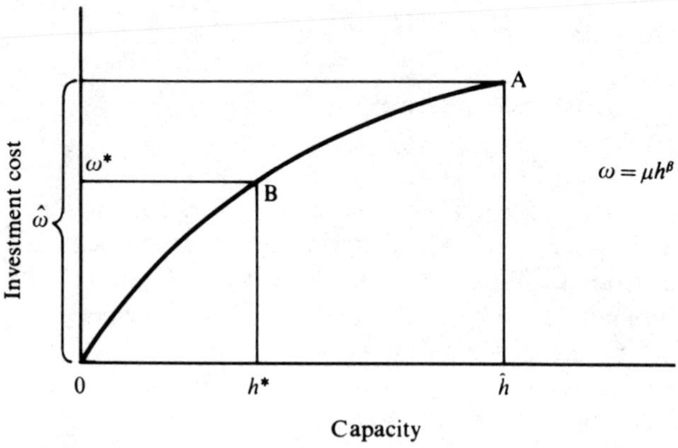

Figure 8-5. *Linearized Investment Cost Approximation*

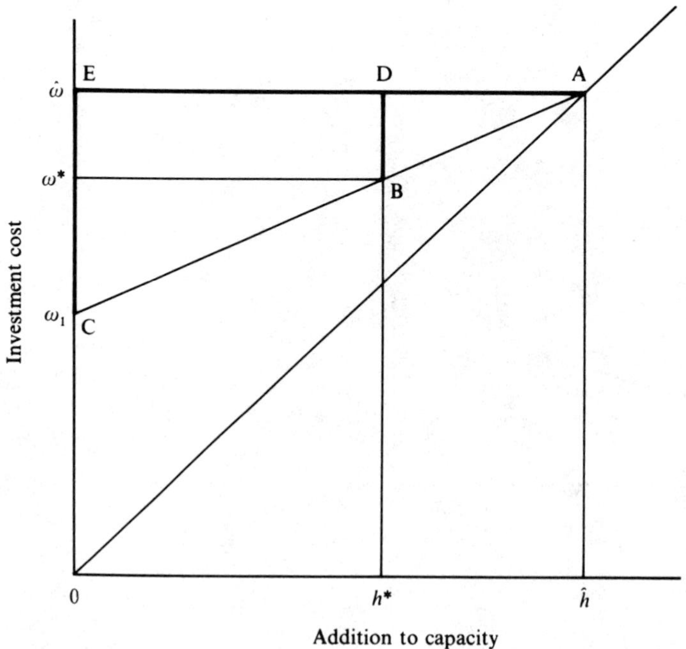

exponential function of the form

$$\omega = \mu h^{\beta} \tag{8.52}$$

where μ = cost parameter
β = scale parameter.

This is shown in figure 8-4. It is fit through the origin 0 and the point A. For the case at hand, the parameter β is chosen to be 0.6, indicating the presence of substantial economies of scale in investment cost.

Next the investment cost function (8.52) is evaluated at a capacity level equal to half the size at which the economies of scale are exhausted, that is, at $h^* = 0.5\hat{h}$. This yields the cost

$$\begin{aligned} \omega^* &= \mu(h^*)^{\beta} \\ &= \mu(0.5\,\hat{h})^{\beta}. \end{aligned} \tag{8.53}$$

The point (ω^*, h^*) is plotted as point B in figure 8-4.

Then two straight lines are constructed. The first one is through the points B and A. The point at which this line crosses the vertical axis is labeled point C, as shown in figure 8-5. Second, the horizontal line EDA is constructed. Using the proportionality of the triangle ACE we can write

$$\frac{\hat{\omega} - \omega_1}{\hat{h}} = \frac{\hat{\omega} - \omega^*}{\hat{h} - h^*}, \tag{8.54}$$

and recognizing the two definitions

$$\begin{aligned} \omega^* &= \mu(\alpha\hat{h})^{\beta} = \hat{\omega}\alpha^{\beta} \\ h^* &= \alpha\hat{h}, \end{aligned} \tag{8.55}$$

we can rearrange expression (8.54) into

$$\hat{\omega} - \omega_1 = \frac{\hat{\omega}(1 - \alpha^{\beta})}{(1 - \alpha)} \tag{8.56}$$

and thus

$$\omega_1 = \hat{\omega}\frac{\alpha^{\beta} - \alpha}{1 - \alpha}. \tag{8.57}$$

The special case of $\alpha = 0.5$ gives

$$\omega_1 = \hat{\omega}\frac{0.5^{\beta} - 0.5}{0.5} = \hat{\omega}(0.5^{\beta - 1} - 1), \tag{8.58}$$

the expression sought in this appendix.

9

Results of the Small Dynamic Model

IN DYNAMIC MODELS the results of greatest interest are the investment activities. Thus in this chapter investment results will be examined first and will be followed by an analysis of mining, steel production, and markets.

As is customary, the results of a base solution will be discussed first in some detail. Then a variety of experimental results will be analyzed in less detail. The specification of and the parameters for the base solution have been described in considerable detail in the previous chapter. However, a few particularly important assumptions made in the base solution need to be reviewed since they will be varied during the experimental runs. In brief, these assumptions are:

1. Natural gas price rises from $14 to $128 per thousand cubic meters over the time horizon covered by the model.
2. The electricity price is constant at $26 per megawatt-hour.
3. The price of energy inputs is 30 percent lower at SICARTSA, Tampico, and Coatzacoalcos than at the other plant sites.
4. No upper bounds are placed on steel production at each site.
5. Reserves of ore and coal are maintained at existing levels.
6. The price of imported coke is held constant at $60 per ton.

The first assumption is one of the most important in this study. The domestic price of natural gas in Mexico in 1979 was $14 per thousand cubic meters (about 40 cents per thousand cubic feet) while the international price was $128 per thousand cubic meters (about $3.60 per thousand cubic feet). Thus it is assumed in the base run that the Mexican government will slowly allow the domestic price to rise from $14 to $128 over the period from 1981 to 1995. Of course, by that time the international price may be higher yet, but this possibility was not considered in the present study.

It can be argued that, since the opportunity cost for the use of the gas is the international price, the base solution should include a price of $128 for natural gas in all time periods. However, the purpose of this study is not to recommend how capacity should be expanded in the Mexican steel industry but rather to analyze the logical consequences of various policy decisions affecting the capacity expansion of that industry.

Second, for the base run the electricity price is held constant across all time periods at the base period price of $26 per megawatt-hour. This corresponds to the domestic price in 1979. The effective coal price in the model does rise somewhat as the higher quality coal is exhausted over the period covered by the model, but the imported price for coke remains constant. One of the experiments discussed below allows the electricity price to rise.

Third, Mexico has a decentralization policy to encourage industry to locate in less congested areas. One part of that policy makes natural gas and electricity prices 30 percent lower at three sites in this model: SICARTSA, Tampico, and Coatzacoalcos. This policy, combined with the policy of keeping domestic natural gas prices below international prices, provides a strong incentive to use direct reduction methods rather than blast furnaces and to install these direct reduction units at one of these three sites.

Fourth, though the model contains an upper bound on the amount of iron which can be produced at any particular site, this bound is so large (30 million tons) as to not limit the solutions very much. If one wished to examine solutions in which there is more decentralization, one could either tighten the iron production bound or add a bound on steel production at each site. The alternative of adding a bound on steel production is used in one of the experiments.

Fifth, it is assumed that the existing reserves of coal and iron ore are not increased during the time horizon covered by the model. Although this is unlikely, it is useful to plan what to do in the event that no new reserves are discovered. An experiment in which the reserves are doubled is also included to see how much impact this has on the investment strategy for the industry. Moreover, the assumption of no new reserves allows one to study the effects of the exhaustion of domestic iron ores on the cost of steel and on the best locational investment strategy for the industry.

Sixth, the price of imported coke is held constant at $60 per ton under the assumption that there are sufficient world reserves of coking coal to hold this price constant. This assumption is modified in one of the experiments discussed below.

The base solution includes the six major characteristics described above and sets the stage for the following experiments:

1. Natural gas price constant at the domestic price level
2. Natural gas price constant at the international price level
3. Rising electricity price
4. Rising imported coke price
5. Removal of energy location subsidies
6. Iron ore and coal reserves doubled
7. Restriction of steel production at each site.

A summary of these experiments is given in table 9-1. It seems likely that, if Mexico should hold domestic prices of natural gas constant at the 1979 level (roughly a factor of ten less than international prices), the best plan for the steel industry is to invest heavily in direct reduction facilities. Similarly, if natural gas prices are allowed to rise immediately to international levels, it seems likely the steel industry should invest in blast furnaces. The first two experiments provide an analysis which shows that both of these conjectures are correct.

Since natural gas prices rise in the base solution, it seems logical that other energy sources such as electricity will also rise in price. If this

Table 9-1. *Summary of Experiments*

Experiment number	*Natural gas price (dollars per 1,000 cubic meters)*	*Electricity price (dollars per megawatt-hour)*	*Imported coke price (dollars per ton)*	*Energy location subsidy (percent)*	*Iron ore and coal reserves*	*Iron output at each site*
Base	14→128	26	60	30	1	+INF
1	14	26	60	30	1	+INF
2	128	26	60	30	1	+INF
3	14→128	26→78	60	30	1	+INF
4	14→128	26→78	60→90	30	1	+INF
5	14→128	26	60	0	1	+INF
6	14→128	26	60	30	2	+INF
7	14→128	26	60	30	1	10

should occur, it would further reduce the attractiveness of investment in direct reduction facilities, since sponge iron is normally converted to steel in electric arc furnaces. So the third experiment provides an analysis of the effects of increasing both natural gas and electricity prices.

If imported coke prices rise along with electricity prices the shift to blast furnaces should be less pronounced. Thus the fourth experiment is used to analyze the effects of the world price of coke rising from $60 to $90 per metric ton.

Some would argue that energy price subsidies at some locations but not at others will produce market disruptions which will be harmful rather than helpful to a country. The fifth experiment shows that the actual subsidies are large enough to have an effect on the desirable investment pattern.

The sixth experiment tests the robustness of the investment strategy for the industry to changes in domestic reserves of iron ore and coal. It shows that increases in the availability of reserves cause only marginal shifts in capacity expansion from ports to interior sites.

In the base solution a large share of the increase in capacity is at SICARTSA. The last experiment imposes a 10 million ton upper bound on steel production at any given site in order to force greater decentralization and to permit an analysis of the cost of this decentralization.

The next section provides a detailed discussion of the base solution. It is followed by discussion of each of the experiments. These solutions are mixed integer programming solutions; that is, all of the y variables are forced to be either one or zero. Even though the problems had 112 zero-one variables, it was possible to solve them for the global mixed integer programming solution because of the particular way the investment cost is modeled and because of the rapid growth of demand for steel products. The investment cost is modeled with economies of scale for small expansions, constant returns for medium expansions, and diseconomies of scale for large expansions. The rate of growth of demand was high enough that most of the expansions were in the range of the medium and large size, so the mixed integer programming solutions were relatively easy to obtain.

Base Solution

This section begins with an analysis of investment variables. In subsequent subsections the solution follows the flow of material from raw material at mines to intermediate and final products at steel mills and then to final products at markets.

Investment

Because this small model does not include investment in mines or in rolling mills, all the investment activities are for either iron or steel production in four types of productive unit: blast furnaces and direct reduction units for iron production, and basic oxygen furnaces (BOFS) and electric arc furnaces for steel production. Because of the simplified technological structure used in the model, the hot metal (pig iron) produced in the blast furnaces must be used entirely in BOFS, and the sponge iron produced in the direct reduction units must be used entirely in the electric arc furnaces:

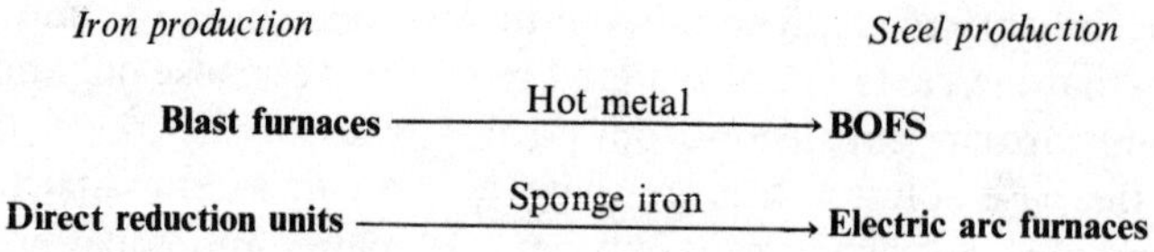

Iron production		*Steel production*
Blast furnaces	Hot metal →	**BOFS**
Direct reduction units	Sponge iron →	**Electric arc furnaces**

Therefore, one can analyze the investment decisions by looking at capacity expansion in either iron or steel and be confident that expansion in the other will match fairly closely. Table 9-2 gives the capacity expansion in iron production by plant site. Mathematically, the results in table 9-2 are

$$h_{it}^{iron} = \sum_{m \in \{\text{blast furnace, direct reduction}\}} h_{mit}. \tag{9.1}$$

The key result in table 9-2 is that almost all of the investment goes to

Table 9-2. *Base Solution: Expansion of Blast Furnace and Direct Reduction Capacity*
(million metric tons of iron per year)

Plant	*1984–86*	*1987–89*	*1990–92*	*1993–95*	*Total*
AHMSA	0	0	0	0	0
Fundidora	0	0	0	1.5	1.5
SICARTSA	2.4	2.4	4.6	5.0	14.4
HYLSA	0	0	0	0	0
HYLSAP	0	0	0	0	0
Tampico	1.9	0	0	0	1.9
Coatzacoalcos	1.6	1.4	0	0	3.0
Total	5.9	3.8	4.6	6.5	20.8

Table 9-3. *Base Solution : Imports of Pellets*
(million metric tons)

Plant	*1981–83*	*1984–86*	*1987–89*	*1990–92*	*1993–95*
AHMSA	0	0	0	1.6	5.1
Fundidora	0	2.2	2.2	2.2	4.6
SICARTSA	0	0	0	0	18.2
HYLSA	0	1.4	1.4	1.4	1.4
HYLSAP	0	2.6	1.4	1.4	1.4
Tampico	0	2.3	2.6	2.6	2.6
Coatzacoalcos	0	0	4.2	4.2	4.2
Total	0	8.5	11.8	13.4	37.5

plant sites at ports: SICARTSA on the Pacific Ocean and Tampico and Coatzacoalcos on the Gulf of Mexico. The reason for this is that the domestic ores are substantially exhausted during the period covered by the model, and pellets are imported to provide an iron source. As shown in table 9-3, there are no pellet imports in 1981–83, but then the imports rise sharply to 37.5 millions tons per year in the 1993–95 period as the domestic ores are used up and it becomes more and more expensive to mine them.

Table 9-3 also shows that the plants nearest the domestic ores (Altos Hornos in the north and SICARTSA in the south) continue to use these ores, while the plants more distant from the ores and/or nearer to ports begin to import. Thus, Altos Hornos does not begin to import pellets until 1990–92 and SICARTSA not until 1993–95.

The complementary pattern of domestic iron ore production is given in table 9-4. Recall that the existing reserves are divided into five groups by quality level, with 1 the highest quality ores and 5 the lowest quality. It is assumed that the ores are equally divided among those five quality groups. For example, the northern mines are assumed to have 130.6 million tons of iron ore reserves. In addition, it is assumed that only 70 percent of these reserves should be used during the time period covered by the model, that is, $(130.6)(0.7) = 91$ million tons. Thus, the reserves in pellet equivalents in the northern mines would be $(91/1.5) = 60$ million tons of pellet equivalents. Dividing this by the five quality groups leaves 12 million tons of pellet-equivalent reserves in each of the five quality groups.

Compare this with the production shown in table 9-4 of 4 million tons of first-quality pellet-equivalent ore per year in 1981–83 at the northern mines. Since there are three years per time period this translates into a

Table 9-4. *Base Solution: Iron Ore Mining*
(million metric tons of pellet equivalents per year)

Quality level	*1981–83*	*1984–86*	*1987–89*	*1990–92*	*1993–95*
Northern mines					
1	4.0	0	0	0	0
2	4.0	0	0	0	0
3	0	4.0	0	0	0
4	0	0	4.0	0	0
5	0	0	0.5	3.5	0
Southern mines					
1	3.4	4.2	0	0	0
2	0	2.2	5.5	0	0
3	0	0	2.9	4.8	0
4	0	0	0	7.7	0
5	0	0	0	3.0	4.8
Total	11.4	10.4	12.9	19.0	4.8

production of 12 million tons of pellet-equivalent ore in 1981–83. Thus, the first-quality level at the northern mines is exhausted in the 1981–83 time period. The second-quality level is also exhausted in this time period at the northern mines, but only part of the first-quality reserves at the southern mines are used up in 1981–83.

From table 9-4 it can be seen that the northern ores are used up in the 1990–92 period while the southern reserves are not all used until the 1993–95 period. This accounts for the fact that in table 9-3 SICARTSA does not import any ores until the 1993–95 period, when it suddenly imports 18.2 million tons of pellets per year.

In summary, most of the capacity additions in table 9-2 are at SICARTSA because of a combination of several factors. First, SICARTSA is located near the largest ore reserves available in the model. Second, it is located at a port so that pellets can be imported cheaply once the domestic ores are exhausted. Third, the energy location factor provides for cheaper natural gas here than at the other established plants.

Most of the remaining capacity additions shown in table 9-2 are at Coatzacoalcos and Tampico. These two sites offer low natural gas prices because of the decentralization policy, and they offer port locations for relatively inexpensive importation of pellets.

The second major result of the small dynamic model is the division of investment in ironmaking facilities between blast furnaces and direct reduction units. This result is shown in table 9-5 which gives the

Table 9-5. *Base Solution: Investment in Blast Furnaces as Percentage of Total Investment in Iron Production Capacity*

Plant	*1984–86*	*1987–89*	*1990–92*	*1993–95*
AHMSA	—	—	—	—
Fundidora	—	—	—	100
SICARTSA	0	0	63	74
HYLSA	—	—	—	—
HYLSAP	—	—	—	—
Tampico	0	—	—	—
Coatzacoalcos	0	0	—	—

—No new capacity installed.
0 Capacity expansion only in direct reduction facilities.

percentage of total investment in iron production capacity that is directed to blast furnaces. Mathematically, this is

$$\rho_{it}^{bf} = (h_{\text{blast furnace}, i, t}/h_{it}^{\text{iron}}) \tag{9.2}$$

where ρ_{it}^{bf} = percentage of new capacity for ironmaking in blast furnaces

h_{it}^{iron} = total new capacity in ironmaking facilities at plant i in time period t

In table 9-5, a dash indicates that there was no new capacity installed in that plant and time period. In contrast, a zero indicates that there was capacity expansion in ironmaking, but it was all in direct reduction facilities. Thus in time periods 1984–86 and 1987–89 all of the investment in ironmaking is in direct reduction facilities. Because of the rising price of natural gas, however, 63 percent of the new investment at SICARTSA in 1990–92 is in blast furnaces and only 37 percent is in direct reduction units. By 1993–95 almost all the new capacity is in blast furnaces, with the exception of some units at SICARTSA. This is probably due to the 30 percent lower price of natural gas provided at SICARTSA under the decentralization policy.

Of course, if the natural gas price in Mexico were not a factor of five below the international price in the first time period, this pattern of investment would be altered. This is discussed later in this chapter.

Before continuing with the other results from the base solution, it is worth discussing the advantages and disadvantages of small models. The small models used in this book have the great advantage over the large models of being much easier to understand. It is also easier to do sensitivity analysis with them because it costs less to solve them. Thus, the small dynamic model offers an extremely useful tool for analyzing questions of the best technology and when and where to add to capacity in a system of plants.

At the same time, one must treat the results with caution because many factors not included in the model may be of great importance. For example, the investment costs at Tampico and Coatzacoalcos are equal in the model, but the terrain may make it much more difficult to build and maintain a steel mill at one location than at the other. This problem could be corrected by simply assigning a higher investment cost to the site with the more difficult terrain. The point is not that the model *could* not provide a good solution, but that it *will* not in the absence of the correct data and specification. For this reason it is advisable for analysts to continually question the results from the model and to test the robustness of the solution to altered data and specifications. Furthermore, the results of the model should be exposed to the most searching analysis by experts in the industry. For example, failure to consider the quality of the subsoil for the foundation for a large plant or the depth of the water at a port could result in an optimal model solution which is in actual fact extremely uneconomical.

Raw Material

The most important result about raw material is the exhaustion of the domestic iron ores. This has been discussed fully above. Coal reserves are treated in a manner similar to iron ore, but the reported resources are sufficiently large that in the time horizon covered by the model only the highest quality reserves are used. This will, of course, differ in some of the experimental runs in which more of the added capacity is in the form of blast furnaces than direct reduction units.

Table 9-6. *Base Solution: Steel Production*
(million metric tons per year)

Plant	*1981–83*	*1984–86*	*1987–89*	*1990–92*	*1993–95*
AHMSA	3.6	2.8	3.6	4.1	4.1
Fundidora	1.7	1.7	1.7	1.7	3.6
SICARTSA	1.3	3.5	5.7	10.9	16.6
HYLSA	1.1	1.1	1.1	1.1	1.1
HYLSAP	0.6	0.9	0.9	0.9	0.9
Tampico	0	1.5	1.5	1.5	1.5
Coatzacoalcos	0	1.5	2.8	2.8	2.8
Total	8.3	13.0	17.3	23.0	30.6

Steel Mills

The production levels for the base solution are given in table 9-6, which reflects the investment results. There is a large increase in production at SICARTSA to exploit the combined advantages of access to domestic ores, location at a port, and subsidized natural gas prices. The buildup to almost 17 million tons of production at SICARTSA by 1993–95 is so large that one of the experimental runs in the next section analyzes a case in which an upper bound of 10 million tons of steel at any one site is placed on the model.

Figure 9-1. *Base Solution: Steel Shipments in* 1981–83
(million metric tons a year)

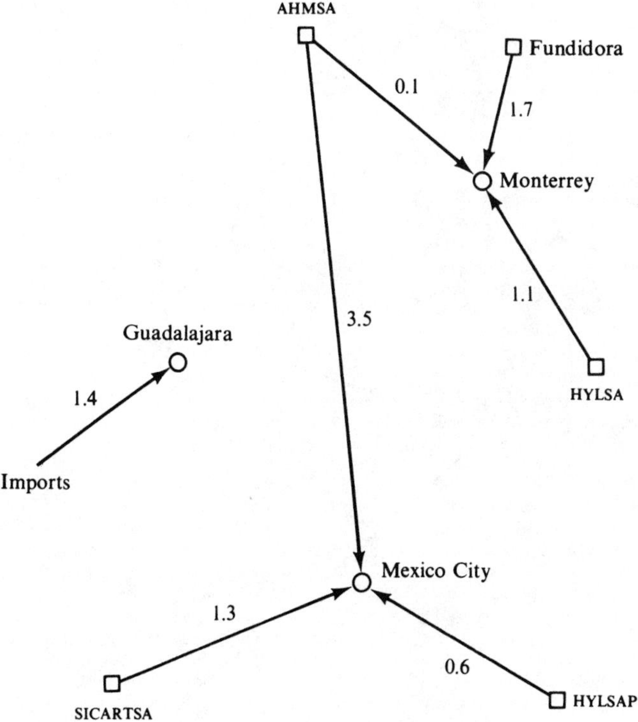

In addition to the buildup at SICARTSA, sizable new steel mills are developed at both Tampico and Coatzacoalcos, the first being 1.5 million tons per year and the second constructed in two stages to reach 2.8 million tons per year.

Markets

Figure 9-1 shows the pattern of final product shipments in the 1981–83 time period. This does not differ very much from the solution to the

Figure 9-2. *Base Solution: Steel Shipments in* 1993–95 (million metric tons a year)

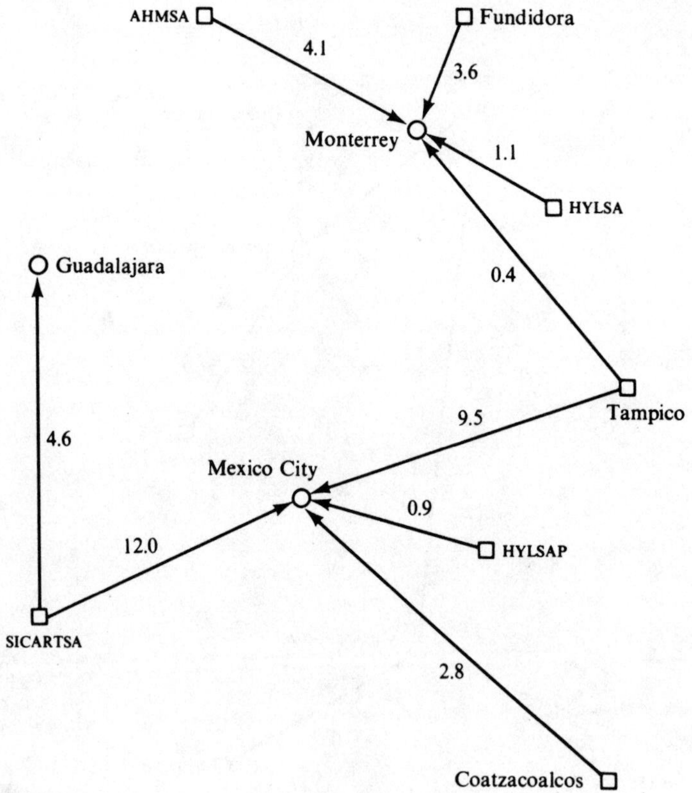

small static model. In contrast, figure 9-2 shows the shipment pattern for 1993–95. The country is divided into two parts with the northern steel mills (including Tampico) serving Monterrey and the southern steel mills (including Coatzacoalcos) serving Mexico City and Guadalajara.

Experiments

Of the seven experiments done with the small dynamic model, four were concerned with energy prices, one with reserves, and one with the limits on the size of plant at any single site. Each solution will be discussed in turn and compared with the base solution.

Natural Gas at Domestic Price Level

In the base solution, natural gas prices, which are controlled by the government, rise from $14 to $128 per thousand cubic meters over the time horizon covered by the model. In contrast, in experiment 1 natural gas prices are fixed at the low level of $14 and held at that level over the time horizon covered by the model. One would expect this to cause investment in ironmaking facilities to be directed more to direct reduction units and less to blast furnaces. Figure 9-3 shows that this does indeed occur. In the base solution most of the capacity built after 1990 is in blast furnaces. In contrast, in the solution to experiment 1 *all* the capacity additions are in direct reduction units.

Lower natural gas prices also cause smaller productive units to be built and to be more decentralized than in the base solution. For example, in the base solution in the 1990–92 period 4.6 million tons of ironmaking capacity is brought on-line at SICARTSA. Of this, 1.6 million tons is in direct reduction units and 3.0 million tons is in a blast furnace or furnaces. In contrast, in experiment 1, 5.6 million tons of capacity in direct reduction units is started up, but it is divided among three locations: 2.4 million tons at SICARTSA, 1.6 million tons at Tampico, and 1.6 million tons at Coatzacoalcos. Thus, it seems that differences in economies of scale affect the solution. The economies of scale in direct reduction units are exhausted at an investment level of 0.8 million tons per year, while in blast furnaces they are exhausted at an investment level of 1.5 million tons per year. Thus, one would expect large blast furnaces to be constructed at fewer locations than direct reduction units. This expectation is fulfilled in this solution.

One other aspect of experiment 1 is of particular interest. Recall that the energy location factors in the model are set such that the natural gas

Figure 9-3. *Investment in the Base Solution Compared with Seven Experimental Solutions*
(million metric tons of iron capacity a year)

	Coatzacoalcos	Tampico	HYLSAP	HYLSA	SICARTSA	Fundidora	AHMSA
Base solution							
1984–86	1.6	1.9			2.4		
1987–89	1.4				2.4		
1990–92					4.6 (1.6, 3.0)		
1993–95					5.0 (1.3, 3.7)	1.5	
1. Natural gas at domestic price							
1984–86	1.6	1.9	1.2		3.3		
1987–89	1.6	1.6			2.4		
1990–92	1.6	1.6			2.4		
1993–95	1.6	1.6	1.6		2.4		
2. Natural gas at international price							
1984–86					5.9 (2.2, 3.7)		
1987–89					3.5		
1990–92		0.8			2.9		
1993–95					4.6 (0.9, 3.7)	1.8	
3. Rising electricity price							
1984–86					4.5 (1.6, 2.9)		
1987–89					3.7		
1990–92					3.7	1.5	
1993–95		1.7			4.5		

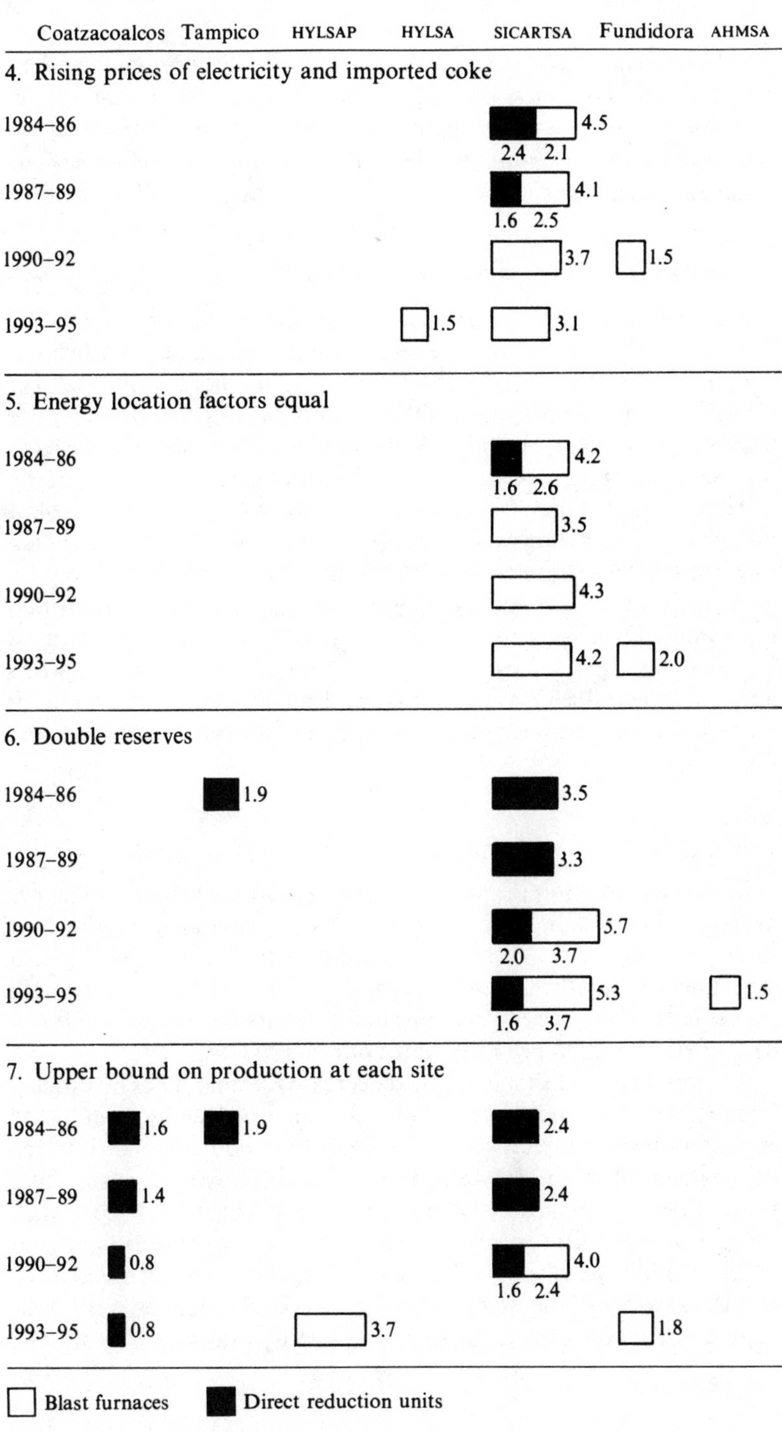

Coatzacoalcos Tampico HYLSAP HYLSA SICARTSA Fundidora AHMSA
4. Rising prices of electricity and imported coke
1984–86 4.5 2.4 2.1
1987–89 4.1 1.6 2.5
1990–92 3.7 1.5
1993–95 1.5 3.1
5. Energy location factors equal
1984–86 4.2 1.6 2.6
1987–89 3.5
1990–92 4.3
1993–95 4.2 2.0
6. Double reserves
1984–86 1.9 3.5
1987–89 3.3
1990–92 5.7 2.0 3.7
1993–95 5.3 1.6 3.7 1.5
7. Upper bound on production at each site
1984–86 1.6 1.9 2.4
1987–89 1.4 2.4
1990–92 0.8 4.0 1.6 2.4
1993–95 0.8 3.7 1.8
Blast furnaces
Direct reduction units

price at SICARTSA, Tampico, and Coatzacoalcos is 30 percent lower than at the other plant sites. This apparently plays a substantial role in determining the location of the new capacity. If natural gas prices are held at the current low domestic level, this policy may therefore have its intended affect.

Natural Gas at International Price Level

Figure 9-3 provides a comparison of the investment results for ironmaking facilities for the base solution and experiment 2, in which the natural gas price is held constant over the time horizon at $128 per thousand cubic meters ($3.62 per thousand cubic feet), the contract price between Mexico and the United States in 1979. This price level is used to represent the opportunity cost for the natural gas.

At this price, as figure 9-3 shows, almost all of the investment is in blast furnaces. The exceptions are 2.2 million tons in 1984–86 and 0.9 million tons in 1993–95 at SICARTSA, and 0.8 million tons in 1990–92 at Tampico. The shift from direct reduction units to blast furnaces also brings with it large unit sizes and a centralization of almost all of the investment at SICARTSA. The energy location factors are no longer sufficient to bring about a decentralization of investment, although they may account for the installation of direct reduction units at SICARTSA in 1984–86 and 1993–95.

Rising Electricity Price

In the base solution the electricity price remains constant at $26 per megawatt-hour. If natural gas prices rise as envisaged in the base solution, however, it is likely that electricity prices will also rise. Thus, in experiment 3 it is assumed that electricity prices rise in the same smooth way as natural gas prices, beginning at $26 per megawatt-hour in 1981–83 and rising to $78 per megawatt-hour in 1993–95.

One would expect that this would decrease the amount of investment in direct reduction units since the sponge iron produced by them is used entirely in electric arc furnaces in this model. (Although sponge iron can be charged to blast furnaces and to some extent to BOFS, those possibilities are not included in this small model.) Figure 9-3 shows that, indeed, all investment in iron production that comes on-line in or after 1987–89 is in blast furnaces. Thus, even if natural gas prices are allowed to rise slowly to the international price level, there is very little investment in direct reduction units if electricity prices are also allowed to rise. The exception to this is 1.6 million metric tons of direct reduction units installed at SICARTSA in 1984–86.

Rising Electricity and Imported Coke Prices

Since rising electricity prices may be viewed as part of a worldwide increase in all kinds of energy prices, it is useful to do an experimental run in which both electricity prices and imported coke prices rise together. Recall that the cost of domestic coke will increase in the model to the extent that the domestic coal reserves are drawn down so that mining costs increase.

In experiment 4, electricity prices rise just as in the previous experiment, and imported coke prices also increase—from $60 per metric ton to $90 per metric ton over the horizon covered by the model. The results, shown in figure 9-3, are best understood by contrasting them with the results for experiment 3. The first difference is that with rising prices for both electricity and imported coke, the expansion at SICARTSA in the first two time periods is in direct reduction units. Thus, 2.4 million tons of direct reduction capacity is added at SICARTSA in 1984–86 in experiment 4, while only 1.6 million tons of direction reduction capacity is added in experiment 3. Similarly, in 1987–89, 1.6 million tons of capacity is added in direction reduction units when the imported coke prices rise, but the expansion is only in blast furnaces when the imported coke prices do not rise.

The other difference in the solutions is not in changes in technology but rather in changes in location and timing. For example, in experiment 3 a 1.7 million ton blast furnace is added at Tampico and in experiment 4 a 1.5 million ton unit is added at HYLSA instead. Caution is advised in interpreting this kind of a result from mixed integer programming (MIP) solutions. The difference in total cost may be very small between two MIP solutions in which the location of capacity increase was the only difference.

In summary, the increase in international coke prices changes only marginally the results of the experiment on rising electricity prices. Blast furnace investments still dominate the capacity expansion.

Energy Location Factors Equal

In the base solution natural gas and electricity prices are 30 percent lower at SICARTSA, Tampico, and Coatzacoalcos than at the other sites. In experiment 5 this subsidy is removed, and natural gas and electricity prices are equal at all sites. One would expect this to result in less investment at the three previously favored sites and more investment elsewhere.

Experiment 5 shows that this occurs, but to a lesser extent than expected. There is a minor shift in investment away from Tampico and Coatzacoalcos, and the largest part of the investment remains at SICARTSA. There is also some shift from direct reduction methods to blast furnaces because the low energy prices at the favored locations work as a subsidy for direct reduction technology.

Thus the location subsidies are sufficiently large to result in almost 5 million tons of capacity being built near energy sources. Without them roughly 2 million tons of additional capacity would be built in Monterrey at Fundidora, and more capacity would be built at SICARTSA.

Double Reserves

One of the greatest uncertainties facing any investment strategy in the steel industry is the availability of reserves. Consequently, in experiment 6 the iron ore reserves were doubled, although the distribution of reserves between the north and south was maintained. Since SICARTSA is both a port and near large iron ore reserves, the most pronounced part of the shift was from Tampico and Coatzacoalcos to SICARTSA.

Experiment 6 helps make clear that the location and quantity of reserves is a very important factor in investment planning for the Mexican steel industry. If the reserves located near SICARTSA in this small model were less than assumed, it would no doubt affect the outcome substantially.

Upper Bound on Production at Each Site

There are many reasons for a country not to concentrate as much of its iron and steel capacity at one site as in the base solution to this model. Of a total capacity expansion of about 21 million tons of iron per year roughly 15 million would go to SICARTSA. Thus, it was decided to obtain an experimental solution in which steel production at any one site was limited to less than 10 million tons per year. In experiment 7 investment in the first three time periods is almost the same as in the base solution. The constraint becomes tight in 1993–95, however, and blast furnaces with capacities of 1.8 and 3.7 million tons per year are installed at Fundidora and HYLSAP. This occurs because the natural gas prices are sufficiently high by 1993–95 that the energy location factors no longer have any effect. Then it is better to build blast furnaces close to markets and (to a lesser extent) to iron ore and coal resources.

Conclusions

One point cannot be emphasized too much. The base solution should not be looked upon as the best or most likely solution. Rather it should be viewed as a basis from which to do experimental runs in order to learn about the model and about the industry.

The general results that emerge from these experiments are:

1. Policies affecting natural gas prices are important in determining investment strategy in the steel industry. At present domestic prices, considerable investment would be made in direct reduction units; at present international prices, almost all investment would be made in blast furnaces instead.
2. The limited availability of iron ore reserves means that almost all expansion of the steel industry will be at ports. In the case of SICARTSA, which is close to a port and existing iron ore reserves, there are very large investments.
3. Rising electricity prices would further shift the investment pattern toward blast furnaces and away from direct reduction units. This basic pattern holds even if imported coke prices are also increased.
4. The lower energy prices at some locations are important. The only solutions in which there was any significant level of investment at Tampico and Coatzacoalcos was when these subsidies were in place.
5. A doubling of iron ore reserves causes only a marginal shift of investment.
6. Placing a 10 million ton limit on SICARTSA results in sizable investment in Monterrey at Fundidora and in Puebla at HYLSAP.

Finally, this small dynamic model is large enough to capture the tradeoffs between dwindling reserves at interior mines, shifts in relative prices of energy inputs, and decentralization policies.

Appendix. Summary Tables of the Results

In this appendix, tables 9-7 to 9-14 present the summary results of the base case and each of the seven experiments. Tables 9-15 to 9-17 compare selected results of the experiments with the base case.

Table 9-7. *Summary of Results for Base Case*

Category	*1981–83*	*1984–86*	*1987–89*	*1990–92*	*1993–95*
Cost (million U.S. dollars a year)					
Capital	0	162.0	263.5	403.3	594.7
Raw material	569.8	693.4	1,048.8	1,604.1	1,558.5
Transport	145.6	160.9	186.5	237.1	324.6
Import	252.9	378.6	513.4	692.4	1,795.2
Export revenues		– 28.0	– 28.0	– 28.0	– 28.0
Total cost	968.3	1,366.8	1,984.2	2,908.9	4,245.0
Total demand (million tons)	9.7	12.9	17.2	22.8	30.4
Production (million tons)					
Pig iron	5.6	5.0	5.4	8.7	13.9
Sponge iron	1.8	7.9	11.7	13.4	14.7
Open hearth	1.7	1.0	1.7	1.7	2.4
Electric furnace	1.7	7.2	10.8	12.3	13.5
BOF	2.3	2.2	0.3	0	0
BOF (max scrap)	2.5	2.7	4.6	9.1	14.8
Pig iron/Sponge iron	3.1	0.6	0.5	0.7	0.9
Imports (million tons)					
Pellets	0	8.4	11.8	13.4	37.5
Coke	0.7	0.7	0.7	2.6	4.9
Steel	1.4	0	0	0	0
Exports of steel (million tons)	0	0.2	0.2	0.2	0.2
Total capacity expansion (million tons)					
Blast furnace	0	0	3.0	5.2	1.0
BOF	0	0	4.2	5.7	1.0
Direct reduction	5.9	3.8	1.6	1.3	1.0
Electric arc	5.6	3.5	1.5	1.2	1.0

Domestic shipments of steel (million tons)					
AHMSA	3.6	2.8	3.6	4.1	4.1
Fundidora	1.7	1.7	1.7	1.7	3.6
SICARTSA	1.3	3.5	5.7	10.9	16.6
HYLSA	1.1	1.1	1.1	1.1	1.1
HYLSAP	0.6	0.9	0.9	0.9	0.9
Tampico	0	1.3	1.3	1.3	1.3
Coatzacoalcos	0	1.5	2.8	2.8	2.8
Total shipments	8.3	12.9	17.2	22.8	30.4
Detailed capacity expansion (million tons)					
AHMSA					
BOF	0	0	0	0.5	0
Fundidora					
Blast furnace	0	0	0	0	1.5
BOF	0	0	0	0	1.2
SICARTSA					
Blast furnace	0	0	0	3.0	3.7
BOF	0	0	0	3.7	4.5
Direct reduction	0	2.4	2.4	1.6	1.3
Electric arc	0	2.2	2.2	1.5	1.2
HYLSAP					
Electric arc	0	0.4	0	0	0
Tampico					
Direct reduction	0	1.9	0	0	0
Electric arc	0	1.5	0	0	0
Coatzacoalcos					
Direct reduction	0	1.6	1.4	0	0
Electric arc	0	1.5	1.3	0	0

Table 9-8. *Summary of Results for Experiment 1: Natural Gas at Domestic Price Level*

Category	*1981–83*	*1984–86*	*1987–89*	*1990–92*	*1993–95*
Cost (million U.S. dollars a year)					
Capital	0	220.3	373.9	527.4	719.8
Raw material	573.7	659.4	687.3	953.7	875.2
Transport	142.1	156.3	167.4	217.2	290.0
Import	252.9	236.0	590.5	848.8	1,618.2
Export revenues	0	−28.0	−28.0	−28.0	−28.0
Total cost	968.7	1,244.0	1,791.1	2,519.1	3,475.3
Total demand (million tons)	9.7	12.9	17.7	22.8	30.4
Production (million tons)					
Pig iron	5.6	3.6	2.9	3.0	3.7
Sponge iron	1.8	9.9	15.6	21.3	28.6
Open hearth	1.7	0	0	0	0
Electric furnace	1.7	9.1	14.3	19.5	26.2
BOF	2.3	2.7	3.0	1.2	1.2
BOF (max scrap)	2.5	1.2	0	2.4	3.2
Pig iron/Sponge iron	3.1	0.4	0.2	0.1	0.1
Imports (million tons)					
Pellets	0	4.9	13.7	20.2	39.4
Coke	0.7	0.7	0.7	0.7	0.7
Steel	1.4	0	0	0	0
Exports of steel (million tons)	0	0.2	0.2	0.2	0.2

Total capacity expansion (million tons)					
Blast furnace	0	0	0	0	0
BOF	0	0	0	0	0
Direct reduction	0	8.0	5.7	5.7	7.3
Electric arc	0	7.4	5.2	5.2	6.7
Domestic shipments of steel					
AHMSA	3.6	2.1	1.9	0.9	1.7
Fundidora	1.7	0.7	0	1.5	1.5
SICARTSA	1.3	4.2	6.4	8.6	10.8
HYLSA	1.1	1.1	1.1	1.1	1.1
HYLSAP	0.6	2.0	2.0	2.0	3.5
Tampico	0	1.3	2.8	4.3	5.8
Coatzacoalcos	0	1.5	3.0	4.5	6.0
Total shipments	8.3	12.9	17.2	22.8	30.4
Detailed capacity expansion (*million tons*)					
SICARTSA					
Direct reduction	0	3.3	2.4	2.4	2.4
Electric arc	0	3.0	2.2	2.2	2.2
HYLSAP					
Direct reduction	0	1.2	0	0	1.6
Electric arc	0	1.4	0	0	1.5
Tampico					
Direct reduction	0	1.9	1.6	1.6	1.6
Electric arc	0	1.5	1.5	1.5	1.5
Coatzacoalcos					
Direct reduction	0	1.6	1.6	1.6	1.6
Electric arc	0	1.5	1.5	1.5	1.5

Table 9-9. *Summary of Results for Experiment 2: Natural Gas at International Price Level*

Category	*1981–83*	*1984–86*	*1987–89*	*1990–92*	*1993–95*
Cost (million U.S. dollars a year)					
Capital	0	160.8	274.4	386.7	576.6
Raw material	653.5	887.3	1,262.5	1,302.1	1,162.6
Transport	142.1	145.8	171.3	235.4	321.2
Import	252.9	268.3	400.6	1,189.8	2,178.3
Export revenues	0	−28.0	−28.0	−28.0	−28.0
Total cost	1,048.5	1,434.2	2,080.7	3,086.0	4,210.7
Total demand (million tons)	9.7	12.9	17.1	22.8	30.4
Production (million tons)					
Pig iron	5.6	9.0	12.5	15.8	21.3
Sponge iron	1.8	2.2	2.2	4.0	4.9
Open hearth	1.7	1.7	1.7	1.7	2.4
Electric furnace	1.7	2.0	2.0	3.6	4.5
BOF	2.3	0	0	0	0
BOF (max scrap)	2.5	9.4	13.6	17.7	23.8
Pig iron/Sponge iron	3.1	4.1	5.7	4.0	4.4
Imports (million tons)					
Pellets	0	2.2	2.2	19.2	40.4
Coke	0.7	3.0	5.2	7.0	9.4
Steel	1.4	0	0	0	0
Exports of steel (million tons)	0	0.2	0.2	0.2	0.2

Total capacity expansion (million tons)					
Blast furnace	0	3.7	3.5	2.9	5.5
BOF	0	4.5	4.3	4.0	6.1
Direct reduction	0	2.2	0	0.8	0.9
Electric arc	0	1.5	0.5	0	0.8
Domestic shipments of steel					
AHMSA	3.6	3.6	3.6	4.1	4.1
Fundidora	1.7	1.7	1.7	1.7	3.9
SICARTSA	1.3	7.1	11.9	15.4	20.7
HYLSA	1.1	0	0	1.1	1.1
HYLSAP	0.6	0.5	0	0.6	0.6
Tampico	0	0	0	0	0
Coatzacoalcos	0	0	0	0	0
Total shipments	8.3	12.9	17.2	22.8	30.4
Detailed capacity expansion (million tons)					
AHMSA					
BOF	0	0	0	0.5	0
Fundidora					
Blast furnace	0	0	0	0	1.8
BOF	0	0	0	0	1.6
SICARTSA					
Blast furnace	0	3.7	3.5	2.9	3.7
BOF	0	4.5	4.3	3.6	4.5
Direct reduction	0	2.2	0	0	0.9
Electric arc	0	1.5	0.5	0	0.8
Tampico					
Direct reduction	0	0	0	0.8	0

Table 9-10. *Summary of Results for Experiment 3: Rising Electricity Price*

Category	*1981–83*	*1984–86*	*1987–89*	*1990–92*	*1993–95*
Cost (million U.S. dollars a year)					
Capital	0	129.9	244.4	412.5	620.2
Raw material	573.7	824.8	1,217.9	1,415.0	1,101.4
Transport	142.1	151.6	178.2	245.7	316.7
Import	252.9	328.3	450.4	1,033.9	2,256.8
Export revenues	0	– 28.0	– 28.0	– 28.0	– 28.0
Total cost	968.7	1,406.6	2,063.0	3,079.1	4,267.1
Total demand (million tons)	9.7	12.9	17.2	22.8	30.4
Production (million tons)					
Pig iron	5.6	8.2	12.0	17.6	23.8
Sponge iron	1.8	3.2	2.9	1.6	1.6
Open hearth	1.7	1.7	1.7	2.4	2.4
Electric furnace	1.7	3.0	2.7	1.5	1.5
BOF	2.3	0	0	0	0
BOF (max scrap)	2.5	8.5	13.0	19.2	26.8
Pig iron/Sponge iron	3.1	2.6	4.1	10.7	14.5
Imports (million tons)					
Pellets	0	4.4	4.4	15.1	39.8
Coke	0.7	2.5	4.9	7.2	11.1
Steel	1.4	0	0	0	0
Exports of steel (million tons)	0	0.2	0.2	0.2	0.2

Total capacity expansion (million tons)					
Blast furnace	0	2.9	3.7	5.2	6.2
BOF	0	3.6	4.5	6.2	7.6
Direct reduction	0	1.6	0	0	0
Electric arc	0	1.5	0	0	0
Domestic shipments of steel					
AHMSA	3.6	3.5	3.6	4.1	4.1
Fundidora	1.7	1.7	1.7	3.6	3.6
SICARTSA	1.3	6.2	10.7	15.2	20.9
HYLSA	1.1	0.9	0.6	0	0
HYLSAP	0.6	0.6	0.6	0	0
Tampico	0	0	0	0	1.9
Coatzacoalcos	0	0	0	0	0
Total shipments	8.3	12.9	17.2	22.8	30.4
Detailed capacity expansion (million tons)					
AHMSA					
BOF	0	0	0	0.5	0
Fundidora					
Blast furnace	0	0	0	1.5	0
BOF	0	0	0	1.2	0
SICARTSA					
Blast furnace	0	2.9	3.7	3.7	4.5
BOF	0	3.6	4.5	4.5	5.4
Direct reduction	0	1.6	0	0	0
Electric arc	0	1.5	0	0	0
Tampico					
Blast furnace	0	0	0	0	1.7
BOF	0	0	0	0	2.1

Table 9-11. *Summary of Results for Experiment 4: Rising Electricity and Imported Coke Prices*

Category	*1981–83*	*1984–86*	*1987–89*	*1990–92*	*1993–95*
Cost (million U.S. dollars a year)					
Capital	0	126.3	241.4	409.5	557.9
Raw material	573.7	831.4	1,271.9	1,810.7	1,703.4
Transport	142.1	156.8	180.9	334.6	439.4
Import	252.9	326.7	444.2	616.8	1,796.1
Export revenues	0	– 28.0	– 28.0	0	0
Total cost	968.7	1,413.1	2,110.4	3,171.6	4,496.8
Total demand (million tons)	9.7	12.9	17.2	22.8	30.4
Production (million tons)					
Pig iron	5.6	7.5	9.9	15.5	20.1
Sponge iron	1.8	4.2	5.6	4.0	4.0
Open hearth	1.7	1.7	1.7	2.4	2.4
Electric furnace	1.7	3.9	5.2	3.7	3.7
BOF	2.3	0	0	0	0
BOF (max scrap)	2.5	7.5	10.5	16.7	22.4
Pig iron/Sponge iron	3.1	1.8	1.8	3.8	5.0
Imports (million tons)					
Pellets	0	4.8	4.4	15.1	37.4
Coke	0.7	2.0	3.6	0	0
Steel	1.4	0	0	0.1	2.0
Exports of steel (million tons)	0	0.2	0.2	0	0

Total capacity expansion (million tons)					
Blast furnace	0	2.1	2.5	5.2	4.6
BOF	0	2.6	3.0	6.2	5.6
Direct reduction	0	2.4	1.6	0	0
Electric arc	0	2.2	1.5	0	0
Domestic shipments of steel					
AHMSA	3.6	3.6	3.6	4.1	4.1
Fundidora	1.7	1.7	1.7	3.6	3.6
SICARTSA	1.3	5.9	10.4	15.1	18.9
HYLSA	1.1	1.1	0.9	0	1.8
HYLSAP	0.6	0.6	0.6	0	0
Tampico	0	0	0	0	0
Coatzacoalcos	0	0	0	0	0
Total shipments	8.3	12.9	17.2	22.8	28.4
Detailed capacity expansion (million tons)					
AHMSA					
BOF	0	0	0	0.5	0
Fundidora					
Blast furnace	0	0	0	1.5	0
BOF	0	0	0	1.2	0
SICARTSA					
Blast furnace	0	2.1	2.5	3.7	3.1
BOF	0	2.6	3.0	4.5	3.8
Direct reduction	0	2.4	1.6	0	0
Electric arc	0	2.2	1.5	0	0
HYLSA					
Blast-Furnace	0	0	0	0	1.5
BOF	0	0	0	0	1.8

Table 9-12. *Summary of Results for Experiment 5: Energy Location Factors Equal*

Category	*1981–83*	*1984–86*	*1987–89*	*1990 92*	*1993–95*
Cost (million U.S. dollars a year)					
Capital	0	123.3	231.9	375.1	569.5
Raw material	573.7	814.2	1,181.5	1,459.9	1,187.7
Transport	142.1	153.0	181.8	238.9	324.5
Import	252.9	336.9	469.3	1,000.5	2,197.7
Export revenues	0	– 28.0	– 28.0	– 28.0	– 28.0
Total cost	968.7	1,399.4	2,036.5	3,046.3	4,251.4
Total demand (million tons)	9.7	12.9	17.2	22.8	30.4
Production (million tons)					
Pig iron	5.6	7.9	11.4	16.1	22.3
Sponge iron	1.8	3.6	3.6	3.6	3.6
Open hearth	1.7	1.7	1.7	1.7	2.4
Electric furnace	1.7	3.3	3.3	3.3	3.3
BOF	2.3	0	0	0	0
BOF (max scrap)	2.5	8.1	12.3	18.0	24.9
Pig iron/Sponge iron	3.1	2.2	3.2	4.5	6.2
Imports (million tons)					
Pellets	0	4.9	4.9	14.2	40.2
Coke	0.7	2.3	4.5	7.2	9.9
Steel	1.4	0	0	0	0
Exports of steel (million tons)	0	0.2	0.2	0.2	0.2

Total capacity expansion (million tons)					
Blast furnace	0	2.6	3.5	4.3	6.2
BOF	0	3.2	4.3	5.7	6.9
Direct reduction	0	1.6	0	0	0
Electric arc	0	1.9	0	0	0
Domestic shipments of steel					
AHMSA	3.6	3.6	3.6	4.1	4.1
Fundidora	1.7	1.7	1.7	1.7	4.2
SICARTSA	1.3	5.8	10.1	15.3	20.4
HYLSA	1.1	0.9	0.9	0.9	0.9
HYLSAP	0.6	0.9	0.9	0.9	0.9
Tampico	0	0	0	0	0
Coatzacoalcos	0	0	0	0	0
Total shipments	8.3	12.9	17.2	22.8	30.4
Detailed capacity expansion (million tons)					
AHMSA					
BOF	0	0	0	0.5	0
Fundidora					
Blast furnace	0	0	0	0	2.0
BOF	0	0	0	0	1.8
SICARTSA					
Blast furnace	0	2.6	3.5	4.3	4.2
BOF	0	3.1	4.3	5.2	5.1
Direct reduction	0	1.6	0	0	0
Electric arc	0	1.5	0	0	0
HYLSAP					
Electric arc	0	0.4	0	0	0

Table 9-13. *Summary of Results for Experiment 6: Double Reserves*

Category	*1981–83*	*1984–86*	*1987–89*	*1990–92*	*1993–95*
Cost (million U.S. dollars a year)					
Capital	0	152.0	251.0	412.8	612.7
Raw material	558.7	804.1	1,194.8	1,680.7	2,553.1
Transport	142.1	170.2	200.4	229.2	299.9
Import	252.9	145.7	200.2	411.9	602.0
Export revenues	0	−28.0	0	−28.0	−28.0
Total cost	953.7	1,244.1	1,846.4	2,706.7	4,039.7
Total demand (million tons)	9.7	12.9	17.2	22.8	30.4
Production (million tons)					
Pig iron	5.6	5.6	5.8	9.4	14.6
Sponge iron	1.8	7.3	10.6	12.5	13.8
Open hearth	1.7	1.5	1.7	1.7	1.7
Electric furnace	1.7	6.7	9.7	11.5	12.7
BOF	2.3	3.6	0.3	0	0
BOF (max scrap)	2.5	1.2	5.1	9.9	16.2
Pig iron/Sponge iron	3.1	0.8	0.5	0.8	1.1
Imports (million tons)					
Pellets	0	2.6	2.6	5.8	7.1
Coke	0.7	0.7	0.7	3.0	5.3
Steel	1.4	0	0.4	0	0
Exports of steel (million tons)	0	0.2	0	0.2	0.2

Total capacity expansion (million tons)					
Blast furnace	0	0	0	3.7	5.2
BOF	0	0	0.5	4.5	6.3
Direct reduction	0	5.4	3.3	2.0	1.6
Electric arc	0	5.0	3.0	1.8	1.5
Domestic shipments of steel					
AHMSA	3.6	3.6	4.1	4.1	5.9
Fundidora	1.7	1.5	1.7	1.7	1.7
SICARTSA	1.3	4.3	7.3	13.6	19.6
HYLSA	1.1	1.1	1.1	1.1	0.8
HYLSAP	0.6	1.1	1.1	1.1	1.1
Tampico	0	1.3	1.5	1.3	1.3
Coatzacoalcos	0	0	0	0	0
Total shipments	8.3	12.9	16.8	22.8	30.4
Detailed capacity expansion (million tons)					
AHMSA					
Blast furnace	0	0	0	0	1.5
BOF	0	0	0.5	0	1.8
SICARTSA					
Blast furnace	0	0	0	3.7	3.7
BOF	0	0	0	4.5	4.5
Direct reduction	0	3.5	3.3	2.0	1.6
Electric arc	0	3.0	3.0	1.8	1.5
HYLSAP					
Electric arc	0	0.5	0	0	0
Tampico					
Direct reduction	0	1.9	0	0	0
Electric arc	0	1.5	0	0	0

Table 9-14. *Summary of Results for Experiment 7: Upper Bound on Production at Each Site*

Category	*1981–83*	*1984–86*	*1987–89*	*1990–92*	*1993–95*
Cost (million U.S. dollars a year)					
Capital	0	162.0	263.5	407.4	599.6
Raw material	569.8	693.4	1,048.8	1,579.0	1,607.5
Transport	145.6	160.9	186.5	237.6	345.7
Import	252.9	378.6	513.4	713.8	1,730.9
Export revenues	0	– 28.0	– 28.0	– 28.0	– 12.4
Total cost	968.3	1,366.8	1,984.2	2,909.8	4,271.3
Total demand (million tons)	9.7	12.9	17.2	22.8	30.4
Production (million tons)					
Pig iron	5.6	5.0	5.4	8.1	13.6
Sponge iron	1.8	7.9	11.7	14.2	15.0
Open hearth	1.7	1.0	1.7	1.7	2.4
Electric furnace	1.7	7.2	10.8	13.0	13.7
BOF	2.3	2.2	0.3	0	0
BOF (max scrap)	2.5	2.7	4.6	8.3	14.4
Pig iron/Sponge iron	3.1	0.6	0.5	0.6	0.9
Imports (million tons)					
Pellets	0	8.4	11.8	14.5	36.5
Coke	0.7	0.7	0.7	2.2	4.5
Steel	1.4	0	0	0	0
Exports of steel (million tons)					
Total capacity expansion (million tons)	0	0.2	0.2	0.2	0.1
Blast furnace	0	0	0	2.4	5.5
BOF	0	0	0	3.4	6.1
Direct reduction	0	5.9	3.8	2.4	0.8
Electric arc	0	5.6	3.5	2.2	0.7

Domestic shipments of steel					
AHMSA	3.6	2.8	3.6	4.1	4.1
Fundidora	1.7	1.7	1.7	1.7	3.9
SICARTSA	1.3	3.5	5.7	10.2	10.2
HYLSA	1.1	1.1	1.1	1.1	1.1
HYLSAP	0.6	0.9	0.9	0.9	5.4
Tampico	0	1.3	1.3	1.3	1.4
Coatzacoalos	0	1.5	2.8	3.6	4.3
Total shipments	8.3	12.9	17.2	22.8	30.4
Detailed capacity expansion (million tons)					
AHMSA					
BOF	0	0	0	0.5	0
Fundidora					
Blast furnace	0	0	0	0	1.8
BOF	0	0	0	0	1.6
SICARTSA					
Blast furnace	0	0	0	2.4	0
BOF	0	0	0	3.0	0
Direct reduction	0	2.4	2.4	1.6	0
Electric arc	0	2.2	2.2	1.5	0
HYLSAP					
Blast furnace	0	0	0	0	3.7
BOF	0	0	0	0	4.5
Electric arc	0	0.4	0	0	0
Tampico					
Direct reduction	0	1.9	0	0	0
Electric arc	0	1.5	0	0	0
Coatzacoalcos					
Direct reduction	0	1.6	1.4	0.8	0.8
Electric arc	0	1.5	1.3	0.7	0.7

Table 9-15. *Comparison of Summary Results*

Category	Base case	Experiment[a]						
		1	*2*	*3*	*4*	*5*	*6*	*7*
Cost[b] (million U.S. dollars)								
Capital	1,422.2	1,869.9	1,405.1	1,370.5	1,313.2	1,271.4	1,411.4	1,429.6
Raw material	6,445.6	4,824.3	6,661.5	6,383.0	7,273.4	6,423.5	7,581.1	6,456.7
Transport	1,297.5	1,213.8	1,240.9	1,266.1	1,451.4	1,272.2	1,298.0	1,313.2
Import	3,815.4	3,694.4	4,235.6	4,308.2	3,567.8	4,272.3	1,897.7	3,789.7
Export revenues	– 129.9	– 129.9	– 129.9	– 129.9	– 83.0	– 129.9	– 94.3	– 118.7
Total cost	12,850.9	11,472.6	13,413.2	13,197.9	13,522.8	13,109.5	12,093.9	12,870.5
Experiment/base case × 100	100.0	89.3	104.4	102.7	105.2	102.0	94.1	100.2
Cost contributions (percent)								
Capital	11.1	16.3	10.5	10.4	9.7	9.7	11.7	11.1
Raw material	50.2	42.1	49.7	48.4	53.8	49.0	62.7	50.2
Transport	10.1	10.6	9.3	9.6	10.7	9.7	10.7	10.2
Import	29.7	32.2	31.6	32.6	26.4	32.6	15.7	29.5
Export revenues	– 1.0	– 1.1	– 1.0	– 1.0	– 0.6	– 1.0	– 0.8	– 0.9
Total capacity expansion (million tons)								
Blast furnace	8.2	0	15.6	18.0	14.4	16.5	8.8	7.9
Open hearth	0	0	0	0	0	0	0	0
BOF	9.9	0	18.9	21.9	17.5	20.1	11.3	9.5
Direct reduction	12.7	26.6	3.9	1.6	4.0	1.6	12.2	13.0
Electric arc	11.8	24.5	2.8	1.5	3.7	1.9	11.3	12.1

a. Experiment 1, natural gas price constant at the domestic price level; 2, natural gas price constant at the international price level; 3, rising electricity price; 4, rising imported coke price; 5, removal of energy location subsidies; 6, iron ore and coal reserves doubled; 7, restriction of steel production at each site.

b. Total discounted value from 1981 to 1995.

Table 9-16. *Comparison of Capacity Expansion by Location and Unit* (million tons)

Location and unit	*Base case*	*Experiment* 1	2	3	4	5	6	7
AHMSA								
Blast furnace	0	0	0	0	0	0	1.5	0
Open hearth	0	0	0	0	0	0	0	0
BOF	0.5	0	0.5	0.5	0.5	0.5	2.3	0.5
Direct reduction	0	0	0	0	0	0	0	0
Electric arc	0	0	0	0	0	0	0	0
Fundidora								
Blast furnace	1.5	0	1.8	1.5	1.5	2.0	0	1.8
Open hearth	0	0	0	0	0	0	0	0
BOF	1.2	0	1.6	1.2	1.2	1.8	0	1.6
Direct reduction	0	0	0	0	0	0	0	0
Electric arc	0	0	0	0	0	0	0	0
SICARTSA								
Blast furnace	6.7	0	13.8	14.8	11.4	14.5	7.3	2.4
Open hearth	0	0	0	0	0	0	0	0
BOF	8.2	0	16.8	18.1	13.9	17.8	9.0	3.0
Direct reduction	7.7	10.5	3.1	1.6	4.0	1.6	10.3	6.4
Electric arc	7.1	9.6	2.8	1.5	3.7	1.5	9.3	5.9
HYLSA								
Blast furnace	0	0	0	0	1.5	0	0	0
Open hearth	0	0	0	0	0	0	0	0
BOF	0	0	0	0	1.8	0	0	0
Direct reduction	0	0	0	0	0	0	0	0
Electric arc	0	0	0	0	0	0	0	0
HYLSAP								
Blast furnace	0	0	0	0	0	0	0	3.7
Open hearth	0	0	0	0	0	0	0	0
BOF	0	0	0	0	0	0	0	4.5
Direct reduction	0	2.8	0	0	0	0	0	0
Electric arc	0.4	2.9	0	0	0	0.4	0.5	0.4
Tampico								
Blast furnace	0	0	0	1.7	0	0	0	0
Open hearth	0	0	0	0	0	0	0	0
BOF	0	0	0	2.1	0	0	0	0
Direct reduction	1.9	6.8	0.8	0	0	0	1.9	1.9
Electric arc	1.5	6.0	0	0	0	0	1.5	1.5
Coatzacoalcos								
Blast furnace	0	0	0	0	0	0	0	0
Open hearth	0	0	0	0	0	0	0	0
BOF	0	0	0	0	0	0	0	0
Direct reduction	3.1	6.5	0	0	0	0	0	4.7
Electric arc	2.8	6.0	0	0	0	0	0	4.3

Table 9-17. *Comparison of Capacity Expansion by Time Period and Technology*
(million tons)

Technology and period	*Base case*	*Experiment 1*	*2*	*3*	*4*	*5*	*6*	*7*
Blast furnace								
1981–83	0	0	0	0	0	0	0	0
1984–86	0	0	3.7	2.9	2.1	2.6	0	0
1987–89	0	0	3.5	3.7	2.5	3.5	0	0
1990–92	3.0	0	2.9	5.2	5.2	4.3	3.7	2.4
1993–95	5.2	0	5.5	6.2	4.6	6.2	5.2	5.5
Direct reduction								
1981–83	0	0	0	0	0	0	0	0
1984–86	5.9	8.0	2.2	1.6	2.4	1.6	5.4	5.9
1987–89	3.8	5.7	0	0	1.6	0	3.3	3.8
1990–92	1.6	5.7	0.8	0	0	0	2.0	2.4
1993–95	1.3	7.3	0.9	0	0	0	1.6	0.8

10
Extensions, Summary, and Conclusions

THIS CHAPTER INCLUDES a discussion of possible extensions of the models outlined in the previous chapter, as well as a summary of the book and its conclusions.

Extensions

The previous chapters describe a small and a large static model and a small dynamic model. In a governmental or commercial application of this investment planning method, two further steps would normally be desirable. One would want to construct, first, a large comparative static capacity planning model, to be followed by a large dynamic model. For the purposes of this volume, neither extension appeared possible because of the effort and resources required.

A static capacity expansion model is constructed for some future year—say, 2000—and contains investment activities for the productive units. It would be constructed before a large dynamic model because the static capacity expansion model would be smaller than a large dynamic model by a factor of four or five and yet would provide an opportunity to analyze investments in the disaggregated setting of a large model.

The results from the static capacity expansion model provide an indication of *where* investments should be made and the *technology* to be used but do not indicate *when* the investments should be made. Therefore an extension to a large dynamic model should be made after the static capacity expansion model has been solved and analyzed. A large dynamic model may contain the level of disaggregation of commodities, processes, productive units, plants, markets, and so on used in the large static model. This is combined with the dynamic structure used in the small dynamic model. The resulting model would be large and expensive to solve but would permit the analysis of when and where to invest and what technology to use. Furthermore, it would do this at a level of disaggregation used by engineers in steel companies; that is, individual productive units such as BOF converters and hot strip mills. It would also permit investment analysis in a model that includes interplant shipments of intermediate products. Thus one can anticipate that the results would include, for example, the efficiency gains from postponing an investment and buying intermediate materials from another plant until demand has grown enough to justify investment in a large productive unit.

The completion of a large dynamic model should not in our opinion be the occasion for discarding the other models. Rather, each of the models discussed in this book has a comparative advantage for use in analyzing certain kinds of operational or investment problems.

Summary

The purpose of this book has been to outline a methodology for the planning of investment programs in the steel industry and to illustrate the application of this methodology with a case study of the Mexican steel industry. This has been done with a series of models. Two static models were solved as linear programs and one dynamic model was solved as a mixed integer program.

The small static model introduces the use of the methodology in the steel industry and is simple enough to be readily understood and easily solved. The large static model provides a basis for a study of operational procedures in the industry. For example, the results indicate that $26 million a year might have been saved in the Mexican steel industry by easing restrictions on coke imports, and that $48 million a year could have been saved by exploiting the possibility of additional interplant shipments of intermediate products.

These two results illustrate the kinds of outcome which can be obtained from large static models of the steel industry. The results from such a modeling exercise should not be treated as definitive but rather should be used to point the direction to possible cost-saving actions. The special capability of this type of model is to do cost studies on a number of steel mills at the same time. By considering the interdependencies between the plants, one can find savings that are not obvious from the more customary studies of *individual* steel mills.

The small dynamic model permits the focus to shift from operational problems to investment problems. Consider the problems faced by the investment analysts in the example of the Mexican steel industry. The ores from the interior mines are declining in quality, as is the coal. Part of the industry uses natural gas for direct reduction while part uses coke. The government is employing a policy of differential pricing of natural gas and electricity at different locations to encourage decentralization of industry. From this matrix of problems the model results indicate that policies for natural gas pricing are crucial to determining the most efficient investment pattern for the industry. If the low domestic price is allowed to rise slowly to the world price level, the choice of technology shifts from direct reduction to blast furnaces. In addition, the price differentials for natural gas and electricity are found to be sufficiently large to encourage decentralization, which is the government's objective. Moreover, almost all of the expansion of the industry is done at ports where imported pellets can be obtained at lower prices than domestic ores as the domestic ores are exhausted.

These results indicate policies which can be used to plan an efficient investment strategy for the industry and also demonstrate the effects of various public policies on that strategy.

Conclusions

The methodology outlined and applied in this book provides a useful vehicle for analyzing both operational and investment problems in the steel industry. The multiplant focus of the large static linear programming model permits the analyst to find cost-saving opportunities which are not so readily perceived when each plant is studied independently. One example of this is in the study of interplant shipments of intermediate products.

Similarly, the multiplant focus allows one to gain a global view for use in investment analysis with dynamic models. Many important factors are changing in the steel industry. Prices of energy inputs have been rising rapidly, the quality of ore has been declining in many locations, and market demand is growing rapidly, particularly in many developing nations. Governments offer energy subsidies for plants at some locations but not at others. All of these changes make investment analysis difficult. The methodology outlined in this book provides no crystal ball for making investment decisions, but it does provide a clear and logical process for considering the alternatives and for analyzing the major factors which affect investment decisions in the steel industry.

11

A Postscript: Observations on Industrial Modeling

THERE HAS BEEN enough experience with industrial modeling that it is useful to begin work to establish some basic principles. As a step in that direction, this last chapter contains a set of "observations" on industrial modeling. Some of these observations may be confirmed by others until they eventually become "principles." Others will be dropped from the literature.[1]

One observation which will surely become a principle is an article by A. M. Geoffrion (1976) entitled, "The Purpose of Mathematical Programming Is Insight, Not Numbers." This is one of the themes of this chapter. The development and use of industrial planning models should not be directed toward the determination of a single optimal solution but rather toward the enhancement of understanding of the problem at hand.

It is hoped that these observations will contribute to high-quality economic modeling. The topics to be discussed are: multiple models, modeling languages, set specification, model size calculations, model debugging strategies, and industry experts. The unifying elements in this diverse list are that all the items are parts of the process of good model building and that several are all too frequently overlooked. Each will be discussed in turn.

1. We are grateful to J. Scott Rogers of the University of Toronto for suggesting this chapter.

Multiple Models

In most industrial modeling projects it is useful to construct not one but a group of models. Two different purposes are served by multiple models: slow increase in complexity and comparative advantage. The first refers to the fact that it is frequently useful at the beginning of a project to construct relatively small models and then slowly but surely increase their size and complexity. This approach is from the school of "keep the complexity under control."[2] Since industrial planning models are difficult to develop and debug, the analyst who attempts to immediately develop a large and complex model may never complete the task. It is better to begin with a small and simple model which is easy to understand and debug and then gradually progress to larger and more complicated models while "keeping the complexity under control" at every step along the way.

This approach also lends itself well to the second purpose served by multiple models: models of various sizes and complexities have comparative advantages that can be exploited. Thus, if a small static model is developed at the beginning of a modeling project, it should not be discarded once larger models are developed, but rather retained for certain kinds of analyses. For example, static models have a comparative advantage for doing operational studies as opposed to investment studies. Small models can be used much more readily than large models for sensitivity testing. Finally, small models are sometimes useful in doing presentations since they are easier to grasp in a short time.

A new theme emerging in the literature of multiple models is the idea of aggregation. This approach to multiple models argues that at times it is advantageous to construct a large and disaggregated model first and then to apply formal aggregation procedures to it to produce a small and highly aggregated model. To do this while maintaining the advantage of a slow increase in complexity, it is advisable to build first a small model and then a large model. Then formal aggregation procedures can be applied to the large model to produce a revised small model in which the data are consistent with the data in the large model.

In summary, multiple models permit slow but steady development from small and simple to large and complex models and provide a set in

2. Verbal communication from Fred Norman.

which each model has its own comparative advantage for use in analyzing the industry.

Modeling Languages

One of the themes of this book is that a modeling language such as GAMS can greatly facilitate industrial modeling. Though this subject alone would merit a separate chapter or book, it is worthwhile here to point out a few of the advantages that accrue to the user who has access to a modeling language (see, for example, Bisschop and Meeraus 1982, and Meeraus 1983).

One of the key advantages is increases in productivity. Models can be developed in much less time when it is not necessary to write Fortran programs or use a matrix generator to prepare the input for a linear program. Moreover, improvements in quality can also be obtained with the use of a modeling language. One improvement is much greater assurance that the model described in the report is actually the one that was solved in the computer. With modeling languages it is much easier to verify that the equations written out in a report match those in the software used to generate the computer model.

The modeling language can also aid in debugging by providing lists of sets, variables, and equations and their locations in the input. Furthermore, a list of unique elements such as set elements can be provided. This type of information is useful in catching spelling errors in the input.

Finally, the use of a modeling language enables the investigator to make specification changes with much greater ease. This is particularly useful as a project nears completion and is presented to others for suggestions and criticisms. When specification changes are easy to make, useful suggestions can be accepted and the model can be improved—instead of defended to the hilt because changes are so difficult to make.

Set Specification

One key element in good model building is set specification. This contrasts with the usual notion that the most important element in model construction is the development of the objective function and the constraints.

Set specification plays two distinct roles in designing models. The first role is to determine the basic degree of complexity of the model. This is done while choosing the number of key sets, that is, the number of basic domains or dimensions of the overall problem. For example, whether to include a set for time periods is a basic and crucial decision. Similarly, whether to include spatial relations may be decided at the time of the set specification.

The second role is selecting the level of aggregation, that is, the number of elements *within* each key set and the number and type of subsets of each key set. An example of the second role is to include in the model only those plants, commodities, processes, productive units, and so on that are crucial in providing insight into the economic problem. Moreover, it is essential to leave out of the set specification those elements that are not crucial. Any unneeded elements only add to the size of the problem and increase the cost of solving and the difficulty of understanding the model.

Another example of the second role is in the specification of commodities. In the small static model the set of commodities was partitioned into three subsets: raw material, intermediate products, and final products. This worked well in that model because each commodity belonged to one and only one subset. However, in more complex models such as the large static model there are more categories of commodities and a given commodity may belong to a combination of categories. In this case the subsets of commodities do not provide a partition of the set of commodities. Then it may be useful to allow the pattern of plus and minus signs in the input-output table to determine implicitly which commodities are raw material, intermediate products, and final products and which commodities are two or more of these types.

Set specification also has important implications for model size, which is discussed next.

Model Size Calculations

In developing high-quality industrial models it is of importance to be keenly aware of the tradeoff between (1) changes in specification of sets, variables, and equations and (2) changes in the model size. Such a consciousness enables the investigator to gain as much insight as possible from the model while keeping it small enough to be efficiently solved and readily understood.

To facilitate this understanding of the tradeoff between model size and specification it is necessary to perform calculations like those shown in chapter 5 on the small static model or to have these calculations performed by the modeling language as was done for the large static model.

It is useful to distinguish between increases in the model size that come from adding an additional key set or dimension, such as the addition of time to a static model, and increases from adding elements to a key set. Of course, increases in the number of key sets or domains may increase the order of the size of the model—for example, from the square of the number of elements in the key sets to the cube of the number of elements in the key sets. In contrast, changes in the number of elements in a key set increase the size of the model much less.

Model Debugging Strategies

There are two major steps in model debugging. The first is checking clerical errors in inputting the model to the computer and the second is finding basic specification errors. Errors in the first stage are usually numerous but relatively easy to find and correct, while errors in the second stage are few in number but difficult to locate and correct. The first stage is similar to compilation errors and the second stage is similar to solution errors in computer programming.

As already indicated, the use of a modeling language greatly facilitates the discovery and correction of compilation errors. These errors are typically misspelled variable names or set elements, misplaced punctuation, and reversed indices. Reversed indices, for example, may be discovered by using the domain-checking facility of the GAMS language.

Solution errors are more difficult to identify and correct. At the first stage they involve the use of common sense. In almost all modeling projects the first solution to the model brings great sighs of relief from the modelers when they discover that it is indeed possible to obtain a solution—any solution—to the problem. However, the first solution is frequently nonsensical. One type of error that produces nonsensical solutions was discussed with the results of the small static model. In that solution a steel plant continued to fully utilize the older and less efficient open hearth furnaces despite unused capacity in the newer and more efficient basic oxygen furnaces. In that case the error was traced to the fact that another process was needed either to supplement or to replace the existing production activity and permit a different mix of inputs. Thus errors which appear after successful compilation but during the solution phase are an extremely important part of debugging, and ample time should be allocated for this phase of the development of any model.

Industry Experts

The results of a high-quality modeling exercise can be impressive. Computers can manipulate large amounts of information extremely efficiently. A skilled modeler can utilize a computer to analyze a myriad of economic factors in searching for improved operational procedures or investment patterns. However, the modeler must be on constant guard against the danger of excluding from the analysis small but crucial pieces of information which can invalidate the results.

Some examples may help illustrate the point. A very careful study of transport and production costs to determine a new location for a steel mill could be organized along the lines suggested in this book. However, the analysis might overlook two small considerations: the quality of the subsoil at each potential site and the depth of the shipping channel that provides access to the site. The result might be the construction of a steel mill at a site where it would slowly but surely sink into the ground while more and more pilings were needed to keep it from doing so. Or the result might be a new steel mill located where only small ships could be loaded and unloaded, thereby greatly increasing the effective transport cost.

When using impressive computers and mathematical models, how is the analyst to ensure that common sense factors are not overlooked? It is clear that subsoil conditions and channel depths and the myriad of other small but important details cannot be included in computer models. The answer lies not in making the models more complicated but rather in keeping them simple enough that their basic structure and approach can be understood by the many experts whose input is important in reaching wise operational and investment decisions. The answer also lies in the determination of the model builders to communicate clearly, crisply, and frequently with a broad range of industrial experts during the model development process.

Models can indeed lead to much improved decisionmaking through the ability of the computer to do rapid calculations. But they will lead to improved decisions only if the analysts themselves develop and adhere to principles of good modeling.

References

Alatorre, Jaime E. 1976. "A Model for Planning Investment in the Mexican Steel Industry for the Period 1974–1986." M.A. thesis, Department of Operations Research, College of Engineering, University of Texas, Austin.

Bergendorff, Hans, Peter Glenshaw, and Alexander Meeraus. 1981. "The Planning of Investment Programs in the Forestry and Forest Industry Sectors." Development Policy Staff, World Bank, Washington, D.C. Processed.

Bisschop, Johannes, and Alexander Meeraus. 1982. "On the Development of a General Algebraic Modeling System in a Strategic Planning Environment." *Mathematical Programming Study*, vol. 20, pp. 1–29.

Chenery, Hollis B. 1952. "Over-Capacity and the Acceleration Principle." *Econometrica*, vol. 20 (January), pp. 1–28.

Choksi, Armeane M., David A. Kendrick, Alexander Meeraus, and Ardy J. Stoutjesdijk. 1981. *La Programmation des investissements industriels*. Paris: Economica.

Choksi, Armeane M., Alexander Meeraus, and Ardy J. Stoutjesdijk. 1980. *The Planning of Investment Programs in the Fertilizer Industry*. Baltimore, Md.: Johns Hopkins University Press. The case study has been translated into French as part of Choksi, Kendrick, Meeraus, and Stoutjesdijk (1981).

Coordinating Commission for the Steel Industry. 1978. "Present Situation and Future Growth of the Steel Industry." Mexico City.

Geoffrion, A. M. 1976. "The Purpose of Mathematical Programming Is Insight, Not Numbers." *Interfaces*, vol. 7, no. 1, pp. 81–92.

Kendrick, David A., and Ardy J. Stoutjesdijk. 1978. *The Planning of Industrial Investment Programs: A Methodology*. Baltimore, Md.: Johns Hopkins University Press. Also translated into French as part of Choksi, Kendrick, Meeraus, and Stoutjesdijk (1981).

Kendrick, David A. 1967. *Programming Investment in the Process Industries.* Cambridge, Mass.: M.I.T. Press.

Kendrick, David A., and Alexander Meeraus. 1981. "Model Reduction through Domain Restriction." Center for Economic Research Paper no. 81–12, Department of Economics, University of Texas, Austin; and Discussion Paper no. 35, Development Research Department, World Bank, Washington, D.C.

Manne, Alan S., ed. 1967. *Investment for Capacity Expansion: Size, Location and Time Phasing.* Cambridge, Mass.: M.I.T. Press.

Meeraus, Alexander. 1983. "An Algebraic Approach to Modeling." *Journal of Economic Dynamics and Control*, vol. 5, no. 1.

Meeraus, Alexander, and David Kendrick. 1982. "Model Reduction in a Large Static Linear Programming Model." Center for Economic Research Paper no. 82–11, Department of Economics, University of Texas, Austin.

Mennes, L. B. M., and Ardy J. Stoutjesdijk. 1981. "Multi-Country Investment Analysis." Development Policy Staff, World Bank, Washington, D.C. Processed.

Russell, Clifford S., and William J. Vaughan. 1976. *Steel Production: Processes, Products and Residuals.* Baltimore, Md.: Johns Hopkins University Press.

United States Steel. 1971. *The Making, Shaping and Treatment of Steel.* Harold E. McGannon, ed. Pittsburgh, Pa.

Vietorisz, Thomas, and Alan S. Manne. 1963. "Chemical Processes, Plant Location, and Economies of Scale." In *Studies in Processes Analysis.* Alan S. Manne and H. M. Markowitz, eds. New York: Wiley.

Wein, H. H., and V. P. Sreedharan. 1968. *The Optimal Staging and Phasing of Multiproduct Capacity.* Studies in Comparative and Technological Planning. East Lansing: School of Business Administration, Michigan State University.

Westphal, Larry E. 1971. *Planning Investments with Economies of Scale.* Amsterdam: North-Holland.

Index

The full range of World Bank publications, both free and for sale, is described in the *Catalog of Publications*; the continuing research program is outlined in *Abstracts of Current Studies.* Both booklets are updated annually; the most recent edition of each is available without charge from the Publications Sales Unit, Department B, The World Bank, 1818 H Street, N.W., Washington, D.C. 20433, U.S.A.

David A. Kendrick is professor of economics at the University of Texas. Alexander Meeraus is chief of the Analytic Support Unit in the Development Research Department of the World Bank. Jaime Alatorre is director of national accounting and economic statistics at the National Institute of Statistics, Geography, and Information of the Mexican Ministry of Programming and Budgeting.